THE FRUIT AND VEGETABLE GARDENER'S HANDBOOK

Marshall Cavendish · London New York Sydney

Edited by Robin Wood from material which has previously appeared
in the Marshall Cavendish partwork *Grow Your Own*.

Published by Marshall Cavendish Books Limited
58 Old Compton Street
London W1V 5PA

First printing 1980

Printed in Great Britain
by Henry Stone and Sons Limited
Banbury, Oxon

ISBN 0 85685 722 X

CONTENTS

INTRODUCTION

No other activity is potentially as satisfying as growing your own food. Moreover, home-grown fruit and vegetables are cheaper, tastier and give better food value than any bought in shops.

The Fruit and Vegetable Gardener's Handbook provides you with all the expert advice needed to grow delicious fruit, vegetable and salad crops. The handbook is divided into four main sections—'Peas, Beans and Greens', 'Root Vegetables', 'Salad Crops' and 'Fruit'. Each chapter is devoted to a single crop, giving a comprehensive guide to successful cultivation.

Essential facts, on the time and effort needed to raise a crop and on its size and yield, are shown at-a-glance using the three symbols explained below. Then, in easy stages, detailed instructions are given on all aspects of cultivation from sowing to harvesting—including how to choose a suitable site and soil, hints on the best varieties to grow, how to identify and prevent the ravages of pests and diseases, even tips on exhibiting your prize crops—in fact, everything you need to know is here.

Fully illustrated throughout with clear and colourful step-by-step diagrams and photographs, *The Fruit and Vegetable Gardener's Handbook* has a place on every gardener's shelf.

Each of the step-by-step guides begins with basic facts about the crop. Three types of symbol are used to give an at-a-glance guide to the nature of the crop

low yield	minimum effort	crops in three months or less
medium yield	needs more care	crops in 4-12 months
high yield	requires special attention	crops in over 12 months

---

Peas,
Beans and
Greens

Broad Beans

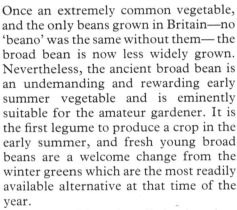

Vicia faba (fam. *Leguminosae*)
Hardy annual
Sowing to harvesting time: 3-4 months
for spring sowings; 6-7 months for autumn sowings
Size: standard varieties 60-90 cm (2- 3′) tall, dwarf varieties
30 cm (1′) tall
Yield: 5 kg (11 lb) per 3 m (10′) double row

Once an extremely common vegetable, and the only beans grown in Britain—no 'beano' was the same without them— the broad bean is now less widely grown. Nevertheless, the ancient broad bean is an undemanding and rewarding early summer vegetable and is eminently suitable for the amateur gardener. It is the first legume to produce a crop in the early summer, and fresh young broad beans are a welcome change from the winter greens which are the most readily available alternative at that time of the year.

The broad bean is a distinctive plant with a square, erect stem, which can be up to 1 m (3′) tall in most varieties, and is occasionally branched. It is pollinated by insects and bears clusters of white, black-blotched flowers in the axils of the leaves. The fertilized flowers develop into pods which hang down from the leaf axils and, depending on the length of these pods and the number of beans in them, broad beans can be divided into two types. Longpod varieties have the longer pods containing about 8 rather oblong beans; Windsor varieties have shorter pods containing fewer large, circular beans. Longpods are extremely

hardy and in most areas can be sown in the late autumn to produce an early crop. Windsor varieties are later, producing a heavy crop of flavoursome beans in summer from a spring sowing.

If you buy broad beans from a shop they are invariably too old and have become hard and unappetizing. Home-grown broad beans, however, can be picked when they are still young and tender—a totally different proposition.

Choosing a site
Broad beans do best on an open site but they are not fussy and will grow quite happily anywhere in most gardens and allotments. You should select your site rather with the interest of other crops in mind. When fully grown the bean will form a hedge up to 1 m (3′) tall which will shade any rows of plants to the south of it. You should make sure that plants on either side get sunshine during at least part of the day by planting the beans so that the rows run north/south. It makes sense, too, to plant the beans alongside a crop, such as lettuce, that will appreciate the shelter the beans provide in early summer; spinach is another crop which benefits from shade in hot weather.

Preparing the soil

The best soil for broad beans is a rich heavy loam, well-manured from previous years and deep enough for the plants not to become short of water in the summer. Although broad beans are leguminous plants which obtain nitrogen from the bacteria in their root nodules (and leave the ground richer than they found it) they appreciate additional nitrogen in their early stages. Organic matter also helps by keeping the ground moist during the summer. If the beans can follow on land well-manured from a previous crop, for example summer cauliflower, this is ideal.

Do not worry, however, if your conditions are not perfect. Broad beans will do well on most soils provided that they are not waterlogged. If the beans are to follow another crop directly, just dig the soil well before sowing. If not, the land should be prepared in the autumn. Dig the soil deeply, adding garden compost or well-rotted manure if the soil lacks it—a good general rate is about 4.5 kg per sq m (10 lb per sq yd). For spring sowings leave the ground rough so that it can be better broken up by the frost and add a further light dressing of compost two weeks before sowing.

Broad beans dislike an acid soil so test

Broad beans are an excellent early summer vegetable.

3

1. Two weeks before sowing add superphosphate at a rate of 60 g per sq m (2 oz per sq yd) and rake in.

2. Use a draw hoe to take out a wide shallow drill 6.5 cm (2½″) deep and 10 cm (4″) wide.

3. Sow the seeds in a double row with the seeds in one row opposite the gaps in the other.

4. If mice are a problem in your garden place traps at intervals along the row.

your soil and, if acid, add lime as indicated by a soil test kit, about six to eight weeks after digging.

A few days before sowing, add superphosphate, at the rate of 60 g per sq m (2 oz per sq yd). Rake in the superphosphate carefully, so as to produce a level seed bed.

Sowing
Broad beans have the biggest seeds of any of the common vegetables, so they can be planted individually just where they are destined to grow. The best method is to prepare shallow drills 6.5 cm (2½″) deep and 15 cm (6″) wide. Then place the beans in a double row with one row down each side of the drill. Leave 25 cm (9″) between each bean in a row. Place the beans in one row opposite the gaps in the other row. If you are planting more than one double row, leave a space of 75 cm (2½′) between each so they do not overshadow one another.

The germination rate of broad beans is low—less than 75%—so sow a few extra plants at the end of the row and transplant them to fill in gaps. Alternatively, if space is limited in a small garden, you can sow two double rows just 10-15 cm (4-6″) apart. As germination is rarely 100%, overcrowding is unlikely to occur. The result of planting like this is a hedge of beans 30-45 cm (1-1½') wide.

Broad bean seeds will germinate at any temperature above freezing and the bright green seed leaves should emerge above ground 1-2 weeks after sowing.

Spring-sown beans
The commonest time to sow beans outdoors is from late winter to early spring depending on local weather conditions. You can plant in the late winter if you have a sheltered garden with a mild climate but should wait until the middle of early spring in colder and more exposed places. The beans from these sowings will be ready for picking from the beginning of early summer. If you want an earlier crop you can sow under cloches, up to a month sooner. Remove the cloches when the plants start to touch the roof.

Broad beans are a cold weather crop and do not do really well during the heat of the summer. Nevertheless, staggered sowings will give you crops throughout the summer. You can sow in mid-spring to pick in late summer and again in early summer for an early autumn crop.

Autumn-sown beans
The hardy broad bean can withstand severe frosts as low as minus 7-9°C (15-20°F) and is thus suitable for autumn sowing in all but the coldest areas. Pick a hardy longpod variety, like *Aquadulce*, and sow in the usual way in late autumn.

There is often little advantage in autumn sowing, however, unless you plan to use the broad beans as wind protection for another crop. Autumn-sown broad beans will crop 2-3 weeks earlier than spring-sown beans and are also less likely to be attacked by bean aphis, but against these advantages there is always the possibility that a cold, wet winter will destroy the crop entirely.

Some gardeners protect autumn-sown beans with cloches but, even if these are available, risks are involved. If the winter is mild the beans will grow so strongly that they will have to be uncovered in the early spring. A sudden cold spell, once the cloches have been removed, could then kill off all the early growth.

Dwarf beans
If you do have cloches available for broad beans you are better advised to grow a dwarf variety. These plants grow to about 30-45 cm (1-1½') tall, so they are unlikely to become too big too early in the season. They are also useful in a small garden or allotment where there is not room to grow taller varieties. Do not expect such a heavy crop as you would get with taller varieties, however.

Sow a dwarf variety in single rows with 25-30 cm (9 12") between plants and 30-60 cm (1-2') between the rows, depending on the variety. The plants will grow to produce a bush with three to five stems about 45 cm (1½') wide.

Care and cultivation
Broad beans grow at a time when weed growth is particularly strong, so regular hoeing around the plants is necessary, especially when they are small. Additionally some weeds, such as thistles, occasionally grow up within the rows very close to the beans. Do not risk trying to remove these with a hoe. Pull them up by hand.

In a wettish year, broad beans will not need watering, as the early summer soil should still be fairly moist. They cannot withstand drought, however. If the soil does begin to dry out, as it may well do for late crops, water generously.

Although they are not true climbers like runner beans, broad beans are, nevertheless, tallish plants with a good deal of bushy foliage, which is supported by quite shallow root systems, so you will need to give all but dwarf varieties some help against the wind to prevent them being blown down. Small plants can be supported by earthing up for about 7-15 cm (3-6") around the stems (this also gives some protection against very cold or very wet weather for beans

1. Draw soil up round the bases of young plants to give them support and to protect them from the weather.

2. Hoe carefully to remove weeds. Pull up any weeds growing very close to the plants by hand.

3. Broad beans may be blown over in windy weather. Support them with stakes and string.

4. Pick off the growing points to deter bean aphis and to encourage bigger pods.

sown in late autumn, and over-wintered) and by placing twigs in the ground alongside the plants in the same way that you would for peas.

Twigs are not sufficient, however, for tall varieties in windy areas, particularly on sandy soils. In such areas, tie the plants in with string. Place thin stakes or canes at 1 m (3′) intervals down both sides of the double rows close to the beans. Then tie round the stakes with twine 30 cm (1′) and 60 cm (2′) above the ground. The beans can then lean against this 'pen' in windy weather. As the plants grow, remove the sideshoots from the base of the stems, while they are still small, so that each plant has only one main stem. As soon as each plant has set about four or five flowers, pinch out the growing points at the top of the stems. This has two uses. It encourages the formation of pods and also discourages

5. Immediately after removing the tops spray with derris or bioresmethrin to deter bean aphis.

6. Harvest the beans with a quick downward twist of the hand. The lower pods mature first.

aphids (blackfly) which like to feed on the growing point and youngest leaves.

If the growing points are clean they can be either cooked and eaten like spinach or added to your compost heap. If they are infected with aphids, however, burn them to destroy the pests.

As broad beans are leguminous plants, obtaining nitrogen indirectly from the soil atmosphere through their root nodules, they do not need any feeding once they are growing.

Harvesting

Harvesting broad beans is a matter of taste. If you like mature, hard beans, then leave the pods on the plant until they are beginning to become bronze in colour, before picking. Most people, however, prefer more tender beans. For these, the pods should be picked as soon as sizeable beans can be felt inside. It is a good idea to open one pod, which will indicate if others of the same size are ready. The beans should be a good size but still soft. Alternatively, for a really tender vegetable, try picking very young pods and cooking them, pods and all, as

you would for runner beans.

When you pick your beans, do it by a quick downward movement of the hand.

Aftercare

After the main crop has finished, broad beans often send up suckers which, if left, flower and eventually produce beans. A second crop can be obtained in this way—especially if the old growth is cut out to encourage the suckers. The number of beans which can be collected is normally very small, however, so, unless space is no problem in your garden (in which case you may as well have this little extra crop), cut off the plants at ground level once the first beans are harvested and use the land for something else. Still leave the roots in the soil, though, as the nodules on them contain nitrogenous salts which will help the next crops. Brassicas would be a good follow-up, as they are a leafy crop, needing quite a lot of nitrogen.

If the ground is required immediately for another crop, add the discarded top growth of the bean plants to your compost heap. If not, dig the entire

1. Sow the seeds individually in 10 cm (4') pots in mid- or late winter. Sow a few more than you actually need.

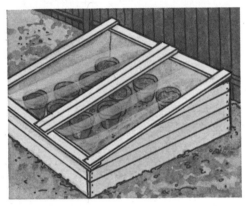

2. After sowing place the pots out in a cold frame or put them on the bench in an unheated greenhouse.

3. The seedlings are ready for planting out in mid-spring. Take care not to damage the root ball.

plants, leaves, roots and stems, well into the soil (chop them up if necessary) and let them rot.

Growing under glass

Broad beans can be successfully sown in pots, either in an unheated glasshouse or in a cold frame, in mid- or late winter and then planted out in early or mid-spring for an early crop. Use one pot for each seed so that the root is disturbed as little as possible when transplanting.

Raising in pots and then planting out is often the only way of getting early broad beans in areas where winters are too severe for autumn planting and the ground is unsuitable to work before late mid-spring.

Exhibition tips

To get really good broad beans for showing, they should be grown on a rich, heavy soil. Add plenty of manure during autumn digging.

You must sacrifice some of the total crop if you wish to grow broad beans for show, since the best beans are produced when only one pod is grown on each cluster. Remove all the pods competing with the one destined for show as soon as the pods have formed. It also helps to grow as many plants as possible, so as to increase your choice when making the final selection.

Select fresh, green, young and well-filled pods without blemishes. They should be large but of a uniform size. The beans inside should be young and tender. Old beans show a black mark on the side, which indicates the point at which the bean germinates; this is considered a blemish.

Broad beans wilt very easily and keeping the beans fresh for show is a problem. Leave picking as late as possible and then store the pods in a damp cloth to reduce transpiration. Sometimes an ugly heel is left on the pod after picking. Remove with a knife.

The normal number of pods exhibited is 18. Simply place them neatly together across a plate or on the bench.

Varieties

The varieties listed here have been separated into Longpod and Windsor types. Nevertheless this classification is rather arbitrary. Modern varieties are often the result of crosses between the two groups and have some of the characteristics of both these groups. Dwarf varieties are separately listed, and all varieties are suitable for freezing.

Longpod

Aquadulce and Aquadulce Claudia: white seeded; hardy early cropper; suitable for autumn sowing; pods 38-45 cm (15-18″) long.

Bunyard's Exhibition Longpod: white-seeded; hardy early cropper; suitable for autumn or spring sowing; well-filled pods about 30-40 cm (12-16″) long; excellent for exhibition.

Imperial White Longpod: white-seeded; spring sowing; long broad pods with up to 9 beans; excellent for exhibition.

Express: green-seeded; spring sowing; very heavy and early cropper; up to 34 pods per plant; excellent flavour, and useful for exhibition work.

Masterpiece Green Longpod: green-seeded; late winter to spring sowing; long pods; excellent for exhibition, very good flavour.

Imperial Green Longpod: green-seeded; spring sowing; heavy cropper; long pods up to 35 cm (14″) long; excellent for exhibition.

Red Epicure: brown-red seeds which become straw-coloured when cooked; spring sowing.

Irish Hardwick

Aquadulce Claudia

Brian Furner

Imperial White Longpod

Brian Furner

Imperial White Windsor

Harry Smith Collection

Imperial Green Windsor

Windsor

Imperial White Windsor: white-seeded; spring sowing; heavy cropper; up to eight beans per pod.

Giant Four-seeded Green Windsor: green-seeded; spring sowing; heavy cropper; short pods, with four or five beans per pod.

Imperial Green Windsor: green-seeded; spring sowing and later; up to seven beans per pod.

Dwarf

The Sutton: white-seeded; suitable for autumn or spring sowing; good as a cloche crop; plants about 30 cm (1′) high; pods about 13-15 cm (5-6″) long; five seeds per pod but dwarf beans will give smaller crops than the normal-sized varieties.

Express

The Sutton

Pests & Diseases

By far the most troublesome pest of broad beans is bean aphis. Happily, however, it is quite easily controlled. If your broad beans escape bean aphis few other pests or diseases are likely to be a serious problem.

Bean aphis: sometimes called blackfly, black aphid, black dolphin aphid, black army, or collier, these tiny insects suck the sap from the plants and also foul the leaf surface with a sticky black substance called honey-dew. The earliest crops are usually unaffected as they produce beans before the aphids have become established, but later crops may be heavily infested.

The aphids congregate particularly on the growing point but are also found on the stem and on the undersides of leaves, which may curl up if badly attacked. Taking out the growing points of the beans reduces the likelihood of attack, but is unlikely to protect the plants completely. Spray or dust the plants with derris or bioresmethrin immediately after removal of the tops. Repeat daily if necessary. The best time to spray is in the evening when bees and other pollinating insects will not be harmed by the spray along with the aphids.

There is some evidence that summer savory discourages attack by the aphids. Try sowing some between the rows of beans.

Chocolate spot: brown spots and streaks on the leaves, stems, petioles, and sometimes also the pods, of the plants are a sure sign of an attack of chocolate spot caused by forms of the fungus botrytis. Good healthy plants, growing on fertile and well-drained soils are never seriously attacked, although autumn-sown plants which have been weakened by frost are susceptible. However, even these plants are likely to recover without treatment. The disease is only serious if the soil lacks either lime or potash and the season is a wet one. The best defence is to plant only in good, well-manured soil, and to space the plants adequately.

Spraying should not be necessary, but Bordeaux mixture or captan can be applied, if the disease becomes troublesome. Destroy infected plants; do not put them on the compost heap.

Bean beetle (Bruchid beetle): These beetles are not a serious threat to a growing crop but rather damage seed which is being stored for future planting. The adults, which look similar to weevils, lay eggs either on the pods of growing plants or on seeds in storage; and the legless and curved grubs which hatch out bore into the seed, feed and pupate inside it. Because of the size of the bean seed, germination is not usually affected but the holes made in the seed reduce the amount of food available to the germinating seedlings, resulting in stunted plants in severe cases. They also expose the seeds to attack by other borers such as millipedes and wireworms, which may be in the soil at sowing time, and to fungal and bacterial diseases.

Seeds containing live grubs or beetles should be burnt to destroy the pest. They should not be placed on a compost heap, as the beatles may spread from it. As the pest is seed-borne the surest precaution against it is to buy seed only from a reputable merchant.

Pea and bean weevil: the same weevil which attacks peas also attacks broad beans. The weevils eat semi-circular holes from the edges of young leaves and also eat the nodules on the roots. As soon as this is seen, dust or spray the plants with derris.

Mice: occasionally seed can be correctly sown in good land, and few or no seedlings germinate. This is probably the result of attacks by mice which take the seed and store it. Set traps at intervals along the rows, and inspect the traps frequently.

Royal Horticultural Society, Wisley, Surry

A. A. Turner

Bean aphis is the worst pest of the broad beans. The bean weevil eats small holes in the leaves.

GUIDE TO BROAD BEAN TROUBLES

Symptoms	Probable cause
Small black insects on stems, leaves and growing points; curled-up leaves	Bean aphis
Chocolate-coloured spots on leaves	Chocolate spot
Seed leaves mis-shapen, seedlings stunted, small holes in seed	Bean beetle
Semi-circular holes along leaf edges	Pea and bean weevil
Complete failure to germinate	Mice

11

Brussels Sprouts

Brassica oleracea gemmifera (fam. *Cruciferae)*
Hardy biennial, usually grown as an **annual**
Sowing to harvesting time: 28-36 weeks
Size: about 90 cm (3′) tall
Yield: 6 plants per 3 m (10′) row, each producing about
1 kg (2 lb) of sprouts

Brussels sprouts—firm, tight, button-like miniature cabbages—are one of the most highly prized of all winter vegetables. These brassicas were practically created for growing in the cool, temperate climates where many other vegetables do not thrive, and they are fairly straightforward to grow. The recent introduction of F_1 hybrids has all but eliminated the once common problem of 'blown' sprouts, those with open and leafy, rather than tight, heads. The flavour of these new varieties is also an improvement, making Brussels sprouts an even more important choice for your garden.

A descendant of the wild cabbage and closely related to Savoy cabbage, Brussels sprouts have a growth habit quite different from other brassicas. The stem of the plant is crowned by a head of inward-curling leaves. From the crown almost down to the base of the stem are closely packed leaf joints, and careful plant breeding has ensured that tight little cabbage-like heads are produced in these joints all the way up the stem. Each of these miniature cabbages is called a sprout. Tradition says that the vegetable originated in the area of northern Europe which is now Belgium, and takes its name from the capital city. It is an economical vegetable to grow, as both the leafy tops and the sprouts make delicious vegetables.

With most brassicas, the buds in the leaf joints do not form until the second season of growth, but Brussels sprouts develop theirs during the first year. The natural tendency of the plant is to form sprouts near the base and then in turn up the stem. After those formed first at the bottom have been picked, the sprouts further up the stem grow bigger, so that a succession of pickings can be made from the same plant. For quite a long time, plants were developed which would produce greater quantities of large sprouts. However, large sprouts have less flavour, and the trend now, started by the commercial growers, is to grow plants which produce a mass of small to

Brussels sprouts—firm, miniature cabbages—are among the most popular winter vegetables.

medium-sized sprouts, all of which come to maturity at about the same time.

It is a good idea to decide what you plan to do with your sprouts before choosing your varieties. For general kitchen use, you will probably want a variety which grows fairly large and produces a succession of sprouts throughout the winter. However, if you plan to freeze most of your crop, choose a commercial growers' variety so that all the sprouts will be ready for harvest and preparation at once. Remember, too, that the picking season can be extended by using a range of varieties which will come into production at different times.

13

The harvesting season for sprouts is from early autumn through to early spring. There are some extra early varieties which will begin to crop in late summer, but, unless you are extremely fond of sprouts, it is rather a waste to begin harvesting them at a time when so many other seasonal vegetables are at their peak.

Brussels sprouts are one of the best cool-climate crops. They are hardy and will withstand considerble frost, although they will not tolerate extreme heat. A hot, dry summer seems to inhibit their capacity to produce tight sprouts in the following autumn. In the initial stages the seeds and young plants need a temperature well above the freezing point, but in the following winter the mature plants will stand quite severe and prolonged frost. The plants will not grow during such extreme conditions, but they will remain alive and will resume growth when the frost is past.

Suitable site and soil

Brussels sprouts are not particular about soil requirements They will grow in almost any type of soil, although they do best in a good deep loam. If the soil is at all acid, correct with an application of lime during the winter, otherwise you may run into trouble with a disease such as club root.

When choosing your site, remember that sprouts can grow into tall plants, and that they will occupy their position for quite a long time. If possible, try to arrange the rows so that the sprouts do not block the sunlight from other crops. A site in full sunlight is not essential, as long as it gets sun for part of the day. And since Brussels sprouts are top-heavy plants, avoid a site which will get the full force of the wind, or be sure to give some wind protection.

Since Brussels sprouts are brassicas, do not plant them in a site previously occupied by another brassica crop, or pests and diseases may build up in the soil. A site last occupied by peas or beans is a good choice. In fact, any position which was manured for a previous crop is good, but if this is not possible, dig the site deeply and work in a heavy dressing of well-rotted farmyard manure or garden compost, as early as possible in the autumn before planting. This will allow time for the soil to settle and become firm, which is very important if you wish to avoid blown sprouts. If you did not manure the site in the previous autumn, apply a top-dressing of a general compound fertilizer (which has slightly more potash and phosphate than nitrogen in it) at the rate of 90-120 g per sq m (3-4 oz per sq yd), about seven to ten days before planting.

Sowing the seed

Brussels sprouts can be sown in a seed-box, in boxes under cloches or outdoors in a seed-bed and then transplanted to their final positions. Transplanting seems to strengthen the plants and gives an improved crop.

Any available plot of fairly fine soil will do for a seed-bed, as the plants will only be there for a few weeks. Rake the soil over lightly, and make drills about 1.5 cm ($\frac{1}{2}$″) deep, and 15-23 cm (6-9″) apart. For a maincrop of sprouts, sow the seed in mid-spring. Like all brassica seed, that of Brussels sprouts is small and round; sow them quite thinly. Germination should take place within seven to twelve days of sowing, a little longer if the weather is cold. If you have any seed left over, keep it, as it will remain viable for three years.

For sowing in containers, choose standard-sized seed trays or pots filled with a good quality seed compost. Sow as you would for seeds in the open ground, and keep the containers indoors or in an unheated greenhouse.

You can also make sowings in frames or under cloches. Again, follow the instructions for sowing in the open ground. For frame cultivation, water the soil thoroughly before sowing, if it is not already moist, so that further watering is unnecessary during the seedling stage. If sown under frames or cloches, the plants

1. In mid to late winter, sow seeds directly in a cold frame, cover with a thin layer of fine sifted soil.

2. In the greenhouse, sow seeds 1.2 cm ($\frac{1}{2}''$) deep in a seed tray, filled with good quality seed compost.

3. As soon as the seedlings show the first pair of leaves, prick them out from seed boxes into pots or trays.

4. Harden young plants off; place pots in a cold frame outdoors and open light on mild, sunny days.

can be thinned and then left in their original positions to mature if you do not wish to transplant them, but remember that the plants may not be as good in the long run. If the seed is sown outdoors without any protection with glass or plastic, cover with netting at once; birds, especially pigeons and sparrows, are very fond of the plants, both when young and mature.

Another alternative, if you do not wish to take the time and trouble to sow seed and grow seedlings, is to buy plants at the transplanting stage. There are always plenty of Brussels sprout plants available at markets and garden shops in late spring. A delay of a day or two between pulling the plants and replanting them should not cause too much harm.

Planting out
As a general rule, young Brussels sprout plants should remain in the seed-bed, without pricking out, until ready for transplanting. They will need thinning, probably twice, so that they are spaced about 10 cm (4″) apart before moving.

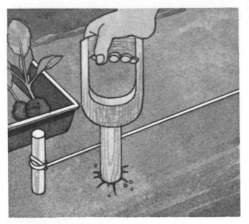

1. Prepare planting holes with a dibber when all danger of frost is past; space plants 45 cm (18″) apart.

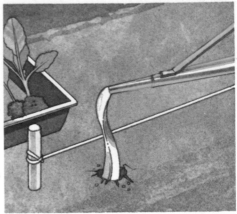

2. If the soil is dry, fill the holes with water; water the seed bed the night before transplanting.

3. Put the plants in carefully, and firm the soil around the roots with a dibber; avoid shallow planting.

4. Test for firm planting by pulling a leaf; it should just tear. If it makes the plant lift up, replant deeper.

Some gardeners transplant most of the crop, but leave a few plants where they were sown, spaced about 45 cm (18″) apart. This can be satisfactory, although those plants left in their original sites will seldom be as good as those which were transplanted, as transplanting benefits Brussels sprouts; the plants grow stronger and produce earlier and better crops.

The time to transplant is when all danger of frost is past, either in late spring or early summer. The plants should be between 10-15 cm (4-6″) high, but not drawn and leggy, with four or five true leaves present. It is essential to allow plenty of space between Brussels sprout plants: allow 75-90 cm ($2\frac{1}{2}$-3′) between rows with the greater spacing for the larger varieties, and 45 cm ($1\frac{1}{2}$′) between each plant in the row. It is important to plant deeply because the plants are mainly shallow-rooting, and the roots have to support a tall, heavy-headed superstructure. A good rule to follow is to plant with the lower leaves just resting on the soil.

A day just after a heavy rain is the best

Birds, particularly pigeons, can do a great deal of damage; protect plants with netting.

time to transplant. If this is not possible, or in a particularly dry season, water the site thoroughly first. If you can water the seed-bed the night before, so much the better, as the plants will then be well watered. Prepare planting holes with a dibber and fill these with water as well. Put the plants in carefully, to the correct depth, and firm the ground well around them to anchor the roots and encourage the development of tight button sprouts. Do not forget to protect the plants from bird attacks; indeed, it is a good idea to have them netted or in a permanent cage.

Early crops

Early sprouts, ready from late summer onwards, are considered desirable by many gardeners, although this is the time of year when summer vegetables such as runner beans and cauliflowers are both plentiful and cheap.

If you are determined to have early sprouts, then sow in mid- to late winter.

Because sprouts require a long period of growth, and the last frosts sometimes occur in late spring, you will have to sow the seeds under glass. For germination to take place, the temperature of the soil must be 10-13°C (50-55°F); if the winter is mild you can use an unheated greenhouse or conservatory indoors, or sow them outdoors under cloches or frames. If the winter is particularly cold, either delay sowing until the weather warms up and accept that early crops will not be possible, or use a slightly heated greenhouse.

Sow the seed in boxes filled with a good quality seed compost. As soon as the seedlings show the first pair of leaves, they are pricked out, or transferred from seed boxes to pots or trays which, like the seed boxes, also need the protection of glass or plastic. The seed boxes, pots or trays should contain a fine soil or potting compost. Transplant the seedlings 5 cm (2″) apart in all directions.

1. **Water young plants in dry weather; insufficient watering will result in blowsy, loose, unattractive buttons.**

2. **In autumn, earth up around the plants to level of lowest leaves, to protect against wind-rock and frost.**

If you use trays or pots, you can place them outside the greenhouse, and take the cloches off, or open the frame light, on mild days, to allow the plants to harden off. Plant them into their final positions in early to mid-spring, depending on their degree of maturity. They may continue to need protection at night if the weather is very cold.

To sow the seed directly in a cold frame, prepare the soil by watering it thoroughly so that further watering will not be necessary for some time. Sow the seed thinly in mid- to late winter and cover with 0.3 cm ($\frac{1}{8}''$) of fine soil. Close the light and cover it with a mat until germination has taken place; on warm sunny days, open the frame so that air can circulate around the plants. They will still need protection with the light in periods of heavy rain or extreme cold, particularly if frost threatens at night, when the mat should be replaced also. Thin them to about 10 cm (4") apart in all directions, and plant them out in mid-spring. Remember your bird protection.

In districts which have a mild winter, the seed is sometimes sown in sheltered borders in autumn and protected by temporary arrangements of glass or plastic against any winter frosts, ready for transplanting in early spring. The main drawback with autumn planting is that autumn-sown plants are much more likely to bolt, or run to seed, without producing sprouts. Also, an unexpectedly cold winter can bring disaster to the whole crop.

Care and development

Remember that sprouts need plenty of water when young, and blowsy, loose buttons often result due to insufficient water at this stage. In hot, dry weather this is particularly important.

A mulch of rotted garden compost or farmyard manure put round the plants about a month after planting will help to keep the soil moist and supply a little more plant food. If you give too much nitrogen while the plants are growing, it will result in blown sprouts later, so any addition of compound fertilizers should be done with caution, and in general only if the soil is very light and quick draining. Avoid sulphate of ammonia and nitrate of soda completely, as they are very rich in nitrates—excessive applications could quickly ruin both taste and quality of your sprouts.

Summer care consists mainly of keeping the surrounding soil free from weeds. Remember, though, that the roots of Brussels sprouts are very shallow and also widespread, so hand weeding is best. If you do hoe, hoe lightly and shallowly across the surface to avoid damage. If any leaves at the bottom of the plant become yellowed or decayed, remove them immediately, or infection may spread to the sprouts and damage the crops.

If the sprouts are a tall-growing variety, or if they are on a windy site, stake the plants in early autumn, placing the stake on the windward side. Two ties are usually necessary. It also helps if you earth-up round the plants to the level of the lowest leaves at this time. Earthing-up, besides protecting the plants from wind-rock, throws excess moisture away from the stems and gives some protection from frost.

Harvesting

You can encourage the formation and early maturity of sprouts by removing the top 2.5 cm (1″) of growing tip. Do this in late summer or early autumn for maincrop varieties and late autumn for late croppers. This practice, however, tends to decrease the yield. As the crop reaches maturity—28-36 weeks after sowing depending on variety—the lower leaves of the plant will start to yellow. Cut or pull them off—they should come off easily if pulled downward.

Sprouts mature from the bottom of the stem upwards, and should be picked in that order. If you leave sprouts on the bottom of the stem, production of new sprouts further up will be diminished, and the lower sprouts will quickly

HARVESTING

1. As the crop reaches maturity, the lower leaves will start to yellow; cut or pull them off when this happens.

2. Pick sprouts from the bottom of the stem upwards; split sprouts off the stem with a sharp, downward tug.

After harvesting is finished, dig up the plants. Burn the roots, to avoid risk of club root disease. Chop up the woody stems with a spade, and put them on the compost heap.

become inedible and subject to infection or infestation by pests.

Begin picking the lower sprouts when they are about 2.5 cm (1″) in diameter, as large sprouts are not nearly as tasty as small ones. Split each sprout off the stem with a sharp, downward tug; if they do not come off easily, use a sharp knife rather than damage the stem by pulling. Spread the harvesting evenly over all the plants; never strip one plant of all sprouts, unless it is to be a once-only harvest, perhaps for freezing.

Once the sprouts towards the top of the stem are well developed, you can cut off the top leafy growth and cook it like cabbage. After the top is cut, the remaining sprouts will mature quite quickly. Otherwise, the top growth can be left on until all the sprouts have been harvested, and will then provide some useful 'greens' in mid-spring. Some gardeners, who want all their sprouts early and small for freezing, cut off the top several weeks before the crop is ready for picking. Most of the sprouts will then mature at the same time.

Care after harvesting

Almost every part of the Brussels sprout plant is used. The sprouts and crown are both eaten, leaving only the stout, woody stem. Some gardeners leave a few stumps of Brussels sprouts in the ground over winter, to produce early spring greens. This is generally a bad idea because the stumps provide a convenient overwintering place for serious brassica pests, such as whitefly and aphids. Having overwintered on the stumps, they then come to life in spring and re-infest newly planted brassica crops.

After harvesting the sprouts and the leafy tops, the best policy is to dig the stumps completely out of the ground. Chop off and burn the root, to avoid the risk of club root. This is why it is much better to dig rather than pull up the stumps. If you pull the stumps out, the root may break off below ground level and remain in the soil to harbour pests and diseases.

The woody stem will rot in time, but should be chopped up with a spade to aid decay. It can be dug into the soil but is probably best incorporated in the compost heap.

A Brussels sprout crop is a heavy drain on soil, which will benefit from a generous manuring before being used again.

Exhibition tips

Brussels sprouts when well grown can make a fine display on the show bench, whether in individual classes or as part of a collection. There are no special cultivation requirements for sprouts intended for showing; good general cultivation should lead to sprouts excellent for both kitchen and show use. They are worth a maximum of fifteen points, and fifty sprouts is the usual number required for both single dishes and collections.

Judges will look for fresh, solid and tightly closed sprouts. As with most vegetables, enormous size is not of paramount importance, and small sprouts which are tightly closed will be favoured over large, loose, blowsy ones.

Try to leave the selection of the sprouts until the last possible moment. Although they will keep for several days when stored in a damp sack in a cool, dark shed or cellar, they really look their best when freshly picked. To ensure that the sprouts are as uniform as possible, it is a good idea to first select one sprout as a control; it should be slightly smaller than average, no more than 3.7 cm (1½") in diameter and tightly closed. Using this sprout as a reference select about one hundred more. This seems like an extravagant number, but you may need a good supply of replacements at the show bench, and it is better to have a few extra. Although they are tough, strong growers, do not handle the sprouts carelessly, or they may bruise.

Little is needed in the way of preparation. If the tiny leaves at the base of the sprouts look yellow or are otherwise unsightly, cut them off with a sharp knife. Do not pick off too many outer leaves, though, because the inner leaves are paler and less attractive. Then cut all stems to the same length, preferably short.

If the sprouts are being packed for transport to the show, make sure they are packed tightly enough; otherwise, they may bump against each other in transit and some damage may occur. If there is extra space in the box, fill it with tissue paper. The sprouts should not be left in the box too long, or the colour will bleach out and rotting may occur. The sprouts are most attractive when displayed on a wire cone packed with moss.

Pests & Diseases

Cabbage aphids: these insects are most troublesome in hot, dry summers following mild winters. The grey aphids heavily infest the undersides of the leaves of sprouts, which then become curled, blistered and discoloured. Because the eggs of cabbage aphids overwinter on the stumps of old brassicas, the best preventive measure is to dig up and either burn or compost the stems immediately after harvesting. Keep the plants well supplied with water, and for severe attacks, remove the worst affected leaves and sprouts and spray the remainder with derris, bioresmethrin or malathion.

Cabbage root fly: these flies are most active from mid-spring through to early summer. The eggs are deposited on or just below the soil surface next to the stems, and the emerging white legless maggots burrow into the stem, and also eat the roots underground. The first obvious symptoms of cabbage root fly infestation are grey-green, wilted leaves and slow-growing plants, smaller than the others. If pulled out of the ground, the roots will be found to contain the maggots, or they may be in the soil round the roots. A preventive measure is to treat the soil with diazinon granules at the time of planting; also treat the seedbed before sowing if an attack occurred the previous year. Surrounding the stems with a small square of tarred felt on the soil when planting will prevent egg laying. If an infestation occurs, remove and burn damaged plants, as well as the soil around the roots.

Cabbage whitefly: these tiny white moth-like insects feed on the undersides of leaves. They are usually a problem in warm weather, although in mild winters attacks occasionally occur. Besides weakening the plants, they exude honeydew, which encourages the growth of sooty mould; in severe cases, young plants will be destroyed very quickly. Prevent serious damage by spraying with a resmethrin-based insecticide as

Cabbage aphid damage: infested leaves become curled, blistered, and discoloured.

This young Brussels sprout plant is infected with club root, a soil-borne fungal disease.

soon as you see them. Remove and burn all heavily infested leaves and spray the remainder with a soft soap solution, as an alternative to resmethrin.

Flea beetle: if the leaves of the seedlings and young sprout plants are perforated with numerous small round holes, then there is probably an infestation of flea beetle. These small black insects are most active in fine weather in mid- to late spring but can also be found at intervals throughout the summer. The best preventive measure is to dust the seeds and soil with gamma-HCH; hoeing frequently round the young plants disturbs the soil and discourages the beetles from laying eggs.

Cutworms: these greyish-brown or grey caterpillars feed at night, when they eat through the stems, severing the plant at or slightly below ground level. If your garden is weed-free and well cultivated, you are less likely to have problems with this pest; if an infestation occurs, dust the soil with gamma-HCH.

Cabbage moth/cabbage white butterfly: the green or greyish-brown caterpillars of these insects feed on the leaf tissues of all brassicas, causing widespread damage. The cabbage moth caterpillars usually attack the inner leaves, where they are not easily reached by insecticide. The caterpillars of the butterfly eat the outer leaves, and also foul the remaining foliage with excrement. Both can do a great deal of damage

and ruin the plants completely. As the eggs of both pests are laid on the leaves, remove and destroy any eggs you find on the plant. They will be small and round or conical in shape, light-coloured and laid in batches. If caterpillars do manage to hatch out, hand pick them off in a mild infestation; otherwise, dust or spray the infested plants with derris or a salt solution, 60 g (2 oz) in 4.5 L (1 gal) of water.

Gall weevil: this occasionally attacks Brussels sprouts, although it is more likely on the brassica root crops such as swede. The roots form round hollow swellings in which white maggots will be found, and young plants will be stunted. Remove and destroy badly infected plants; remove only the galls from the remainder.

Club root (finger and toe): this is the most serious disease the home gardener is likely to encounter; it affects all members of the brassica family. It is caused by a fungus in the soil which infects the roots; the symptoms above ground are bluish and wilting leaves, and stunted, slow-growing plants. The roots, when dug up, will be swollen and distorted, black, and rotting, often with an unpleasant odour. Club root is often associated with heavy, badly-drained soils, so a good precaution is to correct any drainage problems before planting. Excessively acid soils also tend to encourage this disease, so correct the soil acidity by liming so that the pH is neutral or slightly alkaline. A further precaution is to sprinkle calomel dust (using pure calomel, rather than the 4% contained in many proprietary brands) before sowing at the rate of 30 g per 1.5 m (1 oz per 5') run. Alternatively, sow the seed in sterilized soil outdoors, or in containers, or in sterilized soil in individual pots. When transplanting, dip the roots in a fungicidal solution of either 60 g (2 oz) pure calomel, or 15 g ($\frac{1}{2}$ oz) of benomyl or thiophanate-methyl to every 0.5 L (1 pt) of water. Because the fungus is soil-borne, if an infection occurs, the site must not be used for brassicas for at least five years—the spores have been known to survive 20 years. All infected plants must be lifted completely and burned immediately.

Wirestem: this fungal infection attacks young plants, causing the base of the stem to become constricted, turn brown and wither. If the plants are not killed outright, they remain stunted and will never fully recover. Seeds or seed-beds dusted with quintozene or thiram or watered with cheshunt compound will usually be free of attacks.

Downy mildew: the symptoms of this fungal infection are white patches on the undersides of the leaves, and yellow speckling on the upper side, followed by wilting. It is often found on seedlings and young plants under glass, or on the outside of the young buttons later in the season. Spraying with zineb will help control downy mildew in mild cases; destroy any plants or buttons severely infected.

Ringspot; a fungal infection, ring spot attacks older plants, and produces round, light brown spots, about 1.3 cm ($\frac{1}{2}$") in diameter on the outer and lower leaves. Infected leaves eventually turn completely yellow and wither. Remove and destroy all infected leaves, and minimize further damage with a light dressing of potash fertilizer.

Grey mould (Botrytis cinerea): this is sometimes a trouble on Brussels sprouts. Infected sprouts become soft, and eventually covered with grey furry mould. Infection occurs through a broken main leaf stalk just below the sprout, and is more likely where too much nitrogen has been supplied. Removal of the affected parts is all that need be done.

Canker: Brussels sprouts may be attacked by this fungal disease, which produces brown or purple spots and cankers on the stems, and results in stunting and sometimes total wilt. Destroy affected plants and do not plant again in the same site.

GUIDE TO BRUSSELS SPROUTS TROUBLES

Symptoms	Probable cause
Leaves turn grey-green and collapse; roots tunnelled, with white maggots inside them	Cabbage root fly
White patches on undersides of leaves of young plants	Downy mildew
Pale brown spots on leaves	Ring spot
Stunted plants with narrowed brown stem bases	Wirestem
Bluish-green, wilting leaves; swollen, black rotting roots	Club root
Stem severed at or slightly below ground level	Cutworms
Small round holes in leaves of seedlings or young plants, or complete defoliation	Flea beetle
Leaves distorted, discoloured; small grey insects on undersides; stickiness on leaves, sometimes black sooty patches	Cabbage aphids
Leaves skeletonized, covered with excrement	Cabbage moth/ white butterfly
Soft sprouts, grey fur on outside	Grey mould
Brown or purple spots on stems	Canker
Round swellings on roots	Gall weevil

Varieties

The many F_1 hybrids now available on the market have their drawbacks as well as good points. On the positive side, F_1 hybrids tend to be compact growers, and the stems are tightly covered with buttons. However, the sprouts have been bred to mature all at the same time, and this can be a problem if you do not own a freezer.

The ordinary varieties tend to be taller growing, and, hence, less suitable for small gardens. They are the heaviest croppers, though, and they go on cropping for several months.

Peer Gynt

Peer Gynt: F_1 hybrid of outstanding quality; dwarf growing and ideal for small gardens; very prolific cropper of uniform, high quality, dark green sprouts; early crops from early autumn.
Achilles: F_1 hybrid; produces high yields of medium-sized sprouts; begins cropping in mid-autumn; can be picked over a long period, as the sprouts do not rot on the stem quickly.
Citadel: F_1 hybrid; firm, tight sprouts; one of the latest croppers; stands well to give sprouts in early spring.
Fasolt: dark green solid sprouts; mid-to late-winter cropping; good flavour and tightly packed.

Bedford-Winter Harvest

Bedford-Market Rearguard: successful on most soils; very dark green, medium-sized sprouts; will provide continuous supplies from early winter to early spring.
Bedford-Winter Harvest: excellent choice for a mid-season crop; bears medium-sized, dark green, very solid sprouts from mid-autumn to mid-winter.
Cambridge No. 5: prolific cropper of large, high quality sprouts; matures from mid-winter to early spring.
Ashwell's Strain: one of the oldest varieties available; extremely hardy; sprouts can be picked into mid-spring.
Rous Lench: produces small sprouts on fairly short stems; the best variety for an open, windy garden; ready for mid-winter picking.
Perfect Line: F_1 hybrid; mid-season cropper, giving very high yields of medium-sized buttons; slightly earlier that *Citadel;* excellent for early and mid-winter picking.
Bedford-Fillbasket: very large sprouts; harvested from mid-autumn through to early winter; first-class flavour; succeeds on a wide range of soil types.
Roodnerf-Early Button: variety bred for small, deep green sprouts; first-class buttons; excellent for freezing.
Roodnerf-Vremo Inter: early to late

24

Fasolt

Roodnerf-Vremo Inter

winter harvester; sprouts medium-sized; excellent colour.

Roodnerf-Rollo: uniform, small, solid sprouts; mid-autumn to early winter; heavy cropper.

Roodnerf-Seven Hills: early to late winter variety; small, tight sprouts of good quality.

Focus: F_1 hybrid; new variety with distinctive savoury flavour; sprouts small to medium-sized, dark green, firm; ready for cropping from early autumn through mid-winter.

Lindo: new variety; vigorous and heavy cropper; harvests over a two-month period from early to mid-autumn.

King Arthur: F_1 hybrid; popular mid-season variety, with heavy crop of medium-sized, smooth-skinned sprouts; plants fairly tall, uniform and hardy.

Prince Askold: F_1 hybrid; first-class late variety, with heavy crop of dark green, medium-sized sprouts from mid-winter to early spring; plants of medium height.

Irish Elegance: late autumn to early winter cropper, with good yields of medium-sized, smooth sprouts, plants tall and uniform; sprouts keep well on stem for long period of time.

Early Half Tall (Continuity): medium-sized plants cropping from late summer onwards; large sprouts available until late winter.

Stabilo: medium-sized, firm, dark green sprouts; heavy yielder; sprouts keep well on the stem.

Sigmund: F_1 hybrid; hardy, late maturing variety with smooth, solid, medium-sized sprouts; heavy cropper.

Jade Cross: F_1 hybrid; small dark sprouts, very closely packed; early to late autumn; short-growing; ideal for freezing.

Rubine or *Red:* novelty type which produces red sprouts; very decorative plant; good flavour; ready from late autumn onwards.

Rubine

25

Cabbages

Brassica oleracea capitata (fam.
Cruciferae) Savoy cabbages:
Brassica oleracea bullata major
(fam. *Cruciferae*)
Biennial grown as an **annual**
Sowing to harvesting time: 20-35 weeks for red and
autumn cabbages; 28 weeks for winter cabbages; 32 weeks
for Savoys.
Size: green and red varieties average between 23-45 cm (9-
18″) high and 15-60 cm (6-24″) wide; Savoys are about 20
cm (8″) high and 50 cm (20″) wide.
Yield: for red and green cabbages about 10-12 per 3 m (10′)
row, each head weighing between 0.5-1.5 kg (1-3 lb);
Savoys yield about 6-7 per 3 m (10′) row, each weighing
between 1-2 kg (2-4½ lb).

Cabbages are extremely hardy members
of the brassica family, thriving in cold,
damp winters and capable of withstand-
ing conditions which would destroy
many other crops. Their suitability to
most temperate climates and soils, and
the minimal amount of attention they
require, make cabbages one of the easiest
crops to grow.

Spring cabbages, sown in summer, are
a distinct group and won't be dealt with
in this article. Here we look at the types
which can be sown from late winter to
late spring, for harvesting in summer
autumn and winter.

Do not be deterred by the list of pests
and diseases that can attack your
cabbages; as long as you give your crop
reasonable attention it should thrive.

The somewhat unglamorous reputation of cabbage has changed considerably over the last twenty years.
Newer varieties are milder tasting than
the old strong-flavoured types, and
disease resistant varieties have also been
bred.

Suitable site and soil
Cabbages will thrive on almost any well-
drained ground, but they prefer a
medium-light soil which retains a
reasonable amount of water. Prepare the
soil with lime and apply manure at the
rate of one barrow load per square yard
(square metre) several months before
sowing. If the ground has not been
manured, apply a general fertilizer at the
rate of 100 g per sq m (3 oz per sq yd) just

1. Prior to sowing, prepare the ground with an application of a suitable compound fertilizer.

2. Prepare the seed-bed just before sowing by raking the soil to a fine consistency. The soil must be dry.

3. Using the side of a draw hoe blade, take out a narrow drill about 2.5 cm (1″) deep and 2.5 cm (1″) wide.

4. Cabbage seeds are large enough to sow individually. Space them in the drill about 8 seeds per 30 cm (1′).

5. When the drill is filled, use a trowel to cover over the seeds with a thin layer of moist soil or peat.

6. When sowing is complete, use the back of a rake to smooth over and firm the surface of the seed-bed.

7. Cabbages are ideal for frame cultivation. Prepare the seed-bed and sow as for outdoor cabbages.

8. Sowings can also be made in the greenhouse. Sow in seedboxes filled with a good quality seed compost.

Pat Brindley

Winter cabbages can be sown in growing bags which contain specially prepared compost.

prior to sowing.

Choose an open, sunny site, and remember that cabbages must never follow any other brassicas because of the risk of disease being passed on.

Sowing the seed

Cabbages can be sown outdoors or under glass; the method is the same for both. The time of sowing depends on the variety and on the time you want to

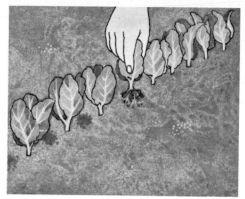

9. When one true cabbage leaf appears, thin the row of young cabbages to about 30 cm (1′) apart.

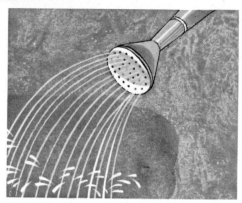

10. Before transplanting the seedlings, water the ground well using a fine rose on the watering can.

11. To transplant, dig a hole in the moistened ground, fill it with water, and gently place in the young plant.

12. Firm the ground around the transplants, and then water. Continue to water liberally as the plants grow.

13. Keep the cabbage patch free of weeds by hoeing frequently with the blade of a small Dutch hoe.

14. Growing cabbage plants will benefit from an occasional watering with diluted liquid manure.

15. Cabbages are bothered by many insect pests, so an occasional dusting with insecticide will be helpful.

16. As the plants begin to mature, check them frequently and remove any yellowing outer leaves.

17. When the cabbages are ready for harvesting, loosen the soil and lift out the plants, roots intact.

18. Cut off the roots and stem, and remove any coarse outer leaves. Put these on your compost heap.

harvest your cabbages. Plan a succession of sowings from mid spring until early summer for a long period of cutting. Rake the seedbed to a fine tilth and prepare drills 1.5 cm ($\frac{1}{2}''$) deep and 15 cm (6") apart. Sow at the rate of eight seeds per 30 cm (1') outdoors.

For a mid to late summer crop, sow the seed thinly in late winter or early spring, in seed beds protected by frames or cloches. Plant into permanent positions in mid to late spring, 30-40 cm (12-15") apart each way. The bed should be prepared in the same way as for winter crops. Protection may still be necessary if the weather is severe.

Cabbages grown outdoors should be transplanted when four or five cabbage-like leaves have formed.

Care and cultivation

Spring-sown cabbages do not require a great deal of care. Never allow them to dry out, as this will check their growth. Water liberally, especially during hot, dry weather. Hoe around the growing plants frequently to control weeds, to aerate the soil and to deter insect pests from laying eggs near the crop.

Some gardeners sow hyssop, a perennial herb, near the cabbage bed. It is supposed to be a protection against club root disease and to repel the cabbage white butterfly, and many gardeners

Another method of harvesting cabbages is to pull back the outer leaves and cut the heart out.

Leave the stump in the ground. In time new shoots will grow and these can produce greens for cutting.

swear that it works well.

Cabbages are greedy feeders, so during the growing period give applications of dried blood or liquid fertilizer. Top-dressings, particularly nitrate of soda, should never be used on cabbages, as they can give a bad taste to the leaves.

As the plants begin to mature, some of the outside leaves may turn yellow. Break off any yellowing leaves as soon as you see them.

Harvesting and storing

Cabbages are ready for harvesting when the hearts are firm; lift the entire plant with a fork and cut the roots off later, or cut the stem with a sharp knife a little above the base of the lower leaves. Remove the outer leaves, which are much too coarse for eating, and put them on the compost heap.

Mature cabbages in good condition with firm hearts can be kept in a cool airy, frost-proof shed for several weeks. Place the cabbages on a rack made from wood or chicken wire in the shed. Do not stack them on the ground.

Aftercare

Once the cabbages have been cut, the crop is finished and the ground may be cleared. Burn the stems, or chop them up and add them to the compost heap, providing they are free of any pests or diseases. Alternatively, you can leave the stems in the ground overwinter to produce shoots again in the spring and provide another source of spring greens.

Red Cabbage

Red cabbages are usually grown as spring-sown varieties for autmn harvesting. Most people use red cabbage for pickling, but it is also delicious cooked simply and served hot. All red cabbage is round-headed, and all varieties need a longer period for maturing than green spring-sown cabbages. The heads are rather smaller than most green varieties.

To have red cabbages ready for harvesting in autumn, sow the seed in an

Store cabbages on a rack of chicken wire in an airy, frost-free place. They should keep for several weeks.

A healthy row of winter cabbages ready for harvesting.

outdoor seedbed in mid spring, and transplant to a cropping position as soon as four leaves have formed. Water well throughout the growing period, especially if the weather is dry, and follow the cultivation instructions for other cabbages.

The plants are ready for cutting when they are firm-hearted, usually from early autumn. Be sure to cut them before the frost can get to them, as they are not very frost-hardy. They will store for several months in a cool, dry, frost-proof place.

Savoys

Savoys are extremely hardy cabbages with wrinkled, curly leaves. They tend to be rather mild in flavour, and for this reason many people prefer them to other spring-sown varieties. There are many different varieties of Savoys, and the range is wide enough to provide crops ready for harvesting in every month from late autumn to early spring.

However, Savoys should never be grown in a city or in an area of high industrial pollution, since their deeply curled and crinkled leaves trap the soot.

Sow the seed in succession from early spring in a prepared seed-bed. Savoys root less deeply than other cabbages, so they will grow well on less fertile soil and need less fertilizers added. Follow sowing instructions for winter cabbage. The site for final planting should be prepared with a hoed-in application of 60 g per sq m (2 oz per sq yd) of superphosphate and 30 g per sq m (1 oz per sq yd) of potash. Transplant the seedlings when they are large enough to handle and set them out at about 45 cm (18″) apart. Cultivation is the same as for other varieties.

Harvest Savoys when they are firm-hearted. Remove the tough outer leaves and put them on the compost heap. If you want to store some, choose very firm ones and keep them in a cool, airy place. Some varieties will stay fresh for two to three months.

Exhibition tips

If you want to grow cabbages for exhibition, choose your varieties carefully for those suited to your soil and area. Think carefully about the timing of your sowing, so that the cabbages will be in prime condition for your particular show. You do not want your plants to mature too early and become wilted or tough before the event.

It is essential to keep exhibition plants completely free of pests and diseases, so take extra precautions. If the outer leaves become damaged, you can remove these before the damage goes any further, providing this does not make the shape unsymmetrical. The remaining leaves surrounding the heart must be perfect.

Cut the cabbages just before the show, as freshness will count high in the judges' marking. If the cabbages have matured too quickly, lift them completely when they are at their prime and hang them upsidedown in a cool dark place. Spray them with cold water twice a day to prevent wilting.

Three perfectly-matched cabbages should be arranged on a plate at the exhibition hall. The judges will look for cabbages which are fresh and well-shaped with firm tender hearts.

Try hyssop (believed to repel cabbage white butterfly) as a companion plant.

Varieties

Green cabbages

Autumn Pride: F$_1$ hybrid; large, flat heads with very solid hearts; stores well.
Babyhead: small-headed type which produces firm, solid hearts; stores well; good choice for a small garden; sow for summer or autumn cropping.
Celtic: F$_1$ hybrid; extremely winter-hardy; heavy yield; firm, solid heads which store well; mature from early to late winter.
Christmas Drumhead: dwarf, compact and hardy variety well suited to small gardens; matures from mid-autumn; sowings can be made later than most varieties to extend cutting time.
Earliest: very early pointed-head type; sow under glass in late winter or outdoors in early spring for summer and autumn cutting; dwarf growing; excellent flavour.
Emerald Cross: round-headed variety; can be sown in succession throughout spring; high yield; firm, solid heads.
Green Express: new and very successful variety; large heads with crisp, sweet centres; stores very well; sow for summer or autumn maturing.
Golden Acre: popular and reliable; dwarf and compact; suited for small gardens; solid, round heads make excellent salads; matures in summer.
Hidena: F$_1$ hybrid; large, crisp oval-shaped heads; well-flavoured, especially for salads; if lifted with roots, will store for two months; crops in winter.
Hispi: all-year-round cabbage, but will mature in early winter if sown in very late spring; large, conical solid heads with a sweet flavour and crisp texture; compact and good for smaller gardens.
Holland Late Winter White: coleslaw-type cabbage with large, oval heads and crisp, white hearts; matures from late autumn to late winter, depending on sowing time.
Jupiter: new F$_1$ hybrid for harvesting throughout winter months; extremely hardy; large, solid heads; will store for two months.

Christmas Drumhead

Golden Acre

Hispi

Savoy King

Pride of the Market: very large, solid roundhead cabbage; matures early; stores well.

Primo: roundheaded variety; sow in early spring for mid to late summer cutting; small and compact; can be sown close together.

Stonehead: F_1 hybrid; small, compact, round, solid heads; sow close together; sow for summer or autumn crops.

Vienna Babyhead: small but heavy heads with smooth leaves around firm hearts; stores well; matures in summer.

Winnigstadt: very old and reliable favourite; tight, pointed heads with little outside leaf; matures from late summer to late autumn; good for exhibition.

Winter Salad: round, hard, compact heads; very good raw for winter salads;

matures late autumn; stores very well.

Red Cabbage

Blood Red: very early-maturing; deep red colour which turns bright red when pickled.

Niggerhead: dwarf red variety; small, round, solid heads which pickle well.

Ruby Ball: F_1 hybrid of outstanding quality; excellent flavour for cooking, salads or pickling; large, solid heads with little wastage; matures in mid-winter and can be harvested for several weeks.

Savoy Cabbage

Alexander's No. 1: largest savoy type; very hardy; firm, dark green heads; cut from mid-winter.

Autumn Green: very dark green heads

Winter Salad

Niggerhead

January King

Late Winter White

with well-curled leaves; matures in mid-autumn for harvesting over several weeks; stores well.

Best of All: large-headed, solid-hearted type matures from late autumn to early winter; excellent flavour.

Dwarf Green Curled: medium-sized, compact and solid heads; very curled dark green leaves; hardy and heavy cropping.

Ice Queen: F₁ hybrid; medium to large heads; very hardy; uniform quality; cut from mid-autumn.

January King: hardiest of all spring-sown cabbages; produces large, round, solid heads with a slight red tinge.

January Prince: smaller-headed variety of *January King:* dark green leaves with a reddish tint.

Ormskirk: very hardy savoy which can withstand even the most severe weather; large, solid heads with curled dark green leaves.

Ostara: matures from mid-autumn to mid-winter; uniform curled heads of good quality.

Savoy King: F₁ hybrid; one of the most vigorous, uniform-quality and high-yielding varieties; large, round heads with well-flavoured solid hearts; matures in early winter; can survive severe weather.

Winter King: similar to *Ormskirk;* extremely frost-resistant; large heads.

Wirosa: F₁ hybrid of *Ormskirk* type; hardy; good colour and flavour; round heads with finely-curled leaves; matures from mid to late winter.

Pests & Diseases

Cabbage aphis: this is a grey or grey-blue aphid which infests the undersides of leaves, from mid-spring through to winter. The eggs will overwinter in the stems. Treat by spraying with derris or malathion.

Cabbage root fly: Spring-sown cabbages are particularly at risk because the flies are most active in mid-spring to early summer. The adults lay their eggs against the cabbage stems, and the maggots hatch and burrow into the stem and devour the roots. The cabbages wilt and die. Lift and destroy any infested plants. An attack can be prevented by dusting the ground with diazinon at the time of planting and again about two weeks later.

Cabbage white butterfly: cabbages in the ground in summer and autumn are liable to attacks by the caterpillars of the cabbage white butterfly. The adults lay eggs on the cabbage leaves, and the caterpillars hatch out and rapidly devour the plants. If unchecked they can destroy an entire crop. Do not wait until the caterpillars are seen to take action. If you see any butterflies, spray the plants with a non-poisonous insecticide such as derris or malathion. Check the cabbage leaves for any yellowish, oval eggs, and remove and destroy them. Should you see any of the yellow-striped green caterpillars, remove them by hand and spray the plants again.

Cabbage moth: Moth larvae can also attack. The moths are nocturnal and rarely seen, so be on the look out for their large, round eggs, laid from mid-spring to mid-summer. The smooth green caterpillars hatch out and burrow into the hearts of the cabbages, destroying them. Remove any eggs by hand, and spray the plants with derris or malathion. Remove and destroy any caterpillars that hatch.

Cabbage white fly: this pest attacks all members of the cabbage family. It is usually a problem during warm weather, although attacks during mid-winter are not unknown. The females lay their eggs on the undersides of leaves, and the flat, scale-like larvae remain attached to the leaves. The secretions of the larvae encourage the formation of sooty moulds, and the cabbages are very quickly destroyed. Prevent a whitefly attack by spraying with a resmethrin-based insecticide at the first sign of the insects. Remove and burn any infested leaves, and spray the undersides of the remaining leaves with a soft soap solution.

Flea beetle: colonies of small, black flea beetles can decimate seedlings and young plants by biting small round holes in the leaves. The crop can be completely destroyed before it has even started to grow. To prevent an attack, dust the leaves of young plants with derris. Hoe

Holes in a head of cabbage caused by the caterpillars of the cabbage white butterfly.

Brian Furner

Adults and larva of the cabbage white fly. Eggs are laid on the undersides of leaves.

K. M. Harris

GUIDE TO CABBAGE TROUBLES

Symptom	Probable Cause
Maggots in stems	Cabbage root fly
Holes in leaves	Cabbage white butterfly caterpillar
	Cabbage moth caterpillar, Flea Beetle
White larva on undersides of leaves, distorted roots	Cabbage Whitefly, Club root
Wilting leaves	Cabbage root fly, Club root
Rotting stems on seedlings	Wirestem
Brown spots on leaves	Ring spot
White fungus on undersides of leaves	Downy mildew

frequently around the plants to disturb the beetles and stop egg-laying.

Club root (finger and toe): this is the most serious cabbage disease the home grower is likely to encounter. It is caused by a fungus which infects the roots. The first signs of infection are wilting,

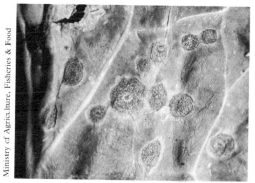

Round brown spots and yellowing leaves caused by the fungus infection ring spot.

Ministry of Agriculture, Fisheries & Food

Young cabbage plants which have been badly infected by the disease club root.

Brian Furner

blueish leaves and dying plants. The roots are swollen and distorted so that they have a club-like appearance. This occurs most frequently on heavy soils which have not been sufficiently limed, so lime the soil before sowing to make it slightly alkaline. Attacks also occur on wet, badly drained soils, so be sure that drainage is sufficient before planting. Dusting the seed-bed and planting holes with calomel dust is another useful precaution and cabbage transplants can be protected by dipping their roots in water containing benomyl, just before planting. The fungus is soil-borne so if an infection occurs remove and burn all plants and do not use the site for brassicas for five years.

Wirestem: Wirestem fungus attacks the seedlings, causing the bases of the stems to turn brown and wither. The seedlings either die or grow into poor, stunted plants. Wirestem can usually be avoided by sowing the seed in slightly alkaline soil or in sterilized compost.

Ring spot: this is a fungus disease which attacks older plants and produces round brown spots about 1.5 cm ($\frac{1}{2}''$) in diameter on the leaves. The infected outer leaves turn yellow, and the inner leaves will also gradually become infected. Remove any diseased leaves as soon as you see them, and prevent further infections with a light dressing of potash fertilizer to harden the growth.

Downy mildew: this disease appears as patches of white fungus on the undersides of the plants. Destroy affected plants.

French Beans

 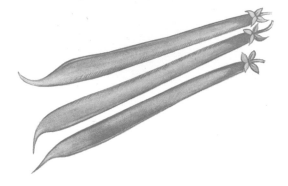

Phaseolus vulgaris (fam. *Leguminosae*) also known as snap
bean and string bean
Half-hardy annual
Sowing to harvesting time: 10-12 weeks
Size: dwarf varieties 15-25 cm (6-10″) high, 10-15 cm (4-6″)
across; climbing varieties up to 1.8 m (6′) high.
Yield: 9 kg (20 lb) per 10 m (30′) row for dwarf varieties;
13.5 kg (30 lb) for climbing varieties; 1 kg (2 lb) as dried
haricots.

French beans make an ideal crop for the home grower; the plants are compact, require little attention, and the yield of succulent, delicately flavoured pods is high compared to the small amount of space needed. Except for protecting early and late sowings from frost damage, little is needed in the way of cultivation, and the plants for the most part take care of themselves. Once they are growing well, the large, attractive leaves form a dense canopy which acts as a weed suppressor. The thick foliage completely shades the soil beneath, and weeds, starved of sunlight, are unable to compete. French beans will crop well in spite of long periods of drought, although heavier crops will result if they are watered regularly in dry conditions. As an additional bonus, the leaves, white or lilac-tinted flowers, and pods, coloured purple or scarlet in some varieties, are exceedingly decorative, and a few plants will enhance any border.

There are both dwarf and climbing varieties available. The dwarf, or 'bush', type, grows 15-25 cm (6-10″) high, while the climbing varieties can be up to 1.8 m (6′) tall; these have growing habits similar to runner beans and will need some form of support. The pods of both dwarf and climbing varieties are 7.5-15 cm (3-6″) long and hang beneath the leaves. There is one exception: the new variety *Remus* carries its pods well above the leaves, for easy picking and early ripening.

Although most varieties have green pods, some are indigo blue, or mottled red and white. French beans with pale yellow pods are called 'waxpod', or 'butter' beans, and are thought by many to have the finest flavour of all. The pods of French beans are round in section, not flat as runner beans are.

Because French beans are only half-hardy in cool temperate climates, they are normally cropped outdoors from

Succulent French beans ready for harvesting; outdoors, cropping begins in mid-summer.

mid-summer through to mid-autumn. By successional sowing, and by giving cloche protection, you can extend the cropping period by a good two months, from early summer through to late autumn. If you have a heated greenhouse available and grow them entirely under glass, then cropping can begin as early as mid-spring.

The beans can be harvested at various stages of development. When the pods are very young and delicate, they are picked for cooking whole. When slightly larger and more mature, the pods are harvested and cut up into pieces before cooking. If left to grow on, the beans inside the pod will begin to swell. These beans are then shelled, and served when green as 'flageolots', or allowed to grow to full maturity, and then dried for winter use as 'haricots'. As a general rule, the more French beans you pick, the heavier the crops will be, as frequent picking encourages the development of more pods.

Suitable site and soil

French beans do best in a sunny, sheltered situation. They will grow in almost any soil, but prefer one that is not too heavy. A heavy soil can be lightened by working in peat, garden compost or coarse sand.

Ideally, you should grow French

39

beans on a plot well manured for a previous crop, such as spinach. If you have no such site available, dig in manure in the autumn before planting, at the rate of one bucketful per sq m (sq yd). The soil pH should be 7.0-8.0. Test your soil some months before planting, and correct if necessary with the addition of lime, (see Improving Your Soil).

This crop does especially well if potassium and phosphorus are given as base dressings, so a fortnight before sowing or planting out, dress with sulphate of potash, at the rate of 15 g per sq m ($\frac{1}{2}$ oz per sq yd), and super-phosphate at 30 g per sq m (1 oz per sq yd) and fork in well.

Sowing

Theoretically, French beans can be sown outdoors from early spring, with fort-nightly successional sowings right th-rough late summer, for late autumn cropping. However, germination will not take place unless there is a minimum temperature of 16°C (60°F), and bean seeds planted in cold wet soil will quickly rot. Secondly, because the plants are sub-tropical in origin, they cannot tolerate even one degree of frost, so early and late sowings will need cloche protection if they are to be at all successful. Local weather conditions are a major factor, and the last frost date varies from year to year and place to place. A basic understanding of the plants' temperature requirements will help you to avoid disappointment, and you can select the right sowing time for your particular garden.

Generally, for early summer crops, sow under cloches in early spring; keep the plants under cloches until the beginning of summer. Main crops can be sown outdoors from mid-spring on-wards, given cloche protection for about a fortnight. French beans which are not given cloche protection should be sown in late spring, or early summer if the site is cold or exposed. Beans grown for drying as haricots should not be sown later than the beginning of summer, as they need plenty of time for proper ripening.

The seeds vary enormously in size, shape and colour, according to the variety selected, but even the smallest are easy to handle and can be sown individually. Because the success rate of germination is relatively low (75%), it is best to sow the seeds in pairs; if both germinate, cut the top off the weaker seedling when the first true leaves appear.

The distance between seeds and rows of seeds varies according to the time of year planted, the planting position, and harvesting requirements. Whatever the planting spacings, make sure the soil has been worked to a very fine tilth. If there are stones or rough lumps of soil, the emerging seedlings will be stunted or mis-shapen. Drills for French beans should be 5 cm (2") deep. If you are growing the beans against a wall or fence, then only one row of plants is needed. Otherwise, sow the seeds in double rows, 30 cm (1') apart. If you have more than one double row, leave 60-90 cm (2-3') between them, so that you can cultivate and pick the crops easily. However, if you are planting French beans for drying as haricots, the rows need only 30 cm (1') between them. This is because the haricot beans are usually harvested all at once, so easy access to every plant is unnecessary.

Sow the seeds at 15 cm (6") intervals for early crops and haricots, and 22 cm (9") intervals for main crops. Germination should take place between 10 days and three weeks after sowing. It is not necessary to water the beans while they are germinating and they should never be soaked before sowing. A word of advice: never leave unused beans on the surface of the soil, or birds will immediately be attracted to the site and quickly peck up the beans. If you have been troubled by birds in past years, it is a good idea to protect the seeds and seedlings with wire mesh netting, similar to that used for peas.

For early sowings which remain under

1. When the soil and air temperature are warm enough, sow seeds in pairs, 15-22 cm (6-9″) apart in seed drills.

2. To keep pods from dragging on the ground, support plants with pea sticks or short lengths of bamboo.

3. While the plants are young, hoe to keep weed competition down, and also to keep soil surface broken up.

cloches for some time, it is best to use the big barn-type cloches, because the plants will need plenty of growing space before all danger of frost has passed. If the weather turns cold, cover the cloches with mats or sacking to give extra protection against frost.

Transplanting

French beans grow best when sown directly where they are to grow. However, for very early crops, and in cold districts, you can sow pairs of seeds in boxes or pots in the greenhouse, four to six weeks before the last expected frost date. Because French beans do not transplant well, and tend to stop growing once disturbed, it is best to sow them in peat pots which can be planted out without any disturbance to the roots. Another method is to sow the seeds in blocks of turf, which can then be planted out in late spring. Those sown under cloches may also be transplanted, but the more usual method is to remove the cloches when no further frosts are expected.

Care and cultivation

French beans will produce heavier crops when regularly hoed and watered. Watering is particularly important in dry weather, when the crop's growth is liable to be checked, and the flowers may not set. If the flowers wilt and droop, the insects cannot penetrate and pollination will not take place. When this happens, spray the plants with a fine misty spray every morning and evening until the flowers have set. This fine mist will not be sufficient to keep the soil moist; a thorough watering, directed at the plants' roots, will also be necessary in dry weather.

Regular hoeing not only keeps weeds under control, it also keeps the surface of the soil broken up. In prolonged dry spells, some soils, particularly if watered by hose, form a hard surface crust. This prevents water penetrating the soil, and it runs off the surface without reaching the plants' roots. Hoeing also creates a

41

1. If it is hot and dry when flowering occurs, spray plants daily with a fine mist of water to aid pollination.

2. A mulch of clean straw, moist peat or leaf litter conserves soil moisture and protects plants from early frosts.

3. When harvesting, cut the pods with scissors or secateurs; never pull the pods off, or you may damage the plant.

dust mulch, which helps conserve soil moisture. A mulch of clean straw or leaf litter has the same effect, provided the soil is thoroughly watered before the mulch is applied.

Small doses of liquid manure are beneficial. To make, soak a bag of manure in a tank of water until the liquid is the colour of weak tea. Take care when applying not to splash the foliage, because liquid manure of this kind is more concentrated than the liquid feeds sold especially for foliar feeding, and can burn the leaves.

Strictly speaking, the dwarf varieties do not need support. However, they tend to get weighed down by the pods, which then rest on the ground and become vulnerable to slug attacks. In wet weather, they will get covered with mud, too. As a precaution, support the plants by tying them to short lengths of bamboo, or else grow them through pea sticks. Occasionally, dwarf varieties will send out runners in an attempt to climb; cut these off as soon as you see them.

The climbing varieties need the support of tall rods or canes around which they will twine in the same way as runner beans (see RUNNER BEANS). Erect one rod or cane per plant; these should be about 1.8 m (6′) high after they have been pushed well into the ground. The framework will consist of a line of pairs of canes, straddling the axis of the row, not less than 45 cm (18″) apart at ground level. Alternatively, use twiggy branches for support, or large mesh netting. Earthing-up around the base of the plant, up to the first set of leaves, gives additional support to the stem, as well as encouraging extra root growth.

If you made late sowings, and plan to harvest right through autumn, give the plants cloche protection from mid-autumn onwards. Alternatively, a thick mulch of clean, dry straw, applied when frost threatens, will help protect the plants.

Greenhouse growing

If you have a heated greenhouse with an

Marshall Cavendish Clay Perry

Planting distances between French bean plants depends on when and where they are sown, and whether they are to be harvested over several weeks, or picked all at once, for drying and storing. Usually, they are planted in double rows, 30cm (1′) apart, leaving 60-90 cm (2-3′) between each set of double rows. This allows for easy access for cultivating and harvesting. Rows of haricots are usually planted much closer together, as they are harvested all at once.

Remember that climbing French beans can over-shadow lower-growing vegetables, so site them carefully.

air temperature of 16°C (60°F) and a minimum soil temperature of 13°C (55°F), you can grow good crops of out-of-season French beans in the borders. Greenhouses which are glazed down to ground level are best, as the French beans need plenty of sunlight. You can also grow them in frames, but only if you live in a really warm and sunny area.

Sow the seeds in good quality seed compost, with enough heat, any time from late summer to late winter. Expect cropping from late autumn through to late spring or very early summer. For minimum root disturbance during trans-

planting, use peat pots or sow the seeds directly onto soil blocks. Once the first pair of true leaves are showing, transplant them into the border or frame. The soil should not be too rich, or the plants will make excessively leafy growth at the expense of pod formation. Ideally, soil which has been manured for a previous crop is best.

Space the plants 22 cm (9″) apart, in single rows 30-37.5 cm (12-15″) apart in frames and in double rows about 30 cm (1′) apart in the borders. Climbing varieties grown in the borders will need support. Use strong garden twine, fixed vertically to two parallel, horizontal wires. The top wire can run under the roof, and the lower one should be about 15 cm (6″) from the ground. Two plants will climb up the same string.

Cultivation is the same as for outside growing, but make sure the plants are kept growing in a reasonably moist atmosphere, otherwise red spider mite could become a major problem, and ensure that the glass is as clean as possible, to allow maximum light to reach the plants.

Harvesting

The beans are ready for picking from ten to twelve weeks after sowing, depending on weather conditions. Once the pods have started to form, check them daily, as they mature quickly. Most varieties are best when about 10 cm (4″) long. Unless you are growing the crop specifically for the seeds (either green, as flageolets, or ripe and dried, as haricots) do not allow the ripe pods to remain on the plant. If you do, the seeds will grow larger, but the texture and flavour of the

pod itself will deteriorate. Secondly, the plant will concentrate its energy on the swelling seeds, at the expense of the pod production, and your crop will diminish accordingly. Daily picking will ensure that cropping continues for five weeks, or more.

When tested, pods ready for eating will snap cleanly in half, without any stringy fibres. The beans inside will be visible, but will not have expanded to their full size. Cut the pods from the plant with scissors or secateurs. You can also sever them with thumb and fingernails. Never try to pull the pods off; the plants are very shallow-rooted and you may pull the whole plant out of the ground. French beans are best eaten on the day of picking, because, although they are excellent for deep freezing, they do not otherwise store well. If you plan to shell the half-ripe beans, and eat them as flageolets, leave the pods on the plants until they are just beginning to turn colour. At this stage, the beans should be pale green. They can either be cooked fresh or dried for later use.

French beans are excellent subjects for growing in pots, either in the greenhouse, or out-of-doors in a warm, sunny spot. Remember that soil in pots dries out very quickly, so water frequently in warm weather. Otherwise, cultivation is the same as for outdoor-grown French beans.

Brian Furner

1. Harvest in mid-autumn, when pods are pale brown and beginning to split; if it is cold and wet, dig up plants and hang indoors to ripen fully.

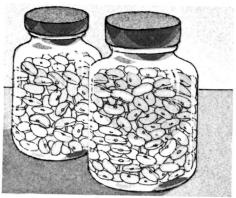

2. Spread shelled beans on trays, and dry them in a well ventilated room.

3. When completely dry, store in glass jars with tight-fitting lids.

Haricots

The beans of some varieties, if left to ripen fully, can be dried and stored for winter use. In mid-autumn, when the pods are pale brown and beginning to split, the beans are ready for harvesting. Cut the plants down, shell the pods, and spread the brown or white beans out on clean paper or wooden trays to dry. The floor of a greenhouse is a suitable drying place, but any room which is light and airy will do.

Some autumns turn cold and rainy before the pods have fully ripened. If this happens, dig up the plants, and hang them upside down in a greenhouse or attic. The pods can then finish ripening under cover; once the pods are brittle, shell and dry the beans in the usual way.

Aftercare

When cropping is over, cut off any remaining growth above ground level. If it is healthy and free from insects, place it on the compost heap. Otherwise, burn all stems and foliage to minimize the spread of pests and diseases. As with all leguminous crops, French bean roots will increase the nitrogen content of the soil as they decay. This is particularly important if the following crops grown on the site are nitrogen-hungry, such as brassicas and potatoes.

Exhibition tips

There is no special cultivation required for growing exhibition French beans; if you follow normal cultivation procedures and your plants are growing well, you should have plenty of pods up to show standard. One useful hint: French beans, when quickly grown, sometimes look a bit pale. To prevent this, give a light dressing of nitro-chalk, at the rate of 60 g per sq m (2 oz per sq yd), when the young plants start forming true leaves.

Mid-spring sowings outdoors should give ripe beans for early to mid-summer shows, provided the weather has been reasonable. If you live in a particularly cold district, it is safer to sow in peat pots in a cold frame in mid-spring, and plant out at the beginning of early summer. For late summer or autumn shows, cover possible crop failures by sowing small successional batches, say, at fortnightly intervals, until mid-summer.

The judges will look for straight, fresh, tender pods without any bumpiness; keep this in mind when selecting the beans. Twenty four beans are usually required, but it is safer to pick about twice this number, so you will have plenty of reserves at the show bench. Never pull the pods off the plant; cut them with scissors. Completely ignore enormous pods, which are likely to be tough and fibrous; they will not gain you any points.

To keep your beans from looking tired and stale, pick them at the last possible moment before the show. Make sure your hands are clean, because it is difficult to wash off stains on the pods without destroying the bloom.

As soon as the pods have been collected, lay them out on damp, clean cloths, and then roll the cloths up into loose bundles. They can travel to the show like this, provided they will not remain in the bundles for more than two days. If there is a longer interval between picking and the show date, it is best to pack the beans dry. A couple of hours before staging the pods, immerse them in cold water to restore their crispness.

Beans look nicest when displayed in a circular pattern on a plate. The tails of the pods should face outwards, towards the edge of the dish.

Pests & Diseases

Bean beetle (Bruchid beetle): because this pest resembles a weevil in appearance, it is sometimes called, incorrectly, 'bean weevil'. The female lays her eggs on the growing seed pod, or else on seeds which have been dried and stored. Once the legless grubs hatch out, they bore into the seeds, and then bite a round, window-like hole beneath the skin surface; it is through this hole that the adult beetle eventually emerges.

Besides feeding on the seed, the holes that they make allow secondary infections, such as fungal and bacterial diseases, to enter. Millepedes and wireworms also find it easier to attack pods which have been initially damaged by bean beetle. Remove and burn any seeds or pods which are holed, or which contain living grubs. Because these pests are usually seed-carried, the best precaution is to be sure your seeds are from a reliable source.

Slugs: these familiar garden pests feed on a wide variety of plants. Active chiefly after dark, they attack leaves and pods, biting large holes in them. During the day, they hide away in dark, moist, cool places. Slugs are often found in decaying vegetable matter, and on soils which are rich in humus and moisture.

One method of destroying slugs is to trap them. Place wet sacks, or heaps of damp vegetable refuse, such as cabbage or lettuce leaves or orange peels, at the base of the bean plants. Inspect the traps daily and destroy any captured slugs.

Alternatively, control slugs with pellets containing metaldehyde or methiocarb.

Capsids: these are sucking insects whose attacks produce pin-prick holes in the leaves and occasionally distort the pods. They attack the growing point of the plant, resulting in stunting of the plant and, if very young, in completely killing it. Control them by spraying or dusting with derris plus pyrethrum, or dimethoate if an infestation is stubborn. Because capsids drop to the ground

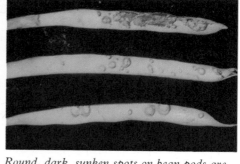

These leaves show the main symptom of halo blight: spots surrounded by yellow rings.

Round, dark, sunken spots on bean pods are telltale signs of anthracnose infection.

when disturbed, remember to treat the soil around the plant as well. Since the damage does not usually show until after the capsids have gone, it is best to start spraying in late spring, when the capsids actually begin to feed, particularly if you had damage the previous year.

Bean aphis (black fly): this insect is most troublesome in late spring, when it completely smothers the growing points of beans. Plants infested with bean aphis stop growing, and the few pods which develop may be covered with a black, sticky substance. Control by spraying with bioresmethrin or liquid derris, or dust with derris powder, and repeat as necessary. Remove and burn infected tops of plants as soon as enough pods have formed.

Bean seed fly: these pests destroy the seeds and the seedlings of newly planted French beans. The pale, legless larvae are most active between late spring and mid-summer. They attack the plants below ground, where they feed on the seeds, roots and underground stems of seedlings.

Because they are more likely to appear on land which has been given manures rich in nitrates, avoid excessively rich nitrogenous fertilizers. A second precaution is to dust the drills with gamma HCH before sowing or planting out.

Red spider mite: this minute sucking insect pest occasionally attacks French beans, especially if grown in hot, dry conditions. Watch for the appearance of leaves heavily speckled greyish-brown or pale yellow, together with webbing and slow plant growth. If it occurs, spray with malathion and give additonal water and ventilation. Remember to allow the correct time interval between spraying and harvesting.

Halo blight: this is a seed-borne, bacterial disease which is encouraged by the unnecessary practice of soaking the beans before sowing. The main symptoms are small, transparent spots which are surrounded by a yellow ring. Eventually the spots dry up, and where many are present, so that they coalesce, the entire leaf will wither. Seedlings may be killed outright, and even older plants can wilt completely. The pods can also be infected with round, moisture-oozing spots. Remove and destroy diseased plants as soon as seen. The best precaution is to only use seeds from reliable sources; never sow seeds which are wrinkled or blistered or have yellow spots on them. The variety *The Prince* is resistant to the disease.

Anthracnose: this fungal disease is usually associated with cool, wet growing conditions. The main symptoms are dark brown elongated spots on the stems which result in the leaves withering. The pods can have small, round, sunken spots, reddish-brown in colour, and the seeds inside diseased pods will eventually develop brownish-black markings. A half-strength mixture of Bordeaux (230 g in 46 litres of water, or 2 lb in 10 gallons of water) sprayed onto the infected plants offers some measure

47

GUIDE TO FRENCH BEAN TROUBLES

Symptoms	Probable cause
Seed leaves mis-shapen; seedlings stunted; small holes under surface skin of beans	Bean beetle
Irregular holes in leaves, stems and pods; faint silvery trails	Slugs
Pinprick holes with brown edges in young leaves; growing points blind	Capsids
Plants, especially growing tips, covered in small black sucking insects	Bean aphis
Roots and underground stems tunnelled	Bean seed fly
Leaves speckled greyish brown or yellow; webbing present	Red spider mite
Small transparent spots with wide yellow rings around them, which later dry up; leaves withered	Halo blight
Dark brown spots on stems, reddish brown spots on pods	Anthracnose
Dark brown or reddish black spots on roots and base of stems; roots withered looking	Root rot
Fluffy grey mould on stems, leaves and pods	Botrytis
Leaves mottled dark green, light green and yellow; stunted plants, mis-shapen pods	Virus diseases

of control, but this spraying must stop when the plants begin to flower. The plants should be destroyed after cropping, and dwarf beans grown in a different place for several years. Because the disease is seed-borne, the best precaution against anthracnose is clean seed, obtained from a reliable source.

Root or foot rot: this fungal infection occurs most often on soils which are cold and badly drained. Roots growing in these conditions will be weakened, and thus will be more vulnerable to attack. Unfortunately, the symptoms of root rot are not visible above ground. If a plant is not growing well, and has yellow, wilted foliage for no apparent reason, gently pry the soil away from the main stem. If root rot is the cause, then dark brown or reddish discolourations will be seen on the roots and base of the stems, and the roots will be withered looking. The crop is likely to be greatly reduced. As with all seed-borne diseases, the best precaution is to obtain clean seed from a reliable source. Affected plants should be destroyed after any crop has been taken. Those only slightly affected may be induced to throw out fresh roots by mulching up and around the stems.

Botrytis: this fungal infection, com-monly called 'grey mould', is usually associated with cold, wet growing conditions; seedlings are particularly vulnerable. As its common name implies, the main symptom is fluffy, grey mould appearing on the stems, leaves and, occasionally, pods.

Sufficient ventilation is important; if you sow your beans under glass, make sure the seedlings are not overcrowded. Thin them as soon as they are large enough to handle, and always remove and destroy weak or damaged plants. If there is an outbreak of botrytis, control by removing badly affected plant parts and spraying the rest with sulphur, or dusting with a fine spray of sulphur dust. Benomyl is also effective.

Virus: two diseases, common mosaic and yellow mosaic, occur on beans. The former produces dark and light green mottling, and distorted leaves. The plants are stunted and the crop reduced. Yellow mosaic produces yellow irregular patches on the green leaves, and the pods can be considerably mis-shapen. Common mosaic can be seed-borne; both are carried by greenfly. As with all virus diseases, there is no remedy, and infected plants should be destroyed. Do not save seed for future sowing.

48

Varieties

Dwarf

The Prince: early crops of long, tender dark green pods, which are nearly stringless and well-flavoured; heavy cropping and very popular variety.

Masterpiece: pods long, straight and tender, best when cooked young; early variety, but with continuous pickings, cropping extends six or seven weeks.

Chevrier Vert: heavy cropper with medium length, dark green pods; sliced, used for flageolets, or dried for haricot beans; virus and anthracnose-resistant.

Kinghorn Waxpod: excellent flavoured wax bean with 15 cm (6") long, fleshy pods, pale yellow; can be cooked whole.

Flair: very early, with heavy crops of straight, 13 cm (5") long stringless, fleshy pods; good for both early cropping and autumn cropping from late sowings.

Glamis: extra-hardy stringless beans, suitable for growing in cold or exposed positions; pods straight and fleshy.

Royalty (Purple-Podded): heavy cropper with stringless, full-flavoured purple pods which turn green when cooked; very good for cold or exposed areas.

Cyrus: new variety with round, very slender pods; heavy cropper; can be cooked whole.

Gold Crop: American variety, with straight, yellow stringless pods about 15 cm (6") long; plants vigorous and disease-resistant.

Remus: new variety with pods carried above foliage; pods 25 cm (10") long, straight, dark green and fibreless.

Climbing

Earliest of All: heavy cropper, with medium-sized pods; crops can be used fresh or dried as haricot beans for winter use; grows to about 1.5 m (5').

Largo: long, straight, stringless pods; can be eaten fresh or dried and stored.

Violet Podded Stringless: heavy cropper with purple flowers and deep blue-violet pods which turn green when cooked; flavour good; pods tender and fleshy.

Blue Lake White-seeded: short, fleshy pods in clusters; particularly well-flavoured; heavy cropper; seeds can be dried for use as haricots.

Haricot

Granda: primarily used for drying, but can be eaten green if required.

Comtesse de Chambord: another dual purpose variety, good for slicing or drying; grows strongly, so good for suppressing weeds in a new garden; very slow to mature, so avoid late sowing.

Left to right: *Cyrus, Royalty, Gold Crop*

Largo

49

Leeks

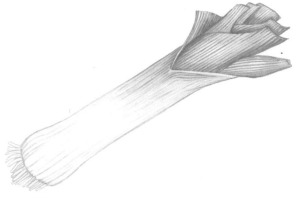

Allium ampeloprasum porrum (fam. *Alliaceae*)
Hardy biennial, grown as an **annual.**
Sowing to harvesting time: 30–45 weeks.
Size: leaves up to 30 cm (1′) long; bulbs 7.5–15 cm (3–6″)
long and up to 11 cm (4½″) in diameter ('pot' varieties),
15–30 cm (6–12″) long and 5 cm (2″) in diameter (long
varieties).
Yield: 10–12 plants per 3 m (10′) row.

One of the finest vegetables, the leek is easy to grow, useful, and very versatile. The blanched, elongated bulb at the base of the leaves makes a tasty fresh vegetable, either on its own or in stews and casseroles. The rich green leaf tops are excellent for flavouring soups. Besides being tasty, leeks are also nutritious; they are rich in vitamin A.

A member of the onion family, leeks are much easier than onions to grow. They are very tolerant of soil conditions, growing in any soil which is not waterlogged, and, unlike onions, they are generally free from pests and diseases. Most varieties are perfectly hardy and can remain in the ground through winter weather until needed. You can, by sowing early under glass, have leeks for harvesting in autumn, but it is really during winter and early spring that they are most welcome. Other garden vegetables are scarce at this time, and those in the shops are expensive.

There are long and short varieties of leeks available; the short, or 'pot' leeks are very popular in the north of England and Scotland, where they are often grown for exhibition work. Pot leeks are thick and stumpy, rather than tall, and have circumferences of up to 37.5 cm (15″).

Of the long leeks, broad flag varieties (sometimes called London leeks) are not frost hardy, and should be lifted before heavy winter weather sets in.

Suitable site and soil

Although leeks are tolerant of a wide range of soil types, they grow best on a moist, light soil that has been heavily manured for a previous crop. Freshly manured soil is not suitable, because leeks grown in very rich soil will be tough and coarse, with too much leaf growth. If the soil is in need of organic matter, it is best to dig in well-rotted garden compost, leafmould or peat

1. If the soil is deficient in potash, apply a potash-rich fertilizer to the soil before sowing is spring.

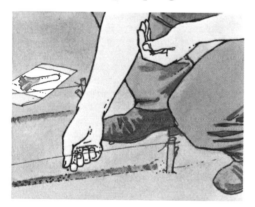

2. Sow the seeds thinly, about 100 seeds to the metre, in shallow drills; cover the seeds with fine sifted soil.

3. Thin the young leeks in two stages, to a final distance of 10 cm (4″) apart; use thinnings for salads.

mixed with hop manure just before planting. If the soil is deficient in potash, apply a fertilizer rich in potash (fertilizers used for tomatoes are suitable).

In crop rotation, leeks follow lettuce, cabbage or peas, but it is not a good idea to plant them immediately after lifting early potatoes though this is often done. This is because the soil will be too loose and disturbed, and leeks do best on a firm soil.

Apart from considerations, the choice of situation in the vegetable plot may be influenced by the fact that leeks are generally left in the ground to be dug up as required throughout the winter, and can remain in the ground for a year or more. If you use a strict rotation system, you should bear this in mind, unless you have reserved a plot for semi-permanent crops like asparagus or artichokes, and there is some free space for your leeks. Do not grow leeks in the same place year after year, or there will be an increased risk of pests and diseases.

Sowing

Sowing in winter under glass is necessary if you want leeks ready for summer and autumn exhibition, but for normal household consumption wait until early to mid-spring depending on weather, when they can be sown outdoors. They can either be sown in a seed-bed for transplanting the following summer, or sown in their permanent positions. If sown in a seed-bed, you have the additional bother of transplanting. Against this must be balanced the fact that if they are sown in their permanent position, they will take up a lot of space for a very long time before producing results.

Sow the seeds thinly (about 100 seeds to the metre) as germination is usually very good, in drills about 0.5 cm ($\frac{1}{4}$″) deep, and cover the seeds with fine sifted soil. If properly stored, the seeds will remain viable for four years so you can keep extra seeds for future use. After covering the seeds, firm the drills down and water if the soil is dry. Drills should

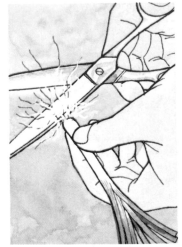

1. Transplant leeks in early to mid-summer, when they are about 20 cm (8″) high; do this in showery weather if possible.

2. Cut back the roots until they are 2.5 cm (1″) long; trim the leaf tips back slightly.

3. Use a thick dibber or trowel to form holes; make the holes vertical and about 5 cm (2″) in diameter.

4. Lower the young leeks into the hole and fill with water; the water will wash soil over the base of the plant, to keep it in position.

be 15 cm (6″) apart in the permanent bed. Germination should take 14–21 days, and thinning should begin as soon as possible, when the plants are not more than thin green shoots, about six weeks from sowing. Thin moderately the first time, as some of the plants may die, and then thin again, when all seems to be going well, so that the plants are about 10 cm (4″) apart.

Planting out
By mid-summer, when they are about as thick as pencils and 20 cm (8″) high, the leeks will be ready for transplanting to the permanent bed. If you can plant during showery weather, the young leeks will get over their planting check much more quickly; otherwise water the seedbed the day before lifting if the soil is dry. To eliminate the bother of sowing, thinning and transplanting, you can buy young leeks from your nurseryman at this stage. Leeks can stand the rigours of transport and once planted will quickly settle in.

There are several methods of planting out leeks, depending partly on soil type and partly on the quality sought. Exhibition leeks are usually grown on the flat, because it suits the special methods used for blanching and is least likely to damage the roots. Unlike those grown for kitchen use, leeks grown for exhibition should never have their roots or leaves cut back when transplanted. You can also grow leeks in shallow trenches, pot holes, or, if the soil is heavy and badly drained, on raised beds.

To plant leeks in holes, use a thick dibber or trowel; make the holes 15 cm (6″) deep, and 15–23 cm (6–9″) apart, depending on what size of leeks you plan to harvest. Many people prefer the taste of the smaller, tender, immature leeks to that of the enormous, prizewinning ones. Make sure the holes are vertical, and move the dibber about from side to side so that they are slightly larger at the top; the holes should be about 5 cm (2″) in diameter. Cut back the roots until they are 2.5 cm (1″) long, and trim the tips of the leaves back slightly. Place the young leeks into the holes so that they lean against one side, and gently fill the holes with water. The water will wash enough soil over the base of the plant for it to become established. As you hoe the rows from time to time, the holes will gradually fill up with soil. Leeks grown in this way will not be completely blanched, but the pale green portions seem to impart the best flavour to a soup. If you prefer thoroughly blanched leeks, this can be done quite easily by earthing up. A useful tip to note when planting is that by the time the leeks have reached transplanting size, it will be possible to see which way the leaves arch. They can then be planted so that the leaves of each plant run along the row and not at right angles to it. This takes up less space and reduces risk of injury during cultivation.

Another way of growing leeks is to plant them 25 cm (10″) apart in a trench. This method is particularly good if you have a deep, fertile soil; otherwise it is best to plant on the flat. The trench should be excavated to a depth of 30 cm (1′), and if there is more than one trench, they should be at least 75 cm (2′6″) apart. If you try to dig the trenches closer together, the walls of the trench are likely to collapse. Into the bottom of each

1. Dig trenches 30 cm (1′) deep and 75 cm (2′ 6″) apart; fork 7.5cm (3″) of garden compost into the bottom.

2. Cover compost with 15 cm (6″) of topsoil, and carefully plant leeks 25 cm (10″) apart; water thoroughly.

3. Grow quick catch crops, such as radishes or lettuce, on ridges, before soil is needed for earthing-up.

53

trench dig about 7.5 cm (3″) of well-rotted garden compost and cover it with about 15 cm (6″) of topsoil. Carefully plant the leeks, perfectly upright, in the bottom of the trench. Then water in as before. Form the remaining soil into flat-topped ridges between the rows. These ridges are excellent places for quick catch crops, such as lettuce or radishes, which will be harvested well before the soil is needed for earthing-up the growing leeks.

Cultivation and care
Water the young plants generously until they are well established. Soon after planting apply liquid manure. If the soil is not adequately rich in fertilizers, nitrate of soda, nitro-chalk or sulphate of ammonia may be applied at the rate of 10 g per metre run (1/3 oz per yard run) about five weeks after planting and watered in; alternatively, apply twice this amount of soot along the row when the plants are well established or liquid feed about once a fortnight through the growing season, instead of giving the single dressing of dry fertilizer.

Hoe between the rows regularly to keep down weeds and also to aerate the soil. Frequent hoeing also creates a dust mulch which helps conserve moisture.

BLANCHING

1. To keep stems free of soil, place collars round stems up to the base of the leaves.

2. Then draw up soil from between rows, using a draw hoe; repeat as necessary, fitting another collar above the first one.

3. You can start blanching with paper collars; support paper collars with bamboo canes.

4. As the leeks grow on, replace paper collars with 10 × 30 cm (4 × 12″) clay drainpipes.

Leaves which grow too long and unmanagable can be cut back slightly, so that they do not trail on the ground. Cut the long, dark green, outer leaves back by about 5 cm (2″) in early summer, again in mid-summer, and a third time, if necessary, in early autumn. If you are growing leeks for exhibition, however, do not shorten the leaves, unless they are decayed.

Blanching

Blanching leeks increases the proportion of plant which is edible, and improves the flavour, which would otherwise be strong and fairly harsh. Begin blanching in early mid-autumn; it is a gradual process and should be done in several stages, rather than all at once. There are several methods of blanching, depending on the way in which the leeks are growing.

If your leeks are growing in a trench, blanching consists of gradually filling the trench with soil to the bottom of the lowest leaves each time, until the plants have ceased to grow, which will probably be mid to late autumn, depending on the weather. This should give you 10–15 cm (4–6″) of blanched stem at least. One word of advice, however: the soil used for earthing-up must be dry, friable and very fine textured. If it is wet when earthed-up, rot is liable to set in. If the soil is lumpy, it will be difficult to handle and will not exclude light properly.

If grown on the flat, push the soil up around the plants, increasing the soil depth by about 5 cm (2″) each time. You can keep the stems free of soil by using collars, which are secured around the leeks up to the base of the leaves. Various materials can be used for the collar: lengths sawn from plastic piping, clay drain pipes, or, at virtually no cost, pieces of strong brown paper secured with string or rubber bands. If you use paper tubes, support them with bamboo canes. Whatever form of collar you use, the minimum diameter should be 7.5 cm (3″); they should be 30-37.5 cm (12-15″) long.

Leeks are very hardy, and can remain in the ground through winter weather until needed.

Marshall Cavendish/Jerry Tubby

Attach the collars before carrying out the earthing-up process. As the plants grow, draw up more and more soil with a hoe, fitting another collar above the first one.

Although it is not strictly necessary, you can put planks of wood, on edge, along both sides of the row instead of using collars. This forms a sort of box into which the soil is put, until the desired height of soil is reached. With this system, you can use silver sand, leafmould or peat instead of soil.

Harvesting and aftercare

Leeks may be harvested from mid-autumn through to the end of late spring, depending on time of sowing and variety. The hardier varieties are left where they grow until needed. Never pull leeks out of the ground by brute force, or they will more than likely break in two, leaving you with a handful of leaves. Instead, lever them out of the ground with a spade or fork. Take the largest first; the smallest, if left until the spring, will put on some weight before running to flower. If the ground is likely to be frozen for long periods of time, it is a good idea to lift any leeks which are ready and store them in sand in a cool place, where they will keep for about a month. If, towards the end of the season, you have a few leeks still in the ground, but need the plot cleared for new planting, you can dig the leeks up and heel them in a shaded place, until needed. Lay them on their sides in shallow trench with the top part of the leaf stalk projecting above the ground, covering the rest of the stalk with soil. This also helps to stop them bolting.

You can, by leaving leeks in the ground and nipping out the flower stems, get a bonus crop: leek bulbs. These small white bulbs will form at the base of the plant; harvest them in early summer and use as onions or shallots.

If you grow prize-winning leeks and want to keep a particular strain for future show work, allow one or two leeks to flower. Tiny, complete plants, or 'pods', will form among the seeds on the seed pod; these can be detached and potted on in the greenhouse.

Exhibition tips

Leek-growing competitions, in which enormous size was the determining factor, have long been a tradition in the north of England and Scotland; today, well grown leeks can be an asset to any display, and perfect leeks are worth 20 points, the maximum for vegetables.

For mid-summer exhibits, seeds should be sown in early to mid-winter. Remember that with exhibition leeks, it is quality rather than quantity that is called for. Six is the usual number shown for single dishes, and nine leeks for collections, so do not get caught up in raising unnecessarily large numbers of leeks. Sow the seeds thinly in John Innes seed compost, so the tiny seedlings do not have to complete for food, air and moisture.

For germination to be successful, temperature should be kept at 13°C (55°F). After germination it can be reduced a little, gradually; remember that leeks are hardy and although they are required to be well-grown for early planting out, too much warmth will force them and make them leggy. When the seedlings are about 5 cm (2″) high, prick them out into pans filled with John Innes No 2 compost. The seedlings should be 7.5 cm (3″) apart in all directions. Be very careful not to damage the tiny single root which supplies nourishment to the plant until additional roots have formed. The young leeks will probably need potting again before planting out, into 12.5–15 cm (5 or 6″) pots. If small pots are full of roots some weeks before planting out

HEELING IN

1. Dig a narrow trench in a cool place; lay leeks on their sides with leaf stalks projecting above ground.

2. Cover leeks with soil and firm down with feet; heeling in helps to stop leeks from bolting.

Well-blanched specimens of Musselburgh, *a good variety both for exhibition and culinary use.*

time, then bigger pots will be essential. In early spring, put the trays in cold frames, to harden the young plants off before planting out in mid-spring.

Lifting the leeks prior to exhibition is a fairly delicate operation; it is all too easy to wreck a season's work by damaging the leeks at this time. Remember that as many roots as possible should remain intact on the plant.

Before actually digging them up, it is a wise precaution to gently tie the top foliage upright with soft twine. Well grown leeks tend to have brittle top foliage, and it will snap off if mishandled.

After tying the foliage, scrape away all sand, soil or peat from the base of the plant. Lift off any drainpipes; occasionally you may have to carefully break the drainpipe with a hammer to get the leek out. If they have been grown in cardboard tubes, it is best to leave the tubes on until the leeks have been lifted. The tubes are then cut open, carefully, with a sharp knife.

Lift the specimens with a fork, digging well under the roots so you do not inadvertently spear the leek. Once the leeks are out of the ground, wrap them in clean, damp cloths or paper; if you leave them exposed to the light, the blanched portions will rapidly turn green. Take them indoors and carefully cut away the first outer layer of soiled leaves. You may have to remove a second layer of leaves, but do not remove more than necessary, or the leeks' appearance will be damaged.

After removing the outer leaves, totally immerse the leeks in cold water, to get rid of all traces of soil. Change the water several times, until the leeks are perfectly clean. They should be cleaned while still tied, or the leaves may snap off in the water.

Leeks must be packed carefully for transport to the show; this is particularly important because their large size makes handling difficult.

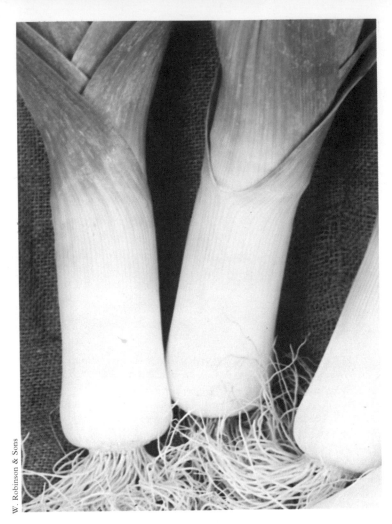

Well grown pot leeks: these thick, stumpy leeks are very popular for exhibition work in the north of England. Pot leeks can be more than 30 cm (1') in circumference, and are judged by their cubic size. Pot leeks for show must not be bulbous at the root end, but should be cylindrical in shape, and free from coarseness.

While in transit the leeks should be kept cool, otherwise the foliage will turn yellow.

Depending on the number shown, leeks are displayed flat on staging, in a basket, or vertically, like columns, on a specially built base. To display them vertically, make a round wooden base, about 2.5 cm (1″) thick, through which you hammer the required number of spikes. These spikes, usually bright metal nails, should be equi-distant from each other, and protrude about 5 cm (2″) above the board. Just· before the show, place the board right side up on the staging, cover the surface with a thick bed of parsley, and fix the leeks securely onto the nails. Because the leeks may tend to lean at slightly different angles, it is best to tie the tips of the leeks together with soft green twine. Three or four bands of twine should be enough to secure them firmly. When this is done, remove the twine which ·tied the individual leaves together, from the lifting stage onwards. If well done, the leeks will look like white columns, seemingly unsupported.

The judges will look for solid, thick leeks, not less than 30 cm (1') long, without any tapering. There should no swelling at the base, or any discolouration. As with all vegetables, the leeks should be as uniform as possible.

Pests & Diseases

Leeks are relatively pest and disease free, as long as they are part of a crop rotation plan and are not grown on the same ground several years running.

Onion fly: Leeks are occasionally attacked by this pest, which is particularly troublesome in the larval stage, when the maggots tunnel into the plant tissue. The fly, which looks like a small grey house fly, lays its eggs in spring and early summer, near the base of the leek, on the leaves and in the soil nearby. Scattering diazinon granules in late spring will help to control the emerging larva. Like onions, young leeks seem particularly vulnerable. Lift and destroy and infested leeks; the main symptoms are yellowing and drooping foliage.

When lifting the infested leeks, make sure there are no maggots left lying on the ground. Because the flies are attracted to the smell of fresh manure, make sure leeks are not planted on freshly manured ground.

Leek moth: this small brown moth lays its eggs on the base of leek plants during mid and late spring. The emerging pale green caterpillars tunnel through the leaves, which are disfigured with white streaks. As more and more tunnels are made, the leeks loose their strength and may collapse and die.

The best method of control is a nicotine wash, applied first when the plants are still in the seed-bed, and again in mid to late summer.

White rot: this fungal infection attacks onions, shallots and garlic as well as leeks, and is most noticeable in hot, dry

Leek leaves damaged by caterpillars of the leek moth, which cause tattering and browning.

Pupae of the leek moth, in their cobwebby cocoons; the moths emerge in mid-summer.

summers. Plants grown in overcrowded conditions are particularly vulnerable. Infected leeks will have yellow leaves, with a white or grey fungus covering the underground base of the plant, looking like strands of white thread. The spores can remain viable in the soil for at least eight years, so proper crop rotation is the best precaution against white rot. Dusting the soil at sowing time with

---

GUIDE TO LEEK TROUBLES

Symptoms	Probable cause
Yellow, drooping foliage, tunnels in plant tissue	Onion fly
White streaks on leaves	Leek moth
Yellow leaves, white or grey fungus at base of plant	White rot
Leaf tips die back, white papery patches on leaves	White tip
Orange, powdery spots on older leaves	Leek rust

These orange, powdery spots indicate leek rust; infected leaves will turn yellow.

Musselburgh

calomel dust gives some additional measure of protection, and leeks grown on fertile, organically manured soil seem less vulnerable.

White tip: this is another fungal infection, which usually appears from late summer through the winter. Symptoms are a white die back of the leaf tips, white patches appearing on other parts of the leaf and stem, and stunted growth. Infected leaves look watery, thin and papery; eventually they rot away. Besides looking unpleasant, infected leeks wilt quickly and will not keep at all. Badly infected leeks should be removed and destroyed, and the remainder sprayed fortnightly with a copper fungicide until all white patches disappear.

Leek rust: this fungal infection is more prevalent when the autumn and winter are unusually mild. Leeks growing in soil which is rich in nitrogen but lacks potassium are particularly vulnerable. The symptoms of leek rust are orange, powdery spots on older leaves, which later turn yellow. Although they are disfigured, leeks with mild rust infections can still be eaten. Badly infected plants should be dug up and destroyed. To control the spread of the disease, spray the remainder of the leeks with zineb.

Varieties

Winter Crop: extra hardy variety, dark green foliage with large white stems; long lasting, keeps till mid-spring without loss of foliage.

Musselburgh: one of most popular varieties, crops very hardy and of good length, will tolerate wide range of growing conditions.

Early Market: early variety, excellent for autumn use; do not grow for late crops.

Malabar: quick growing variety for

Early Market

Malabar

Giant Winter

autumn use; stem medium length, with dark green tops.

Lyon Prizetaker: probably the most popular variety in cultivation; plants hardy and fine flavoured; stems long, thick and white.

Giant Winter (Royal Favourite): very large, pure white stems, leaves very dark; longest lasting, can be pulled in mid to late spring.

North Pole: new variety, late and very heavy cropping; vigorous growth and winter hardy.

Marble Pillar: early variety, suitable for pulling from autumn through mid-spring; produces good, solid, very long white stems.

Northumberland: short, thick, early leek, to be pulled in autumn; original 'pot' leek of Northumberland miners.

Malines Winter: new variety; long, thick, heavy stems, dark green leaves; matures late.

Everest: exceptionally large leeks, perfect for table or exhibition.

Catalina: a new variety with long, thick, fleshy stems, mild flavour; very long standing, and can be left in the ground.

Lyon Prizetaker

North Pole

Peas

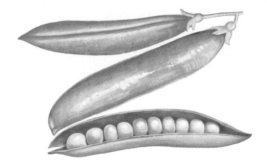

Pisum sativum (fam. *Leguminosae*)
Hardy annual
Sowing to harvesting time: 11-12 weeks for early
varieties; 12-13 weeks for second early varieties; 13-14
weeks for maincrop varieties.
Size: plants vary in height from 30 cm (1') for the smallest
dwarf varieties to 1.8 m (6') for the tallest plants. Pods
range from 7.5 cm (3") to 15 cm (6").
Yield: 40 plants per 3 m (10') row, each bearing up to $\frac{1}{4}$ kg
($\frac{1}{2}$ lb) of peas.

Tender home-grown peas are one of the
finest delights a gardener can enjoy.
Once a treat for a few weeks in summer,
with careful planning it is now possible
to have a variety of fresh peas from late
spring through to early autumn.

Peas have a very long history as a
garden crop and many varieties have
been evolved. There are early, second
early and maincrop varieties, peas that
climb almost two metres high and dwarf
peas that need little support, the small-
seeded and succulent petit pois, mangetout, or sugar peas, with edible pods,
and purple-podded peas. All of these
types can be grown successfully by the
home gardener.

The varieties you choose to plant will
depend on several factors. Peas need a
great deal of space—tall more than dwarf
and maincrops more than earlies—so
consider how much space you have
available. Decide if you like your peas
very sweet, if you want to freeze or dry
part of your crop, and for how long a
period you want to harvest your peas.

Also, bear in mind that all peas are a crop
for cool-temperate zones, as most
varieties will stop producing pods when
the temperature rises above 20 C (70 F).

Two types of seed

There are two types of pea seed, round
and wrinkled. In the wrinkled, or
marrowfat, varieties, some of the starch
in the seed has turned to sugar. Although
the seeds produce very sweet peas, they
hold too much moisture for autumn
sowing, and peas sown in autumn must
be round-seeded varieties, several of
which are hardy.

There are dwarf and tall varieties of
both round and wrinkled seeds. In
general, although there are some exceptions, early varieties of peas tend to be
dwarf and the maincrop types taller and
bushier.

Choosing a site

All peas need plenty of space. Choose an
open, sunny site, but one sheltered from
strong winds. Remember that the taller

1. Dipping seed in mixture of paraffin and red lead.

2. Sow first early varieties in double rows under tall cloches. Put a mousetrap at each end.

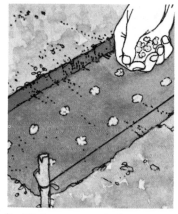

3. Maincrop varieties can be sown without protection.

4. Hoe around the seedlings to keep down weeds and to prevent pea moths from laying eggs.

5. Remove weeds by hand to avoid damaging the roots.

6. If the soil is very poor, apply a low-nitrogen fertilizer when the plants are young.

7. Water the seedlings often, especially in dry spells.

8. Protect young plants from birds with mesh net pea-guards, 12 cm (5″) high and 20 cm (8″) wide.

varieties will shade other crops growing alongside them, so plan your rows of crops with this in mind. Also keep in mind that the large spaces between the tall plants can be used for inter-cropping: quick-growing radishes or shade-loving spinach are both good.

Peas will grow well in a variety of soils, but you should take steps to provide for their special preferences. An acid soil is not very suitable, the ideal being a pH of 7.0. Carry out a soil test and correct any acidity by an application of lime the winter before sowing.

Peas like a rich soil, but not one recently enriched by applications of manure; it is better to sow them in soils which have been well manured early in the winter. Poor soils can benefit from chemical fertilizers containing superphosphate and potash, applied at the rate of 60 g per sq m (2 oz per sq yd) just before sowing. Use nitrogenous fertilizers very cautiously because the pea plant can extract nitrogen from the air for itself, and an excess of nitrogen leads to lush leaf growth at the expense of the pods. Peas need plenty of water and thrive in a reasonably heavy soil which retains moisture, although you must avoid waterlogging. The plants have penetrating roots, so dig the ground deeply and thoroughly.

Sowing the seed

Sow peas where they are to remain for their entire lives because they are deep-rooting and do not usually transplant satisfactorily. The roots must not be disturbed while the plants are growing.

Mice will eat pea seeds as fast as you sow them, so take some precautions. Many seed merchants sell seeds pre-treated with a proprietary mouse repel-lent, and these should be used if mice are a problem. If pre-treated seed is unavailable, another safeguard is to set traps at the end of a protective cloche or mesh net covering.

For all sowings, prepare a shallow drill 15-23 cm (6-9″) wide, and sow the seed 2.5 cm (1″) deep in rows 7.5 cm (3″) apart. Sow 6-10 seeds per 30 cm (1′). A good general rule is to allow a space between rows equal to the height of the fully grown plants. The peas should take between 10 and 20 days to germinate.

Spring-sown peas

Spring-sown peas are divided into three main groups: first early varieties, second earlies (also called early maincrop or mid-season varieties) and maincrops. The division is made according to the time that the varieties take to grow. If sown in early spring, first early varieties will produce peas ready to harvest in 11-

9. Mulch with compost or strawy manure to retain moisture, feed plants and suppress weeds.

10. Use twiggy sticks to support growing dwarf peas.

12 weeks. Second earlies sown at the same time will need 12-13 weeks, while maincrop varieties will require 13-14 weeks. It would be possible, therefore, to provide a succession of pickings by sowing varieties of all three groups at the same time. Alternatively, for a longer harvesting season, you can follow the usual practice and make a succession of sowings, starting with the earlies and proceeding to second earlies and then to maincrop. You can also gain time and produce a very early crop by protecting the first sowing of earlies from frost with cloches.

Autumn-sown peas
Some varieties of peas can be sown in early autumn to crop the following spring. For these early crops, choose hardy round-seeded dwarf varieties. In districts where the winters are mild, they can be sown in the open, but elsewhere they should be protected with cloches. Sow autumn peas more thickly than spring-sown crops, scattering them along the flat drill rather than planting each seed separately; this allows for some mortality. After a mild winter, autumn-sown peas should produce a crop several weeks earlier than those sown in early spring. A severe winter, however, may check them to such an extent that they

offer no advantage, producing at the same time as spring sown peas.

Care and cultivation
Peas are not an 'easy' crop, in that they do require frequent attention throughout their growing lives. Hoe regularly to remove weeds, but be careful not to damage the roots when pulling weeds close to the plants.

Peas need ample moisture, so water them frequently, especially during dry periods. Most of the diseases which infect peas are made worse in dry weather, so be on the lookout for any symptoms of trouble during a drought.

If the peas are sown in well-prepared, well-manured soil, then no additional feeding should be necessary during the growth period. In poorer soils the plants will benefit from an application of a compound fertilizer which is low on nitrogen and high on phosphates and potash. Apply this when the plants are young; use 30 g per metre run (1 oz per yard run). A mulch of garden compost, lawn trimmings, peat (unless the soil is acid) or well-rotted strawy manure will help to retain moisture. Apply this as near as possible to the base of the plants, where it will not only supply nutrients and retain moisture, but will also smother some of the weeds.

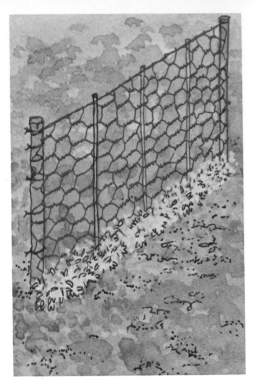

11. Make a supporting trellis for tall peas with a length of wire stretched between poles 1.5 m (5′) high.

12. If birds attack the young pods, drape fine fish netting over the plants and trellis to keep them away.

Staking the plants

Most dwarf and all tall varieties of peas require some staking. The plants grasp the support with their tendrils, so twiggy sticks or wire netting, both of which have plenty of tendril-holds, are the most useful. Unfortunately, traditional pea-sticks made from hazel wood thinnings are now very difficult to obtain and, therefore, expensive. Use conifer thinnings instead, or, for tall varieties, erect a supporting trellis of wire stretched between poles.

Stake the plants when they reach about 10-15 cm (4-6″) in height. Dwarf varieties need only small, twiggy sticks, one stick to each plant. Push the sticks a few inches into the ground close to the plants, but be careful not to damage the roots in the process.

Taller plants must be supported with stronger sticks, or with posts and netting. If you are lucky enough to get traditional pea-sticks or conifer thinnings, push these in the ground about 30 cm (1′) deep, one next to each plant. The stakes should stand about 1.5 m (5′) above ground.

If you decide to build a trellis, place hardwood poles at about 75 cm (2½′) intervals along the row. For a 3 m (10′) row, you will need five poles. Stretch a length of 1.5 m (5′) wide chicken wire or plastic-coated wire mesh along the row, and fasten it to the poles with wire. Make sure your poles are deep enough in the ground and your wire secure enough to withstand the wind.

When the pods begin to form, you can protect your crop from hungry birds by draping fish netting over the trellis.

A well-grown crop of dwarf variety early peas with full green pods ready for cutting.

Peas are ready for harvesting when the pods are full. Use scissors to harvest ripe pods as picking by hand can pull the plant out of the ground.

After picking clear the site. Remove any bits of pea haulm and save the wire for your next crop.

Harvesting the crop

Garden peas are at their best when fresh, young and green. Never let them become fully ripe and hard, as they will lose much of their flavour.

Peas are usually ready for harvesting about three weeks after flowering. Pick them when the pods have filled out and are firm to the touch. During a very dry summer some pods may not fill out completely, but if some of the peas are large pick them anyway before it is too late. Start picking at the bottom of the plant, and cut rather than pull off the pods. Check your plants frequently and harvest the pods regularly as they become ready. Some varieties may have a second, smaller crop after the main one, although these pods are less sweet and tender than the first.

Storing a crop

Peas should go into the kitchen as soon as possible after harvesting. However, if you have several plants and your crop is large you may want to dry and store some for winter use. Reserve a few plants for this purpose, and leave the pods to ripen thoroughly before picking. If the weather is damp, cut the plants and hang them upside down in a dry, airy place to finish ripening. Then shell the peas and dry them completely on fine wire, or mesh, racks before storing them in sacks

or jars in a cool, dry place. If you want to freeze some of your crop, pick the peas when they are at their best and prepare them quickly to retain taste and colour.

Aftercare

There is no point in trying to retain the plants after the pods have been removed. Clear the site and use it for another crop immediately; brassicas are a good choice. The pea haulm should be incorporated in the compost heap, unless there was a bad attack of pea moth. The roots, which are rich in nitrogen, can be left in the ground to benefit the following crop.

There are many different varieties of garden peas, including some very unusual ones. You might want to try one of these less common but delicious types.

Sugar peas or mangetout

There are a number of varieties of peas in which the pods are eaten whole with the peas still in them; the best known is the sugar pea, or mangetout. These plants vary in height from dwarf to tall, 30 cm-1.5 m (1-5′), and they are all heavy croppers.

Sow the seed in late spring in a sunny place, and then follow the cultivation instructions given for other varieties. Sugar peas always need staking, and they must always be protected from birds,

DRYING METHOD FOR PEAS

If you want to dry some peas, cut the plants with pods still on and hang them upside-down until fully ripened.

which for some reason find them particularly attractive.

Harvest sugar peas when they are young and tender, usually in mid to late summer, before the peas have developed in the pods. If you can feel the peas developing, you are too late. Pick and take them straight into the kitchen to enjoy them steamed or stir-fried at their fullest flavour. Older pods make a delicious soup.

Petit pois

Petit pois produce an abundance of small, sweet, delicately-flavoured peas; for flavour they are one of the finest vegetables. The plants are very hardy and grow to about 1 m (3') tall, making them suitable for a small garden.

Sow the seeds in mid-spring, spacing about 15 cm (6") apart in rows 1 m (3') apart. These plants require the same care

as other varieties. They also need a great deal of water, so never let them dry out. Harvest the pods as soon as they have filled out in mid-summer. Cook them whole, as the peas will fall out of the pods then they are ready to be served.

Purple-podded peas

Purple-podded peas are attractive, tall plants with purple pods and green foliage. They can reach a height of 2 m (6'), and they are hearty and vigorous croppers on most soils. Because of their height, they require a lot of space.

Sow in mid-spring, and follow the cultivation instructions for other varieties. Purple-podded peas crop for an unusually long time, so allow for several pickings from mid-summer. Harvest when young, and shell and cook the peas (which are green, not purple) as you would for maincrop varieties.

Exhibition tips

Growing the fifty perfectly-matched pods required for exhibition demands a great deal of skill. If you want to exhibit your peas, choose a heavy-cropping maincrop variety with large, pointed pods. Sow and cultivate as you would for maincrop peas for the kitchen, and take extra care to keep the crop well watered and free from pests. When the pods begin to form, remove any that are weak or misshapen to give the exhibition pods more space to grow. In very hot weather, it is a good idea to shade the plants with cloth draped over the supports to prevent the pods from drying in the sun.

On the day of the exhibition, cut the fullest and best-coloured pods at the last minute, handling them as little as possible to avoid damaging the bloom. Hold them up to a strong light to make sure that they are well-filled and free of maggots, and then pack them carefully between layers of cotton wool. At the exhibition hall, arrange the pods on a plate in a wheel formation, with the stalks pointing inwards. The judges will look for large, green, well-filled and well-matched pods.

Pests & Diseases

Always take precautions to protect your peas from pests, otherwise you are likely to end up with a disappointing yield. Rotation of crops is an important factor in avoiding pea diseases.

Birds Birds are troublesome pests in the early stages, as they attack and devour the pea seedlings. Protect the plants with cloches or with pea-guards, half-cylinders of small-mesh wire netting; these can be home-made or bought from garden centres. Any deterrent you find effective will do: try a traditional scarecrow, entanglements of black cotton placed over the plants, polythene bags hung from stakes, or even twiggy sticks placed flat on the ground.

Mice Many inexperienced gardeners sow good seed in well-prepared soil, and still end up with less than half a pea crop. The culprits are mice, who eat the germinating seed and can quickly clear a row. Seed can be purchased from most merchants already dressed with mouse-repellant. If this is unavailable, another precaution is to dress the pea seeds with a repellent or poisonous substance before sowing. Paraffin and red lead are the traditional dressing with which the seed is coated. Special care should be taken, however, as the red lead *is* poisonous, especially to children.

Maggots from the pea moth can burrow into the pods and ruin the peas.

G. E. Hyde

Greyish-brown mould on the leaves is caused by downy mildew.

Ministry of Agriculture Fisheries and Food Crown Copyright

Pea moth This is particularly troublesome to maincrops; earlies are rarely attacked. The moths are active in summer, when they lay their eggs on the developing pea pods, or on the stems and leaves. The larva, which look like maggots with white bodies and black heads, bore through the pods and into the seeds, producing unusable 'maggotty' peas. Spray with derris or fenitrothion about 7-10 days before flowering to kill the maggots just after they hatch but before they can burrow into the pods. Spray very thoroughly, as peas will be destroyed if the maggots get into the pods where the insecticide cannot reach them. If pea moth is a serious problem in your area, stop growing maincrops and concentrate on the early varieties, which mature before the moth is ready to lay eggs.

GUIDE TO PEA PROBLEMS	
Symptom	*Probable cause*
Maggots in pods or peas	Pea moth
Holes around edges of leaves	Pea weevil
Silvery patches on pods or leaves	Pea thrips
Small holes or maggots in seed	Pea beetle
Powdery white patches on leaves	Powdery mildew
Greyish brown mould on leaves	Downy mildew
Rotting roots or stems	Foot rot fungus; Black rot fungus
Brown patches on leaves or pods	Leaf spot Fungus
Pale green or yellow patches on leaves	Mosaic virus disease

Murphy Chemicals

Regular holes around the leaf edge are typical pea weevil damage.

Ministry of Agriculture Fisheries and Food Crown Copyright

Mottled green and yellow foliage is caused by mosaic virus disease.

Pea weevil Both the adult and the larva of the pea weevil may attack plants. The 0.5 cm ($\frac{1}{4}$") long grey adults feed on the leaves, making regularly-notched holes around the edges. The females lay eggs in late spring in the soil around the plants, and the white, grub-like larva hatch out and feed on the roots. Hoe around the plants in late spring to stop the adults from laying eggs, and control the weevils with a spraying of derris at the same time.

Pea thrips Pea thrips can be a serious problem in very dry weather. They feed on the flowers, stems and pods, distorting the pods and reducing the crop. They are most numerous in late spring and early summer, when they lay their eggs on the pods. The orange grubs hatch out and feed first on the flowers and then on the pods and leaves, causing silvery, mottled patches which later turn brown. Treat the plants just after the flowers have set with a spraying of derris or resmethrin. As with pea moth, early varieties are infrequently attacked, so if thrips are a problem grow earlies instead of maincrops.

Pea beetle Pea beetles, or seed beetles, are a large family of insects which feed mainly on the seed of peas and other legumes. The adult beetles lay eggs on the dried seed, and the larva hatch out and burrow into the seed, leaving a small, round hole. Infected seed will not germinate, or it will germinate poorly. Clean seed purchased from a reputable seedsman should be fumigated and free of pea beetle grubs. If you discover living grubs, burn the infected seed.

Mildew Powdery mildew appears as white, powdery patches on leaves and pods. Maincrop varieties are most often affected, particularly in dry weather. Prevent by spraying the young plants with dinocap. Also, clear out any old haulms left from early plants, as these can spread the disease.

Downy mildew appears much less frequently, and it is only severe in very wet weather. It looks like greyish-brown mould on the underside of the leaves. Try zineb for bad attacks; otherwise destroy individual affected plants.

Other fungus diseases Peas are subject to occasional attacks but fortunately they are neither very common nor very serious. Foot rot and black rot both cause blackened, rotting patches on the roots and at the base to the stems. Plants grown in good soil as part of a rotation system are rarely affected. Leaf spot fungus disease produces tan-brown patches on the leaves and pods. Dig up and burn any fungus-infected plants as soon as you see them.

Mosaic virus disease Pea plants which have mottled pale green or yellow patches on the leaves and pods are probably suffering from a mosaic virus disease. Although not serious, it can cause distorted pods, so pull out and burn any diseased plants you see.

Varieties

There are numerous varieties of peas available to the home gardener, each with different advantages. Many gardeners tend to stick to old and tried favourites, but seedsmen are constantly working on breeding better strains. Study your seed catalogue carefully before deciding what to plant, and give special consideration to those available at your local garden centre, as they are probably those most suited to your area. We list here some of the most popular and widely available varieties.

Early Onward

Early varieties

Feltham First: round-seeded; very early, dwarf; excellent for sowing in late autumn or early spring for very early crops; heavy crop of well-flavoured peas.
Early Onward: very popular round-seeded type; grows to about 60 cm (2′) high; useful for successional sowings; very good type for freezing.
Kelvedon Wonder: one of the earliest of the wrinkle-seeded types; good for successional sowing; heavy cropper of very sweet peas; reaches about 45 cm (1½′) in height.
Kelvedon Triumph: a good variety to choose if growing for exhibition; dwarf; heavy cropper.
Kelvedon Viscount: suitable for autumn or early spring sowing; heavy and reliable cropper; very hardy plant.
Little Marvel: dwarf variety; crops well; particularly good in cooler areas.
Meteor: round-seeded variety for autumn or spring sowing; heavy cropping dwarf plants.

Second early varieties

Hurst's Green Shaft: a new variety; heavy cropper; pods borne in pairs at top of plant, resistant to downy mildew.
Superb: good variety for exhibition; produces large, curved pods; round-seeded dwarf type.
Lincoln: popular variety for its heavy crops of very sweet peas; produces small, dark-green pods; freezes well.

Meteor

Dark-skinned Perfection: medium-sized but well-filled pods; very sweet peas; plants reach about 1 m (3′) tall.
Purple-podded pea: usually treated as a second early variety; small purple pods have excellently-flavoured green peas; grows to about 1.5 m (5′).

Maincrop varieties

Greensleeves (Achievement): superb choice for table or exhibition, produces 15 cm (6″) long, well-filled pods; very heavy cropper; vigorous grower.
Dwarf Greensleeves: enjoys all the advantages of *Greensleeves,* but small enough for the small garden.
Alderman: extensively grown tall variety; long, thick pods with large, well-flavoured peas; high yield.
Onward: one of the most popular and

Dark-skinned Perfection

Pat Brindley

Dwarf Greensleeves

Brian Furner

Gloriosa

Brian Furner

Oregon Sugar Pod

Brian Furner

consistently reliable varieties: extremely heavy cropper of well-filled pods; dwarf plants; good for freezing.

Rentpayer: one of the smallest growing maincrop types; crops heavily with large pods.

Gloriosa: new type which has proved extremely reliable under all conditions; heavy cropper; excellent for drying or freezing.

Lord Chancellor: old variety, but still a reliable heavy cropper; produces long, well-filled pods; height about 1 m (3′).

Senator: grows to about 1 m (3′) tall, heavy cropper of medium-sized pods; peas of outstanding flavour which freeze well.

Trio: new multi-podded variety; good sized peas with an extra high sugar content. Excellent for freezing. The plants grow to about 30 cm (1′) high.

Sugar peas

Sugar Dwarf Sweet Green: one of the smallest mangetout at 45 cm (1½′); exceptionally heavy cropper of sweet, pale green pods.

Sugar Dwarf de Grace: reaches 1-1.3 m (3-4′) in height; early cropper; produces pods 7.5 cm (3″) long.

Oregon Sugar Pea: maximum yield; pods of high quality and flavour.

Petit Pois

Gullivert: attractive plants produce a high yield of small pods; delicately flavoured peas.

Cobri: dwarf plants reaching about 60 cm (2′), heavy cropper of very small, sweet peas.

73

Runner Beans

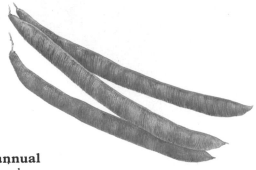

Phaseolus coccineus (fam. *Leguminosae*)
Perennial cultivated as **half hardy annual**
Sowing to harvesting time: 10-14 weeks
Size: This depends largely on the variety used, but
normally they are picked when 15-30 cm (6"-12") long.
Exhibition varieties may attain 60 cm (24") in length. Plants
2-3 m (6'-10') high; dwarf varieties 30-38 cm (12"-15")
Yield: 0.75-1 kg (1½-2 lb) per plant, or 5 kg (10 lb) per
metre run

Reliable and easy to grow, the runner bean is often known as the 'amateur's vegetable'. Its ornamental scarlet or white flowers and succulent green pods have made it a firm favourite. Runner beans are perennial plants in their South American homeland, but in cool temperate areas they are grown as annuals from seed to avoid their susceptibility to frost.

As part of a good rotation plan, runner beans should follow brassicas or potatoes. Like other members of the family *Leguminosae,* runner beans possess root bacteria which convert nitrogen gas from the air to nitrogen compounds, thus enriching the soil for a following crop.

Selecting a site
Runner beans do best in a site that is both open and sheltered. Windswept sites and low-lying frost pockets are not suitable, because in windy or cold weather pollinating insects do not visit the flowers. Avoid siting your beans near

any gaps in fences or hedges through which frost might enter.

When deciding where to plant your runner beans, remember they grow very densely, and a row of climbing beans will make a solid wall of foliage 2 m (6') high. This will shade adjacent rows of vegetables on either side for several hours a day, even if the bean rows run from north to south. Site them accordingly, perhaps at the end of a plot, or next to a wall.

Preparing the soil
The ideal soil for runner beans is a rich, loamy one, well supplied with moisture. Provided that the upper layers are well drained, the more moisture the better; good bean crops are dependant on adequate water. Avoid heavy clay soil as it is generally much too cold at sowing time; very shallow or sandy soils are not suitable as they tend to dry out in summer.

Well before planting time, dig your bean trench. This should be 30 cm (1'

1. Prepare trench well before sowing; double dig and incorporate manure.

2. Two weeks before sowing, apply superphosphate and potash.

3. Rake in the fertilizers, and level off the bed.

4. Sow in drills under cloches for early sowings, or in cold areas.

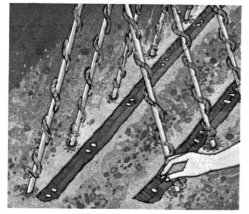

5. Position canes and twine; sow in deep drills, two seeds per cane.

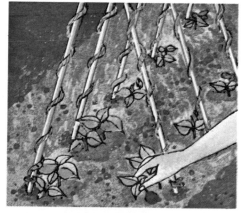

6. As seedlings start to grow, cut or pull out the weaker of the two.

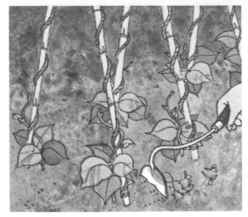

7. Weed around young plants taking care not to damage them.

8. As plants wind themselves up the framework, tie in any stray growth.

9. When plants have reached the top of supports, pinch out growing point to encourage lateral growth.

10. When watering, soak the ground completely to reach the deeper roots. A light sprinkling is simply harmful.

11. Mulch over wet soil in early summer, to preserve soil moisture.

12. Keep picking regularly. Discard yellow, gouty pods—they are too old.

deep and a minimum of 60 cm (2′) wide. On soil with a high clay content, deeper digging to a depth of 45 cm (1½′) will help improve drainage.

It is very important to dig organic matter into the bottom spit, or spade depth, of the trench to help keep the soil open, friable, and moist; it will also serve as a source of nourishment for the growing plants. Well rotted manure or garden compost, at the rate of a litre (2 gallon) bucketful per sq m (sq yd) is sufficient; dig it in during the winter, to allow time for the soil to settle before spring sowing.

When preparing the soil, one point to remember is that too much nitrogen in the soil is sometimes a cause of bean flowers failing to be successfully fertilized, or 'set'. This is best prevented by avoiding fresh manure or artificial fertilizers known to have a high nitrogen content. As a precaution, 45 g (1½ oz) of superphosphate and 15 g (½ oz) of sulphate of potash per sq m (sq yd) applied to the ground immediately prior to planting will balance the presence of too much nitrogen.

Soil in industrial areas or towns is often prone to acidity; beans crop poorly on soil which is too acid. The ideal pH for this vegetable is between 6.0 and 7.0. Test your soil; if it is less than 6.0 add hydrated lime at the rates suggested in the soil test kit.

To train as bushes, pinch out growing point, then growing tips of laterals.

Sowing

Allow five or six plants per person; if you wish to freeze surplus crop allow double that amount.

Runner bean seeds are usually sown outdoors in late spring to provide a crop from mid-summer to mid-autumn. In especially warm and sheltered areas, however, it is possible to sow outdoors during mid-spring, to give a crop starting in early summer. Because the plants are tender and susceptible to frost, and because the seeds will not germinate unless the soil has warmed up, glass protection is needed for earlier sowings. This initial protection is particularly necessary if you live in cold districts such as the north of England.

Glass shelter for the young plants can be cloches, or a greenhouse or cold frame in which the seedlings can be raised in boxes. They can then be hardened off and planted out after all danger of frost has passed. Runner beans can also be raised in pots; peat pots are useful because you won't disturb the roots at planting out time. If you decide to use peat pots, remember to thoroughly wet the pots at planting out time; otherwise the dry pot will impede the flow of moisture from the soil to the plant's root system.

The rate of germination of runner beans is usually very high (80% or more) but it is still wise to sow a few extra seeds at one end of the row, so you will have a few replacement seedlings if there are failures in the row caused by poor germination or by pest damage to the germinating seedlings.

For planting, draw out a 5 cm (2″) deep drill, water it, and sow two seeds every 30 cm (1′) in either one or two lines depending on the method of support. If you are growing the beans up a single row of poles, sow one line only. If you are going to support the plants with pairs of crossed beanpoles, sow the seeds opposite each other in a double row 30 cm (1′) apart. If you are going to use netting, sow two rows, again 30 cm (1′) apart, with the seeds staggered. If you are

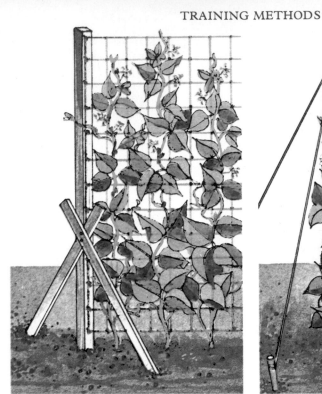

Fix netting to posts placed at 2 m (6′) intervals, sunk 45 cm (18″) into ground.

Rows of canes linked by wires, with stout poles and guy ropes either end.

planting more than one double row of runner beans, they should be at least 1.5 m (5′) apart.

If you plan to train the bean plants as bushes, plant the seeds 23 cm (9″) apart, leaving 60 cm (2′) between rows.

As soon as germination has taken place, earth up round the plants to protect them from possible frost damage. If they do suffer frost damage, pull them out. If it is not too late, make a replacement sowing, because frost-damaged runner beans will never fully recover. Stake the young plants as soon as possible to protect them from wind.

Methods of support

Whatever method of support you use, it must be absolutely rigid. One heavy cropping plant can weigh up to 2 kg (4 lb) and a whole row of them will be enormously heavy. A 3 m (10′) row of beans 2 m (6½′) high will have a surface

area of about 6 sq m (7 sq yd) of dense foliage. This is extremely vulnerable to strong wind; once a row of beans has collapsed, it cannot be re-erected. It will smother neighbouring rows of vegetables, and must be removed at once.

The simplest method of support is to give each plant one cane, or pole, pushing it 45 cm (1½′) into the ground, with 2 m (6½′) above ground. If you have access to a woody area, you can cut your own hazel, ash or sweet chestnut bean poles; alternatively, 2.4 m (8′) long bamboo canes, with a 3.7 cm (1½″) diameter at the thick end, may be used. Each cane is then linked to the next by thin wire or strong twine. At both ends of the row, two much stouter poles are inserted. Lateral stability is provided by straining wires from these heavy end poles to pegs driven into the ground, in the same way as guy ropes are used when

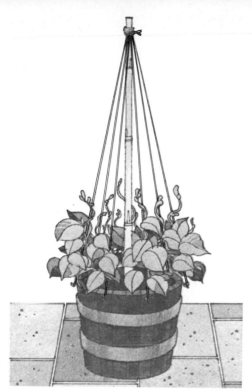

Growing in a tub: use a central pole and twine hooked to edge of tub.

Wigwam of bamboo poles, tied at the top, twine twisted around poles.

putting up a tent. If the row is very long, you may need intermediary posts and struts halfway along the row. Permanent clothes posts or nearby trees can be used to secure the end posts.

Another common method of support is to use the bean poles in pairs; they are inserted into the ground at an angle, so that the tops cross each other at a height of about 1.6 m (5½'). The poles are tied together at the crotch; after a row of these pairs of poles has been erected, 30 cm (1') apart, more poles are laid horizontally in the crotches, overlapping, and securely tied to the intersecting vertical poles where they meet (see figure 8). These horizontal poles help keep the framework rigid. If you are using bamboo canes, it is a good idea to twine string up the length of the smooth canes, to give the climbing bean vines something to cling to.

A third method is to grow the beans up

netting, supported between strong posts. Use 10 cm (4″) mesh wire, plastic coated wire, or plastic netting. Posts supporting the netting should be 2.4 m (8′) long, hammered 45 cm (1′ 6″) into the ground at each end of the row, and at 1.8 m (6′) intervals along the row. Two internal struts are required for each post, to take the weight; these struts reach 90 cm (3′) up each pole and are well buried in the ground (see diagram).

If you are only growing a very small number of beans, wigwams of 6 or 7 poles planted in a circle and tied together at the top will suffice. The plants may be a bit crowded at the top, but will otherwise grow well. Runner beans can also be grown in a large tub, with strings tied to the top of a central pole, and radiating out to hooks which have been fixed to the tub (see diagram). A tripod with three canes is an alternate method of supporting beans grown in a tub.

79

Bush or dwarf varieties, when available, do not need support and are ideal for growing under cloches.

Eric Crichton

When the first vines start to search for something to climb, tie them loosely with raffia or string to their own poles. This is very important; once the beans have begun twining round each other for lack of proper training it will be impossible to disentangle them. Most people give each plant a pole, stick or string; some growers, however, allow up to four plants to use the same support. Choose the method you prefer.

Once the beans have started climbing up the supports, there is no training necessary until the tips reach the tops of the supports. Then pinch off the growing points. This encourages the production of lateral shoots further down the plant, and helps to increase crop yield.

Bush plants

Some gardeners train climbing runner beans as bush plants. This is done by pinching out the growing points at the first joint as soon as the young plants begin to run. When the plants are 30 cm (1') high, nip off the growing tips of the lateral runners to promote bushy growth. You must continue removing these tips at weekly intervals for the plants to remain compact.

These are different from true dwarf runner beans, which grow naturally in a bush form about 45 cm (18") high, and are cultivated as dwarf French beans. Unfortunately, true dwarf runner beans are not always available, as the strains tend to gradually revert to the normal climbing habit. When the seedgrowers' stock has deteriorated in this way, he must find a new source for true dwarfing plants.

Care and development

The main requirements of the growing runner bean plant are simple enough: moisture, weeding and feeding. The crop will not be successful if the plants are allowed to get at all dry. During spells of dry weather, water the plants at least twice a week. You must use enough water to soak the ground completely and reach down to the lowest roots. Light sprinklings are actually harmful, as they encourage the deep feeding roots to come to the surface, where they are vulnerable to hot sun and drying winds. If you are growing your beans in tubs, water them daily during droughts, as soil in tubs or pots dries out very quickly.

In dry conditions, mulching is helpful, as it slows the rate at which water evaporates from the soil. Lawn mowings, 5 cm (2″) deep, are often used as a bean mulch; bark fibre, if you can obtain it, is a particularly good mulch because water and liquid feeds can penetrate to the soil below. Apply mulch in early summer, making sure the soil to be mulched is moist.

Liquid feeding can be occasionally incorporated into the watering pattern as soon as the plants are flowering. Use soot water, alternating with a dilute liquid feeding made by soaking a bag of manure in a tank of water until the fluid is the colour of weak tea.

While the seedlings are developing, you must weed regularly. Hoe the weeds while they are still small, taking care not to harm the delicate roots and stems of the young beans. Once the beans are growing well, they cast a heavy shade which keeps down most weeds; hand weed as necessary. Mulching the plants also helps smother any weeds which might develop.

Failure of the flowers to set is sometimes due to hot, dry weather conditions. When this happens, the flowers wilt and insects and moisture cannot penetrate. Spraying the beans with a fine misty spray every morning and evening, under and over the foliage, during heatwaves may help. Plants grown on moisture-retaining soil should not suffer too badly in a drought.

Harvesting the crop

Runner beans will be ready for picking in mid to late summer, and the golden rule is to keep picking. You must look over plants every few days during the harvesting season, and pick off all young tender pods. Length is not a reliable guide to ripeness, as the length at which they are ready to be picked depends on the variety. In general, beans which have grown too long have coarse-textured, pale pods, and the beans inside are swollen and stand out like gouty finger joints. These are inedible and should be discarded. Be careful to remove all old, stringy beans which have been overlooked under the dense, leafy growth; as long as these remain on the plant, further bean production is reduced.

Remember to remove slug-damaged, badly twisted or muddy pods as well, as they reduce the cropping potential of the plant and may invite infection. Pick the beans early in the morning or evening if the weather is hot. If you don't use them right away, store them in a cool larder, where they will keep for a couple of days, or in a refrigerator, where they will keep a bit longer. The best solution is to either freeze the surplus beans, if the variety is suitable, or share them with friends or neighbours.

At the end of the season, when clearing the plants after final harvest, leave their tuberous roots in the ground. They are rich in nitrogen and will improve the soil for a following crop.

Exhibition tips

If you want to grow beans for exhibition purposes, you will be losing some of the total crop weight the plant would have otherwise produced, as you must remove all pods competing with the few grown for exhibition.

Among the varieties particularly suited to exhibiting are Scarlet Emperor, Yardstick and White Achievement.

Treat the plants normally until you have pinched them out two leaves above the last flower truss when they have reached the top of the bean poles. Then stop all laterals two leaves above a flower truss. Three weeks before the show date, begin feeding your plants regularly with liquid manure. About a fortnight before the show, select the most promising of the pods, marking them with a bit of string. Then thin the trusses to two or three pods, supporting the weight of the beans by tying them in lightly to the poles or netting. Remember to remove the other beans from the plant, so they don't absorb nourishment intended for the show. Some exhibitors run their fingers down the show pods, as they are developing, exerting slight pressure on the beans as they do so. This stretches the pods and keeps them from being bumpy or 'beany'.

The length of the beans exhibited depends on the variety, but they should be from 38-50 cm (15-20″) long and 2.5 cm (1″) wide. Besides length, the judges will consider the beans' colour and texture. A top quality pod will be young, fresh and crisp, without any bumpiness from swelling seeds.

An exhibition dish of runner beans usually contains 24 pods, as alike as possible. If some beans reach their prime condition a few days before the show, cut them off, leaving 2.5 cm (1″) of stalk on the pods. Store them stalk downward, until the show, in a jam jar containing 1 cm ($\frac{1}{2}$″) of water which is changed daily.

On the day of the exhibition, choose your best pods and lay them neatly and as straight as possible on a large plate or across the bench.

Some exhibitors save home-grown seed from year to year. This is a dangerous practice, because of the high risk of seed-carried infections. Halo blight, anthracnose, bean beetle or root rot will effectively end any hope of prize winning.

Varieties

Runner beans have been divided into early and maincrop varieties, according to their time of harvest. Separately listed are some stringless varieties which are now being offered. There is no list of dwarf runner beans because the availability of these varieties fluctuates from one year to the next, due to deterioration of the seed stock. If you intend to freeze any surplus runner beans, make sure you select a suitable variety.

Early varieties

Zebra: attractive mottled pods 23 cm (9″) long; heavy cropper with aromatic flavour, suitable for freezing.

Scarlet Emperor: popular variety, ideal for general garden use; can be grown on poles or as a bush bean, suitable for kitchen and exhibition work; pods 30 cm (1′) long; not suitable for freezing.

Kelvedon Marvel: can be sown under cloches from mid-spring for exceptionally early crops; best results obtained by growing as a bush bean without poles; pods 25-30 cm (10″-12″) long; suitable for freezing.

Sunset: pale pink flowers, heavy cropper; can be grown up supports or as bush beans; if grown in bush form it will produce an early pick of pods; pods 30 cm (1′) long; not suitable for freezing.

Yardstick: pods up to 60 cm (24″) long;

Scarlet Emperor

heavy cropper, exceptionally straight pods; excellent for exhibition work; suitable for freezing.

Maincrop varieties

White Achievement: white seeded, white flowered general purpose runner bean; kitchen or exhibition quality; pods 45 cm (1′6″) long; not suitable for freezing.
Crusader: very heavy cropper; pods 40-50 cm (16″-20″) long; suitable for freezing.
Enorma: heavy cropper; pods up to 52 cm (21″) long; suitable for freezing.
Goliath (Prizetaker): pods up to 60 cm (24″) long; heavy, reliable, and uniform crop; suitable for freezing.
Streamline: pods up to 45 cm (18″) long; scarlet seeded; not suitable for freezing; good flavour.

Stringless varieties

Desiree: very heavy cropper (averaging 40 pods per plant); completely stringless pods 25-30 cm (10″-12″) long; good performance under dry weather conditions; suitable for freezing.
Fry: white seeded, white flowers; pods 35 cm (14″) long; good cropper during hot, dry weather; suitable for freezing.
Red Knight: heavy and early cropper; very good flavour; has pretty red flowers; pods 30 cm (1′) long; sets well in hot, dry conditions; freezes well.

Brian Furner

Desiree

Pests & Diseases

Runner beans are relatively trouble free, but may be affected by any of the following:
Halo blight: this is a seed-borne disease which is encouraged by the unnecessary practice of soaking the beans before sowing. It takes the form of small, yellow transparent spots which are surrounded by a yellow ring. Eventually the spots congeal and dry up and the whole leaf withers. Seedlings may be killed outright, and older plants wilt completely. Diseased plants should be removed and destroyed as soon as seen. The best precaution is to only use seeds from reliable sources: never sow seeds which are wrinkled or blistered or have yellow spots on them.
Bean beetle (Bruchid beetle): these are frequently, though incorrectly, known as 'bean weevils' because of their visual similarity to true weevils. The eggs of this beetle are laid on the growing seed pod, or else on seeds which have been dried and stored. After hatching, the legless and curved grubs enter the seed and bite a round hole beneath the surface skin of the seed; this appears as a little window through which the adult beetle finally emerges. The damage done by these pests is twofold: because the growing grub feeds on the seed, the amount of nourishment for the seedling is diminished, if the germinating seedling is not killed outright. Secondly, the holes made by the beetles allow such other pests as millepedes and wireworms to enter, and expose the seed to attacks by fungal and bacterial growths. Any seeds found to contain living grubs or beetles should be burned; they should *never* be placed on the compost heap or left lying about. Because these pests are seed carried, you must be absolutely certain that your seeds are from a reliable source.
Slugs: one of the most familiar of all creatures which attack plants, they feed chiefly after dark, both above and below ground. They will attack the leaves,

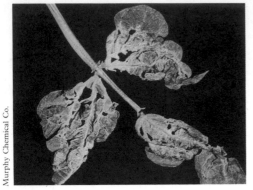

Murphy Chemical Co.

Bernard Alfieri

Damaged and distorted runner bean leaves: the effects of capsid bugs.

An infestation of black bean aphis, commonly known as black fly, on a runner bean shoot.

stems, roots and pods.

During the day they hide away in dark, moist, cool places. Their favourite haunts are decaying vegetable matter, moist, heavy, sour soils or even alkaline soils which are rich in humus and moisture.

It is very difficult to eradicate slugs in heavily infested areas. Because slugs have the ability to cast off poisons or irritants which may fall upon them by excreting slime, to be effective you should always repeat an application of slug pellets on successive nights. Alternatively, use powdered lime and powdered copper sulphate mixed together in equal parts and forked into the soil at the rate of 30 g (1 oz) per sq m (yd). This will kill the slugs, but overuse of copper sulphate may harm the soil, so apply carefully and sparingly.

Another method of destroying slugs is to set traps at the base of the affected bean plants. These traps may be wet sacks, or heaps of damp vegetable refuse, such as lettuce or cabbage leaves or orange peels. It is most important that the traps are inspected daily and the captured slugs destroyed.

Capsid bugs: these are sucking insects which distort the leaves and mark the pods, occasionally attacking the growing point of the plant. They can be controlled by spraying or dusting with nicotine or derris plus pyrethrum. Because capsids drop to the ground

when disturbed, remember to treat the soil around the plant as well.

Botrytis: this is a fungus always present in the atmosphere which appears on the plants as a fluffy grey mould. The fungus usually occurs in cold, wet, weather conditions, and is encouraged by humid, still air. Seedlings are particularly vulnerable and may collapse and die.

Sufficient ventilation is important; if you sow your bean seeds under glass make sure the seedlings are not overcrowded, and any damaged plants removed and destroyed. Botrytis can be controlled by dusting with a fine spray of sulphur dust or spraying with colloidal sulphur.

Bean aphis: this is a black aphis which completely smothers the growing points of beans in late spring. The affected plants stop growing, and the few pods which develop are covered with a black, sticky substance. It can be controlled by spraying with liquid derris or dusting with derris powder, repeated as necessary. The infected tops of plants can be removed as soon as enough pods are formed.

Bean anthracnose: this disease is sometimes called 'blight', 'rust' or 'canker', and thrives in damp, wet conditions. The symptoms are black spots which soon grow into sunken, circular pits surrounded by red lines. Leaves, stems, and pods may be affected. The disease penetrates the pods and infects the seeds,

84

Ministry of Agriculture and Fisheries

Symptoms of bean mosaic: yellowish areas spreading among the dark green of the leaf.

Murphy Chemical Co.

Later stages of halo blight: the transparent ringed spots dry up and leaf begins to wither.

which then develop brownish-black markings. A half-strength mixture of Bordeaux (230 g in 46 litres of water, or $\frac{1}{2}$ lb in 10 gallons of water) sprayed on the infected plants helps control anthracnose, but this spraying must stop when the plants begin to flower. A seed-carried disease, the best precaution against anthracnose is clean seed.

Root rot: this occurs most often on soils which are cold and badly drained; the roots are weakened and made liable to attack from soil fungi. When this happens, dark brown or black spots can be seen on the roots and stems, just below the soil level. As with all seed-borne diseases, the best precaution is to obtain seed from a reliable source.

Bean mosaic: this disease, sometimes called streak, leaf roll, or yellow edge, is caused by a virus which infects the sap. Its symptoms are yellowish-green areas showing among the darker green areas of the rest of the leaf. External applications are not very effective in controlling mosaic, and badly infected plants should be dug up and destroyed. Because this disease is carried by sucking insects, especially aphids, a good precaution against mosaic is to spray the plants with derris or malathion. Because the virus can also be carried on gardening tools, any secateurs, hoes, etc, which have come in contact with infected plants should be thoroughly cleaned in a strong antiseptic solution.

GUIDE TO RUNNER BEAN TROUBLES

Symptom	Probable cause
Small transparent spots with wide yellow ring around them which congeal and dry up; infects pods, stems and leaves	Halo blight
Seed leaves misshapen, seedlings stunted, small holes under surface skin of bean; may be gaps in row	Bean beetle
Pinprick holes with brown edges in young leaves, leaves later tattered, growing points blind	Capsid bug
Fluffy grey mould on leaves, stems and pods; plants rot off at soil level	Botrytis
Irregular holes in leaves, stems and pods; faint silvery trails	Slugs
Sunken black spots, edged in red, on leaves, stems and pods	Bean anthracnose
Plants covered in small, black, sucking insects	Bean aphis

Spinach

Spinacea oleracea (fam. *Chenopodociaceae*), winter, prickly (seeded) or long-standing prickly spinach
Spinacea oleracea inermis, summer or round-seeded spinach
Tetragonia expansa (fam. *Aizoaceae*) New Zealand spinach
Hardy or **half-hardy annual**
Size: height to 20 cm (8"); width 30-37.5 cm (12-15") for summer and winter spinach; trailing, width to 90 cm (3') for New Zealand spinach
Sowing to harvesting time: 6-8 weeks
Yield: 150 g (5 oz) per plant before it bolts for summer type; 240 g (8 oz) per plant for winter type; 360 g (12 oz) per plant for New Zealand spinach

Spinach is a highly nutritious vegetable, rich in protein and vitamin A. It is quick growing and needs a minimum of care; by successional sowings and giving some winter protection, you can have good crops of spinach all year round.

There is some confusion over the name 'spinach' because it is used for many vegetables which are not true spinach but have leaves which are eaten like those of spinach. For example, 'perpetual spinach' or 'spinach beet' is a member of the beet family. Here we are dealing with the cultivation of three types: winter, summer and New Zealand.

True spinach is winter, or prickly spinach. 'Prickly' refers not to the leaves, but the seed capsule. It is a spreading, branching plant, with triangular dark green leaves. At one time winter spinach was thought to be hardier than summer spinach. This has been disproved,

however, and round seeded varieties can be sown right through the year.

Summer, or round spinach is a variety of winter spinach; it has round smooth seed capsules and slightly larger lighter green leaves. Summer spinach has a bad reputation for bolting, or running to seed. When this happens, the plants send up tall leafy stems with small green flowers at the top; the leaves then become bitter tasting and unpleasant to eat. Premature bolting is easily controlled, however, by making quite sure that you meet the basic cultivation requirements. Spinach must never run short of water, and needs some form of shade during the hottest summer months. Equally important is thinning the seedlings as soon as possible so they are never overcrowded. Spinach grown in crowded, starved conditions is more liable to bolt.

Spinach is an excellent, nutritious vegetable, relatively quick and easy to grow.

One sowing of summer spinach will give about three weeks picking; to get continuous supplies, you should sow at three-weekly intervals. Because winter spinach is less likely to bolt, two or three sowings in late summer through mid-autumn should give supplies right through winter and into early spring.

New Zealand spinach is not a true spinach, although it tastes fairly similar. It is not as hardy as winter or summer spinach, and is most successful in hot dry summers. Because it does well in very sunny conditions and does not bolt, it can be planted where ordinary spinach would do poorly. New Zealand spinach is a vigorous spreading plant, with floppy stem and fleshy, arrow-shaped leaves up to 12 cm (5″) long.

Suitable site and soil

To grow year-round supplies of spinach, you must make several successional sowings. The conditions needed for successful growing will change according to the time of year and variety of spinach grown. A warm, sheltered site is required for winter spinach and early sowings of summer spinach. From late spring through mid-summer, however, too much warmth and sunshine may lead to bolting, so a cool shady site is preferable. Spinach is ideal for growing in the shade of peas or beans during hot summer months.

New Zealand spinach needs a light, well-drained soil in a hot sunny position, and will crop well where ordinary spinach would quickly run to seed. New

1. Start sowing under cloches in late winter; continue successional sowing until mid-summer.

2. For free draining soil, make a shallow trench 30 cm (1′) wide, with a central drill 2.5 cm (1″) deep.

3. Thin the seedlings when they are 2.5-5 cm (1-2″) high, to a distance of 12.5-15 cm (5-6″) apart.

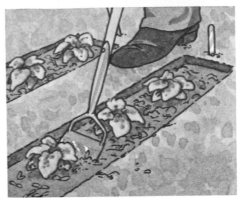

4. Shallow hoeing keeps weeds down and also creates a dust mulch which helps conserve moisture.

Zealand spinach likes soil fairly rich in lime, so it does particularly well on chalk or limestone subsoils; avoid acid soils or lime them well before growing, at a rate determined by the result of a soil test.

The needs of spinach vary throughout the year, so it is difficult to work spinach into a rotational cropping plan. Because it is such a quick grower, however, spinach is an excellent catch crop and can be grown and harvested without interfering with slower-growing crops, such as leeks or cabbages.

Spinach needs a rich moisture retentive soil, and it is a waste of time to sow on a dry, poorly worked site. The ground should be well dug over and watered, using between 5 and 10 kg per sq m (12 and 22 lb per sq yd) of rotted manure or garden compost; the high rate is best if the soil is light or sandy. At the same time a dressing of fertilizer containing 12% nitrogen and 6% each of of phosphate and potassium should be worked in at the rate of 30 g per sq m (1 oz per sq yd). No further feeding should be needed.

Sowing

Besides sowing frequently, you must sow spinach in large enough quantities to provide reasonable supplies for your

5. Water often in hot weather; use a fine spray or rose on your watering can so soil is not washed away.

6. Spinach is good for intercropping, and will grow well in the shade of runner beans or peas.

7. When harvesting, take only a few leaves from each plant at one time; overpicking can kill the plant.

8. After the final harvest, chop up the plants and dig them into the soil to act as green manure.

family. Whereas 'little and often' applies to the sowing of radishes and lettuce, it does not entirely apply to spinach. A whole panful of leaves when cooked will boil down to a couple of spoonfuls; if you then overpick to get enough leaves, the plants will stop producing new leaves and may die altogether. A good rule of thumb is to allow five plants per person per sowing, or a half metre (20″) row per person. 30 g (1 oz) of seed is enough to sow 3.6 m (12′). If you have more seed than you need, you can either share it with friends or store it; properly stored spinach seeds will keep for five years.

Make the first sowings under cloches in late winter, and continue making successional sowings at the rate of one every three weeks until mid-summer. It is best to use bolt-resistant varieties for these early sowings.

If your soil is light and very free draining, you can reduce the problem of drying out and bolting by making a shallow trench in which to sow the seeds. For each row of seeds, hollow out a trench 5 cm (2″) deep and about 30 cm (1′) wide. In the middle of this trench, make a drill another 2.5 cm (1″) deep to sow the seeds in. This shallow trenching system will allow you to flood the trenches, with little water loss. If the soil

1. Sow from mid-summer through to mid-autumn. For heavy soils, make small ridges on which to sow seeds.

2. Protect open grown spinach from winter weather with a layer of bracken or clean straw.

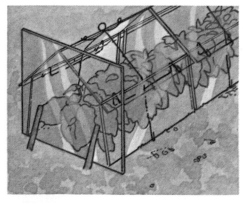

3. Cloches are an alternative way to protect winter spinach; cloches also helps keep the leaves free of mud.

is very dry, water it thoroughly just before sowing, or soak the seeds in water for a few hours prior to sowing. If you are sowing more than one row of spinach, make the rows at least 45 cm (1½') apart. You can grow good spinach with a spacing of 30 cm (1') between rows, but the extra width allows you to cultivate the plants and harvest them without trampling on the bottom leaves. For some of the larger varieties, such as *Sigmaleaf* or *Greenmarket*, 60 cm (2') between rows would be better, and for New Zealand spinach 90 cm (3') is needed.

Germination may be sparse, so it is best to sow one seed every 7.5 cm (3") and thin later. The seeds are actually capsules containing two or three tiny seeds, so you may get two or three seedlings at each station. After sowing, cover the capsules with 2.5 cm (1") of soil, and press down firmly with the back of a rake. Germination should take place one to two weeks after sowing.

Winter spinach should be sown from mid-summer through to mid-autumn, at the same spacing and depth as for summer spinach. However, with winter spinach you have to avoid too much water rather than too little. If your soil is heavy, it is best to form small ridges on which to sow the seeds. Make them 7.5 cm (3") high, with 60 cm (2') from centre to centre. These raised ridges will help keep the spinach dry in the winter, which is important for a good crop.

Because New Zealand spinach is not quite hardy, it is best to sow in early spring in pots under glass and then plant them out in early summer, spaced 60 cm (2') apart in all directions. You can sow them under cloches outdoors in mid-spring or in the open in late spring.

Before sowing, it is advisable to soak the seeds of New Zealand spinach for two or three hours in water to aid in germination as the seed coat is very hard. Whichever method of sowing you use, sow them in groups of threes, to allow for some failure in germination which may occur.

New Zealand spinach is an excellent crop for hot dry sites, as it is bolt resistant.

Cultivation

Thinning the young seedlings is very important; overcrowded plants are more liable to become diseased, unlikely to develop fully, and more likely to run to seed. Thin seedlings of summer spinach when they are 2.5-5 cm (1-2") high, to a distance of 12.5-15 cm (5-6") apart. Thin again when the leaves of adjacent plants begin to touch each other to a final spacing of 22-30 cm (9-12") apart. If more than one seed germinates at a station, select the strongest and thin out the rest. Winter spinach being slightly smaller should be thinned to 22 cm (9") apart; New Zealand spinach grows very large and needs to be spaced 90 cm (3') apart in all directions.

Never let the soil dry out in hot weather, otherwise summer spinach is likely to bolt. Remember, though, that spinach needs a steady, constant supply of moisture: overwatering after a long dry spell can also lead to bolting. Too much water in late summer can also lead to soft rank growth, easily frosted in the autumn. Make sure you use a fine spray or rose on your watering can to avoid washing any soil away.

Keep the beds weed free, although healthy growing spinach will form a dense, impenetrable ground cover leaving little room for weeds. If weeds do appear, either hand weed or hoe. Regular shallow hoeing also prevents the soil from caking in hot weather, and provides a dust mulch which helps conserve moisture.

Although New Zealand spinach will not bolt in hot dry weather, it needs a steady supply of water at such a time. Harvest growing tips frequently, so that the plant will produce a continuous supply of sideshoots.

Cloche protection is very useful if you want to continue picking through winter, and get an early spring crop as well. Winter spinach sown under cloches in early autumn will be ready for picking from late autumn on. Protecting with cloches also helps keep the leaves free of mud. If you have no cloches it is a good

1. New Zealand spinach thrives on limey soil; if your soil is acid, apply lime before sowing.

2. Because the seed coat is hard, soak the seeds in water for a couple of hours before sowing.

3. Sow in pots in early spring; plant out in early summer, spacing 60 (2') apart.

4. Harvest growing tips frequently, so the plants will produce a steady supply of sideshoots.

5. Picking usually starts from early summer onwards, five to six weeks after sowing, and continues until the first hard frosts of autumn. Cut the fleshy shoots with pointed leaves when they are about 22 cm (8") long.

idea to protect open grown spinach from late autumn onwards with a layer of bracken or clean straw placed between the rows. Polythene tunnels are also effective with an occasional airing on mild days, but watch for slugs.

As long as the soil is reasonably rich and has been well prepared, there is no need to apply additional fertilizers once the spinach has been planted. However, you can apply nitro-chalk in early spring, at the rate of 30 g per sq m (1 oz per sq yd) to help winter spinach make a bit more spring growth.

For all types of spinach, after you have finished harvesting, chop the plants up with a spade and dig them back into the soil; they will then be a kind of green manure and enrich the soil.

Harvesting

Winter, summer and New Zealand spinach are harvested in much the same way. The thinnings of spinach are eaten first. Dig these up whole and cut the roots off. Thinnings of summer spinach are very useful for salad, as they are tender, less bitter and less stringy then fully grown leaves. When the main plants are ready, take a few leaves off from each plant. Moderate picking encourages the formation of new leaves; too much picking will kill the plant. A good rule of thumb is to take off no more than half the leaves at any one picking. Select the largest and most fully formed leaves, but do not leave them until they are old and tough.

When you are picking spinach, try to take the leaves only, leaving the stem. If they are young leaves you should be able to nick them off between your finger and thumb. Otherwise, twist the midribs and pull them off outwards or cut them with scissors to avoid damaging the main stem.

Winter harvesting should start in late-autumn. Do not pick the plants as hard as summer spinach. Unfortunately, the thinnings are not suitable for salads, as they are stringy. Pick only the larger outside leaves, allowing the young leaves

to grow on. Light pickings will enable you to have a longer period of harvesting, until spring, when the first crops of summer spinach should be ready.

New Zealand spinach is slightly more difficult to harvest because the plants are larger and tend to sprawl all over the ground. However, if you keep removing the growing tips, the plants will produce an enormous amount of leafy growth from a small area.

Start picking the fleshy shoots with pointed leaves when they are about 22 cm (8″) long. Picking usually starts from early summer onwards, five to six weeks after sowing, and continues until the first hard frosts of autumn. If you miss one or two of the tips, and the plant flowers, it may self-sow and appear again the following year, in mild areas.

Exhibition tips

The main problem with exhibiting spinach is that the leaves tend to go limp as soon as they are cut, and it is difficult to stage an attractive exhibit composed solely of wilted leaves. To help prevent wilting, cut the leaves as close to the ground as possible the night before the show, preferably in cool weather. The number of leaves required for an exhibit is 15-25. It is a good idea to pick two or three times this amount, so you can select the best. Wash the leaves under cool running water to remove any soil. Then place the stalks in a bucket or large jar of water and store in a cool place overnight. The next day, lay the selected leaves on a large plate, with all the stalks pointing towards the centre, like the spokes of a bicycle wheel. Spray the leaves with cool water and cover them with a light cloth until just before judging.

New Zealand spinach is a separate category, although the preparation is similar. After gathering, strip off all the old leaves, and display the remaining leaves in a basket. For both New Zealand and ordinary spinach, pale green or yellow leaves, or those which are small or broken, will be considered defective.

Varieties

Broad Leaved Prickly: long standing; large deep green leaves; good for autumn sowing.

Longstanding Winter (Prickly): best variety for winter use; deep green thick leaves; quick growing; slow to bolt.

Greenmarket: large, dark green leaves; slow to run to seed; winter hardy; very heavy yielding; any virus infection will have only minor affects.

Sigmaleaf: round seeded variety suitable for spring or autumn sowing; can stand for long period of time without running to seed.

New Zealand Spinach: soft thick fleshy leaves; trailing habit; withstands hot dry conditions.

Monnopa: low oxalic acid content; fine flavoured; bolt resistant; winter hardy; for autumn sowing.

Cleanleaf: emerald green leaf; leaves borne well above the soil so they are not splashed by mud.

King of Denmark: large, round thick-leaved summer variety.

Monarch Long Standing Supergreen: dark green, round summer variety suitable for freezing.

Long Standing Round: quick growing; dark leaf; good for spring sowing.

Broad Leaved Prickly

Greenmarket

New Zealand Spinach

Longstanding Round

Pests & Diseases

Spinach blight: this disease is caused by the cucumber mosaic virus. It is a serious disease and any infected plants should be dug up and burned as soon as the symptoms are seen. Usually the first symptom is yellowing of the younger inner leaves, and later the older ones. The inner leaves then become puckered and/or small, the leaf margins roll up, and the leaves die. Because spinach blight can be transmitted by aphids, try to keep your garden free of these pests, and also weeds, which may be infected with the virus, and infested with greenfly. As with other viral infections, there is no absolute cure; the best precaution is to cultivate the plants properly and watch for any sign of the disease, removing any suspect plants as soon as they are seen.

Downy mildew: this fungal infection is most liable to occur where the spinach is grown in crowded or very wet, cool conditions. It spreads very quickly particularly in wet weather, and can rapidly ruin a crop. The symptoms are yellowish patches on the upper surfaces of the leaves and downy grey growth on the undersides. The best precaution is to avoid damp conditions and thin the young plants well. Pick off and destroy any infected leaves; if the attack is severe, spray the remainder with zineb or copper fungicide.

Leaf spot: the symptoms of leaf spot are small light brown spots on the leaves, each with a darker margin. Although they are only 6 mm ($\frac{1}{4}$″) across, if the infection is bad the spots join up into large areas and destroy the entire leaf. As with many diseases, the weakest plants are the most susceptible, especially if growing in badly drained soil. Remove and burn infected leaves as soon as you see them, and spray the remainder with captan or zineb. Spray again a fortnight later.

Damping off: this fungal infection causes seedlings to collapse at ground level and then die. Because it occurs most frequently in close, wet conditions, the best precaution is to sow thinly and make sure the seedlings are not overcrowded or overwatered. Thiram or captan treated seeds will be well protected.

Magnesium deficiency: magnesium is one of the constituents of chlorophyll. If spinach is lacking magnesium, pale areas will appear between the leaf veins. Eventually the pale areas turn brown. The deficiency is most liable to occur in very acid soils, or where an excess of potash makes magnesium unavailable to plants. A good mulch of well-rotted garden compost should help with the problem, and heavy dressings of bulky organic matter when winter digging will gradually eliminate it. On very acid soils, apply lime also. Alternatively, if such

---

GUIDE TO SPINACH TROUBLES

Symptoms	Probable causes
Outer leaves wilt and die; inner leaves turn yellow, curl up and die	Spinach blight
Yellow patches on upper surfaces of leaves, downy grey growth on underside	Downy mildew
Seedlings collapse and die at ground level	Damping off
Pale areas between leaf veins	Magnesium deficiency
Yellow blotches on leaves, leaves curled	Manganese deficiency
Leaves turn brown, wither and die	Mangold fly
Seedlings die (New Zealand spinach)	Millepedes
Irregularly shaped holes in leaves, faint silvery trails	Slugs
Stunted distorted leaf growth	Aphids

Murphy Chemical Co.

These spinach leaves have been damaged by aphids, which feed on the sap.

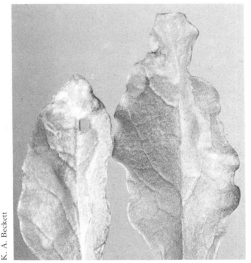

K. A. Beckett

The maggots of mangold fly damage leaves by feeding on them; leaves become blistered.

manures are not available, Dolomite or magnesium limestone can be applied in winter, at about 210 g per sq m (7 oz per sq yd).

Manganese deficiency: the disease called 'speckled yellows' which appears on beet, is really a symptom of manganese deficiency and can also affect spinach. Affected plants have leaves with yellow blotches between the veins, and the leaves tend to curl up, the trouble being most marked in mid-summer. Both very sandy and very alkaline soils can be deficient in manganese, also those which are fairly alkaline and contain a good deal of humus. Some natural

recovery can occur, but if not, foliar spraying with manganese sulphate at 2 oz in 5 gal water with a few drops of liquid detergent, will help the plants considerably.

Mangold flies: the maggots of the mangold fly damage the leaves of spinach by feeding on them to produce large blisters. They are most damaging in late spring when the plants are young; infested leaves turn brown, wither and die. Remove the worst affected leaves and spray the remainder in widespread attacks with trichlorphon as soon as the symptoms are seen; do not forget to allow the specified interval to elapse between treatment and harvesting so that all traces of poison are gone.

Millepedes: these pests are liable to cause problems on soils which are very damp or have a high humus content. New Zealand spinach seems to be the most vulnerable; millepedes feed on the roots of seedlings and young plants, but in general little trouble need be expected in a well worked soil. They are difficult to control; apply gamma-HCH if a severe infestation is apparent while preparing the soil for sowing.

Slugs: if the leaves have irregularly shaped holes in them, and there are faint silvery trails nearby, then slugs are the probable cause. They feed at night, and are most active in the spring and autumn. Thorough cultivation of the soil helps keep the slug population down. You can set traps of piles of decaying vegetable matter near the spinach. Inspect the traps daily and destroy any slugs you find. If the infestation is severe, use metaldehyde or methiocarb slug baits.

Aphids: the damage caused by these insects is twofold. They feed on the sap in the leaves, which results in stunted and distorted leaf growth. They also transmit viral diseases and the honeydew they leave on the plants encourages sooty mould. Handpick affected leaves, as soon as seen, and spray with derris, malathion or bioresmethrin if the infestation persists.

Root Vegetables

Beetroot

Beta vulgaris (fam. *Chenopodiaceae*)
Half-hardy biennial, grown as an **annual.**
Sowing to harvesting time: round and intermediate types
8-10 weeks; long types about 19 weeks.
Size: plants about 30 cm (1′) tall, swollen roots between 2.5
cm (1″) and 9 cm (3½″) in diameter, according to form and
variety at picking time.
Yield: round and oval types, about 40 roots per 3 m (10′)
row; long beet about 20 roots per 3 m (10′) row.

Beet is a fairly straightforward vegetable to raise, and one which has long been popular with amateur growers. It has so many uses in the kitchen that you are never likely to waste any of the crop—as well as adding rich colour and flavour to soups, salads and chutneys it is excellent served as a hot vegetable, and its high sugar content makes it a very good base for home-made wine.

The most common type of beet is round (sometimes called globe, or ball) and deep carmine in colour. These are usually eaten in salads, when they are young and tender, but they can also be grown as a maincrop and stored. There are two other shapes—oval (known as intermediate, or tankard) and long. Long beet is not often grown today, partly because it is less sweet and succulent than the round varieties, and partly because the roots are so large that they will not fit into today's modern saucepans. It does, however, store well and is good for exhibition work.

Although most varieties of beet are red, white and golden beets are now available to the amateur. These are round shaped, and their main advantage over red beet is that they do not 'bleed' in salads. They are doubly useful in the kitchen, because the leaves can be cooked and served like spinach.

By planting several varieties and giving some form of cloche protection in early spring, you can easily have a good supply of beetroot all the year round. A native of the Mediterranean region, it is not frost hardy in colder climates. Winter beetroot should be lifted before the first frosts, and stored until you need them.

Suitable site and soil
Globe beets are reasonably tolerant of soil conditions, and will grow in any well drained soil which does not dry out in summer. However, light sandy soils are ideal for all types of beet, particularly long varieties, which need a deep sandy

loam to grow well. Select a site that is open and sunny for best results.

Begin preparing heavy soils in late autumn; light soils can be prepared early in spring. If the soil is very heavy, dig in plenty of half rotted straw or peat to lighten it. Coarse sand can also be used. Double dig if you are preparing the bed for long beet, otherwise digging to about 17.5 cm (7″) is adequate. Remove all weeds and their roots. If you have dug the soil in the autumn, leave it rough so that winter weather will break it down and make it more friable. If the soil is stony, remove as many as possible, because the roots should be able to grow and penetrate the soil without obstructions which may deform them.

Avoid adding fresh manure when preparing a bed for beet, or you are likely to get forked, mis-shapen roots. Ideally, beet should be grown on part of the vegetable plot which was manured the previous season; beets can sensibly follow celery, peas or runner beans. However, because of beet's maritime associations, seaweed can be added to the soil, provided it is mixed into the bottom spit in autumn.

If the soil has an acid reaction, supply lime sometime in mid-winter sufficient to make the pH neutral or very slightly alkaline. In spring, just before sowing, apply a compound fertilizer at the rate of 60 g per sq m (2 oz per sq yd), but only if seaweed was not added, and rake the soil level.

Sowing

Although beets are reasonably hardy, seedlings can be damaged by heavy frost. If the seedlings are not killed outright, they are liable to be stunted and produce seeds without forming an edible root. There is no point in sowing before mid-spring, unless you live in a very mild area or can give cloche protection. For spring sowings, try to make a point of using bolt-resistant varieties, as beet has a great tendency to run to seed in dry and/or hot conditions.

Round beets for salads should be sown

1. **Prepare heavy soils in autumn, and leave rough over winter; light sandy soils can be prepared in the spring.**

2. **Test the soil; if it is acid, apply lime at a rate to give a neutral or slightly alkaline reaction.**

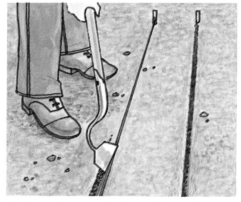

3. **In spring, work the soil to a fine tilth; prepare drills 30 cm (1′) apart and 2.5 cm (1″) deep.**

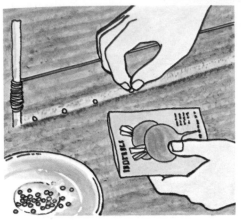

1. Sow seed clusters 5 cm (2″) apart, in small batches, from mid-spring to mid-summer.

2. After sowing fill in the drills with fine soil, and rake the bed lightly to give an even surface.

3. Thin the seedlings as soon as they are large enough to handle; leave one at each station.

4. Thin again, giving a final spacing of 10 cm (4″) for round varieties, and 15 cm (6″) for long varieties.

in small batches until mid-summer. By monthly successional sowing, you will be provided with a continual supply of fresh young roots. Beets to be used for storage should be sown in early summer. Do not sow them earlier in the season, or they will have grown too coarse and woody by the time lifting starts in autumn.

Beet seeds are grouped in capsules, or clusters, each containing four or five seeds. Seeds, if properly stored, will maintain their viability for four years. To hasten germination, soak the seeds in water for a few hours before sowing. The average seed packet will contain enough seeds for several rows, so only soak as many as you intend to use immediately.

Sow each seed cluster 5 cm (2″) apart in rows 30 cm (1′) apart. Make the drills 2.5 cm (1″) deep, and after sowing fill in the drill with soil. Rake lightly to give a fine surface and water if the weather is dry. Germination should be within 12-24 days of sowing. When the seedlings appear, there will be clusters of them at each station. Remove all but the strongest as soon as they are large

1. **Beetroot needs a steady supply of water while it is growing, during the mid and late summer particularly.**

2. **Hoe as necessary between rows, being very careful not to damage the roots with the blade of the hoe.**

3. **For early beet crops, give cloche protection; remove cloches during warm days and replace at night.**

4. **When harvesting, lift the roots with a fork to avoid damaging the long tap root.**

enough to handle. Thin them again, when they are between 2.5-7.5 cm (1-3″) tall for round and intermediate varieties, and 15 cm (6″) tall for long varieties, giving a spacing of 10 cm (4″) and 15 cm (6″) respectively.

Care and development

The cultivation needs of beet are moderate. For the best flavour, beets should grow quickly, otherwise tasteless, cracked, mis-shapen and tough roots will result. This means the plants must have a steady supply of water at the roots, especially during mid and late summer.

If you have thoroughly removed all weeds when preparing the soil, you should have little trouble with weeds while the crops are growing. Once the plants are established, they produce thick foliage which suppresses the weeds. If weeding is necessary, however, hand weed between the plants to avoid damaging the roots; light hoeing between rows is all right if you are very careful and keep well away from the beets.

Beetroot crops are best when grown quickly and given a steady supply of water.

Because beet in its natural state grows near the sea, a light application of agricultural (common or rock) salt is useful. Apply in early or mid-summer, at the rate of 30 g per sq m (1 oz per sq yd) and fork it in lightly.

Birds are much attracted to seedlings and some protection is essential. You can protect the rows with netting, pea guards or black cotton thread twined around and through the leaves.

Container growing

Choose round varieties for container growing. Large tubs are most suitable but, if using pots, the smallest useful size is 30 cm (1′). Fill the bottom 5 cm (2″) of the container with small pieces of broken bricks, pieces of flower pot or hardcore to provide drainage. Fill the container with John Innes potting compost No 3 mixture to within 5 cm (2″) of the rim. Then sprinkle the seeds thinly over the surface and cover with another 2.5 cm (1″) of compost. Water well, using a fine rose on the watering can. Thin the seedlings to allow enough room for them to develop, leaving only eight plants in a

30 cm (1') diameter pot. Water frequently in warm weather.

Forcing

Although you may have stored enough beetroot from the previous year's crop to last through spring, fresh early beet is a real treat and one which is easy to produce. Round varieties are the most suitable for growing under cloches or in frames. Tent and tunnel cloches will accommodate a single row; wider sorts of cloches will take two or three rows, spaced 17.5 cm (7") apart. Sow thinly in early spring in seed drills 2.5 cm (1") deep. Thin as soon as the seedlings are large enough to handle to 5 cm (2") apart; make sure they never run short of water.

After germination, provided that the days are not excessively cold, open the frames or cloches slightly to admit air. Close when night temperatures fall below about 10°C (50°F). Remove the frame lid or cloches entirely on days when temperatures average above 16 C (60°F), but replace in the evening if frost threatens.

Harvesting and storing

Round and intermediate varieties should be ready for pulling when they are about 2.5 cm (1") in diameter, about eight weeks after they are sown. These first pullings are in fact a form of thinning, as the remaining beets will have room to grow larger. For this reason, try to pick evenly over the rows, so the rest of the crop is reasonably spaced. These first pullings will be very tender, and useful for salads. Continue pulling more beet as and when needed, until they reach 6-7.5 cm (2½-3") in diameter. Try to pull the roots as soon as they are fully mature. Once the foliage begins to lose its fresh look and goes limp, it means that growing has stopped and the plants are best harvested immediately.

Maincrops should be ready for harvesting from early autumn, continuing for about two months; this includes the long varieties for winter storing. Loosen the roots with a fork or spade and then lever out; it is best not to wrench the plants out by pulling the leaves. The one exception is the variety *Cook's Delight*, which grows with most of the root out of the ground. These roots will come out quite easily when pulled by the leaves.

Do not cut off the leaves, but twist them off about 5 cm (2") above the crown. This is to avoid breaking the skin and subsequent bleeding, which would detract from the flavour and colour. Then shake the root to remove adhering soil. The leaves of some varieties can be eaten fresh or cooked as greens.

All beets can be stored for future use; if properly stored they will keep until the first of the following year's crop is ready for lifting. Although some varieties are slightly more frost hardy than others, beet can be damaged by severe frost. For this reason, unless you live in a very mild area, you should harvest the crop no later

To store in boxes, line the bottom with sand; place a layer of beetroot on sand, and cover with sand or peat; continue the layers until the box is filled.

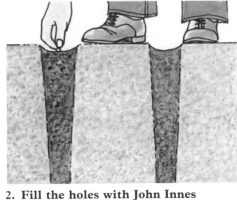

1. Make holes with a crowbar 1.05m (3'6") deep, and 30 cm (1') apart. Leave 45 cm (1'6") between rows.

2. Fill the holes with John Innes potting compost; press the compost in firmly, and sow seeds in the top.

than the first touch of autumn frost. If you do leave them in the ground protect them from frost with a layer of clean straw or bracken. Select a dry day for lifting and be careful not to damage the roots in any way. Damaged, diseased or bruised roots cannot be stored as they may rot and quickly infect the others.

If your crop is moderate-sized, you can store it in boxes. Line the bottom of the container with 5 cm (2") of sand or peat; then lay beetroots on the bottom, not touching each other. Add a 2.5 cm (1") layer of peat or sand and another layer of beet and so on until the box is

Brian Furner

Round varieties are the best sort for container growing; keep them well watered.

fully packed. Then store the boxes in a cool, dry place such as a garden shed, outhouse, garage or cellar. If the storage conditions are too warm or moist, the roots may continue to grow or rot may set in and spoil the crop.

If your harvest is a large one, you can build a clamp, similar to a potato clamp, for beetroot storage (see POTATO).

Exhibition tips

Try to time beetroot sowing so the crop will be just ready for exhibiting; roots which are premature or those which are old and woody will not win prizes. For early summer shows, long varieties should be sown in late winter outdoors with glass protection. Globe varieties should be sown in mid-spring for mid-summer shows, and in late spring for late summer shows.

Globe roots for show can be selected from ordinary crops, and no special cultivation is needed. Long varieties for show are best planted in holes made by a crowbar, 30 cm (1') apart, 1.05 m (3'6") deep, in rows 45 cm (18") apart, filled with John Innes potting compost. Press compost in firmly, leaving a 2.5 cm (1") depression in the top, in which the seeds are sown. Thin out to one strong plant as soon as the seedlings are large enough to handle, and continue cultivating as for normal crops.

3. Before the show, trim back leaf stalks to 7.5 cm (3″) and cut off tiny rootlets with a sharp knife.

When it is time to lift the roots, either round or long, you must take care not to damage the tap root. Do not pull the plants out of the ground by their leaves; it is much better to lift them with a fork or spade.

For both varieties, remove the tiny side rootlets with a sharp knife. Cut off all the outer leaves cleanly; leave 7.5 cm (3″) of leaf stalk from the inner leaves. Wash the roots in cold water to remove any soil adhering, but do not scrub them. Dry the roots and wrap them in paper until the show.

Very large roots are not necessarily prizewinners; it is best to select medium-sized roots which have good colour and are free from blemishes, pale inner rings and damage. The tap root should still be intact. Globe varieties should be symmetrical, smooth skinned, and about the size of a tennis ball. Long varieties should taper evenly from the shoulder to a single tap root. Do not enter roots which are forked or have gall marks, or roots which bulge too much in the middle.

Long varieties are usually shown in a flat basket on a bed of parsley; round varieties can be piled, pyramid shape, in a round basket. Just before judging, spray the beets with a fine mist of water, to make them as visually appetizing as possible.

Pests & Diseases

Mangold flies (beet leaf miner): the maggots of the mangold fly damage the leaves of beet by feeding on them; they mine through the leaves and produce large, pale brown blisters. The worst damage is done when the plants are young; in bad attacks the plants may be killed outright. Infested plants will be stunted; leaves will turn completely brown, wither and die. Pick off and burn all infested leaves. If it is a severe attack, spray the remainder with trichlorphon. Remember to allow the specified interval to elapse between treatment and harvesting. It is a good idea to apply a quick-acting fertilizer to attacked crops to give them a chance to make fresh top growth.

Beet carrion beetle: the grub and adult stage of this black beetle feed on the tender leaves for about three weeks in spring; in severe attacks, the plants may be killed. In general it is not a serious pest, and clean cultivation and frequent hoeing are the best preventive measures. If your plants are attacked, spray with derris as soon as the pests are seen and repeat as necessary.

Swift moth: the dirty white caterpillars of the swift moth can be very destructive; they live in the soil and feed on the roots. Hoe and fork lightly round the beets

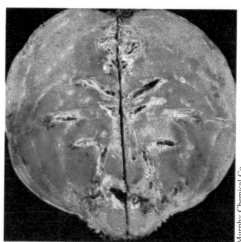

Crown or heart rot is an indication of boron deficiency; roots become cankered and black.

regularly if the soil is infested; this will kill some caterpillars and expose some to insect-eating birds. Because they also feed on the roots of many weeds, such as docks, try to keep your garden weed free. If the attack is severe, try trichlorphon.

Scab: this fungal disease is usually associated with limey soils. Symptoms are small marks or sunken pits; occasionally they are raised above the level of the skin. The small markings will gradually increase in size, until the whole root is disfigured. Although plants are rarely killed by scab, beetroot covered with scab is less pleasant to eat. The best preventive measure is to correct the pH of the soil before planting. You can also dig in green manure, lawn mowings, or moist peat just before sowing as an additional precaution.

Damping off: this is a fungal disease associated with wet, overcrowded conditions. Infected seedlings will collapse at ground level and die; roots of infected plants are usually discoloured reddish-brown. The best preventive measure is to avoid overcrowding the seedlings; thin as soon as they are big enough to handle. If the seedlings are attacked, remove and destroy the infected plants and spray the remainder with Cheshunt compound, captan or zineb.

Violet root rot: this is a very serious

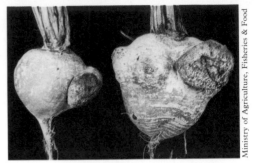

Crown gall is a bacterial infection which causes bumps to form on the sides of roots.

fungal disease. It is soil borne, and infected roots when lifted will show webs of violet strands enmeshing them. The above-ground symptoms of violet root rot are wilting and yellow leaves, but to be absolutely sure you must dig up and inspect the root of the suspect plant. Unfortunately, there is no chemical cure; grub up and destroy infected plants. Do not replant the site with beets, or any other vegetable susceptible to violet root rot for three years. Parsnip, carrots, asparagus and potatoes are particularly susceptible, so avoid planting them if the soil is infected.

Beet rust: this is a less severe fungal infection, the symptoms of which are small red-brown spots on the under surfaces of the leaves. It is most likely to be seen in autumn and is unlikely to

---

GUIDE TO BEET TROUBLES

Symptoms	Probable causes
Brown, withered and blistered leaves	Mangold fly
Leaves eaten	Beet carrion beetle
Roots eaten	Swift moth caterpillar
Small marks or sunken pits on roots; roots disfigured	Scab
Seedlings collapse and die	Damping off
Yellow stunted leaves; roots surrounded by webs of violet fungus	Violet root rot
Small brown spots on leaves	Beet rust
Large hollow cavities in roots	Crown gall
Blackened root and central leaves	Boron deficiency
Pale areas between leaf veins which eventually turn brown and die	Magnesium deficiency
Yellow blotches on leaves; leaves curled upwards	Manganese deficiency

Murphy Chemical Co.

Ministry of Agriculture, Fisheries & Food

These beetroots are infected with scab, a fungal disease associated with limey soils

Beets suffering from manganese deficiency have leaves which are discoloured or curled.

cause much trouble. Pick off and burn infected leaves as soon as you see them; if the disease is severe, spray the remainder with captan or zineb. Spray again a fortnight later.

Crown gall: this is a bacterial infection usually associated with badly drained soils. The bacteria enter the plant through a wound, perhaps made by an insect or damage from a hoe or fork. Once inside the roots, their attack results in the formation of large bumps on the sides of the roots. It is not a serious infection, although the roots may be slightly stunted and less appetizing. However, many other root plants can be seriously attacked and damaged, so infected roots should be dug up and burned as soon as seen. The best preventive measure is to correct any drainage problems before the crop is planted; also avoid damaging the roots during routine cultivation.

Boron deficiency: this is most likely to occur on light sandy soils in dry weather; plants growing on very limey soils are also vulnerable. The symptoms of boron deficiency are commonly called crown or heart rot; the central leaves die back and become blackened, and the roots may turn black on the inside and be cankered on the outside. To correct boron deficiency, mulch with plenty of garden compost, well-rotted manure, leaf-mould, or seaweed, or apply liquid seaweed fertilizer at the recommended rate.

Magnesium deficiency: magnesium is one of the constituents of chlorophyll, and if beetroot is lacking magnesium, pale areas will appear between the leaf veins. Eventually these discoloured areas turn brown and die. The deficiency is most likely to occur on very acid or very limey soils, but in general it is seldom encountered. One or more foliar sprays at two-weekly intervals with magnesium sulphate (Epsom salts) at the rate of 60 g in 4.5 L of water (2 oz in 1 gal) may be tried. A good mulch of well-rotted garden compost should help with the problem in the long term, and also heavy dressings of bulky organic matter when winter digging will gradually eliminate it. On very acid soils, an application of lime is helpful. Alternatively, if such manures are not available, Dolomite or magnesium limestone can be applied in winter to acid soils, at the rate of 210 g per sq m (7 oz per sq yd).

Manganese deficiency: the disease called 'speckled yellows' which also appears on spinach, is really a symptom of manganese deficiency. Affected plants have leaves with yellow blotches between the veins, and the leaves tend to curl up, usually in mid-summer. Both very sandy and very alkaline soils can be deficient in manganese. Some natural recovery can occur; the long varieties seem much less susceptible. In severe cases, apply a foliar spray of manganese sulphate at the rate of 60 g in 22. 5 L of water (2 oz in 5 gal of water) with a few drops of liquid detergent.

Varieties

Long

Cheltenham Green-top: long, tapered shape and good flesh colour; very good variety for sandy soils; excellent for clamping for winter use, or lifting from soil as needed.

Cook's Delight: grows 30 cm (1′) long and 5 cm (2″) in diameter; non-bleeding; good for grating without cooking; no tendency to go woody.

Long Blood Red (Covent Garden): medium sized with small top; excellent for cooking; good in dry years; can be left in sandy soils in warmer areas for digging up as required.

Intermediate

Formanova: deep red, fine-grained flesh; longish oval or cylindrical shape; excellent for cooking.

Round

Detroit: deep red, rich flesh, rough skin; free from rings; fine-grained texture; crops uniform in shape, foliage and texture; suitable for successional sowing and exhibition work.

Detroit New Globe: dark red flesh, fine-grained texture; free from rings; very uniform crops; excellent for kitchen and exhibition work.

Detroit Little Ball: small variety; suitable for successional summer sowings

Detroit

for late autumn and winter use; very quick grower; good for fitting in after a cleared crop.

Boltardy: similar to *Detroit* variety, but can be sown earlier in season due to its resistance to bolting.

Boltardy Mono-seeded: new variety; exactly like *Boltardy* but graded to produce only one plant per seed; eliminates need for thinning.

Ruby Queen: excellent flavour, texture; holds shape well even when crowded.

Globe: dark crimson flesh; good for successional sowings for year round supplies; excellent for kitchen or exhibition work; can be sown mid-summer.

Ruby Queen

Burpees Golden

Early Bunch: deep-red flesh; good round shape; matures in early summer; very bolt-resistant; do not use for maincrop or late sowings.

Avonearly: rich colour, fine texture; very fast grower, maturing in about ten weeks; bolt resistant; can be sown in late winter.

Dwergina: deep-red colour; globe-shaped variety; because it remains small for a long time it is very suitable for bottling and pickling.

Novelty

Burpees Golden: globe-shaped with bright yellow flesh and orange skin; does not bleed like red varieties; leaves can be cooked and served like spinach.

Snowhite: pale white colour; flesh does not bleed; new variety; curled, wavy leaves can be cooked and served like spinach.

Golden Beet: golden flesh; fine flavour; roots best when picked small; good for salads or pickling; tops can be cooked and eaten like spinach.

Sugar beet

Humming Bird: crisp, juicy white flesh; can be eaten raw or cooked as vegetable or used to replace refined sugar in dessert recipes.

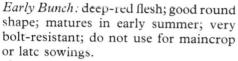

Far left: Formanova

Left: Boltardy

Right: Avonearly

Carrots

Daucus carota (fam. *Umbelliferae*)
Herbaceous biennial, grown as an **annual**
Sowing to harvesting time: early or
forced crops are ready for pulling after about 10-12
weeks, maincrops after 14-18 weeks.
Size: up to 23 × 5 cm (9 × 2″) for long-rooted
varieties; up to 12.5 × 6.5 cm (5 × 2½″) for stump-
rooted types.
Yield: 11.5 kg (25 lb) per 10 m (30′) row for
maincrops, slightly less for early crops.

Carrots are one of the easiest vegetable crops to grow, provided the soil has been well prepared. They are rich in calcium, phosphorus and vitamin A, and are a very popular winter standby, when other vegetables are scarce or expensive in the shops. Although usually considered a winter and early spring vegetable, by successive sowings and giving cold frame or cloche protection, you can crop carrots right through the year.

Carrots can be classified in two different ways: by shape or by the time of cropping. Shapes can be basically divided into three different groups, the short kind, which are round or stump-rooted (sometimes called shorthorn varieties), ideal for early or forced crops; the medium length type, more or less sausage-shaped or with a cylindrical tapering root, suitable for both storage and immediate use, and the long rooted, tapering type, which make a good, late maturing crop and are particularly suitable for exhibition. Long carrots can

reach 90 cm (3′) in length, and should really only be attempted if you have near perfect growing conditions; otherwise, it is best to stick to intermediate or early varieties. A good rule of thumb is: the more difficult the growing conditions, the smaller and quicker growing the varieties cultivated should be.

Carrots, like beetroot, are basically cropped in two ways. Early, quick-growing crops are pulled when quite small and either used raw in salads or cooked. These can be grown under glass or in the open. Their taste and texture when young are considered by many to be superior to fully mature carrot crops; they are sweeter and more tender than maincrops. The larger carrots, sown later in the year and pulled for winter storage, tend to be slightly tougher in texture and less flavourful. Recent developments in plant breeding, however, have resulted in vastly improved maincrop varieties, without the pale, stringy, central core which made them so

The fern-like foliage of carrots; the roots are ready when the leaves begin to curl and die.

unpopular in the kitchen. These new varieties are also tastier.

Carrots are herbaceous biennials grown as annuals. Most people think of all carrots as orange, but the wild carrot from which garden types were developed has a white taproot, and on the Continent purple, white and pale yellow varieties of carrots are grown. Because of their high sugar content, carrots are cultivated for sugar production as well as for use as a vegetable, and for distilling alcohol.

Suitable site and soil

Carrots prefer a deep, light, sandy loam. Early crops grow best in full sun, while maincrops appreciate some shading from hot summer sun. Soil conditions are extremely important, because carrots are a root crop, and must penetrate and build up their structure within the soil. Carrots require a deeply dug bed of friable (crumbly) soil about 45 cm (18″) deep, rich in finely divided particles of humus. Gravelly, heavy clay or stony soil is not suitable, because the roots will be unable to penetrate the soil evenly. Very light, sandy soils are only good for small early carrots; maincrop varieties require more substantial soil. Ideally, carrots should be grown on land with a high water table, so the crop never suffers from drought. This does not mean, however, that waterlogged or badly-drained soil is suitable, as carrots

Carrots grown on stony or freshly manured soils may become forked (left), rather than straight.

will not do well in those conditions.

Carrots should be grown on soil which was manured for a previous crop. If manure, garden compost or similar materials are introduced into the soil immediately before growing carrots, some of the crop will tend to be malformed, the roots being split into two or more forks. Large stones can also result in crooked, deformed roots.

On a plot where crops are being grown in a rotation system, carrots should ideally be grown in the previous year's celery bed, or follow lettuce or peas.

Soil preparation
Carrots grow best in sandy loams, but less suitable soils can be adapted for growing carrots by thorough digging and the incorporation of humus-forming manure or garden compost well before the seeds are sown. Ideally, carrots should follow a crop for which the ground was previously manured but, if necessary, major soil preparation can take place early in the autumn before sowing, the soil being left rough over winter. If the soil is very sandy, leafmould or compost will enrich it and increase its moisture retention. Make sure the organic matter is sifted and

thoroughly mixed with the soil, so there are no pockets of compost or leafmould. Sandy soils are further improved by the addition of peat; peat helps to bind loose, fast-draining soils and also encourages better drainage and crumb structure on heavy soils that need lightening.

A week to ten days before sowing, rake the bed level and create a fine tilth to ensure maximum germination. After raking, work in 60 g per sq m (2 oz per sq yd) of a general fertilizer which has a low nitrogen content. Rake the fertilizer well into the surface of the bed.

When you have raked the bed level, position a line of string between two stakes across the bed to mark out the row of carrots. Run a corner of a hoe or rake along the line to cut out a V-shaped furrow at least 1.3 cm ($\frac{1}{2}$") deep. Make the rows 15-23 cm (6-9") apart for early crops, and 30 cm (1') apart for main-crops.

Sowing
Maincrops are sown from mid-spring to the end of mid-summer, the later the better, to avoid attacks from carrot fly. Early crops are sown outdoors from the beginning of spring, and at fortnightly or monthly intervals until late summer, to have a continuous supply. There are about 18,000 seeds per 30 g (1 oz), and the seeds will remain viable for five years if properly stored. Pelleted seeds are available and, although more expensive to buy, they are easier to handle and cut down the amount of thinning required.

Carrots prefer warm soil and grow best when not checked by cold. Seeds may fail to germinate if sown during a prolonged cold spell. If the weather is bleak at the time you planned to sow, use cloches of horticultural glass or plastic, or plastic mini-tunnels to warm up the soil in advance and to protect the seedlings. Make sure the end flaps of the tunnels are closed, or conditions will be very windy inside them, and their whole purpose will have been defeated.

There are several methods of sowing carrot seeds. They should be sown as

1. At least a week before sowing, apply a compound fertilizer to the site.

2. Take out narrow drills about 2 cm (½″) deep, and 15-22 cm (6-9″) apart.

3. Sow the seeds in the drill as thinly as possible to avoid overcrowding and lessen thinning later.

4. Cover the seeds and firm the soil, and then level the surface by pulling a rake lightly over the rows.

thinly as possible, to avoid waste and the fiddly task of thinning out. Pelleted seeds can be placed singly in the drills, 2.5 cm (1″) apart. A traditional method is to mix the seeds with sand, and then sow the mixture evenly along the drill. You can also mix radish seed with the carrot seed. The radishes will be ready for harvesting early on and this is an easy way of thinning the carrot row. Alternatively, you can sow carrot seed either in pinches between finger and thumb, or by carefully shaking the seed into the drill direct from the packet with the hand held just a few centimetres above the drill. Whatever method of sowing is used, the drill should have been thoroughly watered the day before sowing, if the soil is at all dry.

After sowing, replace the soil by gently covering the drill, so that the seeds are no more than 0.6 cm (¼″) deep, using the back of a rake. A better but more painstaking method of doing this job is to place your feet on either side of the drill, and shuffle forward along the row, with your toes pointing outwards and your feet pushing soil into the drill. This action safely covers the carrot seed and at the same time gives the row a gentle firming. After covering the seed, rake the soil level by lightly pulling the rake down the row—never across it. Raking across the row would disturb or actually displace some of the seeds. Germination normally occurs from 14-18 days after sowing, but may be a few days longer in cold conditions. If a heavy rain threatens immediately after sowing, cover the drills with mats so the rain does not beat down the soil.

Thinning and general cultivation

The essential task of thinning should begin when the greenery is about 2.5 cm (1″) high. The best time to thin your carrots is after a rain shower; the water loosens the soil and makes the seedlings easier to lift. Doing this work in the evening seems to lessen the chance of attack from carrot fly.

If the carrots were sown in groups, pull out the smallest seedlings in each cluster; if sown continuously along the drill, thin initially to 1.2 cm ($\frac{1}{2}$″) apart. The carrots from the first one or two thinnings will be tiny, but the last thinnings in the early crop can be used in the kitchen. Early crops should have a final distance of 5 cm (2″) between each root; the maincrops should be thinned to a final distance of 10-15 cm (4-6″) apart.

Try not to bruise or break the leaves while thinning, as the pungent odour is very attractive to carrot flies. For the same reason, remove all thinnings immediately and bury them well in the middle of the compost heap. Because firm soil discourages the female fly from laying eggs, water the rows after thinning to firm the soil and fill any holes created by the removal of seedlings. If the soil is cracking because of dry weather, it needs water for the same reason, as well as to supply the carrots. Keep weeds under control, and do not allow the crop to run short of water during dry spells.

Frame cultivation

Forcing varieties of carrots can be grown to mature at times when bought carrots are expensive. Sow the seed on a hot-bed in a cold frame in mid-winter if the weather is mild, otherwise wait until the weather warms up in late winter or early spring. Make the hot-bed from a mixture of manure and other humus-containing

Young carrot seedlings just after thinning; try not to damage the leaves while thinning.

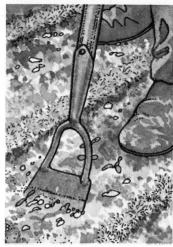

1. Hoe regularly between the rows of seedlings to remove weeds.

2. When the seedlings are 2.5 cm (1") high, thin to a spacing of 1.2 cm (½") apart. Water the soil before thinning.

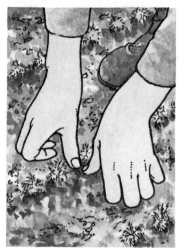

3. Firm in the remaining plants and water the ground to deter the carrot fly, which is attracted by the carrot smell.

4. Sprinkle general fertilizer between the plants in the rows, and water the ground again.

materials that create their own heat by fermentation. The hot-bed for out-of-season carrots should be a gentle one, consisting of a basic layer of straw and rotted manure mixed with rotted leaves. Stack up this mixture until it is about 15 cm (6") deep. Turn it over and moisten it every day for about a week to encourage fermentation, then flatten it and cover it with about 15 cm (6") of good garden loam.

Scatter seeds of a stump-rooted carrot variety thinly over the soil, work them in just below the surface with a hand fork, and firm the bed with a wooden board. Water frequently, give ventilation if the weather allows, and cover the frame with sacking or other protection on frosty nights. Do not allow the temperature to fall below 7°C (45°F). Thin first to about 2.5 cm (1") apart, then to 5 cm (2"); these second thinnings should be big enough to use in the kitchen. When grown in a cold frame, carrots can be sown with lettuce or radishes; these can be harvested fairly quickly, giving the long term carrot crop room to grow.

Carrots can also be forced in unheated cold frames or cloches out of doors, from late winter onwards. Cultivation is the same as for carrots grown on a hot bed. Without the additional warmth of a hot bed, though, the carrots will take longer to mature.

1. Water the ground the night before harvesting so that the young carrots can be easily pulled by hand.

2. To lift mature carrots in autumn, a fork is necessary.

3. Before storing, use a sharp knife to cut off the tops close to the neck.

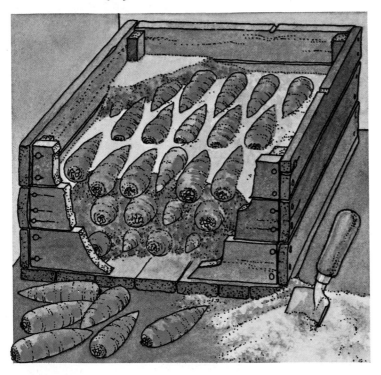

4. Autumn crops can be stored for winter use. Pack them evenly between layers of dry sand in a large wooden box, and keep the box in a frostproof shed.

116

Harvesting and storing

Once they have reached the desired size, short-rooted early varieties can be harvested from early summer, and harvesting can continue for several weeks. These carrots are at their best and most tender when still quite small, between 2.5 and 5 cm (1-2″) long. Earlier thinnings can also be used, although because of their small size they are a bit awkward to deal with in the kitchen. If the ground is dry, water thoroughly the night before pulling, so the carrots come out of the soil without being damaged.

Although carrots are reasonably frost-hardy, it is a good idea to lift maincrop carrots by the end of mid-autumn. If you live in a particularly mild area, you can leave them in the ground well into winter, but cover the crop with bracken or clean dry straw whenever heavy frost threatens. If left in the ground all winter, though, they are vulnerable to attack by frost, carrot fly and slugs.

When carrots are fully mature and ready for lifting, the outer leaves begin to wilt and the remaining foliage curls up. This is an indication that they have stopped growing, and there is no point in leaving them in the ground any longer.

Choose a dry day at the end of the season to lift the crop. Use a garden fork to loosen the carrots from the soil, and then pull them out by the foliage. After lifting, cut off the foliage near the crown and put it on the compost heap. Remove all the soil adhering to the roots and examine the carrots carefully before storing. Any which have been accidentally speared by the fork during the lifting operation should be set aside to be eaten at once, as damaged carrots quickly rot.

Carrots can be stored outdoors in a hole filled with dry sand and covered with straw, or in a clamp like potatoes (see chapter on POTATOES for storing in a clamp). If properly constructed, the carrots can be kept in the clamp through winter and well into spring. These storage methods are most useful if you have a very large crop; for moderate or

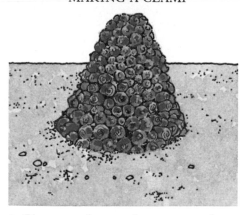

1. Choose undamaged carrots, and pile them on dry ground in a conical heap, thin ends pointing inwards.

2. Cover over the carrots with a layer of clean, dry straw at least 15 cm (6″) thick all around.

3. Cover over the straw with a 15 cm (6″) layer of soil. Leave a ventilation hole at the top.

small-sized harvests, it is more convenient to store them indoors in a box in a cool frost-proof shed or cellar. To do this, fill a box with a 5 cm (2″) layer of sand, and then place a layer of carrots head to tail, on the sand, followed by alternating layers of sand and carrots. The final layer should be sand, and the carrots can be easily removed from the box as needed.

Carrots stored in a clamp will keep firm and fresh for several months; carrots stored in boxes will keep for a slightly shorter period of time.

Exhibition tips

The type of carrot you exhibit depends to a large extent on the show date. For early shows, in mid to late spring, select quick-maturing varieties. These do best when sown on a hot bed in a cold frame in mid-winter. Fresh manure or partially-rotted garden compost, to which an activator has been added, will provide the heat necessary to get the carrots growing. The fermenting material should be covered with 15 cm (6″) of fine sifted soil.

For early or mid-summer shows, you can sow one of the larger varieties of carrots in late winter or early spring. If the weather is not unseasonably cold, a hot bed will not be necessary, although cold frame protection is still beneficial. Make sure the soil is absolutely first class, sandy loam; otherwise, prepare boreholes with a crowbar 45 cm (18″) deep and 30 cm (1′) apart in all directions. These boreholes should be filled with sifted old hot bed soil or fine topsoil mixed with sand. You can also show short quick-growing carrots at mid-summer exhibitions.

As long as you have thinned them to 10 cm (4″) apart in the early stages of growth, you should be able to select good specimens from your garden without any additional work being needed.

For late summer shows, sow in mid-spring and again in late spring, in the open ground. If your soil is badly drained, and you are still determined to produce prize-winning carrots, grow them above ground in large clay drain-pipes filled with good sandy compost. Barrels are also suitable. Remember, though, that containerized soil dries out much more quickly than ground soil. The water supply must be consistant; if the soil dries out and then is thoroughly drenched, the roots will split.

Carrots grown for late shows benefit from a bit of shade, perhaps given by neighbouring plants; shaded soil tends to conserve moisture. Carrots, particularly those grown in boreholes, sometimes grow up out of the ground, and the exposed shoulders then turn green or become otherwise disfigured. As soon as you see them beginning to push out of the ground, gently draw soil up around the carrots to cover them, and repeat as necessary. Leave the carrots in the ground until as near as possible to the show date. The one exception is if prolonged rain threatens. To avoid having the carrots split from excess water, lift and store them in moist sand until the show.

Although you can pull carrots out of the ground by their leaves, the skin will be marred in the process. Dark vertical scratches will appear from the friction between the carrot and soil particles. If the ground is soft, it may be all right to pull out the quick-growing, small varieties, but the intermediate and long varieties should be dug out with a spade. Dig carefully until you have completely exposed one side of the carrot, from the surface of the soil down to the tip of the root, and gently lever it out.

Have plenty of wet sacking nearby to wrap around the newly dug carrots; they should never be allowed to dry out. Wash them fairly quickly at this stage with cold water and a sponge; carrots which have split or otherwise damaged roots will then be exposed and can be discarded for show use, although they will probably be perfectly all right for cooking. At this stage reject any carrots which are pale or weak in colour and those which have green or otherwise

1. To grow long carrots for show, use a crowbar to make holes 45 cm (18″) deep for sowing.

2. Harvest the carrots carefully by digging a trench alongside the row. Lift the roots gently.

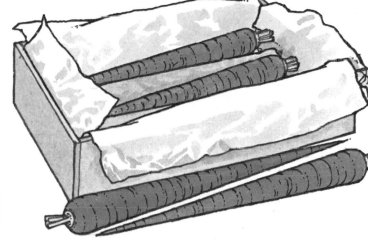

3. Pack long carrots for transporting to the show by placing them tightly, head to toe, in a tissue paper lined box. The carrots must be dry, and the tops cut back to 2.5 cm (1″).

disfigured shoulders. Asymmetrical or bulgy carrots should also be rejected for the show bench. After this preliminary selection has been made, cut off the fine, fibrous roots as close as possible to the main roots with a sharp knife.

If you are packing the carrots to take to the show, remember that much damage can be done if the roots are packed too loosely and can roll against each other in the packing box. Give the carrots a final wash, again with water and a sponge. Never scrub the carrots or you will damage the skin, and never oil them. They should be packed dry and wrapped tightly in tissue paper, with the foliage cut back to 2.5 cm (1″) from the carrot top. Then wedge the roots tightly into the box, the widest part of one carrot adjacent to the narrow root of the next.

Although it may vary from show to show, the carrots are usually divided into two categories: long pointed varieties, and all other types. Six is the usual number required for single displays, and ten for collections of vegetables. Carrots look best when displayed in pyramids on a plate and garnished with parsley. To keep the carrots fresh until judging, spray them with a fine mist of water. The judges will look for well-shaped carrots, as uniform as possible, with clear, bright colour. The texture should be firm, and the flesh tender and juicy.

Varieties

Early

Nantes-Champion Scarlet Horn: cylindrical roots, free from fleshy core; flesh dark red; 10-12 cm (4-5″) long; good for growing under cloches and successional sowings.

Amsterdam Forcing: very popular stump-rooted carrot, earliest to mature; excellent for successional sowings or growing under cloches.

Parisian Rondo: almost completely round roots 5 cm (2″) in diameter when fully grown; useful for forcing or sowing in succession.

Early Nantes: small, cylindrical, blunt-ended carrot; suitable for forcing and eating raw.

Nantes-Tip Top: cylindrical, stump-ended roots 15 cm (6″) long; flesh coreless and sweet; good for maincrop harvesting as well as early crops.

Little Finger: slender, quick-growing carrot of good flavour; useful for early sowing under glass.

Planet: roots round, 5 cm (2″) in diameter; quick-growing, excellent for shallow soils; novelty variety, but crunchy and sweet-tasting.

Pioneer (F_1 hybrid): *Nantes* type; quick grower with heavy, uniform crops; cylindrical roots medium-sized, tender

Early Nantes

and sweet.

French Horn Forcing: round variety; very fast growing.

Chantenay Red-cored (Early Market): very fast grower; crops heavy and uniform; stump-rooted.

Short 'n' Sweet: 7.5-10 cm (3-4″) long, excellent flavour; crops well in light or heavy soil.

Konfrix: round, fast-growing and early carrot; suitable for forcing under glass; very tolerant of soil conditions.

Saber (F_1 hybrid): new variety; very fast-growing carrot, uniform and vigorous; tapered shape.

Parisian Rondo

Nantes-Tip Top

Chantenay Red-cored

Frubund

Sucram: *Nantes* type variety with high sugar content and very sweet flavour; very small, tapered.

Early Horn: very quick-growing variety; stump-rooted with very little core; suitable for successional sowings.

Frubund: new variety, extremely hardy and early; stump-rooted, and excellent for successional sowing through autumn.

Maincrop

Autumn King-Early Giant: long, blunt-tipped, extra hardy; larger than *Nantes* type, good for storing for winter use;

somewhat resistant to drought and carrot fly.

New Red Intermediate: longest carrot, with bright red colour and good texture; good for winter storing and exhibition work.

Chantenay Red-Cored-Concord: large, stump-rooted medium-early strain; suitable for early, as well as maincrop sowings; can be stored for winter use; good flavour.

Chantenay Red-Cored-Favourite: very popular stump-rooted maincrop variety; good for exhibition work in 'short' class.

Royal Chantenay: stump-rooted variety;

St Valery

Autumn King—Early Giant

Juwarot

deep red flesh with very little core.

Scarla: stump-rooted, cylindrical roots; first-class flesh colour; excellent maincrop variety.

Scarlet Perfection: long, stump-rooted variety; first-class flesh; keeps well for winter use.

St Valery: good cropper; long, tapering roots suitable for exhibition work.

Autumn King-Vita Longa: long, large carrot with stump-ended roots giving heavy yields; first-class flavour; good for winter storage.

Flakkee: Dutch variety with large, stump-rooted crops; suitable for winter storage and very good for exhibition.

Long Red Surrey: large, tapered maincrop variety suitable for growing on sandy soils.

James Scarlet Intermediate: large, tapered carrot with heavy, uniform crops; good flavour.

Juwarot: cylindrical-shaped carrot; very good flavour and high vitamin A content; very attractive bright orangy-red colour; stores for a long time.

Zino: new variety; very large, cylindrical carrot; excellent for exhibition work and kitchen.

Pride of Denmark: one of the earlier croppers of maincrop varieties; long, tapering roots; bright orange with red cores; fine flavour.

Pests & Diseases

Carrots are largely pest and disease free; most of the problems occur when carrots are improperly stored in autumn and winter. Conscientious storage preparation is the best precaution against most of the diseases listed below. If there is an outbreak, remove and destroy infected carrots immediately, to avoid spreading the disease.

Carrot fly: this very serious pest attacks other vegetables besides carrots; parsnips and celery are also vulnerable. The worst damage is most likely to occur in hot, dry weather, on very free-draining soil. Large crops of carrots, such as those grown on a commercial scale, seem somewhat more susceptible than the average size crop in a private garden or allotment. The carrot fly, which is about 1 cm ($\frac{1}{2}''$) long, black with yellow legs and transparent wings, is attracted by the pungent smell of the carrot foliage, and finds small areas of disturbed soil near the rows ideal places to lay its eggs. The tiny pale yellow maggots that emerge from the eggs then burrow into the roots and may devastate the crop. Wilting, reddened foliage is usually the chief symptom above ground; seedlings will be killed.

The main carrot fly attack occurs in

Damage to the roots caused by the maggots of the carrot fly; spring sowings suffer most.

late spring, so by delaying sowing until the end of early summer it is possible to miss it altogether. The second generation of adult flies does not start laying eggs until late summer, and the maggots hatching from these are unlikely to cause serious damage.

Since thinning the young plants unavoidably releases the smell of the foliage, sow the seeds as thinly as possible to reduce the possibility of attack. Do this in the evening, when the fly is less likely to be about, and destroy the thinnings. Never use a hoe to thin out the young crops; disturbing the soil encourages the flies to lay eggs nearby.

Some veteran gardeners sow rows of parsley between the carrots, because the scent of parsley is said to counteract that of the carrot leaves and so distract or deter the fly. Rows of onions between carrot rows are said to have the same beneficial effect. Alternatively, a rag soaked in parrafin oil can be pulled along the rows occasionally to introduce a camouflage scent. You can also use bromophos dust according to manufacturer's directions.

Wireworm: this pest is most serious in gardens which have been newly turned over from grassland, and is unlikely to cause any trouble on land which has been under cultivation for

Carrots with the characteristic symptoms of the fungal disease violet root rot.

some time. The larvae of the click beetle are also damaging on weedy, neglected gardens. The larvae, which are about 2.5 cm (1″) long, shiny and golden-yellow with six legs, live in the soil and eat the roots of many plants besides carrots, severely damaging or killing them.

The best precaution against wireworm is to make sure your ground is cultivated well and often. Hand weed between plants to keep weeds down, and also expose wireworms to insectivorous birds. Seeds treated with insecticide are somewhat less vulnerable. If the soil is badly infested, you can apply insecticides, such as diazinon or bromophos, according to manufacturer's instructions.

Aphids: these weaken the carrots by sucking sap from the foliage, and some forms damage the roots, so are doubly damaging. The foliage of carrots will be stunted, wilted, and greyish-green. To control aphids, apply derris or bioresmethrin as soon as the infestation occurs, and again as necessary. Since they attack during dry weather, keeping the plants well watered will help to ward off and minimize the damage.

Eelworm: there are various sorts of eelworm which attack both herbaceous and vegetable crops. The microscopic, transparent worms live inside the root tissue of the carrot and multiply rapidly, eventually killing the host plant. Eelworms are difficult for the home gardener to control with chemical insecticides as the soil remains infested for some time after the host plant is removed. Once the carrots are infested, the symptoms of which are wilted foliage and distorted roots, all carrots must be dug out and destroyed immediately. You cannot use the ground for growing carrots for at least seven years and all weeds should be destroyed. This is the only absolutely certain method of getting rid of eelworm; otherwise, new crops may be re-infested.

Violet root rot: this is a serious fungal disease which attacks asparagus, parsnips, beetroot and potatoes as well as

GUIDE TO CARROT TROUBLES

Symptoms	Probable cause
Wilted, reddish foliage; seedlings killed; irregular holes in roots	Carrot fly
Wilted leaves, round holes in roots	Wireworm
Wilted, stunted foliage, distorted roots	Eelworm
Wilted, grey-green foliage, white particles present	Aphids
Webs of reddish-violet strands enmeshing roots	Violet root rot
Roots split, often exposing core	Split root
White woolly fungal growths with black spots	Sclerotina rot
Soft, greyish, smelly flesh	Soft rot
Black patches on shoulders of roots	Black rot

carrots. It is a soil-borne disease, and infected carrots will have webs of reddish-violet strands enmeshing the roots. The above ground symptom of infection is yellowing of foliage. There is no chemical cure for violet root rot; grub up and destroy infested plants. As with eelworm, do not replant the site with carrots for several years.

Split root: this is a physiological disorder, rather than a disease, which is usually caused by a fluctuating water supply. If there is a heavy rainfall after a period of drought, the inner flesh of the carrot expands faster than the toughened skin, causing the skin to fissure. The best precaution against split root is to ensure

White, woolly fungal growths caused by a severe infection of sclerotina rot.

that the carrots are never allowed to go for long periods of time without water.

Sclerotina rot: this is a problem which occurs under improper damp storage conditions. The symptoms of sclerotina rot are white woolly fungal growths, first seen near the crowns of the roots; in these growths form black resting spore-bodies which can later infect nearby carrots. The best precaution is to ensure that there is proper ventilation in the clamp or box, and that no damaged carrots are ever stored. If there is an attack of sclerotina rot, remove and destroy all infected carrots.

Soft rot: this is a bacterial disease most often encountered in roots damaged during cultivation or by pests; infected carrots become soft, discoloured and unpleasant smelling in the centre, although the outside may look normal. As with sclerotina rot, remove and destroy infected roots so that the bacteria cannot infect healthy carrots. Heavily manured soil, in which carrots are grown in successive years, predisposes them to the disease.

Black rot: a disease found on stored roots, which shows as black sunken patches, usually near the shoulder of the root. As the fungus is carried on the seed, it should always be obtained from reputable seedsmen. No chemical control is known at present, and affected roots should be destroyed, not put on the compost heap, or returned to the soil.

Jerusalem Artichokes

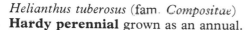

Helianthus tuberosus (fam. *Compositae*)
Hardy perennial grown as an annual.
Sowing to harvesting time: 9-11 months.
Size: tubers about 10 cm (4″) by 5 cm (2″), plants 1.5-2.5 m (5-8′) tall.
Yield: approximately 1 kg (2 lb) per plant, with 5 plants per 3 m (10′) row.

The Jerusalem artichoke is an ugly vegetable, which is a pity, because otherwise it is something of a gardener's dream. It is extremely hardy, nutritious and easy to grow, as well as being virtually disease and pest free, and an excellent vegetable for the home gardener with little time. Although it will repay good cultivation with a heavier crop, it will also grow quite happily with a large measure of neglect.

The tubers may be ugly but the plants themselves are quite attractive and will grow to become a feature of your garden. The plant is closely related to the sunflower, *Helianthus annus,* and grows, sunflower-like, to a height of 2.4 m (8′) and more, although it is usual to cut off the tops at 1.5 m (5′) so that there is less likelihood of wind damage. Cutting off the tops also prevents plants from producing flowers, but in temperate regions they rarely do so in any case. Only after exceptionally hot summers will they form their large, yellow, sunflower-like flowers in early

autumn, and even then they will not set seed.

The parts of the plant which are eaten are the underground tubers, which are storage organs similar to potatoes. Unlike potatoes, however, they are not smooth but extremely irregular in shape and are covered with knobbly projections, rather like ginger. They are about 10 cm (4″) long by 5 cm (2″) wide and have yellowy-white or purple skins and a smoky flavour. Instead of containing starch, as potatoes do, they contain the sugar, inulin, which can be eaten safely by diabetics. Most people, therefore, find them extremely digestible although unfortunately some are allergic to them.

The name 'Jerusalem artichoke' is perhaps misleading. Jerusalem artichokes are in no way related to globe artichokes, whose flower heads, rather than tubers, are eaten, although some people state that they are similar in taste. Nor have they anything to do with the Holy Land. 'Jerusalem' may be a corrupt

125

Jerusalem artichokes grow up to 2.4 m (8′) tall and make an attractive garden feature.

form of the Italian name, girasole (sunflower) or of the Dutch place name, Ter Neusen, where the artichokes were grown in the seventeenth and eighteenth centuries.

But, however they got their name, they are a very worthwhile crop for the gardener. They can be boiled, either with or without their skins, fried, baked or made into Palestine soup. They also make a useful salad vegetable at a time of the year when salads are sparse in the garden and expensive in the shops. Simply dice them raw and dress with a vinaigrette sauce. Alternatively, cook the artichokes and serve them cold, rather like potato salad.

Suitable site and soil

When your Jerusalem artichokes are fully developed they will form a row of plants at least 2.4 m (8′) tall, so plant them to suit the layout of the rest of your garden. This may be alongside a fence or wall, or as a screen to hide an unsightly compost heap or old garden shed. Although they prefer an open, sunny site they grow quite happily in a shaded spot. They also make an excellent windbreak. Plant them on the north side of tomatoes, cucumbers or other tender crops.

Jerusalem artichokes are virtually pest and disease free so you can plant them in the same place year after year without mishap. If you cannot afford to leave a permanent space for them, however, choose their site particularly carefully. It is easy to miss a few of the smaller tubers when clearing the ground at the end of the winter and these will grow up like weeds the next year, so pick a site where it will not matter much if you have the odd plant appearing during the following summer.

The hardy Jerusalem artichoke will do well on indifferent soil— provided it is not waterloged—but a little attention to the soil is repaid with a heavier crop. If you have garden compost to spare, dig it in sometime during the autumn or early winter—a good general rate is one barrowload every 8 sq m (9.5 sq yd). Jerusalem artichokes also like plenty of potash, so dress the soil generously with wood ash a few days before planting. Alternatively, you can use fishmeal at a rate of 100 g per sq m (3 oz per sq yd). Lightly hoe the wood ash or fishmeal into the soil.

Do not give any nitrogenous fertilizer or manure at planting, however, as the result will be a luxurious growth of foliage at the expense of tubers and the whole exercise will have been a waste of valuable time and space.

Jerusalem artichokes are not fussy, but they do not grow so well on very acid soils. A few weeks after digging and adding manure, test your soil with a soil test kit and add lime to achieve a pH of 6.0–6.5.

SOIL PREPARATION

1. Jerusalem artichokes are not fussy as to their soil requirements but dislike very acid soils. Test your soil and if necessary add lime to give a pH of 6.0.

2. Sufficient potash, too, is important to get a good crop. Add wood ash just before planting to remedy any potash deficiency your soil might have.

127

Planting

Jerusalem artichoke tubers are planted in the same way as potatoes. The best tubers to plant are the least knobbly ones, about the size of a small chicken egg. If you can only obtain larger tubers, however, you can cut them into pieces—each with three 'eyes' or buds—and plant these pieces.

Plant the tubers anytime from late winter to early spring, in holes 15 cm (6″) deep and 60 cm (2′) apart. Use a trowel or dibber to make the holes. If you are planting more than one row, space the rows 1 m (3′) apart.

Shoots should start to appear above the ground within two to four weeks, given reasonable weather.

Care and cultivation

Jerusalem artichokes require very little attention but they will need to be weeded during the spring until the plants have grown large enough to shade the soil. Weed, using a hoe, and when the plants reach about 30 cm (1′) tall, draw the soil up around the stems of the plants while weeding. In this way you will build up a mound around the stems similar to that used for potatoes. The mound encourages the production of tubers by increasing the amount of buried stem from which the tubers grow and it will also help you when you come to harvesting, as tubers in mounds are easier to lift than tubers buried deep in the ground.

PLANTING
AND
CULTIVATION

1. If you have no small tubers for planting, save on tubers by cutting large ones into small pieces. Each piece should have three buds.

2. Make holes 15 cm (6″) deep and 60 cm (2′) apart.

3. Plant one small tuber or a piece of a larger tuber in each hole and cover over with soil. Shoots should start to appear above the ground within two to four weeks.

In temperate regions the plants will usually not need to be watered except in very dry years. If the soil becomes dry, however, give plenty of water.

Some gardeners retain moisture in the soil, and also keep down weeds, by mulching round the plants with peat or garden compost once they are about 30 cm (1′) tall. If you do this there is no need to weed or earth up—the mulch itself buries the stems to some extent.

Supporting against the wind
Although Jerusalem artichokes make excellent windbreaks, on exposed sites you run the risk of them being blown down by the occasional gale. Not only would you lose your Jerusalem artichoke crop, but neighbouring vegetables could be ruined at the same time. In a very sheltered spot, alongside a wall for example, you will probably be safe just leaving the plants and giving them no support at all, but elsewhere the plants should be supported with wires. During the summer, hammer a 1.5 m (5′) stake into the ground at either end of each row and at 1.5 m (5′) intervals along long rows. Then join up the stakes with wire at 60 and 120 cm (2′ and 4′) intervals from the ground. When the plants are tall enough, tie them to the wires with string.

Cut off the tops of the plants when they reach about 1.5 m (5′) tall. Taller plants are more likely to be blown over.

4. Weed between the plants drawing soil up around the stems in a mound.

5. On exposed sites, tie the plants to wires to protect them from the wind.

6. Cut the tops off the plants when they reach about 1.5 m (5′) tall if not wanted as a screen.

129

1. When the tops die down in the autumn, cut them off about 30 cm (1′) from the ground. Leave the cut stalks to mark the position of the tubers underground.

2. Fork the tubers up, being careful not to spear any or to leave any in the ground. If tubers are left, they will grow up next year like a weed.

3. Store a few tubers, sandwich fashion, in containers of dry peat or sand for winter periods when fresh tubers cannot be lifted from frozen ground.

Harvesting and aftercare

When the leaves and stems begin to turn brown and die back in the late autumn cut them down to about 30 cm (1') from the ground. Chop the stems up and add them to your compost heap.

You can harvest all the crop as soon as the stems have been cut down in the autumn, but you are better advised to leave the tubers in the ground and to harvest as and when you need them. The tubers can be stored in dry sand or peat, but they taste better eaten fresh from the soil and also have a better texture.

Lift the tubers with a fork in the same way as you would potatoes and add the discarded haulms and roots to your compost heap. Towards the end of late winter, it is best to lift whatever tubers are left in the ground, and use the cleared site to plant new crops in the spring.

Storing the crop

Although Jerusalem artichokes taste best straight from the ground, it is worthwhile lifting some of the crop in the early winter and storing it, so that you have some readily available if the ground freezes hard. To store the tubers, gently rub off any soil adhering to them and place them, sandwich-fashion, in boxes or other containers of dry sand or peat. Keep them in a cool place. All the tubers should be under the surface of the sand or peat as they will deteriorate if exposed to light. Remember to keep some small tubers for planting.

Exhibition tips

Few people bother to show Jerusalem

A fine crop of large, smooth skinned tubers.

Pat Brindley

131

artichokes, which is not surprising as the knobbly tubers are hardly an attractive vegetable. Added to this is the disadvantage that Jerusalem artichokes are rarely ready before late autumn and so can only be exhibited at either autumn or winter shows.

If you do intend to exhibit Jerusalem artichokes, try and grow the variety *Fuseau*, which has more regular tubers. Excessively knobbly tubers will be judged harshly and the other variety, New White, has this tendency.

Lift the tubers with care without damaging the skins and then wash them carefully with a sponge as soon as they are lifted. If damp soil dries on the skins they become discoloured. Allow the tubers to dry.

Once the tubers have dried, select large, less knobbly ones of similar size and colour. The normal number to exhibit is twelve. Select a few more than this to give you a choice at your final selection and immediately store the selected tubers for the show.

Even if the show is a local one they should be stored carefully, as they rapidly deteriorate if exposed to the light and air. Wrap the tubers individually in tissue paper and then again in brown paper or black polythene to exclude the light. Then place them in a box in a cool place until the show.

There is nothing you can do to make Jerusalem artichokes pretty but they can be made to look more attractive with a minimum of effort. Place the tubers in a symmetrical pyramid on a black plate or in a basket.

Varieties

The most likely problem with growing Jerusalem artichokes could well be finding some tubers to plant in the first place. Often the easiest way is to plant tubers bought from your greengrocer; as Jerusalem artichokes are virtually disease-free, you do not run the risk of planting diseased tubers, as you would do if you planted potatoes obtained in the same way. Avoid the old purple varieties, however, as these are usually of poor flavour, and after the first year save your own tubers for replanting.

If you do buy tubers from a seedsman you are very unlikely to be offered any choice. There are only two varieties in general cultivation.

New White: the commonest variety; better flavoured than old purple varieties but with rather knobbly tubers.

Fuseau: a French variety: very worthwhile if you can find it but it is very difficult to find a supplier in England; long smooth tubers with a fine flavour; purple-skinned, but does not produce heavy crops.

New White

Fuseau

132

Pests & Diseases

You will be very unlucky if you have serious problems with Jerusalem artichokes. They are extremely hardy and pest and disease free. In most years you should be able simply to forget them until you come to dig them up. Two pests and one disease might just give you trouble, however.

Slugs: large holes eaten into the tubers are usually the work of slugs. These pests are most active in wet summers and on wet and heavy land. A well-kept garden discourages them by reducing the number of places where they can hide. You can trap slugs in piles of rotting vegetable matter which you should inspect daily, destroying any slugs you find. Alternatively, if their attacks are severe enough to warrant it, use a proprietary slug bait according to the manufacturer's instructions.

Swift moth: swift moths are another soil-borne pest which may also eat holes in the tubers. The dirty white caterpillars which are the larvae of the moths, live in the soil and feed on the roots of Jerusalem artichokes and other plants, particularly weeds. A well-kept garden with few weeds is less likely to become infected. If you do suffer from swift moths, however, try lightly forking the soil to bring the caterpillars onto the soil surface where they are eaten by insect-catching birds. If the attack is severe you can also spray the soil with trichlorphon.

Sclerotina rot: this disease appears as a white, fluffy fungus which eventually produces black resting spores. The disease is worst in cold damp conditions. Stored roots are particularly susceptible but occasionally the stems at ground level and tubers of growing plants are also attacked. Pull up and destroy all infected plants and do not store any damaged roots, as the rot will quickly spread to the healthy tubers.

GUIDE TO JERUSALEM ARTICHOKE TROUBLES

Symptoms	Probable cause
Large holes eaten in tubers	Slugs
Smaller holes in tubers, occasionally with dirty white caterpillars inside them	Swift moth caterpillar
White fluffy fungal growth with black spots	Sclerotina rot

Swift moth larvae eat holes in the tubers.

Sclerotina attacks both the stems and tubers.

G. E. Hyde

Ministry of Agriculture, Fisheries & Food

133

Onions

Allium cepa (fam. *Alliaceae*)
Hardy biennial cultivated as an **annual.**
Sowing to Harvesting Time: 14-23 weeks for bulb onions; 6-9 weeks for spring onions; 12 weeks for pickling onions; 18 weeks for shallots.
Size: average bulb diameter 5-10 cm (2-4″), although much larger ones can be grown; plants grow to 50 cm (20″) high; spring onions about 1 cm ($\frac{1}{3}$″) or less in diameter and 15–30 cm (6–12″) high; shallot bulbs 2–5 cm ($\frac{3}{4}$–2″) diameter, plants grow to 30 cm (12″) high.
Yield: bulb onions 20 bulbs, each about 120 g (4 oz) per 3 m (10′) row; shallots 15 plants, each bearing about 240 g (8 oz) of bulbs per 3 m (10′) row; spring onions about 60 onions per 90 cm (3′) row.

Onions are among the most regularly used of all vegetables, and they are well worth growing at home. Unlike many crops there is little possibility of waste—most onions store so well that whatever you grow you can eventually use up. Another major advantage for many home growers is that an onion crop can be grown on the same site for years, but it can also fit well into a crop rotation, providing a break from brassicas, peas, beans or potatoes.

Onions do best in an open sunny site. The onion grower is rather at the mercy of the weather, in that a period of drought when the bulbs are forming can result in a very disappointing crop. If you can keep watering regularly during a drought this is fine. But if the bulbs reach a point when they get really dry and growth stops, then a sudden drenching can be disastrous, causing distorted growth, split bulbs and thick 'necks'. So, one of the key points to remember is to pull the crop as soon as possible once growth has stopped.

Main types of large onions
The original species of onion has split into several types; the main kinds of interest to the gardener are:
A spring-sown maincrop, harvested in autumn.
Onion 'sets', small bulbs planted in spring for quick growth.
Japanese varieties, a new range of onions, sown in late summer to continue growing over a mild winter and produce a crop the following mid-summer.
An autumn-sown crop, harvested as bulbs in the following autumn.

Preparing the soil
Onions need a firm, loamy soil, although good crops can be obtained on any

1. After manuring in autumn, work in 30 g per sq m [1 oz per sq yd] of a compound fertilizer before sowing.

2. Immediately before sowing, rake the seed bed to a very fine tilth; make the surface as level as possible.

3. Tread down the soil to firm it, but not when it is sticky. Heavy soil needs only a very light firming.

4. Draw drills 1.5 cm [½"] deep and 30-45 cm [1-1½'] apart. Sow seed quite thickly, then barely cover and firm.

5. Sowings under cloches may be made up to 8 weeks earlier than those in the open; warm soil with cloches first.

6. The tip of the onion seedling feeds from the seed at first. Do not disturb it; it will soon straighten (right).

7. To control onion fly, apply bands of diazinon granules between drills; do not thin if the soil is dry.

8. Thin the young plants in two stages to a final distance of 15 cm [6"] apart; use thinnings for salads.

9. Water regularly during the growing season to avoid any check in growth, which can produce inferior bulbs.

10. Weed regularly by hand close to plants to avoid loosening soil around roots; elsewhere hoe carefully.

11. In late summer, when leaves are yellow and dying, bend them over to expose bulbs to light and air.

12. Harvest by lifting bulbs carefully with a fork; remember that Japanese varieties must be used immediately.

suitably prepared ground. The land must be well drained. Onions prefer a light soil to a heavy one, and it is a good idea to correct any acidity to about pH6 by applications of lime at a rate based on the result of a soil test.

For the best results, dig an organic plant food (farmyard manure or a good quality garden compost) into the soil several months before sowing (eg in autumn for beds where you will be sowing in spring). A barrow-load of manure or compost for every 7 sq m (9 sq yd) should be sufficient. A compound fertilizer may also be applied just before sowing at the rate of 30 g per sq m (1 oz per sq yd) and worked well into the soil. All types of onion need a firm, compact seed-bed of fine soil. Rake the ground before sowing and tread well to firm it.

Sowing

The spring-sown maincrop: Sow outdoors as early in spring as soil conditions will permit. The soil should be moist but not wet; if soil does not stick to your boots but still feels damp then it is ready for sowing. Sow the seed in drills 1.5 cm ($\frac{1}{2}$") deep and 30-45 cm (1-1$\frac{1}{2}$') apart, and sow fairly thickly—about 10-20 seeds per 30 cm (1') row—because the thinnings can be used as salad onions. The period from sowing to germination, on average, is 14-21 days. Thin the young plants in two stages, the first to about 5 cm (2") apart, and then to about 15 cm (6") apart.

As with most vegetables, an advantage can be gained in spring by sowing under cloches. These sowings can be made up to eight weeks earlier than those in the open. The extra weeks are particularly useful with onions, as the plants need a long growing period, so that bulbs sown under cloches tend to be larger. Remove cloches when all danger of frost is past.

You can also get a head start by sowing in late winter in a cold frame. Sow as you would for growing under cloches, and harden off for planting out in mid-spring.

Onions sown under cloches or in frames have two other advantages over later-sown crops. In the first place, they

1. Before planting onion sets, cut off old leaves that would attract the birds after planting.

2. By mid-spring, plant sets 15 cm [6"] apart in shallow drills 30 cm [1'] apart, with 'necks' uppermost.

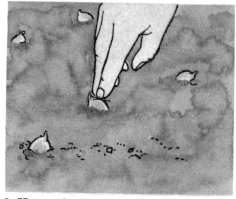

3. Have a look at the sets a week or two after planting; press back into the soil any that have moved.

A fine crop of onions, with their tops bent over to hasten ripening.

grow quickly and make much of their growth while the soil is still moist from the winter rains, thus avoiding a severe check at a critical stage during a summer drought. They are also sufficiently well grown to resist the attacks of the onion fly, which is active in late spring and summer.

Growing onions from sets: Many gardeners achieve a flying start by planting onion 'sets'. These are small onion bulbs which have had their growth arrested in the previous autumn. In the past, gardeners avoided onion sets because they tended to bolt and run to seed. Nowadays, however, sets are carefully treated and stored, and they are often easier to grow and keep than varieties raised from seed, particularly in areas where the summers are cool and wet. Buy only certified sets from a reputable seed merchant.

Onion sets are imported from Europe or sub-tropical zones for planting in temperate climates in mid-spring. Plant them in rows 30 cm (1′) apart with the bulbs 15 cm (6″) apart in each row. Set them in the soil with the 'neck' at the top just visible above the surface.

Like onions sown under cloches, onions grown from sets enjoy the advantage of making much of their growth while the soil is still moist and of being sufficiently well grown to resist onion fly attacks.

Japanese varieties: Sow in late summer, following the instructions for the maincrop but sowing slightly more thickly. When grown successfully, these varieties should fill the gap between using the last stored onions from the previous year's spring sowing and the availability of the new crop next autumn. So far, Japanese onions have not been fully tested in all climatic zones, although they are widely available in the UK and have proved successful in most areas.

Autumn sowing: Sowing onions in autumn outdoors gives the same results as sowing in spring under cloches or planting onion sets. The bulbs from autumn sowings should be ready for harvesting a month or so earlier than those from a spring sowing. But autumn sowings are worthwhile only if your garden is fairly warm, and the site chosen should be quite sheltered.

The seed should be sown in early autumn to give the plants enough time to attain a reasonable size—about 15 cm (6″) in height—before the onset of winter frosts. Sow as you would for the spring maincrop, but a bit more thickly to allow for casualties. Onions are hardy but not completely so, and a severe winter will cause damage. It is important to select the correct varieties, bred for autumn sowing. Onion plants bought from nurserymen for transplanting in spring should also be of the autumn varieties.

Care during growth

Because onions produce tall, thin, hollow leaves, they are particularly susceptible to weed competition. Hoe the soil frequently but shallowly to avoid loosening the compact soil around the onion roots or damaging the bulbs. Hand-weeding, which does not damage the roots, will almost certainly be necessary. A sedge peat mulch will help to control the weeds, but it should not cover the tops of the bulbs.

Onions should be watered well and regularly throughout the growing season to avoid any check in growth, which can result in bulges in the bulbs, in thick necks and thin bulbs, or in splitting.

Examine onion sets a week or two after planting, as they tend to rise out of the soil and may 'travel' several centimetres from the place where they were planted. If this has happened, press the sets back into the soil. They may also be pulled out of the ground by birds.

During the growing period onions

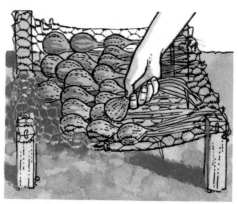

1. If the ground is wet at harvesting time, ripen bulbs by placing them on a platform raised from the ground.

2. If it is raining at harvesting time, ripen bulbs in a cold frame, as shown here, or move them into a shed.

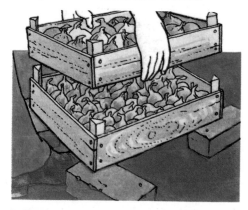

3. You can store ripe, thoroughly dry bulbs in trays with slatted bases in an airy, dry, frost-proof place.

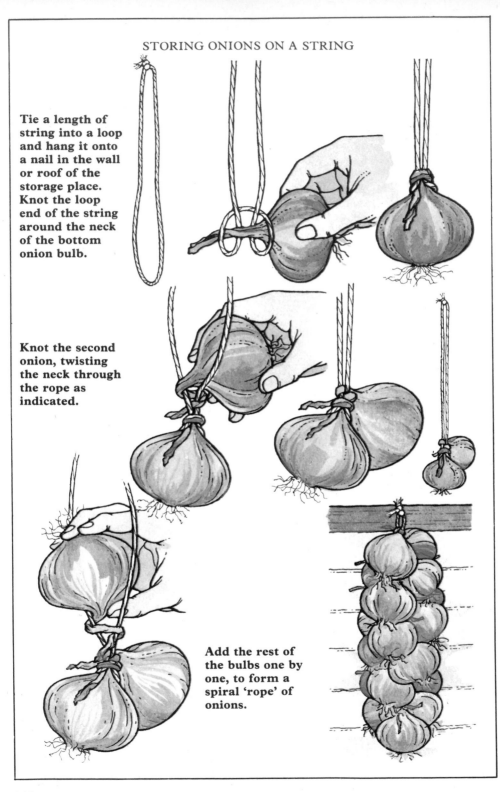

STORING ONIONS ON A STRING

Tie a length of string into a loop and hang it onto a nail in the wall or roof of the storage place. Knot the loop end of the string around the neck of the bottom onion bulb.

Knot the second onion, twisting the neck through the rope as indicated.

Add the rest of the bulbs one by one, to form a spiral 'rope' of onions.

need a lot of nourishment. Feed the plants with either liquid manure at regular intervals until mid-summer, or hoed-in applications of a nitrogenous fertilizer, such as nitrate of soda, at the rate of about 30 g per 3 m (1 oz per 3 yd) in late spring or early summer.

When the bulbs are ripening, as indicated by the yellowing and dying back of the leaves, discontinue any watering or feeding. In dry weather the leaves will bend over naturally but, if the summer is wet and this has not happened, bend over the tops to expose the neck of each bulb to the sun, to hasten the ripening process. It may take

five weeks for large bulbs to ripen.

Harvesting the crop

Bulb onions will be ready for harvesting throughout the summer and autumn, according to the time of sowing. The earliest are the new Japanese varieties which should mature around mid-summer. Japanese onions are for immediate use; most other varieties can be used at once or can be stored. Very large onions do not store as well or as long as smaller bulbs, so use the large ones first.

A dry day is best for harvesting onions. Lift them gently with a fork or pull them by hand and, in dry weather, lie the

Onions can be hung on a wall outdoors if the weather is warm and dry, but take them indoors at the first sign of dampness or of frost.

141

bulbs flat on the ground or on sacking. Turn them now and again to ensure even ripening. The onions are ready for storing when they are thoroughly dry with brittle, papery leaves. In a wet season, the drying process will take longer, and you should lift the onions onto a platform raised above the ground, allowing the circulation of air beneath it. A tray of small-mesh wire netting is ideal. This can be moved into a shed if wet weather persists.

Storing the crop

Bulb onions are normally grown for storing and use in autumn and winter. Onions in store will start to produce green shoots and, if allowed to, flower-heads in the following spring, so only keep them for a limited time and check them for signs of decay or growth.

Bulbs for storing should be perfectly healthy and quite dry. Discard any that are not. Probably the best method of storing is the traditional 'string' of onions: tie each bulb to a length of rope suspended from the roof of a shed or outhouse, arranging them spirally around the rope. Alternatively, onions can be stored on trays of wire netting, suspended in rope or nylon nets, or placed on wooden shelves, although it is best to have air circulating all around the bulbs. The shed in which they spend the winter must be dry, airy and frost-proof.

Aftercare

The onion is among the most economical of plants in its production of foliage. By the time the bulb has ripened there is very little left of other parts of the plant. Consign any dead leaves to the compost heap if they are free from pests and disease; otherwise, burn them.

Salad and pickling onions

Salad or spring onions, also known as scallions, can be sown in autumn, spring or summer, for pulling when young and green to be used raw in salads. Small, silver-skinned onions for pickling are sown in spring and harvested in summer.

Spring onions are sown in the same soil and conditions as for the maincrop. Pickling onions prefer a light, thin soil. Make the drills a bit wider than those for the larger varieties, and sow the seed very thickly. Both are very quick-growing, maturing in about 12 weeks.

Exhibition tips

Sow the seed in mid-winter in a greenhouse heated to 13°C (55°F), so that the bulbs will be fully ripe in time for the early autumn shows. Sow the seeds 2.5 cm (1″) apart in 7.5 cm (3″) deep seed boxes filled to within 2.5 cm (1″) of the top. Use a light compost with a small amount of sharp sand added. Cover the seeds with no more than 0.5 cm ($\frac{1}{4}$″) of the compost and sand mixture and keep the light out by covering the boxes with glass and newspaper until the seed germinates.

Then remove the paper and prop up the glass. Remove the glass altogether after a few days and place the boxes near the light. Keep the compost quite moist. When the seedlings have four leaves, prick them off individually into 9 cm ($3\frac{1}{2}$″) pots and move them to an unheated frame in early spring. If necessary, support the plants with slender canes.

After hardening off, set out the plants into their permanent bed in mid to late spring, spacing them 30 cm (1′) apart in rows 30 cm (1′) apart. Choose only those plants that have firm, green leaves and white, unbroken roots.

After this, cultivate as normal, although you can give more nitrogenous food (as dilute liquid manure) and a light dressing of potash in mid-summer. Just before you are ready to lift the bulbs remove a little of the soil from around the neck, also any loose outer skin, so that the bulbs get plenty of sun and develop the best possible colour.

A few days before harvesting, loosen the roots by partly lifting the bulbs carefully with a fork. After harvesting, when the necks should be limp, place the bulbs in a slightly shaded part of the greenhouse or a sunny room to ripen.

Varieties

This is a guide to the basic characteristics of some of the most popular varieties of onion. Your local garden centre will probably feature a selection of these which are most likely to suit the climate and soil in your area. Other key points to remember are whether you want a strong or mild flavour, and for how long you will want to store your crop of onions.

Varieties for Spring Sowing

Ailsa Craig: an old favourite, and one of the best; the large, golden-brown bulbs have a mild flavour and are very long-keeping.

Bedfordshire Champion: very reliable heavy cropper; well-flavoured, long-keeping bulbs.

Giant Zittau: produces semi-flat, medium-sized, brown-skinned, long-keeping onions.

Rijnsburger: a group of several hybrids; all reliable heavy croppers producing large, long-keeping bulbs.

Hygro: new variety; produces uniform-sized bulbs with pale skin and white flesh.

White Spanish: very large, flat bulbs; will keep for a very long time.

Mammoth Red: very large, sweet bulbs; red-skinned, good for cooler climates.

Varieties for Autumn Sowing

Ailsa Craig: excellent variety equally suited to autumn and spring sowing.

Solidity: very large flattish bulbs; keeps well; not prone to bolt.

Giant Rocca: two types—brown-skinned and yellow-skinned; flattish globe onions; do not store well, however.

Red Italian: medium-sized, flat, red-skinned onions.

Big Ben: large onions with semi-flat shape; non-bolting; golden skin; keeps well.

Japanese Varieties

Express Yellow: earliest of the Japanese types; flattish bulbs with golden-brown skin can crop in early summer.

Sutton Seeds Ltd. Torquay

Much grown for exhibition, Ailsa Craig *is a very large onion variety with a mild flavour.*

Brian Furner

Rijnsburger *varieties are heavy croppers with exceptionally good keeping qualities.*

143

White Spanish *can be sown in autumn or spring and produces mild, long-keeping bulbs.*

For cooler climates, try Mammoth Red *with its large, sweet-tasting, red-skinned bulbs.*

Solidity, *quite bolt-resistant, is good for autumn sowing; it gives solid, flattish bulbs.*

Express Yellow, *an* F$_1$ *hybrid, is the earliest of the autumn-sown Japanese varieties.*

Kaizuka (Kaizuka Extra Early): for sowing in late summer to crop in mid-summer the following year; straw-coloured, flat onions.

Senshyu: heaviest cropper of Japanese types; for sowing in early autumn; straw-coloured, semi-globe-shaped onions.

Presto: of Swiss origin, but very similar to the Japanese varieties and treated as one; sow in late summer for onions the following mid-summer; semi-globe bulbs with a good flavour.

Onion Sets

Stuttgarter Giant: suitable for all regions, particularly where seeds are difficult to grow; resistant to bolting; very long-keeping.

Sturon Autumn Gold: large, solid onions; long-keeping; does not bolt.

Stuttgarter Giant, *grown from sets, is ideal where onions are difficult to grow from seed.*

A long-established spring onion variety, White Lisbon, *has a good, mild flavour.*

Ishiko Straight Leaf *is a Japanese spring onion that can be sown in spring or autumn.*

The most popular pickling onion, Paris Silver-skin, *grows quickly and ripens early.*

Rijnsburger Wijbo (Giant Fen Globe): one of the best varieties; specially treated to stop bolting; very early globe-shaped onions with golden skins; mild flavour.

Spring Onions

White Lisbon: most common variety for spring onions; quick-growing.
White Lisbon Winter Hardy: variety for sowing in early autumn to give the

earliest spring onions; very hardy.
Ishiko Straight Leaf: new type for spring and autumn sowing; leaves straight and green to the tip; winter-hardy.

Pickling Onions

Paris Silver-skin: small, silver-skinned onions; quick-growing; ripens early.
Cocktail: one-inch bulbs which mature rapidly; well-flavoured pickling type.

Pests & Diseases

Onion fly: the most troublesome pest is the onion fly, which resembles a small, grey house fly. It lays its eggs in spring and early summer, on the neck of the bulb, on the leaves and in the nearby soil. When the larvae hatch, from late spring onwards, they tunnel into the plant tissues. Control them by scattering diazion granules in late spring.

Older plants can be attacked, but young onions are particularly susceptible and, if onion fly is prevalent, it may be as well to stop pulling young plants for salad. Lift and burn any affected plants as soon as you see the symptoms of yellowing, drooping foliage, and be sure not to leave any maggots in the ground. Take care not to leave thinnings lying around or to damage roots or leaves.

The flies are attracted to freshly manured beds, so be sure to dig in organic matter several weeks before sowing. Very early sowing will ensure that thinning is done before the onion fly is about to attack the plants. Autumn-sown plants are less likely to be attacked.

Eelworm: eelworms are minute parasites which are invisible to the naked eye. Stem and bulb eelworms may affect onions, causing distorted leaves and swollen bases. There is no really effective chemical control, and an attack is normally a sign of neglect of proper

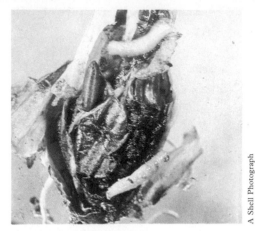

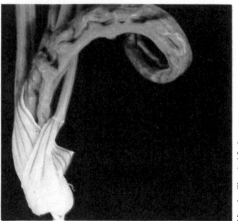

A Shell Photograph

Section of an onion with severe onion fly damage, clearly showing the white larvae.

Murphy Chemical Ltd.

The effects of eelworm. An infestation is usually due to neglecting crop rotation.

crop rotation and a lack of garden hygiene, allowing the pest to build up to dangerous levels. Chickweed can be affected by the same eelworm, so it is important to keep the bed weed-free. Burn any infected plants and make sure that you grow onions in a different place in the garden in the future. After a serious outbreak, it is best to refrain from growing onions in any part of the garden for at least two years. Autumn-sown plants are less liable to be attacked.

White rot: white rot sometimes builds up in crops of salad onions in hot, dry summers. The leaves become yellow and the bases of the bulbs become covered

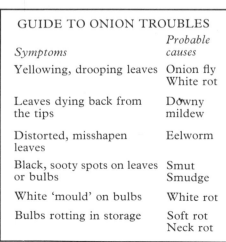

GUIDE TO ONION TROUBLES	
Symptoms	*Probable causes*
Yellowing, drooping leaves	Onion fly White rot
Leaves dying back from the tips	Downy mildew
Distorted, misshapen leaves	Eelworm
Black, sooty spots on leaves or bulbs	Smut Smudge
White 'mould' on bulbs	White rot
Bulbs rotting in storage	Soft rot Neck rot

The fungus disease neck rot may affect bulbs in storage. Avoid damp, stuffy conditions.

White rot damage on salad onions, showing fungus on bulb bases and yellowing leaves.

with a white or grey fungus. It can be combated by dusting the soil at sowing time with calomel dust, but the best control is to keep onions away from any affected plot for at least eight years. Plants grown on fertile, organically manured soil are less susceptible to the disease, and some varieties of onions are more resistant than others. The variety White Lisbon, on the other hand, is particularly susceptible to the disease.

Downy mildew Downy mildew, or onion mildew, is a fungus disease which occurs in cool, wet weather. The fungus causes the leaves to die back from the tips and shrivel. Burn diseased plants and do not grow onions on the site for a year, as the disease spores can remain in the soil. Some varieties are more resistant than others.

Neck rot: this seed-borne fungus disease only reveals itself when the onions are in store—by then it is too late. The preventative treatment is to give onion seeds and sets a dusting of benlate before planting. Keep your storage place cool and well ventilated and dry the bulbs thoroughly. Never store damaged onions or those with green fleshy necks.

Soft rot: soft rot, another disease caused by improper storage, causes the bulbs to become glassy and rot into a soft mass. Again, to prevent this follow instructions for proper storage.

Smudge: smudge is a minor fungus disease which is seen as black smudges on the outer scales of the onions. As it does not usually cause major damage, no special treatment is necessary, other than proper harvesting and careful storage.

Smut: smut fungus disease shows as sooty spots and patches on the leaves and bulbs, and it can kill seedlings. Fortunately it is not common in the UK. There is no chemical control; rest the soil as long as possible, destroy the affected plants as soon as you see them, and be extremely careful not to spread the contaminated soil about the garden to ensure against any further attacks. Only young plants are infected.

Grey mould: autumn-sown onions are susceptible to grey mould, which can be recognized by white spots on the leaves. Eventually the leaves die back from the tips. A spraying of captan or colloidel sulphur in early spring can help to prevent this.

Yellow dwarf and shallot virus yellows: yellow dwarf results in stunted stems and yellow-streaked leaves. It occurs mainly in America, but the disease shallot virus yellows is very similar and is found in the UK, although onions are only occasionally affected. Shallot virus yellows is spread by greenfly, so control by spraying with derris or pyrethrum.

Parsnips

Pastinaca sativa (fam. *Umbelliferae*)
Hardy biennial grown as an **annual**
Sowing to harvesting time: 6-11 months
Size: roots up to 45 cm (1½′) long
Yield: about 14 parsnips, each weighing on average 360–450 g
(¾–1 lb), per 3 m (10′) row.

Before the potato was introduced to
Europe in the late sixteenth century, its
place in European cooking was taken
largely by the parsnip. Few vegetables
are as easy to grow, as nutritious or as
versatile. Parsnips are available as a fresh
vegetable throughout the winter, actually improving as the winter pro-
gresses and frost gets to the roots. They
can be baked, boiled or fried, while some
people eat the leaves as a green vegetable,
getting double value from their crop.

The problem with growing parsnips is
that they have such a long growing
season. They are among the first crops to
be sown—as soon as the soil is workable
in late winter or early spring—and then
occupy the land for the rest of the year
and are perhaps the last crop to be
harvested. They can thus take up land
which could be put to more profitable
use growing a series of crops.

If you have a small garden you may
decide against them for this reason—
although you can raise a catch crop, such
as radish or lettuce, before the parsnips
are established in the spring. But if you
have a fair piece of land, and especially if
you do not have a lot of time, parsnips are
an obvious choice.

Suitable site and soil

Soil is the all-important factor in
growing parsnips. Do not bother with
them if you have a thin gravelly soil, as
you will only get small, mis-shapen
roots. The best soil is friable, rich and
slightly on the heavy side, although it
should not be recently manured as this
tends to cause forking, as do stones.

Do not worry if your soil is not the
best, however. Almost all well-drained
soils will produce a good crop of the
shorter varieties although it is worthwhile to try and follow on to land
manured for a previous crop. Simply dig
the soil about 10 cm (4″) deeper than the
length of your intended variety—this
will be down to about 50 cm (20″) for the
longer varieties—removing large stones.
However, if your garden is very stony
and removing all the stones is impracti-
cal, it may be worthwhile growing in
boreholes as you would for exhibition
parsnips (see Exhibition tips).

Level the bed off, to give a fine tilth, a
day or two before sowing—which will
normally be as soon as conditions allow
in the late winter or early spring. While
you are preparing the bed, rake in a
mixture of four parts by volume

superphosphate, together with one part each of sulphate of ammonia and sulphate of potash, at the rate of 100 g per square metre ($3\frac{1}{2}$ oz per sq yd).

Parsnips dislike very acid soil and do best in one which is slightly acid, neutral or slightly alkaline, so test the soil with a soil test kit several weeks before preparing the seed bed. If necessary, add lime to achieve a pH of 6.5.

The site you choose for parsnips is not as important as the soil. They prefer an open, sunny site, but they will also grow quite happily in a plot lightly shaded by other plants.

Sowing

The traditional time to sow parsnips is late winter but, unless the winter is mild, the soil is often frozen hard or too wet at this time. In most years you will probably have to wait until early spring before sowing. Although parsnips appreciate a long growing season, you can sow later still, up to late spring if you have to, and still get a worthwhile crop.

Sow the seed in a shallow V-shaped drill about 2 cm ($\frac{3}{4}''$) deep. Take the drill out using the edge of a hoe. If you are sowing more than one row, space the rows 30-45 cm (12-18") apart.

Parsnip seeds are fairly large—a little under a centimetre (about $\frac{1}{4}''$) in diameter—but they are very thin and light. Sow three or four seeds at each station along the drill with about 15-23 cm (6-9") between the stations, depending on the size of your variety. It is a good idea to sow several seeds at each station because, although most of them will germinate, you will then have a good choice when thinning and can ensure that there is a really strong seedling in each position. The seed does not store very well, so always use it fresh.

Because the seed is so light, it is inadvisable to try to sow on a windy day; wait until the weather calms down. One way of making life easier is to use pelleted seed. Several parsnip varieties are available in this form. The pelleted seed is heavier so it will not blow away.

Dig the soil a little deeper than the length of your intended variety, making sure to remove all stones.

Test your soil and if it is very acid, apply lime as necessary to achieve a pH of 6.5.

Work the soil to a fine tilth and prepare drills 30-45 cm (12-18") apart and 2 cm ($\frac{3}{4}''$) deep.

Sow three or four seeds at each station, spacing them 15-23 cm (6-9") apart from each other.

It is a good idea to raise a catch crop of lettuce between the parsnips, to mark your rows.

Thin the seedlings when they are about 5 cm (2") tall, leaving only the strongest at each station.

Water if the weather is dry. This is especially important during the crop's early stages.

Hoe as necessary, taking care not to damage the shoulders of developing roots in any way.

After the seeds have been sown in the drill, cover them with soil (sifted soil is best for this) and firm down. Water if the weather is dry.

Germination takes three to four weeks, and in this time it is quite easy for the row of parsnips to be lost among newly germinated weeds. Weed frequently and carefully. Many gardeners sow a quick-maturing catch crop, such as lettuce or radish, between the stations in the row. This not only gives you an extra crop but also helps to mark the row. If you do not wish to do this, leave your marking line in position until the seeds have germinated.

With correct cultivation, you can achieve a bumper crop like this one, ready for harvesting.

Marshall Cavendish/Clay Perry

Care and cultivation

Once the parsnips are sown they need very little attention. When the seedlings are about 5 cm (2″) tall, thin all but the strongest at each station. Do not be tempted to use the thinnings; parsnip seedlings do not produce good roots after the check produced by transplanting. Water, particularly during the early stages of the crop, if the weather is dry, and weed frequently. Be very careful when using a hoe to remove weeds that you do not damage the shoulders of the developing roots; you may open the way for attack by canker.

Harvesting

Once the tops of parsnips turn yellow and begin to die back, they are ready for harvesting. Parsnips sown in early spring should be ready in mid-autumn, but do not rush to pull them all up. The flavour of parsnips is improved by frost, which increases the sugar content of the root, so leave most of them in the ground and dig some up when you want them during the winter. Do not leave any in the ground after February, however, as then they will start to grow again and become woody and useless.

Small parsnips in light soil can be pulled up once the soil around them has been loosened with a fork. Normally, however, the only way parsnips can be lifted without breaking them is by digging. Begin at the end of the row and dig a hole beyond, but close to, the last parsnip. Dig the hole as deep as the parsnip and loosen the soil around the root, which can be then easily removed without damage. Lift the next parsnip by moving the soil next to it into the hole from which the first parsnip has been taken and continue like this to the end of the row.

You will probably find you have to dig down much further than you expect. The end of a parsnip root tapers off for a considerable length, 15 cm (6″) or more, and has a surprisingly strong grip on the soil. In fact, it will probably be necessary to break off the thinnest part of the root, if you want to avoid digging a sizable hole 45 cm (18″) deep for each root.

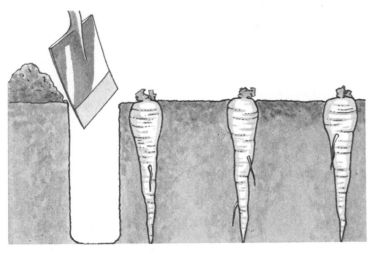

Begin at the end of the row and dig a hole close to the first parsnip, making sure it is as deep as the length you expect the parsnip to be. Loosen the soil around the parsnip and you will then be able to lift it easily without damage. Lift the next parsnip by removing the soil next to it into the hole you made for the first one and continue like this down the row.

Although parsnips are best left in the ground, it is a good idea to store some for when frost makes lifting impossible. Store them in boxes, using layers of peat or dry sand.

Once the parsnips have been lifted, cut off any remaining leaves with a knife. The discarded tops are excellent compost heap material.

Storing

Although the best-flavoured parsnips are those lifted and taken into the kitchen straight from the ground, obviously you will not be able to do this when the ground is frozen hard in the middle of winter. To give you parsnips during this period, therefore, you should dig up some roots in the early winter for storing.

Store the parsnips in the same way as you would carrots. Cut any leaves off close to the crowns and then pack the roots in layers of dry sand or peat in a large wooden box. Put a lid on the top to keep out the light and place the box in a cool, dry and airy place.

Exhibition tips

Exhibition parsnips should be long, straight and unforked. Grow a long variety and sow them as early as you can to get the longest possible growing season. Parsnips are unlikely to be ready for an early summer show but should be large enough for late shows.

If you have a first-class, deep, stone-free and friable loam you will probably be able to produce roots sufficiently good for showing by planting them in the normal way, perhaps just spacing them a little further apart, at 30 cm (12″) intervals. If you are not so lucky, however, you will only be able to produce first-class parsnips by sowing in boreholes.

Use a long straight iron rod to make a conical hole about a metre (3′) deep and about 15 cm (6″) in diameter at the top. Drive the rod into the soil and work it in small circular movements to make the hole. Space the holes about 30 cm (1′) apart.

Fill the holes with a good, moist sandy compost which you have first put through a 1.5 cm (½″) sieve. Firm this soil down and then sow in the normal way.

Keep the parsnips well watered throughout the season to prevent cracking, and weed frequently. It is a good idea also to mulch with peat to retain moisture and to keep down weeds.

Harvest the parsnips as late as possible before the show. Be very careful not to damage or scratch them when you dig

EXHIBITION GROWING

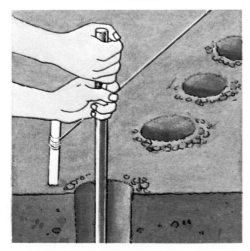

Using a long rod, make holes 30 cm (1′) apart, 1 m (3′) deep and about 15 cm (6″) wide at the top.

Almost fill the holes with sifted soil and sow 3-4 seeds in each. Cover to a depth of 2 cm (¾″).

them up. Use the hole method (see Harvesting).

The normal number of parsnips to exhibit is six in collections and three in single dishes. Pick large, white, straight roots, all of the same size. They should be well-developed with good shoulders and absolutely blemish-free.

After lifting, cut off the tops about 2.5 cm (1″) from the shoulders and shave off all the root hairs with a sharp knife. Then sponge the roots very carefully, and wrap in wet sacking immediately to keep them fresh so that they look their best when you get to the show.

When you get to the show simply lay the parsnips carefully together on the bench in the form of a pyramid, with three roots at the bottom and one at the top. Adjust the roots so that they are close together with as little daylight between them as possible; turn them round so that any bulges on one root fit into a depression in its neighbour. If necessary, tie them together with a piece of soft string, preferably of the same colour as the parsnips. If displayed in a simple manner like this, they will look even better than they are, without appearing over-fussy.

Before the show, trim back leaf stalks to 2.5 cm (1″) and cut off the rootlets with a sharp knife.

154

Varieties

The varieties given have been divided into short, medium and long-rooted. Short and medium varieties normally have rounded ends, long-rooted ones taper to a fine pointed tip. If you are exhibiting parsnips or have a good, deep and stone-free soil, choose a long-rooted variety. Otherwise, choose a short or medium variety which is easier to grow on more difficult or shallow soils.

Short-rooted
Avonresister: the shortest variety of all, producing small, conical roots; because it is so small, thin to only 7.5 cm (3″) between plants in the rows; more resistant to canker than most other varieties.

Medium-rooted
White Gem: white smooth skin; some resistance to canker.
Offenham: a broad-shouldered variety particularly suitable for clay or shallow

Avonresister

Brian Furner

Brian Furner

White Gem

Harry Smith

Offenham

Harry Smith

Lisbonnais

Pat Brindley

Hollow Crown

soils; good, sweet flavour; heavy cropper.
The Student: thick tapering roots with
excellent flavour; heavy cropper.

Long-rooted
Improved Hollow Crown: long symmetrical root; solid white flesh.

Exhibition Long-rooted: clean, smooth
root of fine flavour, a good choice for
showing.
Tender and True: clear smooth skin;
resistant to canker.
Lisbonnais: very good flavour; a large,
well-shaped root; especially good for
exhibiting.

Pests & Diseases

Not much is likely to go wrong with your parsnip crop if it is well-grown as part of a crop rotation. Several diseases, such as downy mildew and leaf spot may be unsightly but they do not seriously affect the yield of an otherwise healthy crop. Canker is the worst problem and good cultivation is the best defence against this.

Wireworm: gardens recently recovered from grassland or badly-tended gardens suffer most from this troublesome pest. The shiny yellow larvae, which are about 2.5 cm (1″) long, bore small regular holes in most root crops, including parsnips. Small roots may be almost entirely eaten up.

Keep wireworm down by careful weeding and cultivation. Treat very badly infected land with diazinon or bromophos, and do not plant parsnips or other susceptible crops for four or five years.

Celery fly: although this pest is not as serious on parsnips as it is on celery, it can still do sufficient damage to reduce growth appreciably, because its attacks interfere with the chlorophyll-making mechanism of the leaves. The tiny 0.5 cm (¼″) adult flies lay eggs on the foliage and the small maggots which emerge burrow into and through the leaves, producing white or brownish blisters as they go. Normally, good cultivation will enable the plants to grow back after attack, but in the worst cases the most badly affected leaves should be removed and the remainder sprayed with malathion. Alternatively, you can kill the maggots by squeezing them, still in the leaf, between your finger and thumb. If you are particularly troubled by this pest, paraffin-soaked rags hung near the parsnips helps discourage the flies from laying eggs.

Carrot fly: the greenish-black carrot fly lays its eggs in the soil near carrots, parsnips or celery to which it is attracted by the smell of the foliage. The eggs hatch to produce small, pale yellow maggots which invade the roots. These pests are also a problem because the wounds they cause provide a starting point for canker.

Carrot fly is most likely just after thinning because the smell of the damaged foliage of the thinned plants attracts them. Thin in the evening when the flies are less likely to be active, and burn all the thinned plants. Firm the soil around the plants after thinning as this fills in the cracks in the soil and deters the flies from laying eggs. As with celery fly, paraffin-soaked rags help to discourage them. If the problem persists, dust with bromophos according to the manufacturer's instructions.

Aphids: in a dry summer, greenfly can infest the foliage in large numbers, so that the leaves curl, become yellowish and even cease to grow. This is more likely to happen in dry weather if the plants have not been watered regularly. Pick off the worst affected leaves and spray the remainder with derris or bioresmethrin.

Canker: this is the most serious problem with parsnips. It appears as firm brown or black patches on the shoulder of the root which then becomes soft and rotten. The secondary rotting which follows the initial discolouration is caused by fungi or bacteria, but the reason for the original discolouration is not known. It is most likely, however,

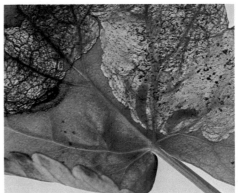

The small maggots of the celery fly burrow into the leaves, causing blisters.

Canker appears as firm patches on the shoulder of the root, which then becomes soft.

Mottled yellow leaves and stunted plants are signs of parsnip virus. Burn affected plants.

that infected roots have been damaged in some way, perhaps by carrot fly, by cracking caused by heavy rain after drought, or by careless hoeing. Because parsnips are not self-healing (as potatoes are, for example), soil-borne fungi and bacteria can enter and rot the root.

The only remedy is better cultivation. Acid soil and over-manuring with unrotted manure are said to encourage canker and these should be avoided. Try, also, later-sown crops, as these are more resistant.

Virus: mottled yellow leaves and stunted plants are signs of parsnip virus. As with all viruses there is no cure. Pull up the affected plants and burn them.

Powdery mildew: parsnip leaves are occasionally attacked by this fungus which appears as a fine white powder on the surface of the leaves. It is most widespread in damp years but even then it does not seriously affect the growth of the plants, and can be ignored.

Downy mildew: downy mildew appears as moist, dark brown or black spots on the leaves but, again, it is not serious.

Leaf spot: a third disease which attacks parsnip leaves is leaf spot which produces small brown spots on the leaves. Again, do not worry. The disease does not do enough damage to merit control measures.

Sclerotina rot: this disease only attacks roots in store, the roots becoming covered with a fluffy, white mould. To prevent rot, only store in a dry, airy place and do not store damaged roots.

GUIDE TO PARSNIP TROUBLES

Symptoms	Probable cause
Small regular holes in the root	Wireworm
White or pale brown blisters on the leaves, leaves shrivelled	Celery fly
Irregular holes in the root sometimes with small whitish grubs inside	Carrot fly
Leaves curling, slightly discoloured, yellowish, and small	Aphids (greenfly)
Reddish brown, dark brown or black patches on the shoulders of the root	Canker
Mottled yellow leaves and markedly stunted growth	Virus
Fine white powder on the surface of the leaves	Powdery mildew
Moist dark brown or black spots on the leaves	Downy mildew
Small brown spots on the leaves	Leaf spot
Roots in store rotten and covered with a white fluffy mould	Sclerotina rot

157

Potatoes

Solanum tuberosum (fam. *Solanaceae*)
Half-hardy annual.
Sowing to harvesting time: approximately 13
weeks for early varieties; 17–22 weeks for maincrop
varieties.
Size: average tuber diameter 6–10 cm (2½–4″), although
this varies greatly depending on the crop and the variety.
Early potatoes are generally much smaller than maincrop
varieties. Plants grow to about 60 cm (2′) high.
Yield: approximately 7–9 kg (15–20 lb) per 3 m (10′) row.

Potatoes are one of our staple foods, but
in recent years they have become
increasingly expensive. For many home
growers, this in itself is sufficient reason
to try raising their own potatoes, but
there are other benefits too. Some of the
best quality varieties do not 'travel' well
so you will find they are never available
in shops or supermarkets, and the
flavour and texture of early 'new'
potatoes is undoubtedly at its best
straight from the garden.

If you want potatoes all year round,
you will need to grow three different
groups: early, second early and maincrop. The earlier the variety, the faster
the growth and the lower the yield.

Many people will have space to grow
only a limited number of potatoes. In
this case, it is best to sacrifice the
maincrop and grow the earlies, which are
harvested when potatoes are most
expensive in the shops. For a 3 m (10′)
row you will need about 1 kg (2 lb) of
seed potatoes.

To grow a continuous supply for a

family of four throughout the winter and
spring you will need quite a large area of
land—it will be feasible only if you have
an allotment or large garden. The
quantities of seed potato to order are 2 kg
(4½ lb) of earlies, 5 kg (11 lb) of second
earlies, and 2.5 kg (5½ lb) of maincrop *for
each person*. You will need 20 sq m (24 sq
yd) of land for this amount, that is 80 sq
m (96 sq yd) for a family of four.

Suitable site and soil
In a simple rotation system, potatoes are
generally grown with roots and to
precede the cabbage family, which
appreciates the clean, well-turned condition in which this crop leaves the soil.
Potatoes are a good choice for a first crop
on old pasture or grassland that is being
taken into cultivation. As a precaution
against disease, they must not be grown
in the same soil two years in succession.
Remember that tomatoes and night-
shade weeds are members of the same
family as potatoes and can transmit
infection; tomatoes should never be

1. Put the tubers in egg boxes, top upwards, to encourage sprouting.

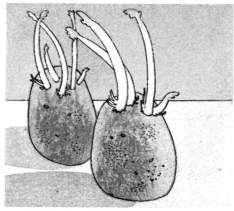

2. Too much warmth or darkness causes shoots unfit for planting.

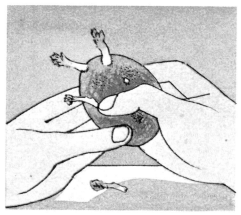

3. Rub off the sprout at the extreme top and all but the two most sturdy.

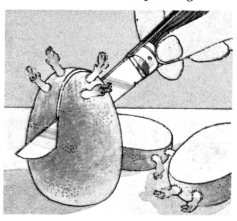

4. Cut large tubers so that each piece has two shoots. Protect cut surfaces.

5. Prepare ground by digging over and then manuring before sowing.

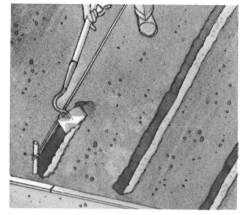

6. Make V-shaped furrows 8–15 cm (3–6″) deep for planting sets.

7. Put manure where each set is to go, then cover with a thin layer of soil.

8. Scatter lawn mowings in drills and position sets with tops uppermost.

9. Protect sprouts by covering sets with soil by hand, before raking level.

included in the same group of vegetables as potatoes in a rotation system.

The site should be open and not overshadowed by trees, walls or buildings. Potatoes are not particular about soil, but on heavy clay soils choose your varieties carefully. Early varieties prefer light land.

In early winter the ground should be well dug and treated with a moderate amount of rotted manure or compost, but not limed. Lime will encourage attacks of scab, and too much nitrogen will produce growth of the haulm, or stem, at the expense of tubers.

Seaweed, dug into the soil the previous autumn, is an excellent manure. If organic matter is not available, apply a fertilizer made up of 2 parts each by weight of superphosphate and sulphate of ammonia with 1 part of sulphate of potash at the rate of 40 g per sq m ($1\frac{1}{3}$ oz per sq yd). Apply this about two weeks before planting.

Preparing the 'sets'

The 'seed potatoes' from which potatoes are grown are dormant tubers known as 'sets'. These are obtained from vigorous plants before they are fully mature and then exposed to the air for a few days. Potato sets come from disease-free tubers produced on government-certified farms. Never purchase potatoes that do not have a government certificate. Most people buy every year, but it is also safe to grow from tubers of your own crop every other year. Sets should be about the size of a hen's egg and look plump and healthy, but a delivery usually contains some larger ones. These may be divided as described overleaf. It is impossible to get a good crop from poor or diseased sets, so if you are using your own sets be sure they are healthy.

Order seed potatoes in time to begin sprouting towards the end of winter (earlier for early varieties).

Right: flourishing rows of healthy potatoes: a good example of earthing up. Sound cultivation will pay off with a heavy crop.

George Hyde

161

10. When haulms are 7.5 cm (3″) high, cover them with straw to give protection against damage by frost.

11. Begin earthing-up when the haulms reach 20 cm (8″) to aid production and protect from light.

Put the sets in trays or empty egg-boxes in a light, well-ventilated, frost-proof place. This enables growth to begin before it would be wise to plant outside in spring. The stacking wooden fruit trays that have a short leg sticking upwards at each corner are also ideal for this. Look for the end of the set where the 'eyes' or dormant buds are crowded together—this is the top. Stand them upwards in the trays or egg-boxes and, if there is any risk of frost, cover with newspaper. Chitting, as this process is called, takes about six weeks and gives both earlier and heavier crops.

The earlies should go into sheltered ground at the end of winter, with second earlies and maincrops following at monthly intervals. You can give some earlies a really good start with cloches, but keep the tunnel end closed until all danger of frost is past. Plant when the sprouts on the potato sets you are chitting are 3 cm (1¼″) long. Just before

planting, rub off all except two or three sprouts with your thumb. The one to get rid of first is the sprout at the extreme top, then any that are still white, as the best ones are purplish and, lastly, the least promising of any surplus remaining. Large sets can be cut into pieces, each having at least two strong sprouts. Dust the cut faces with flowers of sulphate or plaster of Paris to check loss of moisture; alternatively, bring the exposed surfaces together and cover with a damp cloth until planting. Take care not to knock off the sprouts.

Planting out

Potato rows should run north to south so that the plants receive the maximum amount of sunshine and do not shade other crops. The rows should be 50 cm (20″) apart for earlies and 75 cm (30″) for the bulkier maincrop plants. This allows for earthing up later on.

Dig V-shaped furrows; the depth will

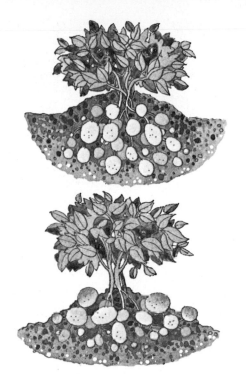

12. Correct (top) and incorrect (bottom) earthing up. Tubers exposed to light will turn green and poisonous.

13. Spray maincrops against blight in midsummer and again in late summer with Bordeaux mixture.

vary depending on your soil type: from 8 cm (3¼″) deep for a heavy soil to 15 cm (6″) deep for a light one. Never use a dibber for planting because it is liable to leave an air-space underneath the tuber. For improved yield spread a forkful of manure where each set is to go and throw 3 cm (1½″) of soil over it, so that manure and set will not be in direct contact. Scatter lawn mowings thinly in and around the drills before filling them in; this will help prevent attacks of the potato scab fungus.

Place each set in position in the drill, top uppermost, 30 cm (1′) apart for earlies and 40 cm (16″) for maincrops, covering each with soil by hand to protect the sprouts from damage when refilling the furrow. Rake the soil level along each row.

Care and cultivation
Protection is necessary for all potatoes when there is any risk of frost—as there

nearly always is with the earlies. Once the shoots are above the surface, ground or wind frost will burn them black, giving a three-week setback. When they are only a few centimetres high, cover them by drawing up a little soil. When they reach 7.5–10 cm (3–4″), they must be covered with straw, bracken or leafy branches.

Wait until the shoots can be clearly seen before doing any hoeing, and then do not work the hoe too close to them. Start earthing up when the shoots are about 17.5 cm (7″) high. The haulms of potato plants are jointed, and the tubers grow out from underground joints in the haulm. Earthing up creates more joints, which means heavier crops.

Earthing up also keeps the tubers well buried so that they will not turn green through exposure to light—green tubers contain a poisonous substance and are dangerous to eat. Several times during the growing period, loosen up the soil

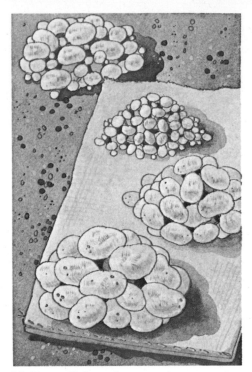

14. Yellowish leaves indicate the crop is ready. Lift with a potato fork which has special tines to avoid damage.

15. Dry off the tubers on the ground, briefly. Clean by hand, discard damaged ones and grade by size.

between the rows and push some up with a draw-hoe on both sides of the haulms, leaving the top 15 cm (6″) uncovered.

Spray against the fungus disease, blight, of maincrops once in midsummer and again in late summer with Bordeaux or Burgundy mixture. These can protect against blight but not cure it. Any flowers that appear during growth should be nipped off.

When growth slows and the haulms turn yellow, the tubers begin to mature. This should happen to all the plants at about the same time and if isolated plants show these signs you must suspect disease—cut their tops down and burn them, although the tubers of these plants may be left in the soil until they are of usable size to be harvested.

Harvesting and storing the crop
Early or 'new' potatoes are eaten immature in early summer, when they are no larger than a pullet's egg.

Carefully lift one or two to see if they are ready for eating; they can be covered up again if they are not. Some people unearth them by hand, pick the tubers they want, and return the soil to let the rest grow on. Dig up the earlies as you need them day by day, because after they are lifted they quickly lose flavour.

A potato fork is a great asset in lifting the crop, as its flat, blunt tines greatly cut down the risk of damaging tubers. Make sure no potatoes or pieces of tuber are left in the ground over winter—they will be a nuisance growing up among the brassicas the next year, and destroy the principle of not growing potatoes in the same soil two years running.

The earlies can go straight into the kitchen as required, but the later crops must be stored. After lifting, let them dry off on the ground for an hour or two, but no longer, before being taken in. Clean off by hand any soil which is sticking to the tubers, discard any that are diseased or damaged, and take the opportunity to pick out any seed potatoes you may require or to do any other kind of grading. Store them in the dark or under cover from light in a dry, frost- and draught-free storeroom. Bags or boxes will do for storing, but put straw under the bags and take precautions against vermin. The potatoes should be inspected once a month, and any rotten ones should be discarded. Also rub off any sprouts.

If you have a lot of potatoes and only a small amount of room, one solution is a clamp raised in a dry open situation out of doors on a thick bed of straw. Heap the potatoes into a ridge on the straw and cover them quickly with more straw, then put some soil on top to keep it in place. After 24 hours' drying cover the straw with 15 cm (6") of soil, obtained by digging a drainage trench all round the clamp. This is then beaten flat with the spade so it will shed rain. Leave ventilation holes at 1 m (1 yd) intervals along the top, pulling up tufts of straw from below to keep them open. When removing potatoes, inspect those exposed to view before closing the breach. If any are rotten you must remake the clamp. Take the haulms away and burn them; do not use them for compost.

Alternative methods of cultivation

It is not essential to earth up potatoes but the traditional method described is still widely favoured. Cultivation time may be cut by planting the tubers individually along the rows with a trowel (without making a trench) and covering the rows with lengths of black plastic sheeting tucked into slits made in the soil, at both its sides and ends, so as to anchor them. When the shoots start to grow and make bumps in the plastic, make openings with scissors in the form of plus signs to release them. The opaque sheeting conserves moisture, inhibits weeds, and shields the shallow-grown tubers from light. Harvest the potatoes by cutting or rolling back the plastic and lifting them up with a hand fork or potato fork.

Growing under glass

Spring supplies of new potatoes can be produced by planting them in warm frames in mid-winter, either directly in the soil or in pots, but few gardeners have this much frame accommodation. Half bury each upright set in a 20 cm (8") pot about a third full, and earth them up as they grow. Potatoes can be successfully grown in pots under glass. Fill 20 cm (8") pots with a good quality compost

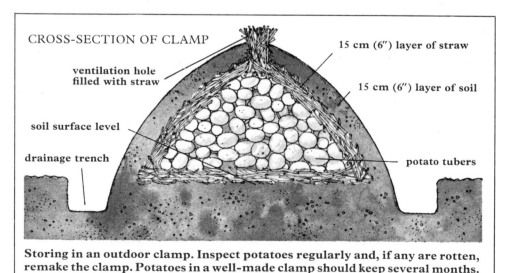

CROSS-SECTION OF CLAMP

15 cm (6") layer of straw

ventilation hole filled with straw

15 cm (6") layer of soil

soil surface level

drainage trench

potato tubers

Storing in an outdoor clamp. Inspect potatoes regularly and, if any are rotten, remake the clamp. Potatoes in a well-made clamp should keep several months.

GROWING UNDER PLASTIC SHEETS

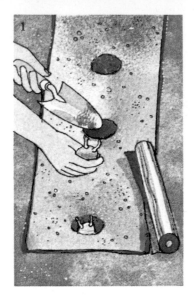

1. There is no need to make a trench. Dig holes along the row with a trowel and plant the tubers individually.

2. Cover the rows with lengths of black plastic sheeting. Tuck sheet in slits dug in the soil, at both sides and ends to anchor.

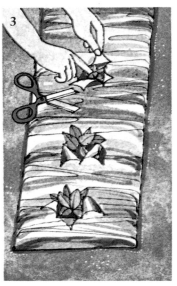

3. When the haulms start to grow and make bumps in the plastic, cut openings in the sheet in the form of plus signs.

4. The sheeting conserves moisture, inhibits weeds, and shields the shallow-grown tubers from the light. Roll back plastic sheeting to harvest. Lift crop with a hand or potato fork.

and plant one sprouted tuber in each pot. If you have a heated greenhouse, plant the tubers in late winter and the potatoes will be ready in late spring. If you have an unheated greenhouse or cold frame, expect potatoes in early summer from an early spring planting.

Growing in containers

If your garden is very small, you may want to grow some early potatoes in containers outdoors, or on a patio or balcony. Tubs made from half wine barrels or 30 cm (1′) whalehide containers are the most suitable. Fill with a good quality compost and plant three seed potatoes in each container. If your containers will be indoors, you can plant at any time; if outdoors, late winter or early spring is the best time.

Keep the containers in a warm, sunny place, and bring them indoors if there is a threat of frost. Use a small hoe to earth up the plants exactly as you would if they

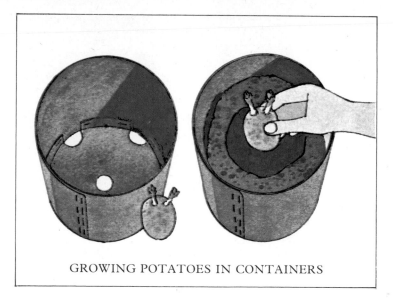

GROWING POTATOES IN CONTAINERS

Yet another way of growing potatoes outdoors is to plant them in 'whalehide' containers. Use good quality compost and plant one seed potato in each 30 cm (1') container. Use a hand fork when harvesting the crop.

were planted in the ground. Your small crop should be ready for harvesting in about 12 to 14 weeks. Use a hand fork to harvest the tubers. You can expect a yield of about 3 kg (6½ lbs) from a barrel or 1 kg from a whalehide tub.

Exhibition tips

You can grow exhibition-quality potatoes in much the same way as you grow tubers for the table, but with special care and with some differences in cultivation details. As with normal cultivation, sets for sprouting should be about the size of a hen's egg, but they should not be cut into pieces for sprouting. Plant them in early spring at intervals of 60 cm (2') in drills 60 cm (2') wide, 15 cm (6") deep and 90 cm (3') apart. As well as lining the drills with garden compost or well-rotted manure, place each set on a mixture of old, crumbly manure, sifted peat and leafmould separated from the set by old (but not diseased) potting soil, and cover them with the same mixture. Take care not to let any manure or compost touch the sets.

During cultivation, be extra careful not to tread on the drills when earthing up; remove any weak, spindly shoots as soon as you notice them; keep the healthy stems upright by tying them

carefully to stakes; keep the plants well earthed-up so that the tubers do not turn green; water the plants, using a fine rose on watering can or hose, during dry weather; and be extra vigilant where pests and diseases are concerned.

Growing exhibition potatoes requires a great deal of space, as you will be required to exhibit either six (for a single dish) or twelve (for a collection) regularly-shaped, shallow-eyed, matching tubers: you will be lucky if you find six such tubers in a 9 m (30') row.

Do not leave the tubers in the ground so long that they are large, heavy and misshapen by the time that you dig them up. Lift them in late summer, handling the tubers very gently. Put them carefully in a container lined with sacks and cover them with dry vermiculite or soft, dry sand. Keep them in a cool place, which should be as dark as possible to prevent the tubers from greening. Near to the time of the show, wash the tubers very carefully (the skins are extremely tender) with a sponge soaked in soapy water. Dry very gently with a soft cloth (pat the tubers; do not rub them), wrap in tissue paper and put them back in the dark until the day of the show. The judges will look for uniformity of size and shape and a clear skin with few eyes.

Pests & Diseases

Potatoes can suffer from many pests and diseases, but the ones given here are those most likely to occur in the garden.

Eelworm: potato root eelworm can be a very serious pest. Eelworm cysts (egg-sacs) can lie dormant in the soil for several years and, when potatoes are planted on infested ground, the larvae attack the tubers, producing potato sickness. Affected plants are stunted and pale green or yellow, they wilt easily and die when immature. Tuber production will be very small. If eelworms are present, there will be tiny dots on the roots, which later become brown. Infected plants and tubers should be destroyed, and infected soil should be put down to grass for eight years. There is no effective method of destroying the cysts. Crop rotation is important in controlling eelworms; never grow potatoes on the same ground two years in a row so otherwise the eelworm population will build up.

Wireworm: these pests can cause much trouble by boring into the potatoes. They are a particular problem in wet summers, and they often occur in freshly dug pasture or on wasteland. If you think wireworms might be a problem, grow

Potato leaves attacked by the virus leaf roll.

Brown patches are a symptom of blight.

early varieties as these are rarely attacked, and lift maincrop potatoes as soon as the tubers mature.

Slugs: slug damage is most likely in wet summers and in heavy, wet soils. Discourage slugs by keeping the garden clear of hiding places and by limiting the use of manure on heavier soils. Use methiocarb or metaldehyde baits to trap them. Early crops are almost never attacked by slugs; damage is usually to maincrop types, and even some of these varieties seem to be immune.

Colorado beetle: colorado beetle is a very destructive pest, fortunately very rare in the UK. The Colorado beetle is a potentially dangerous pest to crops, and its presence must be reported immediately to the government authorities.

Greenfly: greenfly are dangerous to

GUIDE TO POTATO TROUBLES

Symptom	Probable cause
Pale green or yellow leaves	Eelworm Greenfly Virus diseases
Yellowing leaves on blackened stem	Black leg
Brown-black patches on leaves and stems	Potato blight
Curling or rolling leaves	Virus diseases
Large holes in leaves	Colorado beetle
Brown or white dots on roots	Eelworm
Small round holes in tubers	Wireworm
Large holes in tubers	Slugs
Tubers with sunken areas or brown flesh	Potato blight
Large irregular growths on tubers	Wart disease
Rough, discoloured patches on tubers	Scab diseases

Common scab—but only the skin is damaged.

Slug damage produces large interior holes.

potatoes because they spread virus diseases. Destroy by spraying with derris or resmethrin.

Potato blight: potato blight is one of the most common diseases the home grower encounters. A fungus disease, it is most prevalent in warm, wet weather, but it can occur at any time during the growing season. The disease produces dark brown-black patches on the leaves and stems; infected tubers have sunken areas on the outside with brown flesh underneath. The disease can spread rapidly and destroy the top growth completely in mid-summer.

There are several precautions to take against potato blight. Protect plants by spraying with Bordeaux mixture or mancozeb in early midsummer, and repeat in wet weather according to the manufacturer's instructions. Blighted foliage should be cut and burned, and 10 to 12 days should pass before digging the tubers which are still edible if you catch the disease in its early stages. Blighted potatoes should never be stored.

Potato wart disease: potato wart disease is another fungus disease. Affected tubers produce large irregular growths which look like cauliflowers. Infected plants must be burned, and potatoes should not be planted on the soil for at least ten years. The disease must be notified to the government.

Scab diseases: there are several scab diseases, all caused by fungus, which affect potatoes. Common scab is a superficial disease, affecting the skins of the tubers only, but it makes peeling difficult. It can usually be prevented by lining the drills at planting time with small amounts of lawn mowings. Peelings should be destroyed.

Powdery or corky scab is more serious. It causes round swellings on the tuber skins, which rupture and release a brown, powdery substance. The symptoms can be very severe on wet soil, and the potatoes can be destroyed. The soil can remain contaminated for several years, so avoid growing potatoes on the site of an outbreak.

Black leg: black leg is a bacterial trouble which affects an occasional plant within a crop. The stems blacken at the soil level, the leaves turn yellow and the haulm withers; tubers rot where they are attached to the stem. Dig up infected plants and destroy them.

Virus diseases: leaf-roll, mosaic disease and spraing are all virus infections. Leaf-roll, the most common, is easily recognized by the curling, leathery leaves. The plants are under-sized and the tubers are few and very small. The disease is carried in the tubers, so never save tubers from infected plants for planting out the following year. Mosaic also produces yellow markings on leaves; spraing gives brown lines in the tuber flesh. Avoid these virus infections by planting only certified disease-free seed.

Varieties

First Early

Home Guard: white skin and white flesh; good cropper; excellent value.

Arran Pilot: very popular, high quality, excellent cropping potato; immune to wart disease; rarely affected by scab disease; white-skinned; kidney-shaped; floury and well flavoured.

Ulster Chieftan: one of the earliest croppers; oval-shaped with white flesh.

Di Vernon: deserves to be more popular with gardeners as it is a good cropper and immune to wart disease; kidney-shaped with purple eyes and white flesh.

Duke of York (Midlothian Early): does well in most soils; kidney-shaped potatoes with firm, yellow flesh.

Epicure: an old favourite; one of the best-flavoured varieties for new potatoes; very hardy and suited for cooler parts of the country; round, white-fleshed tubers.

Second Early

Arran Banner: white-skinned, large, round, heavy potatoes; floury; good cropper, particularly on light soils.

Red Craig's Royal: red-skinned tubers of uniform shape and size; does best on heavy soils; high quality; immune to wart disease.

Pentland Lustre: new variety which has

Arran Pilot

Kerr's Pink

King Edward

Pentland Lustre

proved very satisfactory; eelworm-
resistant; heavy cropper; firm tubers
with yellow flesh.

Great Scot: popular type which grows
well on most soils; crops and stores well;
immune to wart disease; round, white-
fleshed tubers are excellent for baking.

Maincrop

Kerr's Pink: pink-skinned; good for
areas with high rainfall and/or heavy
soil; good cropper.

Desiree: high quality heavy cropper
suited to all soil types.

Golden Wonder: considered by many to
be the best flavoured potato; excellent
type for exhibition; lemon skin and firm,
white to yellow flesh; immune to wart
disease.

Majestic (Tremendous): most widely
grown variety; well-flavoured, kidney-
shaped potatoes; suitable for most soils,
resistant to blight and immune to wart
disease.

King Edward: large, kidney-shaped
tubers with pale yellow flesh; does best
in medium loam; unfortunately very
prone to most potato pests and diseases.

Pentland Crown: recently introduced
type bred for immunity to blight and
some virus diseases; well-flavoured,
oval-shaped tubers with white flesh;
heavy cropper.

Brian Furner

Majestic

Harry Smith

Red King Edward

Brian Furner

Arran Banner

Brian Furner

Pentland Crown

171

Swedes

Brassica napus napobrassica (fam *Cruciferae*)
Hardy biennial
Sowing to harvesting time: 20-24 weeks
Size: 7.5-17.5 cm (3-7″) in diameter, 12.5-17.5 cm (5-7″) long
Yield: 0.5-1 kg (1-2¼lb) per root

Swede is one of the hardiest vegetables, and one of the attractions of growing the crop is its ability to do well without much attention. It can be left in the soil right through the winter and will be wholesome and edible after being frozen solid for weeks.

This cousin of the true turnip originally came from Sweden, and its name is an abbreviation of Swedish turnip. In some northern areas the swede has almost completely superseded the turnip—when a Scotsman talks about turnips he will almost certainly be referring to swedes.

The crop is grown for its large, yellow-fleshed roots. Swedes are hardier, sweeter and milder than turnips, and rarely get woody. The main harvesting difference between swedes and turnips is that swedes are used in winter, while turnips are harvested in summer and autumn. The growing season of the swede is much longer than the turnip's; growing a combination of two vegetables will give you a long season of use.

Although this crop is grown mainly for its edible roots, swedes left in the ground will produce pale green leaves in spring which can be cooked as greens.

Swedes are divided into three groups according to the colour of the upper part of the root: the Purple-tops, the Bronze-tops and the Green-tops. The green varieties are slower to mature than the purple sorts, which are much freer growing and the heaviest croppers. The bronze varieties are intermediate in habit between the two other types. Seeds of Green-top varieties are sometimes difficult to obtain.

Soil preparation
Swedes grow best on fertile medium loam, although with proper soil preparation they will grow well on a wide variety of soils, from light, sandy loams to medium clay.

Swedes, like other members of the brassica family, are subject to club root disease. Club root thrives in acid soil, so

1. If the soil is not fertile, prepare it by digging in plenty of well-rotted manure or garden compost.

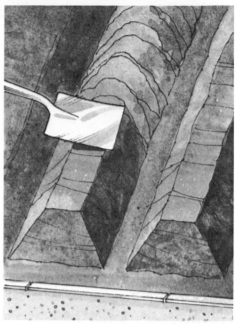

2. In wet areas, prepare rows of ridges 15–20 cm (6–8″) high and sow seeds on ridge tops.

3. Ten days before sowing, apply a compound fertilizer at the rate of 90 g per sq m (3 oz per sq yd).

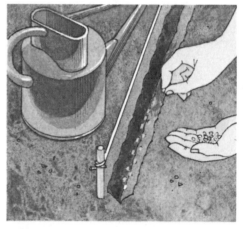

4. If soil is dry, water thoroughly just before sowing; sow seeds thinly and lightly cover with soil.

make sure your soil is between pH 7.0 and 7.3. If the soil is less than 7.0, apply ground limestone at between 0.28 and 1.4 kg per sq m (10 oz and 3 lb per sq yd) depending on acidity.

Provided the soil was well manured for the previous crop, there should be sufficient organic matter for the swede crop. If the soil was not previously manured, dig in well-rotted manure or compost at the rate of one barrowload to 11 sq m (12 sq yd). Do not apply fresh manure or compost, or watery, misshapen roots will result.

1. Three weeks after sowing, or when seedlings are at rough-leaf stage, thin to 15–20 cm (6–8″) apart.

2. Keep down weeds by hoeing between rows and hand weeding between plants.

3. Keep the plants well watered until established; mulch with damp peat in very dry weather.

4. Protect the overwintering swedes from attack by pigeons and rabbits with netting or rabbit fencing.

Swedes have long, ridged necks, and mild, orange-yellow flesh. They are hardier than turnips and can remain in the soil right through the winter.

Harry Smith

The amount of fertilizer applied depends on the nature of the soil, but a good basic feed is 90 g per sq m (3 oz per sq yd) of compound fertilizer applied about ten days before sowing and lightly forked in. On chalk soils apply an extra 60 g per sq m (2 oz per sq yd) of superphosphate. On peaty soils, or those which are acid, fork in 60 g per sq m (2 oz per sq yd) of bone meal. Apply these extra fertilizers at the same time as the compound fertilizer.

When preparing the ground, make sure you get rid of all weeds, particularly the perennial ones, such as couch grass and thistles.

If you live in an area of high rainfall, it is best to grow swedes on ridges. It is hard to precisely define high rainfall, but if you get more than 60 cm (24″) of rain per year, you would do better to grow the crop on ridges. Make ridges 15-20 cm (6-8″) high, and between 60-67 cm (24-27″) from centre to centre (see diagram). Ridges are better drained in winter,

when the ground tends to get water-logged. Fine soil will gradually fall down to the bottom of the trench between the ridges and the roots will grow through into this.

In lower rainfall areas grow swedes on the flat, as ridges would tend to dry out in the summer. For the same reason, do not make ridges if your soil is very sandy or free-draining.

Firm the ground before sowing, whether on ridges or on the flat. Do not attempt to firm the ground if it is too wet, or the soil will become compacted and lose its friable quality.

Seed sowing

The time for seed sowing varies according to local conditions. In Britain, sowing should take place in late spring in the north, early summer in the midlands, and mid-summer in the south and southeast. The temperature required for germination is over 7° C (45° F) and less than 37°C (95°F). By sowing late in the

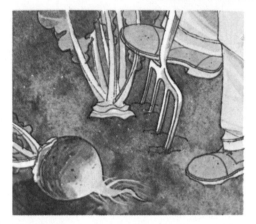

To harvest, gently ease swedes out of ground with a garden fork.

Top and tail the swedes before storing for future use.

season in warmer areas, the plants will be less subject to the worst summer heat, drought and mildews. A last sowing in late summer will provide greens for use the following spring.

If you are growing swedes on ridges, sow the seed as soon as possible after the ridges are prepared. If the soil is dry, water the drills right before sowing. The rows should be about 67 cm (27″) apart; rows on the flat should be 45 cm (18″) apart. Sow the seeds thinly, at a depth of 2 cm ($\frac{3}{4}$″) on light soils, or 1.25 cm ($\frac{1}{2}$″) on heavier ground.

Care and cultivation

The seeds take between seven and twelve days to germinate. Thinning takes place about three weeks after sowing, when the seedlings are at the rough-leaf stage. Do not attempt to transplant the thinnings as, once disturbed, they will not grow. The final spacing of the young plants should be 25-30 cm (10-12″) apart in the rows.

Keep the young plants well watered until established. Cultivate the ground to kill weeds, being careful not to damage the young swede roots. Do not hoe too deeply; lightly loosening the soil surface will create a dust mulch which helps to conserve the moisture below. If the weather is dry, mulch with damp peat,

Storing in a clamp: dig drainage trench; place swedes on a layer of straw.

working it up and over the tops of any protruding roots.

Harvesting and storing

Although swedes may be large enough to use in early autumn, they are often left in the ground until all the summer vegetables have been harvested and frost has set in. They can be pulled as required through the winter, as long as the ground is soft enough to dig. A touch of frost improves the flavour of swedes. The over-wintering roots are, however, vulnerable to attack by rabbits and pigeons, so make sure they are ade-

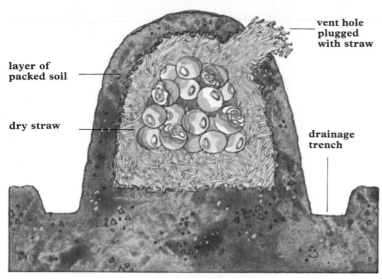

vent hole plugged with straw

layer of packed soil

dry straw

drainage trench

Build up heap of swedes. Cover them with another 10 cm (4″) layer of straw. Put a similar depth layer of soil over the straw, leaving a vent for access and air circulation.

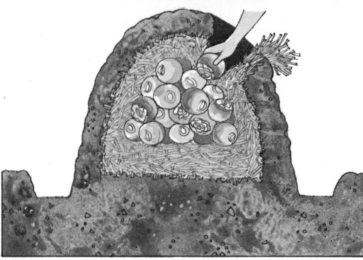

Remove swedes as you need them by unplugging the straw in the access vent and lifting the roots out. Replace the straw plug carefully.

quately protected with nets or rabbit fencing. Alternatively, you can leave them in the ground until spring, when they will produce leaves which can be cut and used as greens.

In the south winters are rarely severe, and you can usually leave the roots in the ground until you are ready to use them. Lift them systematically; do not pull the biggest ones first. You will then have feasible areas of cleared ground to dig over before winter sets in and any swedes left in the ground for spring greens will be grouped together.

An outdoor crop of spring greens is harvested by cutting off the tufts of leaves at the neck as you require them.

If you live in a cold area, have a good supply of roots and some storage space, you can lift some of the swedes and store them in boxes or an outdoor clamp to ensure that you will have a supply when the rest of the crop is frozen hard in the ground.

Lifting the crop can begin in late autumn. Choose a mild day, and gently ease the roots out of the ground with a garden fork. If you are storing them for future use, top and tail them. Removing the leaves and root tails makes them

PRODUCING BLANCHED STEMS

1. Dig up swedes in late autumn; cut back neck and root, plant in box filled with soil or peat. Water well and store in dark place.

2. Cut blanched shoots when they are 20 cm (8″) long.

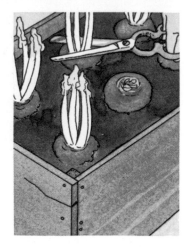

easier to store, and helps prevent rot.

To store them indoors, pack the swedes in layers in a box, and cover them with fine sand. They can also be stored loose in a sack. Whichever method of indoor storing you use, make sure you keep them cool, preferably at a temperature of 0-4° C (32-40° F). Be on the look out for vermin, such as mice or rats; if you see any, put down poison or set traps.

To make a clamp for outside storage in cold districts, select a plot of ground not subject to waterlogging, and clear it of all rubbish. Lay a 10 cm (4″) layer of clean dry straw on the soil, and put the swedes on top. Cover them with another 10 cm (4″) layer of straw. Then place a covering of soil, 7.5-10 cm (3-4″) deep, over the straw, leaving an access vent, or more than one in larger clamps. A shallow trench around the clamp will have been formed by excavating the soil. On heavy soils water would collect in the trench, so build up a pathway at the original soil level to the clamp, to avoid having to walk through the water.

Producing blanched stems
You can induce swede roots to produce blanched stems, like chicory, which are excellent in winter salads or as a cooked vegetable. Dig up medium-sized roots in late autumn or early winter, after a few winter frosts. You do not need the best

roots for forcing, small or misshapen ones will do just as well. Cut off all top growth above 2.5 cm (1″); shorten back the neck and root tail to the swollen root base. These swedes should be about 10 cm (4″) in diameter, and 17.5 cm (7″) long. Then fill boxes with friable soil or peat to a depth of 2.5 cm (1″). Press the roots gently into the soil with a space of about 2.5 cm (1″) between them. Continue filling the spaces between the swedes with peat or soil until the soil is level with the neck of the swedes. Water them well, and keep them in a dark place, with a temperature of 13-15° C (55-60° F). Cut the blanched shoots when they are about 20 cm (8″) long.

Exhibition tips
Swedes for exhibition should be medium-sized, clear-skinned, solid and shapely, with small taproots. Prior to the show, lift the roots carefully, so they are not damaged. Place them on wet sacking in a cool place, and keep them covered. Wash the swedes in cold water, sponging off any soil which is sticking to the root. Cut off any whiskery side roots and dead outer foliage. Then cut back the remaining foliage to 10 cm (4″) and tie with green twine. Usually three or six swedes are shown; these should be displayed on a plate with the roots facing frontwards. Swedes are often used in displays of mixed vegetables.

178

G. E. Hyde

Harry Smith

Varieties

Purple-top: Excellent for eating and for winter storage.

Chignecto: bred for its resistance to club root disease; a first-class table swede, having a fine neck with perfectly round root of the Purple-top type.

Mancunian: greenish-bronze topped root with solid yellow flesh. Excellent keeping, though slower growing than Purple-top varieties.

Western Perfection: a very good quick-growing Purple-top sort with yellow fleshed root; almost neckless; splendid for eating young and stores well.

Acme: excellent for table use; sweet yellow flesh, Purple-top variety.

Above left: Typical Bronze Top variety

Above: Chignecto

Left: Purple Top

Brian Furner

Pests & Diseases

Common sense, clean cultivation and crop rotation will do much to minimize the harmful effects of pests and diseases. The four main troubles which commonly occur in swede crops are club root, also known as 'Finger and Toe', downy mildew, turnip flea beetle, and gall weevil. These will also affect other members of the brassica family; club root, which is particularly destructive, may persist in the soil for many years.

Flea beetle: these are usually most destructive at the seedling stage and occur mainly in dry weather. They eat small round holes in the leaves; in severe cases the plants may be entirely defoliated. Treat the seed before sowing with gamma-HCH, and dust it on the seedlings when they appear, or use derris on the plants.

Aphids: greenfly, blackfly or cabbage aphids will occasionally appear during hot, dry weather. They form large colonies on the under and upper surfaces of the leaves which causes the leaves to curl; stems may also become twisted and distorted. Control them with malathion or derris sprays.

Shell photo

Gall weevil maggots occupy the cavities in the swellings on swede roots.

Ministry of Agriculture, Fisheries and Food

Club root is a very serious fungal disease, causing swollen, foul smelling inedible roots.

Gall weevil: white maggots attack the roots, causing round swellings to appear on the upper part of the roots. Treat the seed with gamma-HCH (BHC).

Wireworms: these shiny yellow worms occasionally tunnel into the roots; they usually occur on ground freshly turned over after grass. Gamma-HCH (BHC) dust raked in before sowing will help to minimize the attacks.

Murphy Chemicals Ltd.

Turnip flea beetle damage; the beetles can defoliate young plants.

Slugs and snails: these pests do twofold damage. They eat the leaves and roots, and the holes they make allow root rotting disease organisms to enter. Control slugs and snails with any proprietary bait.

Club root disease: this fungus attacks not only other brassicas, but most members of the *Cruciferae* family. The symptoms of the disease are stunted and weak plants having swollen roots. The infected roots are gnarled and galled, slimy, rotten, and foul smelling. Prevention is the best defence. Ensure that ground is not too acid before sowing, as club root thrives in acid soils. It is prevalent on badly-drained soils; make sure drainage problems have been corrected before sowing. Do not grow swedes on land which has grown any brassicas in the last two years. Lastly, avoid using manure or compost containing infected roots or leaves.

Liming the soil will help control the disease; sprinkle hydrated lime at the rate of 6 kg to every 30 sq m (14 lb every 30 sq yds). Sprinkle 4% calomel dust in the seed drills before sowing, at the rate of 30 g per 1.5 m (1 oz per 5' run).

Downy mildew: the first sign of this infection is the appearance of greyish-white patches on the leaves, generally on the undersurface, followed by wilting and yellowing. Spray the plants with zineb.

Powdery mildew: this appears as whitish powdery patches on the leaves. Pick off affected leaves and spray plants with dinocap.

Root rots: dry rot, or phoma rot, occurs as a brown, sunken, elongated canker-like areas on the side of the roots. Prevention is again the main control of this problem. Eliminate slugs and snails and avoid using manure or compost containing infected roots. Use the same preventive measures against soft rot, which causes brown or grey mottling and eventual softness and sliminess of the root.

Wirestem: this causes damping off of seedlings, but stem bases of older plants may be attacked; the stems turn brown, shrink and break off easily. It is not necessarily fatal to the crop, but infected plants will be stunted. Prevent wirestem by treating soil with quintozene dust at sowing time.

GUIDE TO SWEDE TROUBLES

Symptoms	*Probable Cause*
Curled leaves, twisted stems with colonies of green, black or bluish insects on leaves and stems.	Aphids
Small round holes in leaves of seedlings or plants.	Flea beetles
Swellings, on upper part of roots, containing white maggots.	Gall weevil
Slime trails, holed leaves, stalks and roots.	Slugs and snails
Shiny, yellow worms and tunnels in the roots.	Wireworms
Weak, sickly plants with swollen, galled, bad smelling and rotting roots.	Club root disease
Greyish-white downy patch or leaves turning yellow and wilting.	Downy mildew
Whitish powdery patches on leaves.	Powdery mildew
Brown, sunken elongated canker-like areas on the side of the roots.	Phoma rot
Grey or brown mottled areas, some being soft and slimy in the advanced stages.	Soft rot
Seedling stems constricted and brittle, some falling over and dying.	Wirestem Damping off

Turnips

Brassica rapa (fam. *Cruciferae*)
Hardy biennial
Sowing to harvesting time: maincrop 10–12 weeks: early crops 6–8 weeks
Size: maincrop roots average 7.5–10 cm (3–4″) across, but can grow much larger; early crop roots about 4 cm (1½″); leaves to 30 cm (12″) long.
Yield: maincrop roots average 260–480 g (½–1 lb), but can be much heavier; early crop roots weigh about 90 g (3 oz).

Turnips are quick and easy to grow, and their swollen white roots provide a delicate flavour when used in stews or casseroles, or served on their own as a vegetable. Although often thought of as an autumn and winter crop, turnips are much more versatile. By selecting your varieties carefully to suit the season, and by meeting their few cultivation needs, you can extend cropping over many months.

In the annual garden cycle, turnips can be regarded as three distinct crops. Early turnips are those which are ready to harvest as quite small roots from mid-spring to early summer. They may be grown outdoors on a hotbed in a frame, or started in a greenhouse or outdoors under cloches. These quick-growing tender varities have long or spherical roots, white flesh and white skin, sometimes with purple or red shading. They are French or Italian in origin and are not hardy. Because they are so quick growing, they make excellent catch crops.

Maincrop turnips are sown in the summer to produce roots 7.5–10 cm (3–4″) in diameter in autumn. In mild areas they can be lifted as needed through the winter; in colder areas they are lifted all at once in late autumn and stored. These larger, hardier varieties were developed in England and Scotland to withstand winter weather. They are usually round and white fleshed, and either white or white and green skinned. There is a yellow fleshed variety, which is a mutation, or 'sport', of the white fleshed turnip. It is used for maincrops, and its flesh is considered by many to be superior in taste to most of the other turnip varieties.

Finally, you can grow turnips in spring or autumn for their leaves, which are cooked like cabbage and are rich in vitamin C and iron. The leaves can either be harvested as thinnings, before the roots have fully formed, or the roots can be left in the ground over winter to produce a continuous supply of spring greens.

Turnips are one of the easiest garden vegetables to grow; both leaves and roots are edible.

Suitable site and soil

Turnips require an open, sunny position. If grown in the shade of trees, they will produce foliage rather than roots. For early turnips, the site should have some shelter from north and east winds.

Although turnips will grow on a wide variety of soils, the main requirement is that the soil is moisture retentive; rich sandy loams are ideal. Turnips like calcium and are grown extensively on chalk and limestone soils; they also need a soil well supplied with phosphates.

Turnips grow best on a soil which has been manured for a previous crop, such as potatoes. If the site has not been previously prepared, dig the soil over in autumn or early winter. If it is dry or heavy, dig in plenty of well-rotted manure or compost to improve moisture retention and drainage. If you are digging in manure, bury it deeply or the roots will be mis-shapen and earthy tasting. Unless the soil is chalky or limey, apply a top dressing of carbonate of lime to ensure that the soil is neutral to slightly alkaline. Allow two months to elapse between manuring and liming, otherwise the nutrients in the manure will be released into the air.

Sowing

In theory, the gardener can grow a succession of crops from early spring until late autumn. Two crops are more practical, an early one harvested in spring or early summer, and a maincrop harvested in autumn and stored through the winter. An intermediate crop would coincide with the main summer veget-

1. Begin digging the soil in autumn or early winter; work in plenty of well rotted manure or garden compost.

2. Unless your soil is chalky or limey, apply a top dressing of carbonate of lime to make the soil neutral in pH.

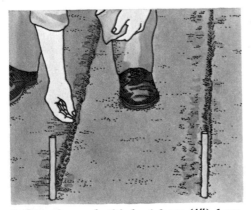

3. Sow the seeds thinly, 1.2 cm ($\frac{1}{2}''$) deep, in drills 30-40 cm (12–16″) apart; any extra seed can be stored for later use.

ables, and any seed sown in late spring for harvesting in summer would quickly bolt under hot, dry weather conditions.

For the first sowing, choose an early, quick growing variety and start under glass or cloches. For maincrop turnips, sow in mid to late summer, again selecting a suitable variety. A final sowing in early autumn will provide turnip tops in spring, with a cutting, if required, in late autumn, within a few weeks of sowing.

The early varieties generally have white roots. A succession is provided by more white varieties, by white turnips with red or purple tops, and lastly by golden ones. Green top white varieties are among the hardiest and best for overwintering to supply early spring greens.

Sow the seeds thinly, 1.5 cm ($\frac{1}{2}''$) deep, in drills 30–40 cm (12–16″) apart; 7 g ($\frac{1}{4}$ oz) of seed is enough to sow a 9m (30′) row; if you have more seed than you need, you can store it; the seed remains viable for three years.

Thin the seedlings as soon as they are large enough to handle to a distance of 5 cm (2″) apart. Pairs of seedlings occasionally grow very close together and appear as one seedling, so thin carefully. Thin early crops and turnips grown for greens to a final spacing of 15 cm (6″) between plants. Turnips grown as maincrop should be thinned to a distance of 23–30 cm (9–12″) apart. If you spread the second thinning over a period of several weeks, you can use the thinnings as spring greens. The sowing to germinating period varies according to soil warmth, but in reasonably warm weather germination is rapid and can take less than a week. Like most other root crops, turnips do not transplant well.

Cultivation and care
The cultivation needs of turnips are moderate and fairly basic. For early sowings in the open, protect the plants with cloches if the weather turns cold. Turnip seedlings are particularly vul-

1. The first thinning takes place when the seedlings are large enough to handle; thin to 5 cm (2") apart.

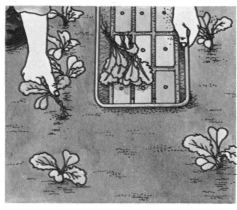

2. Thin again to 15 cm (6") apart for early crops and those for greens; space maincrops 22-30 cm (9-12") apart.

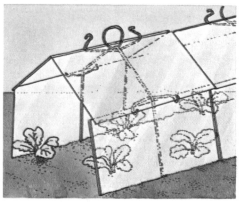

3. For early sowings in open ground, protect the plants with cloches if the weather turns cold or frost threatens.

4. Dust the young plants with derris as a precaution against turnip flea beetle; reapply as necessary.

5. The turnips should receive a steady supply of water while growing, or they will bolt without forming roots.

6. Keep the soil well hoed, being careful nor to damage the roots; this controls weeds and keeps soil aerated.

1. Pick early turnips when they are the size of a tennis ball; maincrops can be left in the ground until needed.

2. Pull turnip tops when they are 15 cm (6″) high; do not pull more than two leaves from a plant at one time.

3. In cold areas, lift maincrops in late autumn for storing; place roots in boxes between layers of peat or sand.

nerable to attack by flea beetle, so dust the drills with derris as soon as the seedlings emerge and continue dusting with derris as necessary.

Spring turnips should be grown as quickly as possible, without any checks. This means there must be a constant and steady supply of water. If the turnips grow in dry soil, they will either run to seed without forming roots or else the roots will be coarse, stringy and unpleasant. On the other hand, if the turnips are watered heavily following a long dry spell, their roots will split.

Keep the soil well hoed, being careful not to damage the roots. This helps to control weeds and also keeps the soil aerated.

Harvesting and aftercare
Turnips are best when grown quickly and harvested while still young and tender. Pull spring turnips when they are about the size of a tennis ball, and cut the leaves off close to the root. The spring crop of leaves may be picked or cut at any time after they are about 10–15 cm (4–6″) high. Most of the turnip varieties which are grown for pulling when young are not frost hardy, and if you make a late sowing, they should be out of the ground before the onset of hard frost.

Hardier winter varieties can withstand a moderately mild winter, and in the south of England may be pulled as required. Alternatively, if you live in a cold, wet area, or where the ground is likely to be frozen hard, lift the turnips for storage in clamps or boxes until needed. Begin harvesting for storing when the outer leaves show signs of ripening in late autumn; leave about 2.5 cm (1″) of leaf stalk attached to the roots. If storing them in a box, pack the roots between layers of dry peat or sand, and store in a cool place where they will keep until early spring.

Lift the roots systematically for immediate use or storing; do not pull the biggest ones first. In this way you will have a feasible area of cleared ground to

Turnip leaves, or 'tops', are rich in vitamin C and iron; cook them like spring greens.

dig over before planting the next crop; any turnips left in the ground for spring greens will be grouped in one place. These spring greens will be particularly useful at a time of the year when cabbages are scarce. Do not pick all the leaves off one plant, or it will stop producing new growth. Pick just one or two leaves from each one, so the plants will continue producing fresh foliage. As soon as the plants form flowerheads, however, scrap them, as the leaves will be bitter and unpleasant tasting.

To avoid pests and diseases, clear away all surplus roots and the remains of vegetation after harvesting and take them to the compost heap. If you have had serious trouble with pests or diseases, do not risk spreading them through the compost heap; dig up and burn all debris instead.

Growing turnips under glass

Turnips may be produced very early in the season if you grow them under glass. They will not stand hard forcing, however, so if you grow them in a frame on a hotbed use gentle bottom heat only. Fermenting manure or leaf litter covered with 15 cm (6″) of fine soil should be adequate. Insert the seeds, two or three together, in holes about 12.5 cm (5″) apart in mid to late winter. Thin to one seedling per hole when the seedlings are large enough to handle. The bed should be covered by sacks or mats to help retain the heat until the seeds have germinated; remove the sacks once the seedlings

1. For growing in a frame on a hotbed use gentle heat only; cover a layer of manure or leaf litter with fine soil.

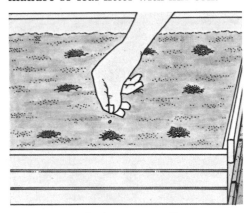

2. Insert seeds, in groups of two or three, in holes 12.5-15 cm (5-6″) apart, in mid to late winter.

3. Cover the lights with sacks or mats to help retain heat until seeds have germinated; then remove the sacks.

appear. Allow plenty of air to circulate round the plants after this, and water every day. It should be possible to harvest the crop within four to eight weeks of sowing.

Alternatively, if you want early turnips without using a hotbed, you can grow them under cloches in early spring. Keep them covered with the cloches and thin the seedlings so they are 15 cm (6″) apart. You should have tender roots for pulling in about six weeks. Turnips left in the soil over winter to produce spring greens may also need cloche protection if the weather turns very cold.

Exhibition tips

It is risky to try to time a single sowing of turnips to be ready for a show date, because unforeseen changes in weather can retard or advance the growth considerably. Make several small sowings, nine, ten and eleven weeks before the show, and select the best roots for exhibition. Six turnips is the usual number shown in single dishes, and ten turnips in a collection of vegetables.

The globe turnips should be a little larger than a tennis ball, and as uniform in size, weight, and general appearance as possible. Globe varieties should be perfectly round, without any taper to the tap root. Long varieties should be 3.7 cm ($1\frac{1}{2}$″) in diameter, and 12–15 cm (5–6″) long. For all varieties, the judges will look for clear skins and symmetrical, solid roots, with small tap roots.

Lift the roots carefully with a fork, and put them in wet sacking so they do not dry out. Wash any soil off carefully with cold water and a sponge; do not scrub them or the skin will be damaged. Remove the small outer leaf stems entirely, and cut the leaves away so that 12 cm (5″) of leaf stem remains. Trim away any small root hairs from the tap root with a sharp knife.

The roots can be displayed in a circular basket, on a flat plate or board, or hung from wire cones; try to make the display as pleasing and attractive as possible.

Varieties

Early

Early Six Weeks (Early White Stone): fast, first class white globe turnip; early cropper and sweet flavoured; good for growing under glass.

Tokyo Cross (F₁ hybrid): globe shaped roots; very quick growing, ready five weeks from sowing; well flavoured, uniform crops.

Jersey Navet: cylindrical shaped, white fleshed variety; excellent for cold frames or cloches for early crops, or can be sown in open for maincrops.

Golden Perfection: nearly flat golden skinned roots, small to medium sized; tender flesh.

White Milan: very early turnip, excellent for growing under frames or cloches; dwarf, compact roots, flat shaped and medium sized.

Sprinter: early selection of *Purple Top Milan,* but slightly smaller; suitable for growing either under glass or outdoors in the open ground.

Purple Top Milan: white variety with purple top; very early cropper; distinctive, heart-shaped leaves.

Red Globe: round, medium sized roots; white flesh, red and white skin.

Snowball: early variety, quick growing; well formed, round white roots; can be cooked or grated raw; suitable for table and exhibition work.

Jersey Navet

Golden Perfection

Purple Top Milan

Red Globe

Snowball

Green-top White

Maincrop

Golden Ball: dwarf and compact; tender yellow flesh; hardier than white-fleshed turnips and lasts well in open; best variety for autumn sowing; flavour only moderate.

Green-top White: round variety, with half green, half white, skin; leaves used as spring greens; heavy cropper; well-flavoured roots.

Manchester Market: excellent green-topped, globe variety; mild flavour; especially recommended for winter use as a table variety.

Pests & Diseases

Club root disease (finger and toe): this is one of the most serious fungal diseases affecting members of the *Cruciferae* family, mainly brassicas; turnip crops can be completely destroyed by severe infections of club root. Yellow fleshed varieties have slightly more resistance to club root than white fleshed varieties. The above ground symptoms are stunted and weak plants with wilted greyish leaves. The roots, when dug up, will appear gnarled and galled, slimy, rotten and foul smelling. Once a soil is infected with club root, it is a lengthy process to eradicate the fungus completely; it is better to try to prevent an attack of club root than to cure it. Because club root is associated with acid soils, ensure that the ground is not too acid before sowing. Correct any drainage problems at this time as well, as plants grown on waterlogged soil are particularly vulnerable. To protect seedlings, sprinkle calomel dust, used according to manufacturer's instructions, in the seed drills before sowing.

Make sure you practice crop rotation, and do not grow turnips on land which has grown any brassicas in the last two years. Lastly, dig up and burn any infected plants as soon as you see them; do not put them on the compost heap or the infection is likely to spread.

Liming the soil will help control the disease; sprinkle hydrated lime at the rate of 6 kg to every 30 sq m (14 lb every 30 sq yds).

Dry rot: although swedes are usually more vulnerable to dry rot than turnips, the latter are sometimes infected. The symptoms of dry rot are brown, sunken, canker-like areas on the roots. Prevention is again the best method of controlling the infection. Keep your garden free of slugs and snails, as they cause the wounds through which dry rot enters the roots. Avoid using manures of composts containing pieces of infected roots or leaves. Destroy any infected roots immediately.

This leaf shows the damage done by flea beetle; in severe cases it may be skeletonized.

Wounds made on the leaves and roots by slugs allow infections like soft rot to attack.

Soft rot: this bacterial infection causes brown or grey mottling and eventual softness in the inner root, although the outer skin may remain firm. As with dry rot, the infection usually enters the root through a wound, perhaps from hoe or insect damage. It is also likely to occur where the roots are stored in damp conditions. Dig up and destroy any infected plants, make sure your garden is pest free, and avoid hoeing. Too heavy liming can predispose plants to this trouble, so try to avoid this condition.

Powdery mildew: this mildew is most likely to occur in dry summers. The symptoms are white powdery patches on the leaves. The best precaution is to make sure your plants do not run short of water in dry spells. If powdery mildew does appear, pick off and burn infected leaves and spray the remaining leaves with dinocap.

Brown heart (Raan): the symptoms of this physiological disorder, which is due to boron deficiency, do not appear until the turnip roots are cut open. The plants will show grey or brown areas in the bottom half of the root; the flesh will be bitter, stringy and unpleasant to eat. Brown heart is sometimes associated with very dry soil conditions; if your soil is very free draining, make sure you dig in enough humus when preparing the

site to make the soil moisture retentive. Excessive liming can also cause brown heart, as it makes the boron in the soil unavailable to the plants. Mulching the soil with well rotted compost and digging in manure is the safest method of correcting this deficiency.

GUIDE TO TURNIP TROUBLES	
Symptom	Probable cause
Wilted grey leaves, roots mis-shapen, slimy and rotten	Club root
Brown, sunken, canker-like areas on roots	Dry rot
Brown or grey mottling in inner root	Soft rot
White powdery patches on leaves	Powdery mildew
Grey or brown areas in bottom half of root	Brown heart (Raan)
Pale grey patches on undersides of leaves	Downy mildew
Base of stem shrivels and turns brown	Wirestem
Small round holes in leaves	Flea beetle
Galls in roots containing white maggots	Gall weevil
Leaves and roots eaten	Slugs and snails
Tunnels in roots	Wireworm

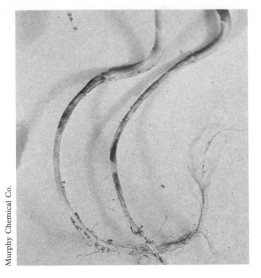

Wireworm: this pest is most troublesome on soil freshly turned over from grass.

Wirestem causes brown, hardened and shrivelled stems; plants will not crop well.

Downy mildew: the first sign of this infection is the appearance of greyish white patches on the undersurfaces of the leaves; seedlings are most likely to be infected. Eventually infected leaves wilt, turn yellow and die. Remove and destroy infected leaves, and spray the remainder with zineb.

Wirestem: this infection causes damping off in seedlings, but older plants may also be infected. Plants infected with this fungal disease will have stems which shrivel, narrow, turn brown and toughen. Although not necessarily fatal, diseased plants will be stunted and poor croppers. Prevent damping off and wirestem by treating the soil with quintozene dust at sowing time, or with a thorough watering of Cheshunt compound.

Flea beetle: this is the most serious pest you are likely to encounter with turnip crops. The most severe attacks occur in hot dry weather, when the plants may be entirely defoliated. The main symptom is small round holes in the leaves; eventually the holes may join up and the leaf skeletonized. Seeds treated with gamma HCH before sowing are less vulnerable to attack. As a further precaution, dust the seedlings as soon as they appear with derris, and repeat if you see holes in the leaves.

Gall weevil: the symptoms of infestation by gall weevil are sometimes confused with those of club root, as in both cases swollen disfigured roots occur. If the suspect roots are cut open and galls are found containing white maggots, then gall weevil is the cause. It is much less serious than club root; the best precaution against gall weevil is to treat the soil with gamma HCH prior to sowing; destroy infected plants.

Slugs and snails: besides damaging turnip crops by feeding on the leaves and roots, the open wounds they make allow more serious secondary infections, such as soft rot and dry rot, to attack the plant. Keep your garden free from debris and litter where snails can hide during the day. Trap slugs in piles of old vegetable matter; inspect the traps daily and remove and destroy any slugs you find. Alternatively, control them with a proprietary slug bait used according to manufacturers' instructions.

Wireworms: these shiny yellow worms are only likely to be a problem on soil freshly turned over after grass; land that has been cultivated for any length of time is usually free from wireworm. The symptoms of wireworm attacks are tunnels through turnip roots; gamma HCH dust raked in before sowing will help to minimize the attacks.

Salad Crops

Celery

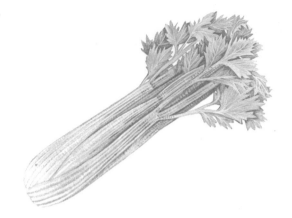

Apium graveolens
(fam. *Umbelliferae*)
Biennial, grown as an annual
Size: 30-50 cm (12-20″) high,
7.5-10 cm (3-4″) in diameter
Sowing to harvesting time: 6-8 months; mature plants of
winter celery may be left in the ground for several more
months and lifted as required
Yield: 12-15 plants, each 0.7-1 kg (1½-2 lb), per 3 m (10′) row

Celery has long been considered a specialists' crop, largely because of the labour and skill thought to be involved in trenching and blanching. In fact, these operations are not particularly difficult or time-consuming. Self-blanching and green varieties are now available if you want to grow celery with a minimum of effort.

There are three basic types of celery; winter, or blanching; summer, or self-blanching, and American green, grown for its green stalks.

Winter celery may be white, pink or red. The white varieties are rather tender and are the first to mature, followed by the pink and then the red varieties. Winter celery is available in dwarf or tall forms. If you have a small family, or do not use a lot of celery, select a dwarf variety for planting. Celery is at its best when eaten fresh; there is no point in growing giant varieties if it takes days for your family to finish one head.

The summer varieties are creamy-white, stringless, and have a milder flavour than the winter types. These are less hardy, and must be harvested before the first autumn frosts. They are not strictly speaking self-blanching, but simply contain less chlorophyll than the winter varieties.

American green celery, also for autumn harvesting, is hardy and grows happily outside, requiring no blanching. Both green and summer celery require less work than the winter varieties, and are quicker to come into crop. If you are a beginner or have little time to spend in your garden, it might be advisable to grow a summer or green variety.

Suitable site and soil

Choose a sunny open spot; celery does not do well in the shade. Like wild celery, which grows in marshes, cultivated celery needs plenty of water. The water supply must be continual as well as abundant; if celery suffers from lack of water at any time during its growing period, stunted plants or bolting will result.

SOWING CELERY

1. Sow the seeds under glass from early to mid-spring. Sow them thinly in seed compost; cover with a fine layer of compost.

2. When you can hold the seedlings between finger and thumb, prick them out 5 cm (2″) apart into boxes.

Celery needs deep, fertile, well-drained soil. It also needs soil which can retain moisture; it grows best in Fenland conditions. Sandy soils are least suitable because they tend to dry out in summer. Avoid badly-drained or heavy clay soils, which can become waterlogged. Celery is a very greedy feeder, and can be grown on well-rotted manure or garden compost without any soil added.

Raising seedlings

The sowing procedure for winter and summer celery is basically the same. Sow white winter varieties in early spring to eat in early winter. Sow pink and red sorts a month later, for harvesting in mid or late winter. Summer and green celery are usually sown in mid-spring, because earlier sowings may bolt, while later ones may be injured by frost.

If you are growing celery from seed, make sure it is guaranteed disease-free. Always wash your hands after dealing with celery seeds as they are treated with strong chemicals to prevent disease. Never use seeds intended for sowing to flavour food.

Celery seeds are slow to germinate, and may take up to six weeks under a cloche or cold frame; germination can be patchy under these conditions. Because celery has a long growing season, you should start the seeds under glass. Sow the seed thinly in John Innes seed compost and cover with a thin layer of compost. Germination will not take place unless a temperature of 15–21 °C (60–70 °F) is maintained; germination will be quicker if the temperature is higher.

When the first true leaf appears, prick the seedlings out into boxes, spacing them 5 cm (2″) apart. Now you can lower the temperature to 15 °C (60 °F). When they are growing well begin to harden them off before finally planting out. To get a longer season for celery, and avoid a sudden glut, do not plant the seedlings out all at once. Prick out and plant the most advanced seedlings first, leaving the slower ones to plant out at weekly intervals.

If you do not have a greenhouse, you can buy plants ready for transplanting.

Growing winter celery

Preparation for planting should be done well in advance, preferably in late winter. For winter celery, dig a trench 37 cm (15″) wide for a single row of plants, 45 cm (18″) for a double trench. If you are digging more than one trench, leave 1.2-1.5 m (4-5′) between trenches.

Dig out 30-60 cm (1-2′) to start with and fork over the bottom of the trench.

WINTER CELERY

1. Dig a trench 37-45 cm (15-18") wide and 30-60 cm (1-2') deep in late winter. Fork over bottom of trench to loosen soil; work in organic matter. Then cover with 7.5-10 cm (3-4") topsoil. Make finished trench level 15-20 cm (6-10") lower than ground. Space plants 22 cm (9") apart.

2. If your soil is not too dry, plant quick catch crops on the ridge of soil next to the trench. Lettuce, dwarf beans, or radishes can be raised this way and harvested before the soil is needed for earthing-up in late summer.

Replace some of the soil with plenty of manure, garden compost or grass cuttings. If you cannot get farmyard manure, hops manure is a good substitute. Then cover the organic matter with 7.5-10 cm (3-4") of soil until you have the finished trench level. The final depth of the trench varies according to soil and drainage conditions. A finished trench level of 22 cm (10") is best for light sandy soil. On heavy clay soil the trench can be 15 cm (6") deep.

Pile up the soil from the excavation alongside the trenches in neat ridges. If the soil is not too light, you can grow quick catch crops, such as lettuce or radishes, on them until you need the soil for earthing-up in late summer. The crops will be harvested before then.

Planting out

Two weeks before planting, apply superphosphate at the rate of 60 g per sq m (2 oz per sq yd). Right before planting, clean out of the trench bottom any soil which has crumbled in from the sides.

3. In late summer begin earthing-up. Remove side-shoots, suckers and tiny leaves; remove and destroy slugs. Wrap plants in newspaper and tie with raffia to keep soil from getting into celery heart. Place 10 cm (4″) soil from adjacent ridge around base of each plant. Earth-up gently to avoid bruising.

4. Earth-up twice more, once in late summer and again in early autumn. Each time add another 10 cm (4″) to the soil around the plants. After the final earthing-up, only the leaves should be visible. Finish the ridge off neatly with smooth sloping sides.

Then thoroughly drench the trenches with water.

Plant out the young celery in late spring, if the weather is not too cold, or early summer. Be careful not to disturb the rootballs when transplanting; it is best to use a trowel when lifting and planting them. Set the plants in either a single or double row, with a spacing of 22 cm (9″) in all directions. For the first few nights after they have been planted out, or if the weather turns frosty, cover the plants with cloches.

Care and development

The main requirement of all young celery plants is a continual supply of water. If the plant is allowed to dry out, coarse growth and tasteless hollow leafstalks will result. Organic top dressings are not usually needed. Do not apply nitrate-rich fertilizer because excess nitrogen makes the stalks cracked and frothy. Keep the trenches weed free; pick off and burn any leaves infected with celery fly. If the plants are throwing out side-shoots or suckers, remove them,

5. Harvesting can begin in mid-autumn. Scrape back the soil until you see the roots.

7. When the roots are exposed, place your fork well down into the soil to avoid damaging the stems. Lever out the plant, being careful not to damage adjacent plants.

as all growths should come from the centre of the plant.

Blanching

This is usually started in late summer, when the plants are 30-45 cm (12-15″) high. Choose a fine day, when the ground is reasonably dry. Check again for sideshoots and suckers, and remove any tiny leaves which would be buried by the process of earthing-up. Remove and destroy any slugs in the trench.

Wrap the plants in newspaper and tie with raffia. This keeps the soil from getting into the heart of the celery; once soil gets into the centre of the plant rot may set in. An alternate method of tying the stalks together is to use a long length of garden twine, twisting it round the top of each plant. Remove the twine when the final earthing-up is completed.

To begin earthing-up, rake the loose soil from the adjacent ridge down into the trench bottom. Place around the base of each plant 10 cm (4″) of soil. Do this gently, as earthing-up is done to keep out light, not to physically constrict the plant. Never apply fertilizer to the soil which is used for earthing-up, as it can damage the stalks. Earth-up around the plants twice more, in late summer and early autumn. Each time add another 10

cm (4″) to the soil around the plants, until only the top leaves are showing.

When earthing-up is finished, the trench should be filled in and formed into a ridge on the top. Finish the ridge off neatly, with smooth sloping sides. This helps throw off the rain.

Another method of blanching is to use celery collars. These are about 15 cm (6″) high and are tied round the celery. Collars are placed one on top of the other over the plant at three week intervals until celery is completely covered. Heap soil around collars to keep them from blowing in the wind.

Protection and harvesting

Once earthing-up has been completed, winter celery can remain in the ground for several months. Leave the plants in the ground for at least six to eight weeks after the last earthing-up. This will complete the blanching process, and moderate frost improves the flavour. Lift the heads from late autumn onwards, as you need them.

In very bad weather, protect the plants from frost and rain by covering the ridges with clean straw or bracken. Alternatively, place two boards on edge along the ridge; this will help throw off the rain as well. A third method of

SUMMER CELERY

Transplant young plants into frames in mid to late spring, depending on weather conditions. Space them 22 cm (9″) apart in each direction. Cover only the roots with soil; if the stems are covered, suckering will be encouraged. Water in well after planting.

protection is to place waterproofed paper along the ridge, folded down the middle in a tent shape. Fix the paper with crossed canes so it cannot be blown away by the wind.

When harvesting, work your way down one row at a time, lifting the heads in order. Carefully remove the earthed-up soil from around the plant you are lifting until you can see the roots. Then place your fork under the plant and lever it out. Be careful not to damage adjacent plants.

If a heavy or prolonged frost threatens, you can lift a few heads of winter celery in advance and store them until needed. Dig the plants out, before the ground becomes frozen solid, complete with roots. Remove any damaged stalks and outside leaves and pack them upright in a box filled with a layer of moist sand. Store the boxes in a cellar or shed, where the temperature is just above freezing point. Keep the soil moist until all the celery has been used.

After harvesting, put the leaves, outer stems and roots on the compost heap and level the ridges. The soil is already enriched for succeeding crops. Do not replant the site with carrots, which are a member of the same family, to prevent the build-up of pests and diseases.

Growing summer celery

Summer, or self-blanching, celery is not grown in trenches, but in prepared beds or cold frames. They are basically less hardy than winter celery, and mature earlier in the season. Bring on your seedlings as already described, or buy young plants.

Although it is called 'self-blanching', summer celery will be whiter if it is shaded from sunlight. You can either grow it in the open or in a cold frame. If you are growing it in the open, plant the celery in large, square blocks, say seven rows of seven, so that the outer plants cast shade on the inner ones and blanch them. As this method only works with large quantities of celery, the average household would do better to grow a smaller crop in a cold frame.

To grow summer celery in the open, prepare the soil as in late winter, digging in manure or compost at the rate of one bucketful load per sq m (sq yd). Do not dig a trench; the plants are grown on flat beds, spaced 22 cm (9″) apart in each direction. Erect a framework around the plants, and cover it with sacking, hardboard, or black plastic sheeting to keep the outside plants blanched. As with winter celery, keep the weeds down and never let the soil dry out.

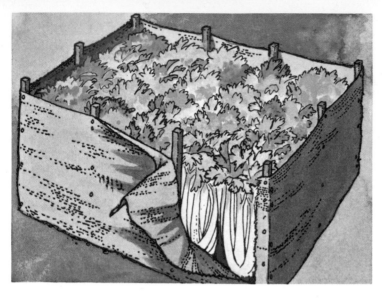

To improve the blanch of summer celery, plant it in square blocks. Erect a framework of stakes and sacking or plastic around the plants to exclude light. As rows are harvested move the frame in, to shade remaining celery.

It is easier to blanch summer celery in a cold frame, because the frame sides keep out the light. Prepare the soil well in advance, mixing in manure or garden compost. The soil mixture must be moisture-retentive, so add plenty of peat. Set the plants out in mid to late spring, depending on sowing time and weather conditions. Plant them in rows 22 cm (9″) apart covering only the roots with soil. Carefully firm the soil round the roots. Do not bury the stalks, as suckering will be encouraged. Immediately after planting water them thoroughly. Keep the frame light on for the first couple of days after planting. For a further week or so, leave the frame light open during the day, shutting it at night to keep out frost. When all danger of frost has passed, leave the frame light off.

To make full use of the cold frame, interplant the young celery with lettuces sown in mid-spring. The lettuce should be ready for harvesting in mid-summer, before the celery is ready for blanching.

Keep the frames well weeded, inspect frequently for slugs, and make sure the soil never dries out. In mid-summer, after the lettuce is lifted, dress the celery twice at ten-day intervals with a mixture of one part old soot to three parts lime.

Dust the plants with this mixture early in the morning and wash if off the next morning with a hose or watering can with a fine rose. Alternatively you can improve the blanch of summer celery, whether open grown or in a cold frame, by packing clean dry straw in between the plants to a depth of 22 cm (9″). Dust the straw with pyrethrum powder to keep the woodlice away. Loosen the straw with a fork after heavy rains, so that it does not compact around the stalks and damage them.

American Green celery
This celery is eaten green. As it is hardy and is not meant to be blanched, it is best grown in the open ground rather than a cold frame. Cultivate as for summer celery, setting the young plants outdoors in early summer, 22 cm (9″) apart and 30 cm (12″) between rows. Give cloche protection to young plants. If there is the threat of frost, give protection to all growing plants.

Harvesting and aftercare
Summer and American Green celery are harvested from late summer to mid-autumn. They should be cleared before the first autumn frosts. If the summer celery is open-grown, remember to

move the framework as you lift the plants, to keep the remaining plants blanched. Fill holes left by individual plants with clean dry straw, to prevent sunlight reaching the other celery.

Exhibition tips

Timing is a main consideration when planning to show celery at summer exhibitions, because only winter celery will grow to the standard required, and it is not normally ready until mid-autumn. For a late summer show, you must sow the seeds in mid-winter in a well-heated greenhouse. Prick out the seedlings into 12 cm (5″) deep containers, and continue growing them under glass until they can be hardened off outdoors in frames. Plant out in late spring, with cloche protection for the first fortnight. Then follow blanching and cultivation for ordinary growing.

To select celery for showing, unwrap and throw away all coverings. Tie string gently around the tops of the plants so that the stalks do not fall away. Dig them up, chopping away most of the root.

After carefully lifting the celery you wish to exhibit, wrap it in clean damp paper with roots standing in water. Do not expose the celery to light, or it will turn green.

Right before the show, lay the celery out on a table, removing the temporary tie from the top. Also remove any damaged or unwanted stalks and leaves. Trim the roots back to the hard base, leaving a pointed shaped piece at the butt. Then hold it upside down and wash with a strong spray of water from a tap or hose until it is free of all soil. Never scrub celery. Tie around the celery where the foliage joins the stalks and wrap again.

A single dish should contain three heads of celery, exhibited so the heads lie flat on the bench. If the celery is entered as part of a collection of vegetables, then six heads of celery are shown.

The judges will look for large solid heads without any coarseness or flower stems. The leaf stalks should be thick, well-balanced, clean and brittle.

Pests & Diseases

Celery fly: this is the most serious pest likely to attack celery. The insect reproduces twice, and sometimes three times a year: a first brood appears in mid or late spring, again in mid and late summer, and some years a third time in early and mid-autumn. The flies, which are 5 mm ($\frac{1}{4}$″) long, lay eggs on the leaves; the emerging maggots tunnel through the leaves causing blisters. Eventually the whole leaf shrivels and dies. If a plant loses too many leaves, it cannot grow properly and the sticks will be stunted and bitter.

Before planting out, check all plants carefully for blistered leaves; remove and burn any you find. Never leave them on the ground or put them on the compost heap. To deter the flies from laying eggs on the leaves, dust very lightly once a week with a mixture of three parts soot to one part lime. Alternative methods are to spray occasionally with derris or hang paraffin-soaked cloth near the celery. If the leaves are attacked, spray with malathion, as advised by the manufacturers, to kill the maggots, or crush them in their burrows between finger and thumb.

Celery beetle: these metallic blue oval beetles are 3 mm (1″) long and attack celery crops in mid and late summer. Swarms of them may settle on the plants; they eat the leaves first and then the hearts. Apply derris dust as soon as the beetles are seen.

Carrot fly larvae: these small yellowish maggots will occasionally attack celery roots, causing the plants to wilt and die. They are particularly active on light soils and in dry weather. In early summer the adult flies lay eggs on the soil near the plants; the emerging legless, colourless grubs tunnel through the soil into the roots. A second generation of carrot flies occasionally appears in late summer. As a preventive measure, treat seeds with a dressing containing g-HCH (BHC), or water a trichlorphon solution into the soil near the plants. Mulch the beds with grass mowings, as this tends to repel the flies.

Slugs: these common garden pests may feed on the leaf stalks if the celery is not properly earthed-up. Eventually, considerable damage may be done to the heart, and the celery may be ruined for eating or exhibition. They feed at night, leaving silvery slime trails behind them; during the day they hide in dark plant debris, under pots or boxes.

Apply metaldehyde spray to the soil and plants or bran mixed with Meta fuel, repeating if necessary. An alternative method is a 10 cm (4″) wide strip of Jeye peat around the base of the plant. Proprietary slug baits are more effective; the most effective method is to strip away all cover once a week, remove and destroy any slugs, and apply metaldehyde to the soil before replacing the cover.

Celery leaf spot: this is the most serious fungal disease. It is prevalent in wet summers and can spread rapidly by means of spores. It is seen on the leaves and sometimes the stalks as small brown spots with little black fruiting bodies developing eventually. The disease is seed-born; the best precaution is to buy seed advertized as 'thiram-treated' or 'hot-water-treated'. But remember that these treatments are only a precaution, not necessarily a guarantee that the disease will not occur.

If an attack develops, spray seedlings and young plants with benomyl, Bordeaux mixture or a fungicidal compound containing copper. Remove and destroy all infected leaves as soon as you see them. Give the plants an extra application of potash-high fertilizer to avoid soft growth, which is particularly susceptible. Where the attack is very bad, disinfect the frames with a 2% formalin solution.

Celery heart rot: this is due to a bacteria which can turn the centre of the plant into a soft, brown, slimy mess which frequently extends up the stalks. The bacteria can only enter the plant through wounds, such as those caused by slugs, careless cultivation, or frost. Keep the plants carefully earthed-up, doing so when the soil is friable and dry. Apply copper lime dust at the same time as a precaution. In severe weather protect the foliage, as the rot sometimes enters from the top of the plant and works its way down. Another precaution is to change the site for planting celery every four or five years, as the bacteria builds up in the soil. Make sure slugs are controlled, as they are often a cause of the primary wound that allows the bacteria to enter.

Boron deficiency: if your celery is stunted, with yellowing, withered leaves and dark cracks in the stalks, it is probably suffering from boron de-

Damage to the leaves of celery caused by the leaf-mining caterpillar of the celery fly.

Damage caused by slugs feeding on the stalks of celery. Control with slug baits or traps.

GUIDE TO CELERY TROUBLES

Symptom	Probable cause
Leaves develop blisters, then shrivel and die	Celery fly
Leaves and stalks eaten	Celery beetle
Roots eaten, plants wilt and die	Carrot fly larvae
Leaf stalks eaten, silvery slime around plants	Slugs
Small brown spots with black fruiting bodies on leaves	Celery leaf spot
Centre of plants brown, slimy, rotten	Celery heart rot
Celery stunted, yellow withered leaves, dark cracks in stalks	Boron deficiency
Young plants, seedlings die; roots discoloured reddish brown	Damping off
Plants stunted, leaves mottled, distorted	Arabis mosaic virus
Celery bolts, stalks split and frothy	Nitrogen excess

ficiency. To correct, step up feeding with organic mater; seaweed is particularly good.

Damping off: young plants and seedlings will wilt and die when infected with damping off fungus. The roots are usually discoloured reddish-brown. Overcrowded seedlings, or those growing in too wet soil or very high temperatures are particularly susceptible. Seeds prepared with a thiram or captan dressing are less susceptible. If seedlings are attacked, spray with a Cheshunt compound, captan or zineb.

Virus diseases: there are several virus diseases which affect celery, including cucumber mosaic virus and arabis mosaic virus. Yellowing, mottling or chlorosis of the leaves and stunting of the plants are symptoms of virus infections. Cucumber mosaic virus can be transmitted from cucumbers, spinach and marrows, so do not plant celery too close to them. Arabis mosaic virus is transmitted by eelworm, so avoid planting in eelworm-infested soil.

Nitrogen excess: if there is an excess of nitrogen in the soil the celery will bolt and stalks split. Correct this by applying 45 g ($1\frac{1}{2}$ oz) of superphosphate and 15 g ($\frac{1}{2}$ oz) sulphate of potash per sq m (sq yd) or give less organic matter.

Varieties

Winter
Giant Pink—Unrivalled Pink: pale pink colour, excellent flavour; solid sticks of extreme length, good for exhibition and for the table.

Giant Red: reliable keeping quality, solid stem of dark red colour, robust grower.

Superb Pink: good for exhibition work, blanches easily and quickly, crispy texture.

Giant White-Solid White: large solid, good for table use from mid-autumn to mid-winter, recommended for exhibition work.

Prizetaker White: excellent for table and exhibition; solid, crisp stems.

Summer
Golden Self-Blanching: dwarf variety, very early cropper, ready for use in late summer; tender stringless heart and stems.

Green
American Green (Green snap): pale green stems, crisp excellent flavour; starts cropping in mid-autumn; blanching is not necessary.

Chicory

Cichorium intybus (fam. *Compositae*)
Perennial, grown as an **annual**
Sowing to harvesting time: 26-29 weeks from sowing to lifting the roots, which are then stored and forced at intervals during winter and spring.
Size: leaves grow to a height of 25-30 cm (10-12″) in the first year, when harvested green; chicons (blanched shoots) 12.5-23 cm (5-9″) long.
Yield: 12-15 plants per 3 m (10′) row; each yielding 125 g (4 oz).

A fresh, crispy vegetable harvested in winter and early spring, chicory is becoming increasingly popular as an unusual, easy-to-grow, and delicious crop. Its blanched creamy white, tightly packed shoots, called 'chicons', are a real delicacy, and are available to the home grower for very little outlay in time or money. Occasionally, you can buy this vegetable from luxury food shops, but only at prohibitive prices. However, if you grow chicory, for the cost of a packet of seeds you can have heavy crops of fat chicons over a period of several months, at a time of the year when fresh vegetables are especially appreciated.

Although it is most widely known for its blanched chicons, chicory is harvested in a variety of ways, from summer onwards. At first, its unblanched green leaves, which resemble those of a dandelion, are picked and either used fresh in salads or cooked and eaten like spinach. In autumn the roots are lifted and stored for forcing chicons through the winter. Lastly, the roots of some varieties can be cut up, roasted, and ground for use as a coffee substitute, or blended with coffee to give a pleasantly bitter taste to the drink. In these days, with coffee so expensive, growing crops of chicory root for this purpose can be a real money-saver. Usually varieties which are grown for their roots have less tasty leaves than those grown for chicons, but there is one variety, *Belgian Witloof,* which can be used both as a vegetable and as a coffee substitute.

Sugar Loaf chicory is a third, and quite distinct, variety. In autumn it produces a very close head of inwardly curled leaves, a bit like a Chinese cabbage or pale cos lettuce in appearance. Because it can stand a moderate degree of frost, it is a valuable asset to the winter vegetable garden. It makes a very pleasant salad at a time when lettuce has to either be grown in artificially heated conditions or bought from the shops at top winter prices.

The chicory plant is a hardy perennial, and its bright blue, daisy-like flowers can often be seen in the countryside, particularly on chalky soils. Do not, however, dig up wild chicory and attempt to blanch it or use the roots for essence of chicory; it is a poor substitute for a named variety, and is bound to give disappointing results.

Many people are put off by the fact that blanching is necessary before chicons can be produced. This is not at all difficult, and can be done in very little space. A bit of room in an airing cupboard, attic or warm cellar is all you need. Alternatively, under the greenhouse staging is another out-of-the-way place which can be put to good use. Once the roots have been prepared and packed into boxes or pots (both very simple operations) there is nothing left to do but harvest the chicons a few weeks later.

Suitable site and soil

An open site with not too much shade is ideal; make sure it is well away from overhanging trees. The best soil for growing chicory is a light but reasonably fertile one, which is at least 60 cm (2′) deep. Avoid badly drained soils, and shallow or stony ones, which cause the roots to fork. During the autumn before sowing the following spring, double dig the soil, working in plenty of well-rotted manure or garden compost, so that it is completely absorbed during winter. Soil which has been manured for a previous crop will only need light forking over before planting.

Chicory is found growing wild on chalky soils, and prefers an alkaline soil. If your soil is acid, work in carbonate of lime (chalk) a week or two before sowing; the rate will depend on the pH of your soil.

Sowing

Dormant chicory roots are not widely available commercially, so you will probably have to raise plants from seed. This is not at all difficult, if you wait until the end of late spring before sowing. Seeds sown earlier than this will form very big roots by the time they are lifted the following autumn or winter. These large roots are more liable to bolt,

1. In the autumn before sowing, double-dig the soil; work in plenty of well-rotted manure or compost.

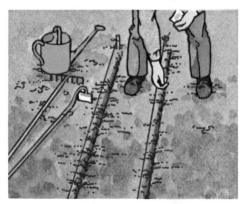

2. At the end of late spring, sow seeds thinly, in drills 1.5 cm (½″) deep, and 30-38 cm (12-18″) apart.

3. As soon as the seedlings are large enough to handle, thin them to 23-25 cm (9-10″) apart.

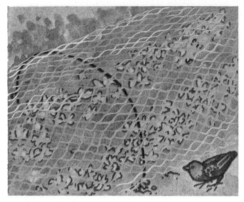

1. Birds find seedlings of *Sugar Loaf* **chicory attractive; protect seed rows with netting if necessary.**

2. Chicory is deep-rooted, so water the growing plants only if there is a severe drought.

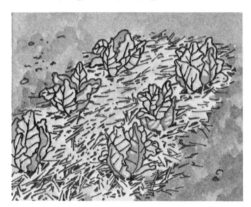

3. Mulch with clean dry straw in mid-summer to keep weeds down and also conserve soil moisture.

4. Occasionally, plants will attempt to flower; if this happens, cut out flowering stems at ground level.

or go to seed, without producing chicons. If they do not bolt, they tend to form several small chicons instead of single, large, tight ones.

Before sowing, rake the soil surface to a fine tilth. Make the drills 1.5 cm ($\frac{1}{2}''$) deep, and 30-38 cm (12-15″) apart. If the soil is dry, flood the drills a couple of times with plenty of water. Sow the seeds thinly and firm the soil over the drills 25 cm (9–10″) apart. Varieties such as *Sugar Loaf* should be started in early or mid-summer, so they will be ready when few lettuces are around.

Chicory flower

PREPARATION FOR FORCING

1. Lift the roots from early autumn onwards; only keep those with a crown diameter of 2.5-5 cm (1-2").

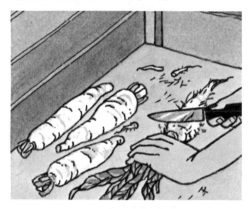

2. For storing in boxes. trim back foliage to within 2.5 cm (1") of crown and remove all side roots.

3. Pack roots horizontally in boxes containing moist sand, and store in a frost-free shed or cellar.

Cultivation

Little cultivation is needed: water in severe droughts and hoe if weeds become a problem.

Alternatively, mulch with clean, dry straw in mid-summer, to keep weeds down.

You may find the occasional plant attempting to flower. If this happens, cut out the flowering stems at ground level.

The *Sugar Loaf* variety is sometimes troubled, in the seedling stages, by attack from birds, and some netting may be necessary. Once the plants get going, the birds find them less attractive, and they are usually left alone.

Unblanched salading

A bonus crop may be taken from some varieties by cooking the leaves like spinach, or using them fresh as green salading. During the summer, either take a few leaves from a number of plants, in order not to weaken any one of them, or reserve certain plants for this purpose.

Sugar Loaf chicory will form tightly packed white hearts in autumn, and may be cut for salad as required. Cut off the heart with a sharp knife. Alternatively, pull up the plant and trim it afterwards. The roots can be put on the compost heap, as this variety does not blanch at all well.

Preparation for forcing

Chicory roots are normally lifted in autumn and either stored in boxes indoors, or heeled in the ground until they are needed for forcing. Forcing can begin in early autumn for chicons before Christmas, and can continue through late winter—*Normato* is the best variety for early forcing. Some people leave the roots in the soil, undisturbed, until needed, but in mild weather the roots may begin sprouting prematurely.

When lifting, remember that the quality of the chicons produced is directly related to the quality of the roots. Select only strong-growing, healthy roots and consign the rest to the

207

Brian Furner

These healthy, strong-growing roots have been lifted for forcing. Roots with a crown diameter of less than 2.5 cm (1″) tend to produce poor chicons. Those with a crown diameter larger than 5 cm (2″), on the other hand, produce several small chicons instead of one large one.

compost heap. Roots with a crown diameter of 2.5-5 cm (1-2″) are best. Any roots you leave in the soil will complete their perennial life cycle and produce flowering stems the following spring. This is only useful if you plan to save seed; otherwise, clear the site completely of all chicory roots so it can be used for another crop.

If you are heeling in the roots, lift them from early to late autumn. Pack them tightly into a deep trench, and cover the plants with enough soil or clean straw to keep the frost off. You need not trim the roots or foliage at this

stage, and heeling in should be a fairly quick operation. Dig up a few roots at a time, as you need them, from mid-autumn through early spring. Cut off the foliage to within 2.5 cm (1″) of the crown. Leave them in a frost proof shed for a week or so, to allow them to dry out. Then trim the root back to 20 cm (8″) and cut off all side roots with a sharp knife, to prepare them finally for forcing.

If you have nowhere in your garden to heel the plants in, store them in boxes. Lift and select the roots as for heeling in; late autumn is the best time to do this. Prepare them completely by trimming

1. A month before the chicons are needed, fill pots with damp sand, moist peat, potting compost or soil.

2. Put the prepared roots in vertically, 5-7.5 cm (2-3") apart so that crowns are 2.5 cm (1") below soil surface.

3. Invert another pot over the roots to keep the light out; remember to plug the drainage hole with a cork.

4. Begin inspecting pots a month later; the chicons are ready for harvesting when 12.5 cm (5") tall.

5. Pull up the root and cut off the chicon afterwards; cut as close to the crown as possible.

back the foliage and removing all sideshoots. Pack the roots horizontally in boxes containing moist sand; the moisture prevents them drying out. They can be packed quite close together. Store the boxes in a cool, dry place. Temperature is most important during storage, because if it is too warm the roots may start producing shoots. On the other hand, if it is frosty the roots may be killed; ideally, the temperature should be a couple of degrees above freezing.

Forcing

About a month before the first chicons are required for the table, take out as

1. Chicons can be forced in boxes under greenhouse staging; keep out light with black polythene sheeting.

2. You can expose the crown and cut the chicon off in situ; the root will then produce a second, smaller crop.

many roots as you need; each root normally produces one chicon. For a continuous supply, lift a few roots every week or fortnight. Lifting all your roots at once will lead to a glut of chicory.

Any container which is reasonably light proof will do, provided it is deep enough to take the roots comfortably. You can use barrels, large flowerpots, black plastic bags or wooden boxes. Fill them part way up with damp sand, moist peat, potting compost or light soil. Then put the roots in vertically, 5-7.5 cm (2-3″) apart, and fill up the container with the remaining compost until the crowns are about 2.5 cm (1″) below the surface.

The problem of excluding light can be solved in three ways. The containers can be placed in an absolutely dark room or shed, in which case they will not need covering. Alternatively, cover the containers with boxes, black plastic, sacking, or inverted pots to keep the light out, remembering to allow sufficient headroom for the developing chicons. Lastly, you can cover the crowns with about 17.5 cm (7″) of additional peat, sand, or compost. Although it is a more tedious method, chicons which are forced through soil or other material tend to have more tightly packed heads than those growing without covering.

You can also force chicons in the soil under the greenhouse staging. Use a dibber to make holes 5 cm (2″) apart. Fill the holes with water, and when it has drained away, put the roots in. Exclude light either by draping black plastic from the staging to the floor of the greenhouse, or by earthing up. Use 23 cm (9″) boards along the edge of the border to form a temporary retaining wall. Cover the planted roots with 17.5 cm (7″) of suitable material; sprinkle with water.

The roots need a minimum temperature of 10°C (50°F) to start producing shoots. If the surface of the sand or compost looks bone dry any time during forcing, sprinkle with warm water.

Depending on the heat, chicons should be ready for cutting from a month to six weeks after the roots have been planted. Begin inspecting the containers or greenhouse border after a month. Chicons are best when about 15-20 cm (6-8″) long; those forced without earthing up will be about 12.5 cm (5″) above the soil. The spear-like tops of those being forced under sand or compost will be slightly below the surface; a small mound of disturbed soil will appear directly above them. This mound indicates that the chicons are ready.

To harvest, pull up the root and cut off the chicon afterwards.

A second, smaller crop of chicons may

sometimes be taken by replacing the roots in the same container after cutting, but you will get far better results if you use fresh roots.

Exhibition tips

Blanched chicory is not often seen at major shows because there are few taking place when chicory is at its best, in winter and early spring. However, well grown chicory is worth a relatively large number of points and, should you have occasion to show blanched chicory, it is worth having a go. Twelve is the usual number of chicons required for collections, and nine for single dishes. They look best when shown upright on a small, spiked board. The board surface can be easily concealed with sprigs of fresh parsley after the chicons have been fixed into position. Remember, though, it is the chicory and not the parsley which is being shown, so use sparingly.

There are no special cultivation requirements for growing exhibition chicory. Proper packing and presentation is all-important though and, if badly presented, valuable show points can be lost. As close to the show time as possible, cut the heads with a sharp knife. Make sure there is a tiny bit of root attached, so the leaves hold together. Wipe away any soil or sand adhering to the outer leaves with a damp cloth. Roll the heads up, individually, in tissue paper, and lay them side by side in a shallow box. Exposure to light will cause the leaves to lose their blanch and turn green, so keep them covered until the last possible moment. Once they are on the staging, cover the chicons with brown paper until the judges appear.

Points will be awarded for long, solid, crisp chicons, which are well blanched and uniform in size and shape.

Unblanched chicory can be shown as part of a collection of 'salading', which is made up of three or four vegetables normally served cold. The chicory should be fresh, crisp, and perfectly clean, and displayed with the other vegetables in a shallow bowl or plate.

Pests and Diseases

Slugs: Chicory is singularly free from pests and diseases, and slugs are the only problem you are likely to encounter. These will attack chicory both above and below ground, feeding chiefly after dark. During the day they hide away in leaf litter, piles of debris, or anywhere where it is dark and moist. They are particularly prevalent on heavy, sour soils, or alkaline soils which are rich in humus and moisture.

The main signs of slug infestation are irregular holes in the leaves and roots, and faint, silvery slime trails nearby. Any poison put out for slugs must be repeated on several consecutive nights to be fully successful. Use baits based on methiocarb or metaldehyde, according to manufacturer's instructions.

Alternatively, trap the slugs in bits of decaying vegetable matter or wet sacks placed along the rows of chicory. Inspect the trails daily and remove and destroy all captured slugs.

Irregular holes in leaves and faint silvery slime trails are symptoms of slug infestation.

Varieties

Occasionally, named varieties of roots are available commercially, prepared for forcing, but it is more likely you will have to start your chicory from seed. Check with your local nurseryman.

Brussels Witloof: very popular and widely available; leaves can be blanched for spring salads, or eaten like spinach in summer; roots can be ground for coffee substitute.

Red Verona: variety with reddish tinge to foliage; when blanched, produces compact red head.

Sugar Loaf (Pain de Sucre): similar to a well grown cos lettuce in appearance; very useful for winter salads; will stand for long periods without going to seed.

Madgeburg: grown primarily for its root, which is dried, roasted and ground and used as a coffee substitute; blanched leaves and young shoots can also be used as vegetables.

Normato: new Dutch variety which is self-folding; excellent for early forcing, up to Christmas.

Red Verona

Brussels Witloof can be harvested in three ways. Although primarily used for forced chicons, the unblanched leaves produced in summer are good for salads, and the roots when roasted and ground can be added to coffee, or used as a coffee substitute.

Sugar Loaf

Normato

Cucumbers

Cucumus sativus (fam. *Curcubitaceae*)
Half-hardy annual
Sowing to harvesting time: 10–14 weeks
Size: plants to 2.4 m (8 ′) tall in the greenhouse, and 1.2 m (4′) in a frame or the open.
Yield: greenhouse cucumbers average 20 fruits per plant, ridge cucumbers 12-15.

Like many other salad crops, cucumber really is at its best fresh from the garden. With a little care it is not a difficult crop to grow well, either in the greenhouse or outdoors, and the relatively high yields per plant make it well worth the effort; just three plants will produce sufficient for the average family's needs.

Main types of cucumbers
There are two basic sorts of cucumbers. The first is the large, smooth skinned type up to 38cm (15″) long. This is often called the frame, or greenhouse, cucumber because in cool temperate climates this variety needs the protection of a frame or greenhouse. These plants are grown as climbers, so the fruits can hang down. The other main type is the ridge cucumber, so called because of the old market garden practice of growing the plants on ridges outdoors. Ridge cucumbers, which include gherkins for pickling, are shorter than the greenhouse type. They are about 13cm (5″) long, with knobbly or spiny skin.

The new, recently available Japanese varieties produce long, slim cucumbers, like the greenhouse varieties, but have the advantage of being hardy and can be grown outdoors. They are also heavy and reliable croppers.

Apple cucumbers are a novelty variety with round fruit the size of a small apple, a pale, yellowish-white skin and a good texture. They are generally regarded as more digestible then the green-fruited varieties. A trailing variety, they can be grown in pots or boxes in the greenhouse, in a frame, or outside in a warm, sheltered part of the garden.

Pollination
Cucumbers produce fruit in two ways. Wild and ridge cucumbers bear separate male and female flowers on the same plant, and the female flowers need to be pollinated before fruits are produced. Greenhouse cucumbers also bear male and female flowers, but the female flowers produce fruit without pollination. These unfertilized fruits are

what you should aim to produce in the greenhouse. If your greenhouse cucumbers are fertilized the fruits swell at one end, containing hard, inedible seeds. They are spoiled for exhibition use and are bitter tasting and unpleasant to eat.

Growing under glass

You can either grow your plants from seed, or buy seedlings from a reliable source. If you buy plants, choose dark green, short, stocky ones. Select ones with three or four true leaves, and the seed leaves still intact. Do not buy chilled plants from windy shopfronts. After buying the plants, stand them in the greenhouse for a few days in their pots. This will acclimatize them to new conditions; you can then transplant them successfully into the hotbed.

Sowing

If you grow cucumbers from seed, it is best to sow them in a propagator or warm greenhouse, at an absolute minimum temperature of 15°C (60°F), but 18-25°C (65-75°F) is better. Select only plump, clean seeds and throw away any which are flat, discoloured, or very small. Sow the seeds singly in clean, 6-7.5cm (2½-3″) pots, which have been filled with John Innes seed compost to within 1.5cm (½″) of the top of the pot. Place the seeds on

edge, sideways, about 1.5cm (½″) deep and lightly firm the surface. Water the compost and then cover the pots with black plastic or a sheet of glass and brown paper. Make sure the compost is thoroughly damp, because the seed casings are fairly tough. If there isn't enough moisture in the soil to penetrate the casing, the seed may not germinate. After germination, remove covering; place plants in a light position in the greenhouse. The young plants should grow rapidly and will need staking with a small, split cane. Keep the temperature at 15°C (60°F), minimum; do not let the temperature drop at night.

White roots should show on the outside of the rootball within a month of sowing; when you can see them pot the plants on into 10-12.5cm (4½-5″) pots of John Innes potting compost No. 2, or into their final positions if you can maintain a high enough temperature.

Making a hotbed

Cucumbers require a rich, moist, well drained and aerated rooting medium. Greenhouse varieties are most successfully grown in beds raised above ground level. These beds should be heated; you can use hot water pipes, ducted warm air, electric heating, or heat produced by fermenting organic matter.

RAISING GREENHOUSE CUCUMBERS

1. **Sow seeds in seed compost. Gently firm the surface and water.**

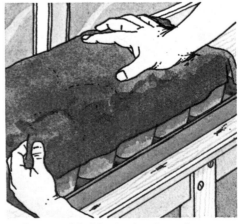

2. **Cover with black plastic or brown paper and glass, until germination.**

3. When white roots show on outside of rootball, pot on young plants.

4. When roots have filled 12 cm (5″) pots, nip out growing point.

5. When plants are 45 cm (18″) high, plant them into the hotbed.

6. Train the young plants up strings fixed to horizontal wires.

7. Damp down the greenhouse often, particularly in hot weather.

8. Top dress with 2.5 cm (1″) of potting compost to encourage roots.

The base of the bed can be soil, ash gravel, or concrete. Make sure the base is absolutely clean before building the bed.

If you plan to heat the bed by fermenting organic matter, put a layer of fresh manure on the base 45cm (1'6") wide and 15cm (6") deep. Turn this over occasionally for a few days, to allow excess nitrogen to be given off as ammonia. Another way of producing heat is to use straw. Put down a 60cm (2') thick layer of straw, firmed down. Sprinkle it with sulphate of ammonia and saturate the straw with water. On top of the straw or manure, place a 30cm (1') deep and 45cm (1'6") wide layer of good soil, or John Innes potting compost No. 2, forming it into a ridge.

Planting

When the pots are full of roots, and two to four leaves have fully expanded, nip out the growing point and plant the young cucumbers into 23cm (9") pots. When these plants have eight or nine leaves and are 37cm (1'6") high, plant them directly in the hotbed. They should be 60cm (2') apart, in one line down the centre of the bed.

Training

The cordon training of cucumbers is roughly similar to that of tomatoes. Fix three wires horizontally, the top one 2.1 m (7') high, the centre wire about 1 m (3') high and the bottom wire along the surface of the bed; all three wires should be 30cm (1') from the outside glass of the greenhouse. Next fix a vertical string for each plant, tying it to the top, centre and base wires. Tie the leading shoot to this string at regular intervals. When the plant reaches the top wire, pinch out the growing point and tie in the lead growth. Remove all side shoots up to a height of 38cm (15") above the base of each plant. If fruits form in the first or second leaf joints of the laterals, pinch out at two leaves beyond the fruit. If there are no fruits, stop the laterals at the second joint.

Continue tying the plant to the

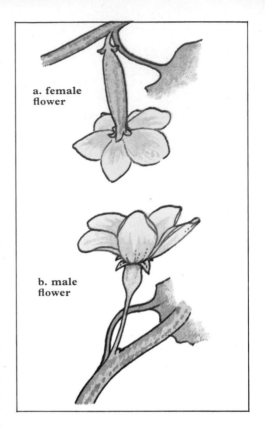

a. female flower

b. male flower

vertical string, stopping side shoots and removing all tendrils and male flowers until the top wire is reached. You can easily recognize male flowers, as they have no miniature cucumbers behind the petals. Continue removing the male flowers until the last fruits of the season are swelling. Remove any cucumbers which start to develop on the main stem.

Care and development

Cucumbers must be given plenty of moisture and warmth at all times, but particularly in hot weather. If you allow them to dry out at all, wilting plants, flabby fruits, pests and diseases will follow. The atmosphere in the greenhouse should be very humid. Damp down two or three times a day, always using water which is the same temperature as the greenhouse. Use a rotary spinkler attachment to a hose, a syringe, or a watering can with a rose spray to moisten the floors, walls, staging and

Do not remove any flowers from ridge varieties; pollination is essential to produce fruit.

pots, as well as the plants. When the temperature in the greenhouse rises above 24°C (75°F), you should provide ventilation, to keep the air circulating around the plants.

It is difficult to lay down hard and fast rules concerning feeding. It is generally considered best to apply a high nitrogen feed when the fruits start to swell; continue feeding twice weekly.

Top dress the beds with a 2.5cm (1″) layer of John Innes No. 2 potting compost once a month. This helps nourish the surface roots and also encourages new adventitious, or extra, roots to form at the base of the stem. The cucumber's thick coarse rooting system is particularly vulnerable to infection by fungus and bacteria, and may rot partway through the cropping season, so the continual production of healthy new roots is very important.

You must remember to remove the male flowers every four days, picking them off by hand. It is also a good idea to fix fine gauze to any ventilation openings in the greenhouse to exclude bees and flies which may enter and pollinate the female flowers. There are 'all female' varieties on the market; these produce very few male flowers and are capable of extremely high yields. *Femspot, Femden,* and *Femina* are some examples.

Growing cucumbers in frames

Where a greenhouse is not available, cucumbers can be grown successfully in a cold frame. The frame should have a stout wooden, concrete or brick base to retain warmth. Raise the seedlings as for greenhouse cultivation. In late spring place the young cucumber plants in the centre of the frame on a hotbed, as described earlier. If you have no hotbed, delay planting until early summer. Keep the frame closed, except for occasional ventilation on warm days, but when the weather is very warm leave the frame light off all day. Remember to replace it at night, when the temperature drops.

Pinch out the growing tips when four or five leaves have formed on each plant. Shortly afterwards, shoots will be produced in the axils (joints) of these leaves. Select the four strongest shoots and train one towards each corner of the frame. Carry out watering, feeding, and pinching out side shoots as described above. As the fruits develop, place a sheet of glass or piece of slate under the fruits, to keep them from becoming soiled or discoloured. Remember to remove any male flowers. Shade the plants from strong sunlight to prevent scorching.

Growing outdoors

Ridge cucumbers will grow and crop under lower temperatures and drier atmospheric conditions than the greenhouse varieties. In a mild climate you can sow the seeds directly outdoors, or under cloches in a sunny, sheltered position.

Cucumbers will grow in any well-drained soil, as long as it is not too acid. Dig in a generous helping of garden compost, well-rotted manure, or leaf mould 30cm (1') deep and the same width. Cover this manure with the excavated soil, which is then moulded up into a low, flat-topped ridge. This allows the water to drain away from the main stem; although the roots like a lot of moisture, stem canker may set in if the base of the stems get wet. If you are having more than one ridge, leave a good 1.2m (4') between them.

If your soil is very light, the ridge system will not work because enough moisture will not reach the roots. A good alternate method is to dig the organic matter into holes 90cm (3') apart and 30cm (1') deep by 60cm (2') square. Over this place a 10cm (4") layer of John Innes potting compost No. 3, making sure it is flush with the level of the surrounding ground. Use the soil which has been excavated from the hole to form a low mound on the north side of the plant stem. This acts as a shelter. Lightly fork in a general fertilizer at the rate of 60g per sq metre (2 oz per sq yd) two weeks

1. Dig compost or manure into trench and cover with soil ridge.

2. For light dry soil, dig in manure and plant cucumbers on flat.

3. Sow groups of 3 seeds 90 cm (3') apart and 2.5 cm (1") deep.

POT-RAISED SEEDLINGS

1. Before planting out, form a hole in the soil using an empty pot.

2. To remove plant from pot, up-end the pot and tap out on a table edge.

3. Put plant into preformed hole and water in with tepid water.

before planting and again when the plants are beginning to grow well.

Sow the seed in the open in late spring or early summer, as soon as the soil has warmed up, or two or three weeks earlier under cloches. Sow a group of three seeds, point downwards, on each prepared trench, 2.5cm deep (1″), or 90cm (3′) apart on the long ridges. Keep the seedlings covered with a cloche or jam jar until they are established. Then select the strongest of the three and discard the others. Never transplant seedlings sown in the open.

If you plant out seedlings sown in the greenhouse, harden the seedlings off first so they can withstand the lower temperatures.

Because cucumber roots are delicate, there is a special method of transplanting pot-grown seedlings to the open ground. First, plant an empty pot of the same size the cucumber is growing in. Firm the soil around the empty pot, and remove it with a slight twist. Now turn the cucumber plant out of its pot into the preformed cavity. Push the surrounding soil into contact with the rootball. Water it well with tepid water.

Remove the growing tips when the plants have produced six leaves. Train out the resulting side shoots, evenly spaced, stopping those which have produced fruit at the seventh leaf, and stopping further shoots if the plant needs restraining. This practice encourages the plants to devote more energy and nourishment to the swelling fruits and less to unproductive vegetative growth.

Do not remove the male flowers, as the female flowers must be fertilized before the fruits will develop. Insects usually pollinate the flowers; alternatively, you can hand pollinate the female flowers with the male flowers. Remove the male flower by its stem and carefully take off the petals. Then shake the powdery central core into the centre of the fully open female flower.

Water the plants frequently in dry weather, being very careful to keep water off the base of the main stem. Spray both

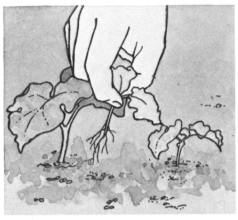

1. If directly sown, thin to one plant per group when first leaves appear.

2. Keep the plants well watered if the weather is dry.

3. Nip off the ends of side shoots one leaf beyond the young fruit.

4. To pollinate female flower brush with the anthers of a male flower.

5. Protect cucumbers from soil by placing a pane of glass under them.

6. Harvest the ridge cucumbers when they are about 12 cm (5") long.

Greenhouse cucumbers ready for harvesting; plants should crop from early summer onwards.

sides of the foliage with tepid water on dry evenings to keep red spider mite away. Feed the plants as for greenhouse varieties, first when the fruits begin to swell, and again at fortnightly intervals. Whenever fine white roots appear on the surface, cover them with a 5cm (2″) layer of moist compost, pressed firmly down.

The outdoor Japanese varieties need supporting frames on which to grow. Buy 2.2m (7′6″) poles and insert them so they are 1.8m (6′) above the ground and 1.8m (6′) apart. Run wires between them and attach netting with a 20cm (8″)

mesh. At each end of the row, use much stouter posts, with straining wires to pegs in the ground for lateral stability. Plant the cucumbers 30cm (1′) apart. Train the plants upwards, pinching out the lead growth when they reach the top of the net. Stop the side shoots as described for ridge varieties.

Harvesting

Greenhouse cucumbers will start to crop in late spring or early summer, and fruits should be cut when about 30-37cm (1′-1′3″) long. Cropping should continue until autumn. Ridge cucumbers sown under cloches will begin to crop in late summer, or early autumn if they have been sown in the open ground. Outdoor cropping will continue until the first frosts, when the plants will be killed. Harvest the cucumbers when they are young and crisp; old fruits go to seed and if left on the plant cause further fruit production to cease. If you have a bumper crop, pickle them if they are the ridge variety, or give the extra cucumbers to friends or neighbours. Cucumbers are at their best when freshly picked; they do not store vell.

Exhibition tips

The judges will look for straight fruits of uniform thickness, with short necks and noses. Cut the fruits early in the morning or late in the evening when they are fully charged with water. They are at their best when the two sides are approximately parallel and straight. A pointed cucumber is not yet ripe; a misshapen yellow one will not win prizes.

Cucumbers are usually shown in pairs, when between 30cm (1′) and 37cm (15″) long. Cut the fruit with a length of stem; it can then be handled by the stem and the bloom will not be damaged. The flower should still be on the end; the fruit should be young, crisp and tender.

If the fruits you intend to show are at their best a few days before the exhibition, cut them off the vine, and place them stem downwards in a jar of water. Change the water every day.

Pests & Diseases

The warm, moist conditions in which cucumbers flourish provide the perfect environment for bacterial and fungal infections. Since many of these are encouraged by improper watering and ventilating, make sure you are cultivating the plants properly. Be on the lookout for any sign of infection and act quickly to control it, because disease will spread rapidly in close greenhouse or frame conditions. When you use an insecticide on cucumbers, be sure to choose one that will not damage the plants; the *Curcubitaceae* family are sensitive to some chemicals sprays.

Red spider mite: this pest causes the leaves to turn yellow; if severely infected, the plant will become bronze

GUIDE TO CUCUMBER TROUBLES	
Symptoms	Probable causes
Leaves turn yellow; silky webs on plant	Red spider mite
Small green insects; leaves turn yellow	Greenfly
Clouds of minute insects	Whitefly
Holes in stems of young plants, silvery slime	Slugs
Holes in leaves and surface of young fruit, grey, hard shelled creatures	Woodlice
Leaves discoloured, plant collapses	Root knot eelworm
Grey fluffy growth on stems fruit and leaves	Botrytis
Leaves wilt, stem becomes dark, plant dies	Collar rot
Leaves mottled yellow; plant wilts, dies	Mosiac virus
Leaves turn yellow from base upwards	Verticillium wilt
Sunken, oozing spots on fruit	Gummosis
Wet, dark wounds on stems, leaves and fruits	Sclerotinia disease

Adult whiteflies on the underside of the leaves of cucumber foliage.

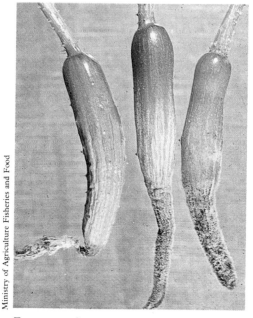

Furry growths on young cucumbers produced by a severe attack of botrytis.

coloured, wilt and collapse. Another sign of red spider mite is the appearance of silky webs around the leaves and stems. The best preventative action is to maintain damp conditions in the greenhouse or outdoors. The best control is to spray the infected plants with derris or soft soap.

Greenfly: these small green insects are usually found in colonies on or near the growing points and under the leaves, which may turn yellow green and wither. Control greenfly by smokes or sprays of malathion or nicotine. Use the nicotine with care, as overuse may blanch the leaves; if this happens, cut off the bleached leaves immediately and spray with a nicotine soap wash.

Whitefly: if, when you disturb the leaves of cucumber plants, clouds of minute insects appear, then the plants are infested with whitefly. These insects are very destructive and weakening; they feed chiefly on the sap and excrete honeydew which encourages the growth of sooty mould. Spray with malathion as soon as whiteflies are seen.

Slugs: slug damage can usually be spotted by holes in the stems of young plants and the presence of silvery slime trails. Proprietary pellets are the most effective control.

Woodlice: these are grey, minute armadillo-shaped creatures which roll up into small balls when touched. They eat holes in the leaves and may also attack the surface of young fruits. Woodlice are most likely to occur in old greenhouses or frames; spray or dust around the roots of infected plants with BHC (HCH).

Root knot eelworm: plants indoors and outdoors may be attacked by these microscopic pests which invade the roots. Leaves may become discoloured; in bad cases the whole plant may collapse. Although some plants may survive mild infections, it is best to dig up and burn any diseased plant. There is no absolutely effective control, but if one plant is infected, it is a good idea to treat the soil with a sterilant such as formaldehyde before growing susceptible crops in the same place.

Botrytis: this grey fluffy growth on the stems, fruits, and leaves is best controlled by benomyl sprays. Badly infected plants should be removed and burned, as they will never crop well.

Collar rot: this usually affects greenhouse cucumbers which are growing in

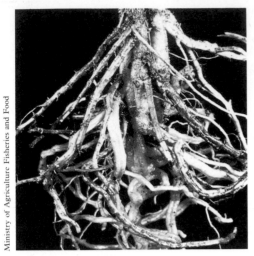

The roots of plants infected with collar rot are swollen, discoloured and distorted.

Leaves infected with cucumber mosaic virus display characteristic yellow mottling.

badly drained soil or have been over-watered. The plants are attacked by soil-borne organisms at or slightly above ground level. The leaves wilt, the stems become dark and the plants die. Preventive measures of raised beds, well-aerated soil, and good hygiene are useful. Plants which are not too badly damaged may be saved by removing all decaying tissue and dusting the infected areas with captan. Then raise the level of the soil 3.5cm (1½″) around the stem to encourage the growth of new adventitious roots. In 10 days top dress again. Pull out and destroy badly infected plants; treat the soil around adjacent plants with benomyl or captan.

Mosaic virus: the leaves of plants infected with mosaic virus become yellow and mottled; the whole plant then rapidly wilts, shrivels up and dies. As there is no effective control for the virus, and it is carried by greenfly, the best prevention is to control greenfly.

Verticillium wilt: this soil-borne fungus causes the leaves to turn yellow from the base upwards. The disease is more liable to occur in cold wet conditions. It usually attacks the roots of young plants; older plants are vulnerable if they have open wounds. Eventually the diseased plants wilt, and should be dug up and burned. Apply Cheshunt compound to the soil before replanting.

Gummosis of cucumber: this fungus disease affects plants grown in a greenhouse or frame; it spreads quickly in cold, wet conditions. Infected fruits develop sunken spots which ooze a gummy liquid; this spot is eventually covered with dark spores. Occasionally small spots appear on the stems or leaves. Keeping the greenhouse or frame warm and well ventilated is a good preventive measure. Control gummosis by spraying with zineb or captan; destroy all diseased fruits. Disinfect the greenhouse or frame before replanting.

Sclerotinia disease: wet, dark wounds appear on the stem, leaves and fruits, followed by fluffy, white growths with black central areas. Dig up and burn any infected plants.

Anthracnose: the leaves will have small pale patches which quickly turn brown and grow bigger until the whole leaf dies; stems are sometimes affected. Remove and destroy badly infected plants. Spray the remaining plants with 1 part lime sulphur to 60 parts water with a spreading agent. Make sure that the greenhouse is well ventilated, and spray with formalin when it is empty or between crops.

Telegraph

Femspot

Varieties

Greenhouse

Telegraph Improved: reliable cropper for cold or heated greenhouses, useful for exhibition; uniform fruit of deep green colour; fine quality.

Butcher's Disease Resisting: medium-sized, slightly ribbed fruit; heavy cropper; highly resistant to leaf spot; easy to grow.

Conqueror: dark green fruits; very prolific; suitable for unheated greenhouse or frame in northern areas.

Femden: F_1 hybrid produces mainly female flowers; prolific cropper; disease resistant.

Topsy: F_1 hybrid female flowering type; sweet juicy fruits 30-40cm (12″-16″) long.

Femspot: F_1 hybrid; female flowering variety; early cropper; fruits 35cm (14″) long; disease resistant.

Femina: produces mainly female flowers; heavy yield; disease resistant.

Topnotch: F_1 hybrid; vigorous grower; enormous crops; suitable for greenhouse or frame.

Ridge varieties

Marion: Virus-resistant; fruits no tendency to bitterness; 22 cm (9″) long.

Greenline: fruits retain colour over long period; especially recommended for growing under cloches.

Burpee Hybrid: F_1 hybrid; vigorous; prolific; extra large, dark green fruit; crisp, white flesh.

Perfection: prolific cropper; fruits 12–15 cm (5 6″) crops well into autumn.

Patio-Pik: early F_1 hybrid of bushy, prolific habit; produces up to 30 fruits per plant.

Baton Vert: F. Hybrid; very early cropper; long, slender; good flavour.

Burpless Tasty Green: fruits low in acid; dark green, smooth-skinned, small white spines; 20-25cm (8-10″) long; can be sown on open ground; resistant to heat, and to powdery and downy mildew.

Nadir: F_1 hybrid; long fruited; prolific habit; outstanding variety.

Venlo Pickling: grown for gherkins for pickling; heavy consistent cropper; gather fruits when young and tender.

Japanese varieties

Kyoto: straight fruits, containing very few seeds; 5cm (2″) in diameter, 37cm (15″) long.

Chinese Long Green: smooth skinned; up to 60cm (2′) long; keeps well after harvesting.

Kaga: up to 35 cm (15″) long; early cropper; dark green with yellow stripes.

Novelty variety

Apple-Shaped: produces pale green, round fruit; prolific cropper of good flavour.

225

Lettuce

Lactuca sativa (fam. *Compositae*)
Half-hardy annual.
Sowing to harvesting time: 8-14 weeks
Size: Cabbage and American types between 15-38 cm
(6-15") in diameter; cos types between 20-40 cm
(8-16") tall.
Yield: 9-12 heads, each weighing about 224-340 g (8-12 oz),
per 3 m (10') row.

The most popular salad vegetable, lettuce is easily grown and, with careful planning, you can have a high all-year-round yield. Tender young lettuce, freshly cut, has an unbeatable flavour and the crop is a must for every kitchen garden.

There are three main types of lettuce: cabbage varieties, which are hearted and look like cabbages, taller and crisper cos types, and the frizzy-headed loose-leaf American lettuces. Cabbage lettuces can be further divided into butterheads, with tender, butter-coloured hearts, and crispheads, which are crisper and have hearts that blanch to white. The hearts of cos lettuce are also blanched—many varieties of cos are now self-blanching with leaves which fold in by themselves. American varieties are harvested by picking single leaves, rather than by cutting the whole plant.

Lettuce has been much hybridized since the early sixties, and there are all sorts of varieties now available for growing at particular periods of the year. There are also several new dwarf lettuces available for the small garden or for container growing. Before buying your lettuce seed, study the catalogues carefully. Most catalogues specify which varieties are suitable for which season. When growing out of season, in particular, it is important to choose varieties which have been bred specially for that particular purpose, such as early spring cropping or heated greenhouse winter cropping.

Preparing the soil

Lettuces will grow well on almost any garden soil, although they prefer soil that is rich and light, well drained and dug. Clays which are well broken down produce very good plants, as will sandy or gravelly soils which have been bulked with organic matter. The site should have its humus content renewed every year with an application of farmyard manure, rich compost or green manure worked into the ground at a rate of 6 kg per sq m (13 lb per sq yd) the autumn before a spring sowing. This will also aid in water retention, which is important because lettuces are 90 per cent water and must have very moist soil to grow

1. Lettuces like an alkaline soil, so prepare the ground prior to sowing with an application of lime.

2. For early spring sowings outdoors, prepare shallow drills and sow the seed very thinly.

3. Thin when two leaves have formed. If thinnings are to be transplanted, handle gently by one leaf only.

4. Prepare the holes before transplanting, put the seedlings in and water the ground well.

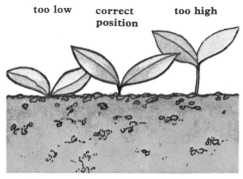

too low   correct position   too high

5. Take care to transplant the seedlings with the neck exactly level with the soil.

6. Seedlings can be put into the ground which has been covered with sheets of plastic to retain moisture.

	RECOMMENDED VARIETIES	GROWING CONDITIONS
SUMMER LETTUCE	Windermere	Sow outdoors at 2-week intervals for a long harvesting period.
	All the Year Round	Has one of the longest periods for cutting. Sow outdoors in spring or under cloches in autumn.
	Lobjoits Green Cos	Good summer cos type to grow outdoors.
	Salad bowl	Sow outdoors. Pick by pulling outer leaves.
AUTUMN LETTUCE	Winter Density	Good autumn cos for early cutting.
	Appia	Quick-maturing butterhead which can withstand a hot summer.
WINTER LETTUCE	Amanda	Must be forced in a heated greenhouse.
	Kordaat	Good for growing under glass with heat.
	Kwiek	For growing in a cold frame or greenhouse.
SPRING LETTUCE	Premier	Sow in frames or under cloches to protect over the winter.
	May Queen	Prefers a heated greenhouse, but can be successful under cloches in a mild winter.

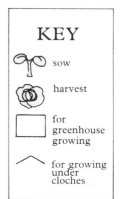

KEY

- sow
- harvest
- for greenhouse growing
- for growing under cloches

Summer lettuces grown from successional sowings. The ones on the left are ready for cutting.

Bernard Alfieri

YEAR-ROUND LETTUCE

WHEN TO SOW AND HARVEST			
SPRING early mid late	SUMMER early mid late	AUTUMN early mid late	WINTER early mid late

rapidly and form well. Lettuces also need lime (a pH of 7.5 is best), so test soil and apply lime before sowing if necessary. Poor and ill-prepared soil will produce floppy leaves and failure to heart-up.

Quick-growing lettuce is a good vegetable for intercropping between rows of other vegetables, such as tall varieties of peas, providing you have prepared the soil carefully.

Planning your sowings

Lettuces can be available for harvesting throughout the year if you make successional sowings of different varieties. Classification is by the season for harvesting, not the time of sowing, so choose your varieties, whether cabbage, cos or loose-leaf types, according to your harvesting needs.

Summer lettuce: sowing outdoors can start in early spring with the first of a succession of fortnightly sowings designed to maintain a supply of lettuces from early summer until the autumn. Choose cabbage, cos or American varieties; plant a mixture to give a varied crop. Sowing several different kinds also gives varied rates of germination and development, and extends the period for cutting.

Unfortunately, a routine of successful sowings does not guarantee an uninterrupted supply of prime lettuces. Except in a steadily favourable climate, there are times when the lettuces are checked. And when the weather is hot, the whole crop engages in a race to see which plant can bolt (run to seed prematurely) first. Bolting used to be a serious problem to lettuce growers, but

To catch crop, sow lettuces between rows of peas, preferably running north to south to avoid shading.

Lettuces are ideal for growing in cold frames: sow the seed in late winter for harvesting in spring.

Extend the period of harvesting by successional sowings. Plant some lettuces every two weeks in spring.

For late winter and spring crops sow hardy varieties in autumn and protect with cloches or tunnels.

newer varieties are less likely to bolt in high temperatures, so long as they are kept well watered.

Sow the seed fairly thinly in short shallow drills about 1.5 cm ($\frac{1}{2}''$) deep and 30 cm (1') apart. The seed should germinate in about 4-12 days, and you should thin as soon as the first pair of true leaves have formed. Aim for a spacing of one plant every 23-30 cm (9-12") depending on the size of the variety.

It is best to sow lettuces where they are to remain, as transplanting can cause a check in growth. In any case, transplanting is only satisfactory very early in the growing season, as later transplants are liable to bolt. When transplanting

lettuces, lever the plants gently out of the ground with a spatula and handle only the leaves with your finger and thumb. Lower the transplants into prepared holes, then firm them down and water them well to ensure that the rootlets make good contact with the soil. Do not plant too high or the lettuces will not heart; too low planting can cause grey mould infections of the lower leaves. The neck of the plant must be exactly at soil level.

You can give transplanted lettuces a better start by putting them in a row covered by a strip of black plastic. Secure the edges of the plastic by weighting down with stones, then make

Butterhead lettuces grown under cloches and ready for cutting. These soft, round cabbage types usually grow very quickly.

cross-shaped cuts about 30 cm (12″) apart, and transplant the lettuces in the usual way. The plastic will help retain moisture in the soil.

Autumn lettuce: choose cabbage or cos types for autumn lettuce. Sow the seed as you would for summer lettuce, in succession from mid-summer to late summer. Sow where the plants are to mature. Thin the 5-7.5 cm (2-3″) high seedlings so that you have about 23-30 cm (9-12″) between plants. Your first sowings should be ready for cutting by early autumn; the last by late autumn to early winter. However, the latest sowings may be slow to grow and may not be ready by early winter. If you protect these plants with cloches or tunnels they should withstand the winter and will certainly be ready for cutting by early spring.

Winter lettuce: if you have a heated greenhouse, you can enjoy fresh lettuces from early winter through to early spring. A well-constructed and well-designed greenhouse where you can maintain a temperature of 15°C (60°F) is a necessity. However, you should keep in mind the amount of fuel needed to maintain this temperature, and consider that in a cold winter it could prove very expensive to grow your own lettuces.

If you decide to grow winter lettuce, make successive sowings in early to mid-autumn of a cabbage variety. Sow in seed trays filled with good quality compost.

7. Weed between the young plants with a draw hoe. In addition to keeping down the weeds, this will help to discourage egg-laying insects.

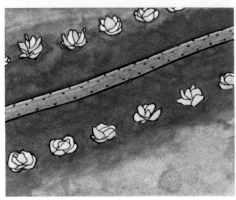

8. Lettuces need a great deal of water to grow well. Keep the soil very moist; a trickle hose is ideal because water seeps out slowly.

9. Mulch the young lettuces by applying well-rotted garden compost with a fork. This will keep down the weeds and retain moisture.

10. Slugs love sweet, tender young lettuce plants. Discourage these pests by scattering slug pellets on the ground between the rows.

11. To test for firmness, apply gentle pressure to the heart with the back of your hand.

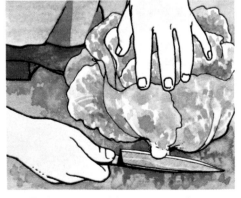

12. To harvest cabbage or cos lettuces, use a sharp knife to cut just below the lowest leaves.

Germination must take place at temperatures between 10-15°C (50-60°F). Prick out the 5 cm (2″) high seedlings into boxes and plant them in cropping position, 23-30 cm (9-12″) apart, as soon as the first pair of true leaves is fully developed. The greenhouse temperature should be kept at 15°C (60°F) for three weeks after planting, and thereafter maintained at 10-13°C (50-55°F). Maintaining humidity in the greenhouse (through controlled watering and ventilation) is also important, as the lettuces need a moist environment.

Spring lettuce: spring lettuce can be grown outdoors or under protection. Sowing outdoors is satisfactory only in areas where the winters are fairly mild, and even then you must choose hardy types. The crop will not survive on cold, heavy ground, so choose an open, sunny site with land well manured for a previous crop. Sow the seed in a seedbed in late summer, and plant out between mid and late autumn in rows 30 cm (1′) apart, allowing 23 cm (9″) between plants. Hoe the rows just before winter sets in; then leave them alone until growth restarts in early spring, when they will need the same care as spring-planted types.

Spring lettuces are generally more successful if they are protected over the winter. Follow the basic instructions above, but protect the rows with barn cloches. Thin seedlings to about 23 cm (9″) apart in early winter. When growth begins again in early spring, remove the cloches a few at a time. Cutting for the plants uncloched first should begin in mid-spring.

Care and cultivation

All lettuces require warmth, moisture and a weed-free environment with protection from garden pests. The soil must be well prepared so that it is rich enough in humus to retain moisture adequately. Give the lettuces as much water as the roots require, but do not try to hurry growth by overwatering. It may

13. If you are growing a variety of cos which is not self-blanching, blanch by tying around the middle and then around the top a week later.

14. Loose-leaf lettuces are picked by pulling the outer leaves. Pull them off gently and take them straight into the kitchen.

15. To store, pull up the whole plant and tie a plastic bag around the roots. Keep in refrigerator.

be difficult in hot weather to keep soil moist and prevent a crust from forming; overcome this by mulching with well rotted organic matter. Strips of black plastic placed on the ground close to the plants will also help to retain moisture, especially if placed down just after rain.

Hoe frequently between the rows and the plants. This will kill the weeds before their roots are big enough to compete with the crop.

If you are growing one of the varieties of cos lettuce which is not self-blanching you may want to blanch the plants to increase their crispness. About two weeks before the lettuce is ready for harvesting, apply a tie of raffia or a rubber band around the thickest part of the plant. One week later, make another tie about 15 cm (6″) further up. The harvested lettuces will be firm and crisp.

Cutting your lettuces

Harvest lettuces as soon as they are at their best and fully hearted. When the heart begins to form a point and push upwards, the plant is beginning to bolt and the quality will fall off rapidly. The lettuces should feel firm, so test for firmness by pressing with the back of your hand, not with your fingers which will bruise the plants.

Cut lettuces with a sharp knife, just above the lowest leaves, or pull out by the roots and cut them off. If the lettuces are going to be stored, it is best to pull the whole plant, enclose the roots in a plastic bag, and chill. The lettuce will keep fresh for about a week. If the roots are disease-free, put them on the compost heap.

If you are growing American lettuces, harvest these like spinach by pulling off individual leaves from the outside of the plant when they are firm, but still young and tender. The plant will continue to produce new leaves for quite a long time.

Growing in containers

If you do not have a heated greenhouse, you can grow lettuces in containers indoors for winter supplies of fresh salad. Lettuces are a good vegetable to

Loose-leaf lettuces are ideal for growing in individual pots on a sunny windowsill. Pick leaves as required.

grow in containers, as there are several dwarf varieties available. Cabbage lettuces which require a lot of space are unsuitable, so choose from the smaller varieties available or plant cos or the loose-leaf American types. Tom Thumb lettuce, a cabbage type specially bred for small gardens or containers, needs only 15 cm (6″) when mature and will grow well in 20 cm (8″) plant pots.

Sow the seeds in containers, tubs or individual pots filled with a good quality compost. Sow about 7.5 cm (3″) apart and cover with a fine layer of compost, or with compost mixed with peat. If you have the space for several containers, make successional sowings to extend the period of cutting. Thin the 5 cm (2″) high seedlings to a distance of 15 cm (6″) apart for loose-leaf varieties and 20 cm (8″) apart for cos types. If you use individual pots, sow about 3 seeds to each one, and then thin to the strongest seedling.

Keep your containers in a warm sunny position, and remember that all lettuces need a great deal of water and the soil must never be allowed to dry out.

Cut your lettuces as soon as they have hearted, or pull off mature leaves from the American types. When one plant is cut, you can replant new seed in the same pot and have a succession of lettuces.

Varieties

There are hundreds of varieties of lettuces available to the home grower, a vast selection of different types for sowing at different seasons. Consider what type of lettuce you prefer, and plan your succession of sowings according to season. Some seed merchants offer lettuce variety packs containing seeds of several types to be sown throughout the year. We have divided our list of selected varieties into cabbage, cos and loose-leaf American types, and we have indicated under each variety the best time for sowing.

Cabbage lettuces (summer and autumn varieties)

All the Year Round: butterhead; good for sowing throughout the year, but does best in spring or autumn sowings; crisp, well-flavoured lettuces.

Appia: quick-maturing, high-quality lettuces; excellent for mid-summer sowings because it is resistant to mildew.

Webb's Wonderful: one of the most consistantly popular and reliable of the crispheart types; large heads with well-flavoured crinkly leaves; slow to run to seed even in hot, dry weather.

Great Lakes: high-quality crisphead which makes large, solid hearts; slow to bolt; one of the best varieties for areas with hot summers.

Windermere: smaller, earlier, more compact version of *Great Lakes;* also slow to run to seed in hot weather; good choice for a small garden.

Tom Thumb: the smallest variety; well flavoured butterheads; needs only 15 cm (6″) when mature; ideal for small gardens, frames or containers.

Buttercrunch: popular butterhead; small, dark green heads with creamy yellow central heart; keeps better than most types.

Avondefiance: dark green butterhead for early or mid-summer sowing; resistant to mildew and root aphid.

Webb's Wonderful

Great Lakes

Tom Thumb

Ilo New!: excellent new variety which is highly disease-resistant and slow to bolt; crisp, sweet butterhead with yellow hearts; sow in succession from early spring.

Ballerina: new variety similar to Great Lakes; neat and compact crisphead; can be grown closer together than most varieties; slow to bolt.

Cabbage lettuces (winter and spring varieties)

Artic King: good for autumn sowing; small, compact heads with pale green, crumpled leaves.

Imperial Winter: extremely hardy; one of the largest varieties for autumn sowing; very reliable.

Valdor: excellent, very large winter lettuce; crisp, solid, deep green hearts; resistant to cold, wet conditions, so good for autumn sowing; new introduction.

Kordaat: one of the best varieties for greenhouse sowing; produces lettuces throughout the winter.

Kwiek: large-headed variety for greenhouse growing; sow in early autumn for crisp, well-flavoured lettuces in early winter.

May Queen: cut in early spring from early autumn greenhouse sowing; small heads; pale green leaves with slight pink tinge.

Premier: sow under glass in mid-autumn or mid-winter for transplanting outdoors in mid-spring; early variety; fairly large green heads.

Hilde: pale green, compact, smooth-leaf heads; early hearting; not prone to bolt; good for frame or outdoor sowing to crop in summer.

National Vegetables Research Station

Arctic King

Harry Smith

Amanda

Brian Furner

Hilde

Amanda: quick growing variety for greenhouse or frame; makes heavy, solid hearts.

Ramcos: new variety which is very disease-resistant; good for forcing in a cool or heated greenhouse; quick maturing; small enough for a windowbox.

Cos lettuces

Lobjoits Green Cos: very large heads;

Lobjoits Green Cos

self-folding crisp leaves over dark green hearts; suitable for spring or autumn sowing; slow to bolt.

Little Gem: dwarf, compact, very early cos; crisp, bright green leaves; sow outdoors from early spring to mid-summer; also succeeds under cloches; one of the best flavoured lettuces.

Winter Density: hardy; successful for autumn, spring or early summer sowing; dwarf and compact; very crisp with green hearts.

Lobcross: new variety to harvest in autumn; grows well in most conditions; very solid and well flavoured.

Paris White: noted for its resistance to bolting; very large cos with self-folding leaves; crisp and sweet.

Island Cos: thick and fleshy very dark green leaves; yellowish hearts.

Loose-leaf American lettuces

Salad Bowl: the best of the loose-leaf varieties; deeply curled green leaves resemble endive; large with crisp and tender leaves; does not bolt; sow outdoors from mid-spring to mid-summer; excellent for containers.

Grand Rapids: tasty non-heading lettuce for greenhouse growing; will also grow outdoors from spring or summer.

Little Gem

Salad Bowl

Pests & Diseases

Lettuces can be bothered by a number of pests and diseases and, although most of them are not serious, precautions should be taken to ensure a healthy crop.

Lettuce root aphids: lettuce root aphids can attack the roots and collars of growing plants, causing the lettuces to turn yellow, wilt and rapidly decay. Different varieties have different levels of susceptibility. Attacks are most serious in late summer, and can be a particular problem in dry weather, when the moisture content in the plants is already low. The roots appear yellow and covered with a white woolly substance. The flies will be attracted to any decaying lettuces in the area, so pull out and burn any lettuce stumps or remains of plants. Lettuce rows should be hoed regularly to destroy weeds which could act as hosts to the pests. A dressing of naphthalene at 60 g per sq m (2 oz per sq yd) or watering between the rows with diluted derris in early summer are useful precautions.

Eelworm: eelworms (nematodes) are microscopic creatures which attack the roots of lettuces, producing small knobs on them and weakening the plants severely. The lettuces wilt and die. Destroy any affected plants immediately, and do not grow lettuces on the same ground for at least five years, as the eggs can remain there dormant.

Lettuce root maggot: this maggot, also called the chrysanthemum root maggot, causes severe injury to the roots of lettuces and chrysanthemums. The flies lay their eggs in the soil near lettuces, and the small, yellowish maggots hatch out and bore into the roots, causing the plants to wilt and die. Lettuces should never be grown too close to chrysanthemums, and never on the same ground. Reduce egg-laying by dusting around the base of the lettuces with flake naphthalene at weekly in-

Plants with mottled yellow leaves and stunted growth—the symptoms of mosaic virus.

Greenfly attack lettuces in spring, checking growth and spreading diseases.

National Vegetable Research Station

Grey mould fungus causes the lettuce stem to blacken and the roots to rot away.

Ministry of Agriculture Fisheries and Food

Ministry of Agriculture Fisheries and Food

tervals in late spring and early summer. Maggots can be killed by watering with a solution of g-BHC applied according to the manufacturer's instructions. However, it is better to prevent an attack of flies than to try and deal with the maggots.

Greenfly: both young and mature lettuces are at risk from greenfly attacks. The flies swarm on young summer lettuces in mid to late spring, checking growth and preventing them from hearting. Attacks are usually worse in a dry spring, as there is no rain to wash off the flies. Older plants can also be attacked, whether grown outdoors or in a greenhouse. Prevent greenfly attacks by spraying with a non-poisonous spray, such as pyrethrum, in spring. A fumigated greenhouse should be free of aphids, but if any are seen then spray the plants. Never put infested plants on the compost heap.

Slugs: as with all leafy crops, slugs are a menace to lettuces. They eat holes through the leaves and can quickly destroy a crop. Destroy slugs with methiocarb or methaldehyde baits.

Grey mould: grey mould fungus is the most common problem a lettuce grower will encounter, and you can easily identify it by the grey mouldy spots found on the leaves. The disease can attack plants at all stages of growth, and the result is always rapid decay. The disease usually enters the stem at soil level, often through a dead outer leaf, or through yellowing seed leaves in young plants. Carefully remove any bits of dead or dying leaves from lettuces and, if the disease appears, remove and destroy any infected plants, along with the soil from around their roots. Spraying with dichlofluanid or benomyl according to the packet instructions can be quite effective. Under glass, if grey mould has been a problem sterilize the soil six weeks before sowing by watering with a formalin solution.

Downy mildew: certain varieties of lettuces are subject to downy mildew, often seen as whitish spots on the leaves

GUIDE TO LETTUCE TROUBLES	
Symptom	Probable cause
Wilting, dying plants	Lettuce root aphids
	Eelworm
	Lettuce root maggot
Yellowing roots covered in white wool	Lettuce root maggot
Larva in seed	Lettuce seed fly
Holes in leaves	Slugs
	Ring spot
Mouldy grey spots on leaves	Grey mould
White spots on leaves	Downy mildew
	Ring spot
Brown patches on leaves	Bacterial spot
Mottled yellow leaves	Mosaic virus

of overcrowded seedlings, or on mature plants. To prevent, thin seedlings at an early stage, regulate watering and ventilation under glass. Zineb or thiram sprays applied according to the manufacturer's instructions give quite effective control.

Mosaic virus disease: greenfly spread mosaic virus disease of lettuces, which produces yellow mottled leaves and stunts the growth of plants. The infection can also be carried in the seed, so be sure your seed is certified clean. There is no cure for mosaic virus disease: burn infected plants and destroy any greenfly with pyrethrum.

Leaf spot disease: lettuces can be affected by several leaf spot diseases. Bacterial spot causes browning of the leaves along the veins and at the edges. Autumn lettuces which have been heavily manured or over-watered and those grown under glass are most often affected. Maintain a careful balance of moisture to avoid this disease.

Ring spot is a fungus disease sometimes seen in cold, damp weather. It starts as brown spots on leaves, and the spots turn white and fall out, leaving big holes. The lettuces are quickly made unusable. Good ventilation in frame or greenhouse will discourage the disease, and crop rotation will lessen attacks outdoors. Destroy infected plants.

Mushrooms

Agaricus bisporus (fam. *Agaricaceae*)
Capped fungus
Sowing to harvesting time: 4-12
weeks; the harvest then continues for
11-12 weeks longer.
Size: mushrooms up to 7.5 cm (3″) high; caps vary from
about 2.5 cm (1″) across for button mushrooms to 10 cm
(4″) across for mature ones.
Yield: at least 0.45-1.0 kg (1-2 lb) per sq m (sq yd); can be
much higher, depending on the quality of compost.

One of the most popular foods,
mushrooms are different in character,
shape, and method of cultivation from
other vegetables. They are widely grown
commercially, but mushrooms can easily
be cultivated on a smaller scale by the
home grower. Mushrooms are expensive
in the shops all through the year, and it is
much more economical to grow them
yourself, as the initial outlay is quite
small. A second point in favour of
homegrown mushrooms is that
mushrooms are at their best when
freshly picked; they quickly lose their
flavour and become tough and stale. The
best guarantee that the mushrooms are
fresh is to harvest them yourself just
before cooking. A third point is that you
can superintend the ingredients and
making of the growing medium yourself,
and so choose materials for the compost
which will ensure the same rich flavour
in your home-grown mushrooms that
the wild field mushroom has. In the
kitchen, mushrooms can be used whole
or chopped, and eaten raw in salads or
cooked by almost any method. Most of
the work in growing mushrooms is
connected with the preparation of the
special compost in which they grow;
after the compost has been prepared,
very little is needed in the way of
cultivation and care.

Botanically, mushrooms are the
fruiting bodies of the fungus *Agaricus
bisporus*. The entire growth above the
ground is edible; it consists of a white,
creamy or brownish cap on a brownish
stalk. Mushrooms change shape slightly
as they mature. Young mushrooms first
appear as white pinheads on the surface
of the mushroom bed; they develop short
stalks as the buttons, or caps, grow
larger. At this stage the caps are
spherical in shape and the gills are
covered with a membrane, or veil, which
is connected to the stalk. As the
mushroom matures, the stalk grows
longer and the cap grows larger and
begins to flatten out. The membrane
tears as the cap expands, and exposes the
brownish gills beneath.

The usual method of propagation is by
spores, which are produced in the gills
and correspond to the seeds of green
plants. Because the brownish black

Although they are cultivated differently from other vegetables, mushrooms are easy, quick, and very economical to grow. Well-established beds will crop for several months.

Grant Heilman

powdery spores are microscopic in size and difficult to germinate except under special conditions, mushrooms are normally grown from spawn. Spawn, or mycelium, is the germ tube produced by the spores; each appears as a long, thread-like white filament. The spawn absorbs food and moisture from the compost and eventually produces the fruiting bodies, or mushrooms, which are then cropped.

Cultivated mushrooms are closely related to the edible wild mushrooms (*Agaricus campestris*) found in summer and autumn in fields and meadows. A word of warning, however: there are several species of wild mushrooms which are highly poisonous, and very similar in appearance to those which are edible. Unless you are fully knowledgeable about mushrooms, and can identify them accurately, it is best not to pick wild mushrooms for eating.

Suitable sites

Mushrooms are grown commerically in purpose-built mushroom houses and artificial caves, but the home grower should be able to find a suitable site, either indoors or out, for growing smaller crops of mushrooms. The main factors in growing mushrooms

When mushrooms are harvested at a young stage, they are called 'buttons'; as they mature they expand into 'cups' and, finally, 'opens', or 'flats'.

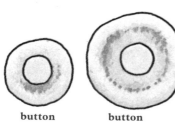

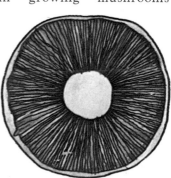

button   button   cup   open, or flat

successfully, besides suitable compost, are stable air temperature and moisture; you must select a site where these can be controlled. Indoors, you can use the floor of a cellar or shed; outdoors, they can be grown in greenhouses, cold frames or, in mild areas, in the open. Wherever they are grown, it is probably most convenient if you use boxes, other than beds, to contain the compost, remembering that boxes have the disadvantage of being wasteful of space.

If you are growing them in a shed or cellar, it must be clean, waterproof and dark. It is a good idea to disinfect old buildings before attempting to use them for mushroom growing, and dust the floor with lime as an additional precaution. It will be much easier to regulate the temperature inside a building if it is insulated; mushrooms will not grow if the temperature rises above 27°C (80°F) or falls below 7°C (45°F). There should also be some form of ventilation, so that the air can circulate freely. You can grow your mushrooms in wooden boxes or trays, with a depth of about 20 cm (8″) and any convenient size. You can also make up ridges directly on the floor, each about 45 cm (1½′) deep, and with a base of 60 cm (2′), rounding the top of the ridge. Or you can use a flat bed about 20-25 cm (8-10″) deep, but make it convenient for picking.

You can grow mushrooms in your greenhouse from mid-autumn through to mid-spring, if it is heated; under the staging is the best place to grow them, putting the compost either in boxes or directly on the greenhouse floor. They can also be grown on the staging, in containers; you will have to shade the glass fairly heavily as mushrooms become brown when exposed to sunlight, or make some arrangement to cover the containers or bed so as to exclude the light to some extent.

Outdoors, mushrooms can be grown in frames which are fairly deep; you will need a depth of at least 45 cm (1½′), though 60 cm (2′) is better. This allows a depth of compost of between 30 and 45 cm (1-1½′) and also gives reasonable conditions in which to keep the right temperature and humidity and allow the mushrooms room to grow. Lights will also be needed, and mats to shade the growing mushrooms. In very mild areas, mushrooms will grow outdoors on ridges from late winter through early summer and again from early autumn through late autumn. Make the ridges 60-75 cm (24–30″) wide and 45 cm (18″) high, and as long as is suitable. You can have them higher but not lower, since less good results will be obtained. You will need a good supply of straw and plastic sheeting in case of heavy, prolonged rain.

You can also grow mushrooms in a lawn or field. This is a chancy method, but can sometimes produce successful results. Simply lift a piece of turf in late

**You can grow good mushroom crops on ridges outdoors in mild areas.
Make ridges 60-75 cm (2′ 6″) wide, 45 cm (1′ 6″) high, and as long as is suitable.**

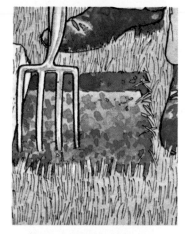

1. **Lift a section
of turf in late
summer, when
soil is moist and
air warm and
humid.**

2. **Using a small
fork, loosen the
exposed soil.**

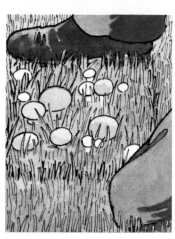

3. **Scatter the
spawn on the
surface, then
replace the turf
and firm lightly.**

4. **The first flush
should appear
about a month
later, depending
on weather and
soil conditions.**

summer and place the spawn beneath it.
The soil should be moist, and the
atmosphere warm and humid. A touch of
frost will not damage outdoor grown
mushrooms. Finally, it is possible
nowadays to buy mushroom kits which
take the backbreak out of mushroom
cultivation. They consist of a bucket
containing prepared compost, which has
already been spawned; you simply add
water to start the spawn growing, carry
out a few other simple instructions and
pick mushrooms a few weeks later.

Compost preparation
As it is important to know the
temperature of the compost during the
various stages of making it, you should
obtain a soil thermometer.

**The easiest way to grow small crops
of mushrooms is to buy mushroom
kits. These buckets contain prepared
spawn and compost, plus instructions
for growing and harvesting the crop.**

Manure being prepared for compost is stacked in a heap and kept moist by watering.

Mushrooms are usually grown on a compost made from strawy horse manure. Other materials can be used, such as pig or cow manure or any animal manure; wheat straw with fertilizer added has been tried and is much used commercially, also barley or bean straw, and bracken, again with the addition of nutrients. If you are making compost from horse manure, make sure it is fresh and has not been exposed to the weather for a long time. You should begin preparing the compost about a month before it is needed. Stack the manure in piles about 1.2 m (4′) high. This can be done outdoors in the summer; otherwise the stacking must be done in a shed or similar building to protect the manure from wet weather. If it is at all dry, water the manure; it should be moist but not really wet. If it is almost pure dung, without much litter, add wheat straw in the proportions of 1 part straw to 10 of dung (by volume) and mix thoroughly. Leave the stack alone for about seven days, during which time it will begin to ferment; the temperature inside it should be in the region of 65°C (150°F). This will kill all insect pests and should destroy most fungal diseases. Once it has reached this temperature, you can turn it, putting the manure that was on the outside into the centre of the new heap, and breaking up all lumps as you proceed. Shake it at the same time to aerate it. Turn the stack another four or five times, at about four-day intervals, moistening the manure if it is at all dry. In about three to four weeks time, the compost should be brown, crumbly and moist, with the straw still recognisable but only just, and there should no longer be a smell of ammonia. It will now have a temperature of about 27°C (80°F) and is ready for use. Commercial growers often add gypsum, at the rate of about 0.45 kg (1 lb) gypsum to 40 kg (88 lb) manure compost—during the first turn—to prevent the finished product from being excessively sticky.

When horse manure is unavailable, you can use other animal manures as a substitute, ready-made mushroom compost, or home-made compost. The latter is made with the aid of an activator. A proprietary brand of this chemical can be bought from your seedsman or garden shop. Specific instructions will be provided, but the general principle is simple. Make a heap with alternate layers of straw or any other similar materials suggested, and activator and then follow the same procedure outlined for manure. The heap must also be kept moist but not wet.

Spawning and casing

The spawn, generally shaped into fibrous blocks (though now also available in granular form) can be bought from seedsmen or garden centres. For the spawning of your mushrooms, you need an air temperature of about 21°C (70°F); after covering it can be dropped to about 15°C (60°F). Mushrooms will grow at any temperature above 10°C (50°F), but more slowly at the lower temperatures. Too high temperatures can kill the spawn. This is, of course, more easily maintained within a building than outdoors.

When filling boxes or trays put the compost in firmly, but not packed down hard so that air is completely excluded. Beds and ridges should similarly be

PREPARING COMPOST

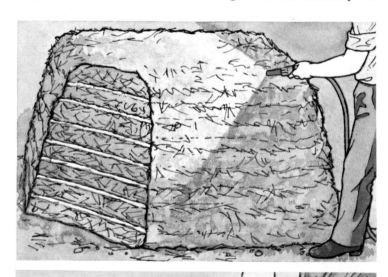

1. Build manure stack about a month before compost is needed; spray with water to promote fermentation, but do not soak.

2. Use a fork to turn the heap four or five times every few days to ensure it rots evenly and stays moist. When ready, it should be brown, moist and crumbly.

1. Test the soil and plant spawn when temperature falls to 21°C (70°F).

2. Break walnut-sized pieces of spawn from the cake and plant them 2.5 cm (1") deep and 20-25 (8-10") apart.

packed firmly and evenly, but not trodden—disease can come in on footwear. Ridge beds, which give slightly higher yields from the same floor space, are usually made in pairs. Make the base of the ridges 60 cm (2') wide, gently tapering at the top to 15 cm (6"). Height should be 45 cm (1½') from top to base.

When the compost has been put into position, its temperature will again rise, to about 38°C (100°F) and will then gradually fall. Keep the bed moderately well watered during this period—when squeezed, the compost should feel damp but should not drip water. After a few days, the temperature will fall to 21°C (70°F). This is the correct moment to

3. If using grain spawn, scatter it on surface; cover box with black plastic.

Heather Angel

These rye grains have been impregnated with mushroom mycelium spawn.

R. J. Corbin

Cake mushroom mycelium spawn is sold dry, and is activated by warmth and moisture.

4. **Prepare casing of sterilized soil, or a mixture of peat and chalk or gypsum. Mix thoroughly.**

5. **Ten days after white threads of mycelium spawn appear, spread casing lightly over compost to a depth of 2.5 cm (1″).**

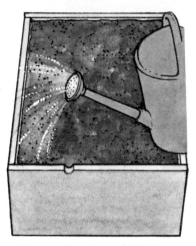

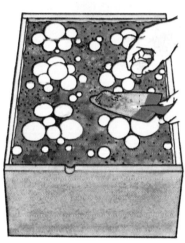

6. **If the casing seems to be drying out, water sparingly; always keep box well ventilated.**

7. **Pull mushrooms from compost with a twist of the hand; do not cut.**

insert the spawn; if the temperature is lower, growth may be very slow.

Break the cake into fragments about the size of a walnut and insert pieces about 2.5 cm (1″) deep in the compost, at a spacing of 20-25 cm (8-10″) in each direction. Press the compost firmly around and over the spawn, so that no air pockets develop.

After a week or so, the mushroom mycelium will be seen spreading like fine greyish to white threads through and on the compost. Leave it for a further ten days, then cover it with a casing of fine, moist soil whose pH is between 7.0 and 8.0. The casing helps to retain the heat of the bed and also helps to conserve moisture. A fine, rich, loamy soil is ideal, and if it has been sterilized, so much the

better. Cover the compost evenly to a depth of 2.5 cm (1″). Alternatively, the casing can consist of a mixture of moist peat and chalk or gypsum, in the ratio of three to one by volume.

Care and development

The mushrooms should appear about two to three weeks after casing, according to the temperature. During this period water sparingly, and only if the casing seems to be drying out. If the beds are over-watered, and the manure beneath the casing is drenched, the spawn will be killed. If, on the other hand, the beds are too dry, the spawn will grow away from the surface of the bed, and deeper into the compost, with the result that no mushrooms will appear

Commercially, mushrooms are cultivated on shelves in purpose-built mushroom houses.

on the surface of the soil. Ideally, the casing should be kept moist with lukewarm water, applied as a fine spray. During this time, the temperature of the bed must not be allowed to rise above 21°C (70°F) for more than brief periods, or the mycelium will be damaged. On the other hand, it should not become cool, and it is a good idea to cover outdoor beds or ridges with a layer of loose straw up to 45 cm (1½′) thick, depending on the time of year. Keep the beds well ventilated, but avoid draughts. The air around a mushroom bed should be moist but also fresh.

Harvesting and aftercare
One to two months is the normal span of time from spawning to cropping, but it can sometimes take longer. If the manure has not fermented properly, or there is inadequate moisture or heat at

any time, it may take up to twelve weeks for the mushrooms to be ready.

The developing mushrooms appear directly over the spawn, so the crops should be evenly distributed over the surface of the bed. Mushrooms tend to reach maturity all at the same time, in 'spates', or 'flushes'. When the first flush is ready for picking,' twist out each mushroom and break it off from the cluster. You should clean out the stem bases from the compost as you pick the mushrooms, to avoid infections and infestations gaining a hold on the beds. After this routine cleaning, fill the holes in the bed with fresh soil. Water the bed thoroughly, although not to the point of saturation. A second flush should appear in about ten days.

Cropping will continue for about three months. If the bed stops cropping prematurely, give it an additional thorough watering. This is often all that is needed to start production again.

Beds in production will need a good steady supply of water as long as cropping continues; make sure that the temperature of the water is the same as the temperature of the bed.

When the last of the mushrooms have been gathered, the compost should be immediately cleared. Never use any of the old compost and soil for growing mushrooms again, although it makes excellent manure for other crops. Give the frames, boxes or other containers a thorough disinfecting to remove any traces of insects or infections. You should also lime-wash the walls and scrub the floors.

Exhibition tips

Timing mushrooms for a particular show date can be a bit risky; mushrooms can be ready for harvesting from one to two months after the spawn has been planted. To avoid disappointment, prepare a small mushroom bed two months before the show, another six weeks before, and a third bed a month before the show date.

Mushrooms can either be shown as buttons, with the gills still covered by the membranes and not visible, or as cups, when the gills are open but have not yet fully expanded. Twelve is the usual number required, either as single exhibits or as part of a collection of vegetables. Because mushrooms deteriorate rapidly once they are picked, delay the picking until the last possible moment. Pick more than you need for the exhibit, so you will have replacements at the show bench, should they be necessary. Whether they are shown as cups or buttons, they should be as uniform as possible.

There is very little pre-show preparation needed. Simply trim the stems to a uniform length of 2.5 cm (1″). At the show, the mushrooms can be displayed in a shallow basket, box or tray. They will look best displayed near the front of the staging.

Varieties

There is only one kind of mushroom available to the amateur grower; this is the species *Agaricus bisporus*. Commercial names attached to mushroom spawn only indicate the particular firm which has produced and marketed the spawn.

Pests & Diseases

White mould (Bubbles): this is a fungal disease which covers the mushrooms with white mouldy growths; the gills are particularly vulnerable to infection, and a badly attacked mushroom may simply be a rounded mass, completely covered with the mould. In very bad attacks, whole clumps of young mushrooms can be enveloped in white mould and killed. Because white mould usually enters the beds in the casing soil, the best precaution is to use only peat or sterilized soil. Once an attack of white mould has occurred, remove and burn all infected mushrooms and stumps immediately. After the final crop, spray the containers and the inside of the building or greenhouse with a solution of formalin, or zineb.

White plaster mould: this is another fungal infection, which shows up on the surface of the beds as a pale powdery growth much like a top dressing of lime in appearance. It prevents the growth of the mushrooms and usually appears as a result of improper composting of the manure. It is favoured by alkaline conditions; the use of gypsum in the compost will generally prevent its appearance. If the beds have suffered from white plaster mould, disinfect the containers or building after the final crop.

Brown plaster mould: a relatively minor fungal infection, this appears on the surface of the bed first as a white fluffy patch. In a few days, the centre of the white patch will turn brown;

The fungal disease white mould, or bubbles, covers mushrooms with white, mouldy growth.

These brown, sticky mushrooms display the symptoms of brown blotch infection.

eventually, the whole fungus turns brown and powdery. As with white plaster mould, improper composting is the main cause. Hygienic conditions and properly made compost will help to prevent its appearance.

Brown blotch: this bacterial infection makes the caps brown, sticky and inedible. Because it thrives in warm, moist still air, proper ventilation and moderate watering can avoid it.

Mushroom bed sclerotium: if you find branch-shaped, hardened growths in the casing soil, often with pinkish tips showing just above the soil surface, then your beds are infected with mushroom bed sclerotium. Pull them out of the soil and destroy them; you should still be able to harvest good crops.

Dry bubble: light brown spots and blotches appear on the mushroom cap, and later the mushrooms become distorted and the stalks split and peel. They become dry and leathery in time: Treat as for white mould; chlorinated water is also helpful.

Cobweb disease: a downy or fluffy mould appears on the compost surface and grows all over the mushrooms also, which then rot completely. Sometimes the mould has a pinkish tinge. Treat as for white mould.

Rose comb: the symptoms of this physiological disorder are deformed or cracked caps. Often gills are produced on top of the caps. Rose comb is caused by exposing the beds to fumes from oil

stoves, or by applying mineral-based sprays.

Woodlice: these pests thrive in the humidity, darkness and decaying manure which are necessary for growing mushrooms. Once they enter the beds, either with the manure or else through cracks or holes in the shed, they will multiply rapidly. They eat holes in the developing buttons, and in severe infestations the entire crop can ruined. Gamma-HCH or pyrethrum applied to the bed are the best methods of control.

Slugs: slimy, silvery trails on the surface of the bed and ragged holes in the buttons indicate the presence of slugs. Hand pick if possible, at night when they feed, or trap them with proprietary slug baits as soon as they are seen, but put the bait near to the beds or boxes, rather than on them, as slug baits are poisonous to humans also.

Springtails: these tiny jumping insects often appear in great numbers and can do an enormous amount of damage. They attack the stalks, gills and outer edges of the caps, which then become slightly pitted. Once they have attacked the developing buttons, no further growth takes place, and the crops will be severely stunted. Compost which has heated up to the temperature recommended should not be troubled, but spraying or dusting the growing medium with gamma-HCH, pyrethrum or derris should control an infestation.

Sciarid flies: these tiny black gnats lay

250

The physiological disorder rose comb appears as extra gills growing on top of the caps.

Mites have eaten holes in the cap and stalk of this mushroom; control is difficult.

eggs on the surface of the compost and at the base of the mushroom stalks. The emerging tiny legless larvae, which are white with black heads, enter the base of the stalk and tunnel upwards; infected mushrooms decay. Treatment is the same as for springtails. High temperature composting in the first place will destroy larvae.

Mites: there are several species of mites which attack mushrooms, all of which eat internal holes in the stalks and caps. Unfortunately, mites have developed a resistance to most organochlorine-based insecticides, but derris or pyrethrum offer some measure of control. If the infestation is severe, the only completely effective method of control is to clear out all the beds, discard all the soil and manure, and disinfect the walls and floor of the shed with boiling water.

Phorid flies: these are similar to sciarid flies, and both insects do much the same damage. Phorid flies, however, are active mainly in the summer months, while sciarid flies occur all year round. The best preventive measure against phorid flies is to cover all ventilators, doors and windows with fine mesh screening. If an infestation does occur, spray or dust the beds with derris or pyrethrum.

GUIDE TO MUSHROOM PROBLEMS	
Symptoms	*Probable cause*
Holes eaten in buttons	Woodlice
Ragged holes in mushrooms; slimy trails on casing	Slugs
Pitted stalks, gills and outer caps	Springtails
Tunnels in stalk, decayed mushrooms	Sciarid flies Phorid flies
Holes eaten inside stalks and caps	Mites
White mouldy growths on mushrooms	White mould (Bubbles)
White powdery mould on casing	White plaster mould
White fluffy patches on casing, later turning brown	Brown plaster mould
Caps turn brown	Brown blotch
Pink tipped, branch-like growths in casing soil	Mushroom bed sclerotium
Light brown spots on cap, later distortions of mushroom and splitting of stalk	Dry bubble
White downy or fluffy mould on compost and mushrooms, sometimes pinkish	Cobweb disease
Deformed, cracked caps; gills on top	Rose comb

Peppers

Capsicum annuum, C. frutescens (fam. *Solanaceae*)
Annual or perennial, but most culinary capsicums are grown as **half-hardy annuals.**
Sowing to harvesting time: 20–28 weeks
Size: plants vary in height from 30–90 cm (1–3′). Fruit of dwarf varieties about 2.5 cm (1″) across; large varieties from 7.5–12 cm (3–5″) long.
Yield: 0.45–1 kg (1–2 lb) per plant.

Originally a native of tropical America, peppers are becoming increasingly popular as a flavourful vegetable cooked in stews and casseroles, or served fresh in salads. Widely grown in southern Europe and warmer areas of the United States, recent developments of F_1 hybrid strains have made growing peppers in cooler temperate climates possible; they are now grown commercially in parts of southern England.

Peppers have much to recommend them; their bright red, green or yellow colour and flavour add zest to any meal. They are relatively expensive to buy in the shops, but the home grower can produce healthy-sized crops with little initial expense. In good years, when crops are abundant, excess peppers can be frozen or dried and stored like onions. Unlike tomatoes, which are virtually inedible in their unripe state, unripe peppers are very tasty, and indeed preferred by some people to the milder, sweeter ripe pepper. Unripe peppers are dark green, and brilliant red or yellow when ripe.

Peppers are relatively pest and disease free, and their cultivation requirements are few. Rich growing medium, warmth and a steady water supply are necessary, but they require no training, tying or pinching out of sideshoots.

Peppers, besides their food value, make very decorative pot plants; they can be grown indoors and stood out on a balcony, windowsill or paved courtyard during the summer months. In a greenhouse, they have much the same growing requirements as tuberous begonias; a mixed display of flowering plants and bushes hung with peppers can be very attractive.

There are many varieties available from seed catalogues, some of which have inedible fruits and are grown solely for decorative value. The two main categories of edible peppers are sweet

Chilli plants are very decorative as well as useful. The vivid, bright red hanging fruits which adorn the branches are visually attractive; when dried they are ground into chilli powder or cayenne pepper. These spices are used in the making of curry powder, pickles and tabasco sauce.

Derek Fell

peppers (*Capsicum annuum*) and hot peppers, or chillies (*Capsicum frutescens*). Sweet peppers, also called bull-nose, bell or pimiento peppers, generally have larger fruit than chillies. The paprika made from these is much used in Hungarian cooking. The taste of peppers in general varies greatly in intensity, depending on ripeness and variety; some are sweet and mild, while others can be incredibly pungent. The peppery flavour is due to the presence of a chemical compound, capsicin, in the fruit; the more capsicin, the hotter the flavour. All peppers have a very high vitamin C content. The shape, size and texture varies; they can be round, oblong or conical in shape, wrinkled or smooth skinned, and from 5–15 cm (2–6″) long.

The small, tapering fruits, about 2.5 cm (1–2″) long of the *C. frutescens* types are renowned for their strong 'hot' flavour. Because of their pungency, these peppers are mostly used for flavouring only, the bright red flesh being dried and ground into chilli powder or cayenne pepper, or shredded. When green, chillies are pickled or made into chilli vinegar. Because they are so intensely flavoured, though, most households need only one plant to keep well supplied with chillies.

Suitable site
Peppers are tropical in origin, and will be killed by frost. For this reason, they are most successfully grown in greenhouses, either in pots or in the border under

**In mild sheltered
areas, peppers
can be grown
outside, at the
base of a south-
facing wall. In
early summer,
transplant
peppers started
under glass to a
growing-bag
outside.**

**Alternatively, in
early summer
plunge the pots
containing the
pepper plants up
their rims in a
sunny border.
Lift them in
autumn, and
return the pots
to the
greenhouse to
finish ripening.**

staging. In very mild, sheltered areas, peppers can be started under glass and planted outside in early summer, against a south facing wall. New F_1 varieties have been bred for hardiness, and growing peppers out of doors is certainly less risky than it used to be. A late frost, however, can still be disastrous. Cloche protection lessens the risk somewhat, but because strong growing pepper plants are taller than most cloches, the cloches will have to be raised to accommodate them.

You can combine the advantages of greenhouse and outdoor cultivation: start the plants in a greenhouse, and in early summer, plunge the pots up to the rims in sunny borders outdoors. They will then have the benefit of the hot summer months. When summer is over and autumn comes, lift the pots from the borders outdoors, and bring them into the greenhouse. Here they will be able to ripen off in the warmer atmosphere.

Suitable soil

Outdoors, and in the greenhouse border, peppers thrive in rich, well worked soil containing plenty of manure. For growing in pots, standard

254

1. Begin sowing seeds from late winter onwards. Space seeds 2.5 cm (1″) apart in all directions in the tray.

2. At the three-leaf stage, prick the seedlings out into 7.5 cm (3″) pots and lower the temperature slightly.

3. Do not allow plants to become root bound; repot them into 12 cm (5″) pots and richer compost as necessary.

4. Harden plants off in a cold frame or under cloches prior to moving them outdoors into the open ground.

potting composts, such as John Innes No 3, are suitable. Alternatively, use plastic growing bags filled with prepared compost, such as those used for tomatoes.

Sowing and planting out
The timing of sowing depends on whether the plants are to be grown entirely in a greenhouse, or a combination of greenhouse and out of doors. Seeds for greenhouse peppers can be sown in late winter or early spring; for plants intended for cloche or outdoor

fruiting without protection, the beginning of mid-spring is the best time. You can sow peppers out of doors, either directly in the ground or in peat pots after the last frosts, in mild sheltered areas. Peppers need a long growing season, though, so it is really best to start them off in a warm greenhouse or propagator, or even in a warm room.

Sow the seeds in trays, spaced 2.5 cm (1″) apart in all directions, and push them about 1.3 cm ($\frac{1}{2}$″) below the surface of the compost. John Innes No 1 is the most suitable medium. Peat pots can also

FEEDING PEPPERS

Prepare home-made liquid manure; dilute it to the colour of weak tea before feeding the plants.

Alternatively, buy liquid food and dilute according to manufacturer's instructions; feed while fruits form.

be used, sowing two or three seeds in each pot. A soil temperature of 18°C (65°F) is ideal, but seeds will still germinate if it drops a few degrees below this for short periods of time. The first leaves should be showing two to three weeks after sowing, depending on temperature.

When the seedlings reach the three-leaf stage, prick them out into 7.5 cm (3″) pots. The temperature can be lowered now to 13°C (55°F) during the day dropping to 10°C (50°F) at night. Do not allow the plants to become root bound;

as they grow re-pot them into larger pots and richer compost to encourage the development of good growth. If they are to fruit indoors, use 15 cm (6″) or 17.5 cm (7″) pots for the final potting ; if they are to be planted outdoors, 12.5 cm (5″) pots are large enough. In the early stages they are very slow to grow but, provided they remain a good colour, there is no need to worry.

Never move half-hardy pepper plants straight from a warm greenhouse or kitchen windowsill into the open garden. The plants should be hardened off gradually, until they are completely used to the lower outdoor temperature. Do this by putting them in a cold frame for a short period of time, or giving them cloche protection outdoors during the day, while they are still in their pots, and bringing them back to the greenhouse at night. After one or two weeks, the plants can be left out permanently.

It is safest to wait until the beginning of early summer before planting out permanently; do this about the same time as you plant out tomatoes under cloches. If the spring is exceptionally cold, delay planting out until the weather and soil warm up. Do not let the plants starve, though; if they have to remain in their pots longer because of cold weather, top dress with nitro-chalk and water it in.

Set out the young plants 37.5–60 cm (15–24″) apart, depending on variety. Always water the soil well before planting unless it is already moist.

Cultivation and care
Peppers need a steady supply of water if their growth is not checked. If the soil becomes dry, even for a short period of time during mid-day, the plants will droop at once. The leaves, being thin, tend to dry up more quickly than most; syringing them daily in hot weather helps reduce transpiration, as well as keeping red spider mite away. A position where they are shaded from the late morning and mid-day sun is ideal especially when the plants are young.

1. If using peat pots, sow two or three seeds per pot; remove all but the strongest seedling.

2. If cold weather delays planting out, top-dress the plants with nitro-chalk and water in thoroughly.

3. Plant out in early summer when the weather warms up; the plants should be about 20 cm (8″) tall.

4. Give plants cloche protection at night or if weather turns cold; take cloches off during the day.

5. Peppers need plenty of water, particularly at mid-day in hot weather; their thin leaves dry out quickly.

6. Mulch with clean dry straw once the plants are established, to keep weeds down and conserve moisture.

Remember, though, to water steadily and moderately, because over-enthusiastic watering can lead to botrytis infections, especially in cool weather.

In very warm weather, provide some form of light shading, particularly to those grown under glass.

Peppers grown in pots respond well to liquid feeding once the fruits have begun to form, using a potash-high feed, and this can be done at routine watering times, applied according to manufacturers' instructions. Alternatively, you can make liquid manure by steeping a bag of rotted manure in a tub of water; use this after diluting it to the colour of weak tea and apply once a week.

If you have been thorough in preparing the soil for outdoor plants, you should have no trouble with perennial weeds. Any annual weeds which appear can be kept down with a hoe, worked between rows. Be careful not to damage the roots of the pepper plants; hand weeding plants is best. A mulch with clean straw, once the plants are established, will keep the weeds down, as well as conserving soil moisture.

Artificial pollination is not really necessary as the greenish-white flowers set fruit readily, and may indeed need thinning to get the best sized peppers. However, misting the plants daily while they are flowering improves the rate of pollination. Never grow sweet peppers and hot peppers in the same greenhouse, because the cross-pollination which may occur would have disastrous results.

You may need to give support, in the form of bamboo poles to the taller growing varieties; the dwarf kinds stand up well without support. Some people advise pinching out the growing tips when the plants are 20 cm (8″) high, but eventually, when the plants are fully grown, there is little difference between plants treated in this way and those allowed to develop naturally.

Harvesting and aftercare

Peppers grown under glass should be ready for picking in mid-summer; if the

Harry Smith

Peppers grown under glass will be ready for harvesting in mid-summer; those grown out of doors can be picked from late summer.

greenhouse is heated, harvesting should continue until early winter. Those grown outdoors will normally be ready for picking before late summer or early autumn, and harvesting will stop as soon as the weather turns cold. The length of the harvesting season depends to some extent on local climate, and can also vary from summer to summer. The fruits should be picked as soon as they are of sufficient size, and the flesh is firm and well filled out. A good quality pepper has a smooth pleasing shape and an even colour. Peppers taste delicious at all stages, and many people prefer them when they are still green and slightly under-ripe. Peppers left on the plant to ripen fully will turn a rich red or yellow, depending on variety; they are somewhat sweeter than the green ones.

In some varieties, the fruit hangs down from the shoots; in others, the peppers grow erect from the upper sides of the stems. Cut the fruit from the parent plant with a sharp knife or secateurs, leaving the remaining peppers, which develop at different rates, undisturbed. Handle the peppers carefully, so that they are not bruised. A

1. Pinch out the first few flowers by hand to encourage the formation of larger fruit. Keep well watered.

2. Prevent infestation by the pest red spider mite with a daily spray of water on the undersides of the leaves.

strong plant should produce between at least six and eight peppers. One word of warning, however: the peppers will remain in good condition on the plant for sometime after they are ripe, but if you do not pick them the production of additional peppers will cease. It is best to harvest peppers as soon as they are ready, except perhaps towards the end of the season, when the plant has finished forming fruits. Because peppers continue to flower over a long period, you are unlikely to be faced with a sudden glut of them. Any which are picked green in mid-autumn will ripen slowly until early or even mid-winter.

Hot peppers are picked in much the same way as sweet peppers; in their unripe state they are used for pickling, and when ripe, for drying and grinding into chilli powder. Fruit can be stored by threading string through the stalks and hanging them to dry in a cool place. If picked when green, for storage, they will gradually change colour until they are red or yellow.

Do not leave the plants in the soil after harvesting has been completed; in temperate climates they are treated as annuals and there is no point in keeping them longer. Pull up and burn or compost old plants. Remember never to put on the compost heap any plants showing signs of pests or diseases.

Exhibition tips

Because of their intensely bright colour, peppers and chillies will enliven any display, either on their own or as part of a collection. Although botanically fruit, the Royal Horticultural Society classifies them as vegetables for the purpose of exhibition. Although peppers are not worth as many points as some vegetables, it is not difficult to grow first class specimens to give you the maximum that are available. As they are extremely attractive, they are particularly useful for bringing colour to sombre displays.

Peppers can be displayed while they are still green, or when they have ripened fully and are red or yellow. This means that timing the date of sowing is not as tricky as it is with some other vegetables, which are at their best for a few days only. As general guide, sow under glass in early to mid-spring for late summer or early autumn shows.

If you particularly want to exhibit fully coloured peppers, and due to unforeseen weather changes it is unlikely that they will ripen naturally in time for the show, you can force ripening. A few days before the show, pick the peppers and wrap them individually in tissue paper. Pack them in a single layer in a box so that all light is excluded. Place the box in a warm room or greenhouse, and inspect the peppers daily. Take out any which have ripened and have begun to shrivel, and store them in a cool dark place until the show.

Twelve peppers is the usual number shown; because chillies are much smaller, twenty-four is the usual number required. Try to have double this amount ready for showing, so that you can select the best. Because peppers are by their very nature irregular and unsymmetrical in shape, it is unlikely you will find perfectly uniform specimens. Try to select fruits which are approximately the same size and colour, however, for the best visual effect.

Cut the peppers with secateurs, leaving a good sized stalk attached to the fruit. This stalk will come in handy if you are wiring the peppers to a display stand. They should not need much preparation; just wash them lightly and dry afterwards. If the pepper is left wet for any length of time, rot may set in and

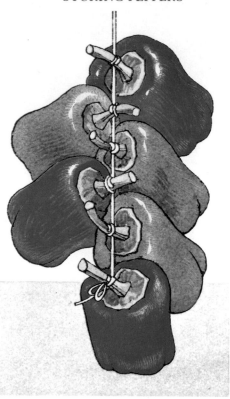

Sweet red and green peppers can be stored; thread a string through the stalks and hang in a dry place.

ruin your display.

If you are packing them for transport to the show, wrap them individually in tissue paper. Pack them tightly enough so they do not move about in the box and rub each other, or they may be bruised when you take them out.

Peppers can be displayed on plates or in shallow baskets, or wired to cones or other display shapes. If wiring them up, use tight bunches of parsley to fill the spaces between the peppers. Keep the parsley on short stalks and close to the wire form; if the parsley is loose or sloopy looking it will detract from the exhibit. Make sure you leave plenty of time to set up the exhibit before the show; chillies are particularly troublesome and time consuming to prepare because of their small size.

Varieties

Canapé (F₁): very early and suitable for outdoor cultivation; fruit sweet flavoured and bright red when ripe; heavy cropper.

Ace (F₁); new variety, early; heavy and uniform cropper; equally good for forcing or outdoor use; widely used commercially.

Californian Wonder: bull-nose type; forms large plants; mild, delicate flavour; this variety is good for deep freezing.

Worldbeater: well known variety; heavy cropper; fruits 12.5 cm (5″) long; skin dark green turning deep red when ripe; best grown under glass.

Emerald Gem: excellent taste; suitable for sheltered border outdoors or cultivation under glass.

Outdoor: blunt-nosed variety; red when fully ripe; half-hardy, needs cloches outdoors.

Slim Pim (F₁): small peppers, about 5 cm (2″) long with mild, sweet flavour; suitable for freezing; very heavy cropper; suitable for outdoor growing in mild areas.

Vinedale: very early variety; fruits mild, sweet, thick-fleshed and pointed; this variety does best in a warm sheltered position.

Bell Boy (F₁): new variety; heavy cropper; popular for commercial growing; this variety is excellent for home growing.

Novelty varieties

Tompa: similar to a tomato in shape and colour; juicier and sweeter than other peppers; suitable for growing in a greenhouse or close to a warm, south-facing wall.

Gold Topaz: unusual variety; peppers golden yellow when ripe, with mild, spicy flavour; best grown in cold frame or greenhouse.

Mexican Chilli: hot, spicy flavoured, small peppers; fruits dried and ground into chilli powder; must be grown in greenhouse.

Pests & Diseases

Capsid bugs: these bright green, quick-moving insects occasionally attack the growing points of pepper plants. They pierce the leaves and stems, and suck the sap, from mid-spring onwards. Infested leaves will be mis-shapen, puckered and tattered; infested growing points will be severely stunted or will die outright.

If your plants are attacked by capsids, which is unlikely, control them by spraying or dusting with malathion or derris plus pyrethrum. Capsids drop to the ground when disturbed, so remember to treat the ground around the plant as well.

Red spider mite: capsicums grown under glass seem particularly vulnerable to attacks by greenhouse red spider mite. The young and mature mites feed on the undersides of the leaves; the upper surfaces then become pale and speckled. If the attack is very bad, the leaves will turn yellow and fall prematurely. Leaves and stems covered with a fine web is another indication of red spider mite.

Because the insects are most destructive in hot, dry, overcrowded conditions, make sure your plants are properly spaced apart, with plenty of air circulation. Regular syringing, up to three times a day in very hot weather, is a good precaution. Use lukewarm water, and make sure both sides of the leaves are thoroughly dampened. If you find one or two leaves with a few mites on them, usually close to the main vein, removal of these leaves completely may well be enough to prevent any further outbreak.

If, however, there is a serious infestation, fumigation of the greenhouse with azobenzine will help control the pest. Alternatively, you can use derris or malathion as a spray. Red spider mites can develop a resistance to a particular chemical if it is used too frequently, so make sure you use insecticides according to manufacturers' instructions, and if there are no positive results after a couple of weeks, try another method of control.

G. E. Hyde

Bruce Coleman

*Whiteflies attack a wide range of plants;
control with bioresmethrin.*

*Greenflies feed on the sap, resulting in
yellow, puckered, curled leaves.*

Botrytis (grey mould): this fungal infection attacks a wide variety of fruits and vegetables, and is usually associated with cool, damp, overcrowded conditions. Peppers grown under glass are particularly vulnerable. The disease can enter the plant through a wound or through dead or dying tissue. Because botrytis spores are present in the air, poor growing conditions can quickly lead to severe attack. The best precautions are to ensure that seedlings and young plants are not overcrowded, and that air can circulate freely. Quintozene applied to the soil just before planting gives some measure of protection. If there is an outbreak of botrytis, remove and burn all infected leaves and improve the growing conditions; badly infected plants should be removed and destroyed, as it is unlikely they will recover.

Whitefly: these insects, which look like small white moths, are more troublesome some years than others. They thrive in hot, dry weather, and whitefly attacks in these conditions can be severe. Like red spider mite, they live and feed on the undersides of leaves, where they suck the sap. They also exude honeydew, which encourages secondary infection from sooty mould. Spray with bioresmethrin as soon as they are seen, and again as necessary to destroy any newly hatched insects.

Greenfly: these are one of the many types of aphids which attack cultivated plants. Greenfly feed on the plant sap, the removal of which results in puckered, distorted and yellowed leaves, especially the young ones. Because greenfly breed rapidly, it is vital that you take action as soon as you see them. Spray with derris or malathion; repeat as necessary. In very severe cases, use a systemic insecticide, such as dimethoate. Remember to allow the recommended time to pass before harvesting the peppers.

GUIDE TO PEPPER TROUBLES

Symptom	Probable cause
Mis-shaped, puckered, tattered leaves	Capsids, greenfly, whitefly
Leaves pale, mottled, turn yellow and fall prematurely	Red spider mite
Leaves, fruits and stems covered in grey mould	Botrytis

Radishes

Raphanus sativus (fam. *Cruciferae*)
Hardy annual or biennial.
Sowing to harvesting time: three to six weeks for
summer varieties, five months for winter varieties.
Size: varies with type, spring and summer radishes average
2.5 cm (1″) in diameter, winter radishes much larger,
weighing up to 0.45 kg (1 lb) each.
Yield: 1.6 kg (4 lb) per 3 m (10′) row for summer varieties.
4.3 kg (10 lb) per 3 m (10′) row for winter varieties.

Radishes are one of the easiest and quickest vegetables to grow, giving a high yield of crisp roots with minimum effort. Because their cultivation needs are so few, and quick-growing varieties can be harvested three weeks after sowing, growing radishes is one of the best projects for children as an introduction to gardening. Radishes are, of course, an extremely useful crop in general; they can be sown between other plants, as catch crops, or in the odd corner of the garden. As long as the soil has been prepared properly and the plants do not run short of water, a good crop will be ready for pulling a short time after sowing. By giving some protection against the extremes of winter and summer weather, you can harvest good crops of radishes all year round.

Most commercially grown radishes, seen in the greengrocers in spring and summer, are the round red variety. The amateur gardener has a much wider selection of varieties from which to choose. Besides red radishes, there are white, yellow, red and white, and black-skinned types, round, long and tapering or oval in shape. Some varieties are suitable for early forcing, others are grown for autumn and winter harvesting. Packets of mixed strains are available; these contain seeds of several varieties of mixed colours, shapes and sizes. The different varieties of radish in these packets mature at different times, so the season of harvesting will be extended.

The most familiar types of radishes are the round red one and the slightly longer red and white type, which are popular for garnishing and for use in summer salads. These are sweeter-tasting than the long white variety, which has a peppery flavour and is also used in salads. The slower growing winter varieties form enormous roots, weighing up to about half a kilogramme (1 lb) each, and can be red or black-skinned, with white flesh. These are pungent and tasty, but not sweet. They can be cooked like turnips or eaten raw, in which case they are sliced or grated, rather than served whole. Winter varieties are peeled before eating but the summer varieties are eaten whole.

Summer radishes are quick growing and ready to pull three or four weeks after sowing.

Suitable site and soil

Success with radishes depends to a large extent on soil conditions. The soil must be rich and moist; warm, light fertile sandy soil is best. As with most other root crops, manuring the soil right before sowing is not a good practice, as it leads to coarse, badly shaped roots. You can lighten heavy clay soil by adding peat. Very dry soil can also be improved by the addition of peat, which increases the moisture-holding capacity of the soil. Whatever the soil type, it should be deeply dug well before sowing, and worked to a very fine tilth. There should be no lumps in the top 15 cm (6″) of soil. Work in sifted leafmould or ripe sifted garden compost, and add a dressing of bonemeal at the rate of 120 g per sq m (4 oz per sq yd).

Site requirements vary according to the time of year. For early outdoor sowings, a warm, sunny sheltered site is best, preferably with a south-facing slope. From early summer onwards, radishes need a cool, shady position. If they are grown in full sun during the summer months, they tend to bolt, or run to seed. Do not, however, plant them in a dry, shady place, such as under a hedge, or you will have a disappointing crop of thin, drawn roots. Shade given by pea or bean plants is ideal. If you are planting radishes in early autumn, select a sunny open site, protected from frosts if possible. Later sowings should have some form of glass protection.

Sowing in the open

Like lettuces, radishes should be sown little and often. Because most varieties are at their best for only a short while after reaching maturity, there is no point in sowing an enormous number of seeds at one time. Successional sowing, every two or three weeks, will give a con-

1. Well before sowing, dig the soil deeply; add moist peat to very dry or very heavy soils.

2. Work in sifted leafmould or ripe garden compost; avoid digging in heavy manures.

3. Apply a top dressing of bonemeal at the rate of 120 g per sq m (4 oz per sq yd) and fork in lightly.

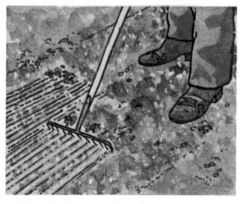

4. Just before sowing, rake the soil surface to a fine tilth and break up any lumps of soil.

5. Make the drills 1.8 cm (¾″) deep, and 10-15 cm (4-6″) apart; be sure they are absolutely level.

6. Sow the seeds thinly, overcrowding leads to foliage rather than root growth.

tinuous, reasonable harvest. An average packet of seeds will be plenty for sowing three 3 m (10') rows, and should produce over 300 radishes. If you have more seeds than you need, you can share them with friends or store them; under proper conditions, the seeds will retain their vitality for five years.

Radishes are often intercropped with other vegetables—sowing them, for example, on the ridges adjacent to celery trenches. When intercropping in this way, make sure the radishes will not interfere with hoeing and weeding, and there is enough space for access to both crops. Radish seeds are sometimes mixed with slow-germinating seeds, like onion or parsnip. Their distinctive heart-shaped seed leaves mark the rows and the radish roots are soon ready for pulling, leaving space for the long term crops to grow. When you are mixing radish seeds in with another crop, make sure you remove all small slow-growing radishes as soon as the bulk of the radish crop is pulled, to avoid crowding the long term crop.

If you have a very warm, sheltered site, you can sow in the open in early or mid-winter. Do not attempt very early outdoor sowing if the soil is cold, wet and heavy. To improve drainage and to speed growing in winter-sown radishes you can make a slightly raised hot bed in the open. Cover the fermenting material with a 15 cm (6") layer of fine soil. Some people sow early crops of radishes outdoors in the 10 cm (4") gap between lines of cloches. The cloches protect the radishes from wind and keep the soil slightly warmer, but you may have difficulty caring for and harvesting the radishes when grown in this way.

Normally outdoor sowings are made from early spring onwards. Sow in drills 1.8 cm ($\frac{3}{4}$") deep and 10-15 cm (4-6") apart. Make sure the drills are dead level, so that all the seeds are covered with the same depth of soil.

Radishes must be sown thinly. If you sow them too thickly, you will get a very poor crop; overcrowding leads to foliage rather than root growth. Try to aim for 12-15 seeds per 30 cm (1') run. Because the seeds are relatively large, you should have little difficulty in sowing them this thinly.

After sowing, rake the soil gently over the radishes to cover them. Never cover the seeds with more than 1.8 cm ($\frac{3}{4}$") of soil. Then firm down the soil, with the back of a rake or spade. The seeds should germinate from four to ten days after sowing. If thinning is necessary, it should be done as soon as the seedlings are large enough to handle. The smaller salad varieties should be spaced 2.5 cm (1") apart; the larger salad varieties 3.7-5 cm (1$\frac{1}{2}$-2") apart.

Radishes for harvesting in winter should be sown in mid to late summer in drills 22 cm (9") apart, and thinned if necessary so that there is 15 cm (6") spacing between plants.

A less satisfactory method of sowing radish seeds is sowing them broadcast instead of in drills. Although initially easier and quicker to do, broadcast sowing has several drawbacks. It is much more difficult to control weeds because the radishes are sown over a large and indefinite area; hoeing becomes impossible. Because you cannot control the density of sowing, you will also have more thinning to do. Like other root vegetables radishes do not transplant very well, so the thinnings will be wasted.

Sowing under glass
The earliest radishes of all can be had by growing them on a hot bed in a cold frame in early to mid-winter. For sowing under cold frames select varieties with short leaf growth. Cover the fermenting material with 15 cm (6") of good soil. Do not mix the soil with the fermenting material as it is the heat and not the rich fertilizer which is essential. Mixing the radish seeds with carrot seeds is an excellent way to make the best use of the frame. The radishes should be ready for pulling in three weeks, and the carrots can grow on. You can sow the radishes in

1. After sowing, tamp down the soil with the head of a rake, so the seeds are in contact with the soil.

2. Thin the seedlings as soon as they are large enough to handle, to 2.5-5cm (1-2″) apart.

3. Dust seedlings with HCH powder as they emerge and again 10 days later, to avoid damage by flea beetle.

4. Protect the seeds and seedlings from birds with small mesh wire netting, bird scarers, or cotton webs.

5. Harvest radishes as soon as they are ready; do not leave them in the ground to get hot and stringy.

6. Large winter radishes can be pulled in autumn and then stored in a box filled with damp sand.

a cold frame in late winter, without a hot bed, but it will take six to eight weeks before they are ready for pulling. Another method of giving glass protection to very early crops is to sow radish seeds in the borders of an unheated greenhouse. Radishes grown under glass should be a minimum of 7.5 cm (3") apart, with 15 cm (6") between rows with more space for large types.

Under cloches, radishes can be sown between rows of early lettuce or peas. Grown on their own, five rows of radishes will fit under an average size cloche; with this protection they can be grown outdoors from mid-winter onwards, though cropping may take longer.

Care and development

For early sown crops, under glass and in the open, protection from frost is essential. Cover cloches and frames with newspapers or sacks if a frost is expected. It is best to open the frames during the day to keep the plants well ventilated once they have germinated, shutting the frame at night and covering as necessary. For radishes sown in the open on hot beds, a covering of litter or mats at night helps protect the plants from frost damage. Remove the covering during the day, unless the weather is very cold. A 15 cm (6") layer of clean straw or branches of evergreen trees or shrubs are also useful for covering the plants in cold conditions.

Moisture is essential; water regularly in warm weather and particularly during the summer. Radish crops will fail if they are checked by lack of water. If you have prepared the ground properly, weeds should not be a problem. Radishes grow very quickly and should be ready to pull before any weeds have time to become established.

Birds like radish seeds and seedlings; if necessary protect them with small mesh wire netting, bird scarers, or webs of black cotton. Birds do not seem to attack radishes past the seedling stage, so the protection need only be temporary.

To avoid damage by flea beetle, dust the seedlings with HCH powder as they appear and again about ten days later.

Although summer radishes do not need additional fertilizers, winter radishes benefit from a dressing of nitro-chalk in early autumn. Apply it at the rate of 30 g per 3 m run (1 oz per 10' run), to help the radishes make good growth before winter.

Harvesting

Summer radishes are normally harvested three to four weeks after sowing, while they are still young and crisp. If you leave them in the ground until the flowering stems develop, the roots become stringy and have a hot, unpalatable taste. If you have a bumper crop, and more radishes are ready for pulling than your family can sensibly use, harvest them and share them with friends or neighbours. If there is still some surplus, put them straight on the compost heap, as they are rich in nutrients and make good compost. There are some varieties, such as *Cherry Belle* and *Red Prince*, which can remain in the ground for relatively longer periods without splitting or going to seed. The best way to avoid a glut, however, is by frequent and small sowings.

Large winter radishes can either be harvested in autumn and stored in damp sand like carrots, or left in the ground and lifted as needed. They will not become hollow in the centre, as do summer radishes if they are left in the ground for any length of time.

Summer radishes grown on hot beds must be watched very carefully, and picked as soon as they mature, because they are at their best for a few days only.

Exhibition tips

Although four weeks is the average time from sowing to harvesting, it can vary according to weather conditions. Because it is difficult to time the radishes exactly for a particular show date, it is best to make a few small sowings at

1. Sow seed under glass from early winter onwards. Sprinkle the seeds thinly at a depth of 0.5 cm ($\frac{1}{4}$").

2. Open the frame during the day once the seeds have geminated; shut it at night to keep the cold out.

3. If you expect a frost, cover the frame light with sacking or paper to protect the seedlings.

You can also sow radishes in the borders of an unheated greenhouse; make the rows 15 cm (6") apart.

Early radishes can be grown outdoors between rows of cloches used for forcing other crops.

weekly intervals, starting six weeks before the show date.

Do not gather the radishes until just before the show, to avoid wilted foliage. Twenty-four radishes is the usual number shown; they should be as uniform as possible, and all of one variety unless otherwise stated. Select roots of moderate size. The judges will look for fresh, brightly coloured roots with the foliage still attached. Just before the exhibition, wash the radishes under running water until all the soil is removed, and tie the roots in a bundle with green twine. Display with the roots pointing towards the front of the staging.

Black Spanish

China Rose

Varieties

Winter radish

Black Spanish Round: black skin, white flesh; very hardy; lift in winter and store, or leave in the ground and lift as needed. Slice or grate and serve as salad.

China Rose: rose, white-tipped skin, white flesh; oval shaped, 12–15 cm (5–6") long, 5 cm (2") in diameter; serve sliced.

Black Spanish Long: black skin, white flesh; similar to Black Spanish Round.

Mino Early: large Japanese variety; roots 37 cm (15") long, 5 cm (2") in diameter; mild flavour; useful in autumn and winter.

Spring and summer radish

Cherry Belle: round, smooth, cherry red radish; sweet, mild taste; quick-growing; remains in harvestable condition for a long time.

French Breakfast: red, white-tipped; olive-shaped; crunchy texture; mild and sweet-tasting.

Sparkler: bright red, white-tipped; globe-shaped; very quick-growing.

Inca: bright scarlet; globe-shaped; very firm-textured, even when large.

French Breakfast

Red Forcing

Yellow Gold

Scarlet Globe

Saxerre: round variety, especially suited for early sowings; neat tops; quick to mature.

Half Long: rose red, white-tipped new variety; resistant to pithiness.

Red Prince: new variety; can stand for a long time without going to seed or splitting; grows very large.

Yellow Gold: golden radish, white flesh; egg-shaped; medium flavour.

Red Forcing: early-maturing round variety; useful for cloches, frames, greenhouses.

Scarlet Globe: scarlet roots, pure white flesh; quick-growing.

Red White Tipped: red roots tipped with white; useful for spring and summer sowings; suitable for growing under cloches.

Long White

Long White Icicle: white, tapered shape; 7.5 cm (3″) long; crisp and sweet-tasting; very quick-growing and good for early crops.

Minowase Summer Cross: F_1 hybrid; white, tapered shape; 15 cm (6″) long; can be pulled over long period; remains crisp, mild and white without any hot, peppery flavour.

Long White Icicle

Minowase Summer Cross

271

Pests & Diseases

Radishes are pleasantly trouble-free; because they grow so quickly they are usually harvested well before disease or pests can do much damage. However, like other members of the *Cruciferae* they are subject to infection by several fungal diseases. Provided your garden is clean and weed-free, the radishes are grown as quickly as possible and never allowed to dry out, you are unlikely to encounter much difficulty.

Damping off: this disease is caused by a fungus and infected seedlings will collapse and die at ground level. It is particularly likely to occur if the seedlings are overcrowded or grown in very close, damp conditions. The best preventive measures are to sow seeds thinly and thin them if they are at all overcrowded. Avoid sowing in very wet conditions. Seeds treated with thiram or captan are less vulnerable. If damping off does occur, spray the seedlings with Cheshunt compound.

White blister: if glistening white pustules appear in rings on the leaves of your radishes, they are probably infected with the fungus known as white blister. Although not a serious disease this does disfigure the crop. It is most likely to occur if the radishes are crowded or weak. If white blister does occur, remove and burn all infected leaves. The weed Shepherd's Purse harbours white blister, so make sure your garden is free of this and other cruciferous weeds.

Downy mildew: this is another fungal disease encouraged by poor cultivation. It appears on seedlings and young plants usually on the undersides of the leaves, as white tufts or downy patches. Remove and destroy infected seedlings or leaves. If the plants are badly infected, spray with Bordeaux mixture or zineb.

Club root (finger and toe): this fungal disease usually infects brassicas, but radishes are occasionally damaged. The symptoms are bluish and wilting leaves, and swollen, black, rotting roots which have an unpleasant odour. It is most likely to occur on acid, badly drained soils, so make sure any drainage problems and excessive acidity are corrected before planting. Calomel dust sprinkled in the seed drills before sowing offers some protection. Apply it at the rate of 30 g per 1.5 m (1 oz per 5') run.

Scab: this fungal disease appears as

Fungal infections appear as woolly growths on the roots or leaves. Radishes grown in wet or overcrowded conditions are most vulnerable.

White downy patches on these radishes are the result of severe infection with downy mildew; it is encouraged by poor cultivation.

circular, sunken scabby patches on the roots, although occasionally the patches may be raised. The infection is most likely to occur on light, gravelly, hungry soils lacking in organic matter. The most effective preventive measure if your soil is light is to dig in plenty of well-rotted manure, leafmould or vegetable compost well before planting. Avoid overliming your soil, as. excessive lime seems to encourage the disease.

Flea beetle: these are the only pests likely to harm radishes. They eat small circular holes in the seedlings and young leaves and will eat older leaves until they are skeletonized and lace-like. They are particularly active in sunny weather from mid to late spring. Adult flea beetles vary in size and colour, but are usually dark blue or black, occasionally with yellow stripes. Because the beetles overwinter in garden debris or rubbish in hedge bottoms, practising good garden hygiene is the best preventative measure. Because they feed on weeds of the *Cruciferae* family, such as Shepherd's Purse and Charlock, make sure your garden is weed-free. Never leave stumps of Brussels sprouts or cabbages in the ground after winter, because flea beetles will feed on them until they can move onto new crops.

If your radishes are healthy and growing quickly, it is unlikely that flea beetles can do severe damage. Water the radishes in dry weather to make sure they are not checked. If the beetles do appear, dust the beds with derris.

GUIDE TO RADISH TROUBLES

Symptoms	*Probable causes*
Seedlings collapsing at ground level	Damping off
Rings of white pustules on leaves	White blister
White downy patches on undersides of leaves	Downy mildew
Bluish wilting leaves, swollen, foul-smelling roots	Club root
Circular sunken dark scabby patches on roots	Scab
Small circular holes in leaves of seedlings especially	Flea beetle

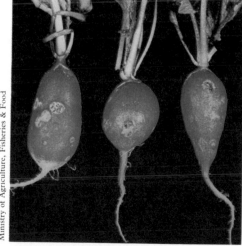

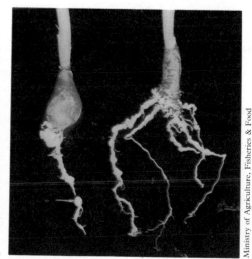

These radishes show the main symptom of scab: circular sunken scabby patches on the roots. It is most likely to occur on light soils.

These swollen and distorted roots are infected with club root, a fungal infection associated with badly drained soils.

Tomatoes

Lycopersicon esculentum (fam. *Solanaceae*)
Perennial, cultivated as an **annual,**
Sowing to harvesting time: 12-15
weeks, depending on variety.
Size: plants 15 cm-1 m (6″-3′) tall, depending on variety.
Yield: greenhouse tomatoes about 3.6—5.4 kg (8–12 lb) per
plant; outdoor tomatoes 1.8–2.7 kg (4–6 lb).

Tomatoes have always been one of the most popular crops for the amateur gardener. Once regarded almost solely as a greenhouse crop, with the development of new, hardier varieties many people now grow them successfully outdoors. However, it is important to remember that the crop is native to a fairly hot, dry climate. High summer temperatures suit them perfectly, but since that kind of weather cannot be expected every year in a temperate climate, some care must be taken to give tomatoes the right situation.

Tomatoes do not like damp, cool, cloudy conditions, and they cannot stand frosts. Bearing these facts in mind, there is no reason why anyone should not do well with the crop.

Tomatoes cannot be grown outdoors without protection before all danger frost is past. Since frosts can occur right up to the end of spring and may return in early autumn, the time left for cropping is short. Allowing for a growing period of from 12 to 15 weeks, it is possible to sow the seed outdoors in early summer and harvest a crop in late summer, although the farther north one lives the more

hazardous this is. Alternatively you can buy young tomato plants from a nursery. Cloches and frames can be used in several different ways to give you a better chance of a good outdoor crop.

Tomatoes in a cold greenhouse
Most gardeners save growing time by starting tomato plants under glass, even if they are to be transplanted outdoors later. There is no doubt that a greenhouse gives the very best conditions for a successful crop.

Soil
Tomatoes will grow in almost any reasonably rich soil, or even in a basically poor soil if plenty of nutrients are supplied during the season. A greenhouse border soil can be prepared for tomatoes by flooding with water about a month before planting to ensure good water reserves in the subsoil (this is very important) and then, when the soil·is workable, by working in rotted organic matter such as farmyard manure at the rate of one barrowload per 3.5 sq m (per 4 sq yd). About 7-10 days before planting, fork into the top few inches a

1. Sow tomato seeds in a propagator from late winter onward. Space the seeds about 1.5 cm (½") apart.

2. When the seedlings are large enough to handle, prick them off into 7.5 cm (3") pots filled with compost.

3. When the plants are 12.5-15 cm (5-6") high, transplant them to permanent beds and tie to stakes.

4. If growing single-stem varieties, remove axillary-shoots with a clean knife to control the plant's growth.

5. Give liquid fertilizer as soon as the fruit begins to swell, and repeat every two weeks until harvesting.

6. If growing bush varieties, put dry straw on the ground under the plants to protect them from soil and slugs.

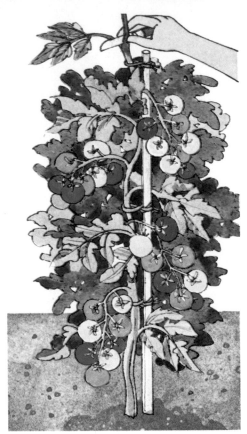

7. When six or seven trusses are ripe, stop the stem one leaf above top truss.

8. Harvest tomatoes as they ripen, leaving the calyx on the fruit.

dressing of a proprietary tomato fertilizer at the rate recommended by the makers. However, after a few years of growing tomatoes in the same soil, pests, bacteria and fungi will multiply in a greenhouse, so precautions must be taken. Either sterilize the soil each year or introduce new compost. A home-made compost can be made of four parts good, sieved loam (preferably a fairly heavy one), one part well-rotted farm-yard manure or garden compost, one part coarse sand (all parts by bulk), together with 120 g (4 oz) of a tomato fertilizer, and 22 g ($\frac{3}{4}$ oz) lime per bushel of the mixture. Mix together well, and leave for ten days before use.

Isolate this compost from the soil of the greenhouse floor by growing the plants in boxes or containers separated from the ground by staging or a sheet of polythene.

An increasingly popular method is to use 'grow-bags', which are polythene sacks filled with a suitable compost. Normally bought complete and ready for use from garden supply centres, they prevent the tomato roots coming into contact with contaminated soil.

Sowing
Sow the seed in boxes, pots or trays of well-draining sieved loam or seed compost from mid-winter to early spring. Sow each seed separately, about 0.5 cm ($\frac{1}{4}$") deep and 2.5 cm (1") apart. Cover the seed-box with glass and brown paper or black polythene until the seeds start to germinate in about 7-14 days. Then remove the covering and

9. Pick by severing the stalk at the knuckle just above the calyx.

10. To ripen green fruit, lay the plants on straw and cover with cloches.

expose the seedlings to as much light as possble, without burning them.

Tomatoes require a germination temperature of about 15 C (60 F). That temperature should be maintained, if possible, throughout the life of the plant; 10 C (50 F) is about the lowest permissable level. 27 C (80 F) is generally considered to be the upper limit. If you are sowing before spring, sow more seed than you might think necessary. This earlier sown seed has a tendency to produce a percentage of inadequate, fern-like plants with ragged leaves—because of poor light. These must be rejected, as they will never crop well.

Transplanting
Transplanting is done in two stages. When the seedlings have grown two seed leaves, and the first true leaf is starting to appear, they need to be moved to give them more growing space. It is usual to transplant them into 7.5 cm (3″) pots, often into peat pots or pots made of black polythene, containing a suitable potting compost for tomatoes. The young plants remain in the pots, in maximum light, to grow into strong, bushy specimens. When they are 12.5-15 cm (5-6″) high they are ready to transplant into their permanent bed, which in the greenhouse can be a pot, box or grow-bag, or a border in the greenhouse floor. At this stage each plant will probably have its first truss of flowers begining to open.

When transplanting, handle carefully, keeping the soil in a ball around the roots. Make sure that both the soil around the plants and the soil into which they are to be set are thoroughly damp, but not saturated. Dig a hole large enough to take the entire contents of the pot in which the plant has been growing. Fill the hole with water if the weather is very dry and quickly transfer the plant and its surrounding compost into it. Press the soil firmly around the stem.

Support
Well-grown tomatoes should yield 3.5-5.5 kg (8-12 lb) of fruit per plant in a season. This is a heavy weight for a plant with a thin stem, so the plant needs support. A string (3 or 4-ply fillis) may be suspended for each plant from an overhead wire, attached at the lower end to a wire hook plunged into the soil, about 23 cm (9″) deep, or to a wire running horizontally about 3.5 cm ($1\frac{1}{2}$″) above the soil, along the row of plants. As the plant grows the string is twisted gently round it taking great care not to snap the top of the plant.

Ventilation and shading
Adequate ventilation is essential—stagnant air allows diseases to develop. Open doors and ventilators as much as possible, avoiding draughts to the plants. Attempts to save on heating costs by keeping ventilators closed may result

**1. Support plants
by twining with
fillis string tied
to horizontal
wires at the top
and bottom of
the greenhouse.
For easy
removal later,
tie the string to
the top wire, as
shown in the
insert.**

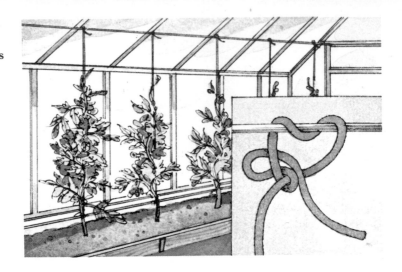

in attacks of moulds and mildews, which
thrive in stuffy atmospheres. It is better
to keep the plants well aired, albeit
slightly chilly.

Provide shade for the plants whenever the temperatures rise above 27°C
(80°F), by painting the glass with a
proprietary shading compound—there
is one which is opaque in sunny weather,
and translucent in rain. Alternatively a
mixture of quicklime in enough water to
make it milk-like, with a little size added
for sticking, can be used. You may of
course have Venetian or roller blinds
attached to the ridge outside the
greenhouse which can be used as needed,
on the south side. Without shading,
leaves will burn and have brown patches.

Pollination
Greenhouse plants may need some
assistance with pollination. The pollen
needs exactly the right atmospheric
humidity to adhere to the female parts of
the flowers and to grow down towards
the ovule, and sometimes the air in the
greenhouse becomes dry. The remedy is
to spray the plants and the air with water,
preferably in the early morning.

Sideshooting and stopping
As soon as flower trusses start to form,
the plant will begin to produce shoots in
the joints between stem and leaf. By

nature, the tomato is a bushy plant, but
allowing these shoots to grow will result
in a mass of bushy foliage and a lot of
under-sized fruits. Remove sideshoots
by pinching them out with thumb and
finger as soon as seen. This pinching out
should be repeated every two or three
days, for the shoots grow quickly. Early
morning is the best time for the job.

Towards the end of the season, when
the plant is bearing six or seven trusses of
fruit, stop the plant, i.e., break off the
growing tip cleanly, just above the
second leaf above the top truss. The
plant can then concentrate all its
resources on developing and ripening
the fruit on the existing trusses, rather
than trying to form more leaves.

De-leafing
Removing the lower leaves of the plant
will encourage it to channel its resources
into fruit production and improve
ventilation close to the soil. But leaves, as
long as they are green, are important to a
plant—they are food factories—and
removal should be approached with
caution. Remove only the leaves beneath
the lowest truss of fruit and one or two
which may be shading it. Using a sharp
knife, remove the chosen leaves completely, so that a clean cut is made flush
with the stem. Later on in the season,
when the life of the plant can be a few

2. As fruit set and swells, remove the leaves below the bottom truss in stages to allow for free air circulation.

3. Spray plants with water each morning to encourage pollination.

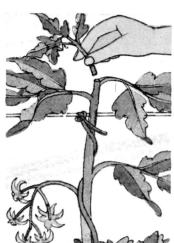

4. Keep plants well watered and mulch with peat to conserve moisture. Shade from the hot sun with blinds.

5. To ensure that the fruit swells remove the growing tip at the top wire at least two leaves beyond the last truss.

weeks more at most, remove the leaves more drastically to promote ripening before the cold weather comes.

Any leaves that turn yellow should be removed completely whenever they appear.

Feeding and watering

Tomatoes need plenty of moisture, but not a saturated soil. In borders, they should be watered heavily whenever the soil has become dry on the surface. In containers, daily watering is usually necessary, twice daily in hot weather. In greenhouses, a daily dampening in hot weather is important. This involves spraying the plants, paths, staging and walls of the greenhouse in the morning and at midday.

To produce the highest possible yield tomatoes need generous feeding. Greenhouse tomatoes will certainly benefit from regular application of nutrients. It is quite satisfactory to use a proprietary tomato fertilizer, following the instructions on the container. If you do want to mix your own, 2 parts sulphate of ammonia, 3 of superphosphate and 2 of sulphate of potash (all by weight) make a good, general fertilizer, applied every seven to ten days from the time the fruits begin to swell, at the rate of about a teaspoonful sprinkled in a wide circle round each plant.

Proprietary tomato fertilizers generally contain a fairly high proportion of potash, of which the plant needs liberal supplies for most of its life. Towards the end of the season, however, it will require more nitrogen to support its long stem and foliage. If the top shoot becomes thin and spindly before the plant is at the stage of pinching out, switch to a fertilizer with a higher nitrogen content and lower potash.

If, as the plant grows larger, the lower leaves start to turn yellow between the veins, the plant is probably deficient in magnesium. Correct this by spraying the plants with a solution of magnesium sulphate (Epsom salts) at the rate of 60 g per 4.5 L (2oz per gallon) of water, about once a week. This condition sometimes occurs when a tomato fertilizer with a high potash content has been used too heavily. The plants absorb potash in preference to magnesium.

Harvesting and aftercare

The bottom trusses ripen first. Pick tomatoes before they are quite ripe. Remove the fruit by severing the stalk at the 'knuckle' just above the calyx. Orange-red tomatoes can complete their ripening on a windowsill within a few days, and their removal before they are fully ripe will enable the plant to divert its resources to fruit at an earlier stage of development.

When the first frosts are imminent, harvest all the tomatoes, whatever their colour. Orange, yellow and even some of the green ones will ripen indoors if each is wrapped in paper, and placed in a warm dark place, although they may take several weeks to do so. Those too small to ripen can be used for chutney.

Burn old plants including the roots. Do not put them on the compost heap, for they may well be carrying disease.

Extending the tomato season

The main advantage of taking the trouble and expense of heating a greenhouse in spring to bring on tomato plants is to have tomatoes quite early in the season, in late spring or early summer when prices are still high in the shops. There is not much point in sowing seed in autumn to try for a late winter or early spring crop, because the daylight hours are so short in late autumn and winter that seeds sown before winter will usually lie dormant for many weeks unless artificial lighting is employed, and even then extra lighting will be required for the plants.

It is possible, however, to extend the tomato season until the very end of the year by planting young plants in a greenhouse in mid-summer and providing them with heat when the frosts come.

Ring culture

Ring culture is an excellent method of growing tomatoes. It is best suited to the greenhouse, but may also be used outdoors. With this method, the plants are grown in bottomless 'rings', 23 or 25 cm (9 or 10") wide and 23 cm (9") deep, set on a base of moist aggregate (coarse sand, gravel or pebbles). The base may also be made of weathered ash or clinkers, or three parts (by volume) of gravel to one part of vermiculite. The plants develop fibrous roots which draw nourishment from the compost in the rings, and longer roots which derive moisture from the aggregate below it.

The rings should be placed 38 cm (15") apart in rows 45 cm (18") apart. Fill each ring to within 1.25 cm ($\frac{1}{2}$") of the top with potting compost two weeks before planting, in order to give the compost time to warm up. Water compost and aggregate two days before the plants are set out. Give an initial 1 L (2 pts) of water to each plant through the rings, but do not water through the rings again unless the plants wilt in hot weather. Keep the aggregate wet. In about ten days, the roots should reach the aggregate. After this, water the aggregate only, keeping it permanently moist. In a hot summer you will need to give about 2 L ($3\frac{3}{4}$ pt) daily for each plant, but less if the weather is cool and dull.

Make sure plants are properly sup-

Eurocross *variety of tomatoes, thriving in pots against a sunny wall.*

ported, either with stakes put in a week after planting, or with wire and string, as for border plants.

When the fruit begins to form on the first truss, begin giving weekly liquid feeds through the rings at the rate of 1 L (2 pt) per plant. The feed should be high in potash. Halfway through the season, add a 2.5 cm (1″) deep top dressing of fresh potting compost or granulated peat. Otherwise, follow all cultivation and pruning instructions as for greenhouse or outdoor tomatoes.

Outdoor tomatoes

Because the natural home of tomatoes is sunny, choose a plot which gets the maximum amount of sunshine. A site near a wall facing the sun, unshaded by trees, is ideal since the plants also need shelter from wind.

Ideally the soil should be dug over during the autumn and allowed to weather. If it is available, plenty of well-rotted farmyard manure or garden compost should be dug in at the same time, especially if the soil is light.

For outdoor tomatoes the seed is sown in early spring in seed-boxes or other containers in a heated greenhouse. Follow the sowing instructions for greenhouse tomatoes. Transplanted to their outdoor site in early summer, they should produce fruit by late summer and

Grow plants in bottomless rings on a bed of aggregate; feed and water via the rings.

Set bush tomatoes in frames; train forward.

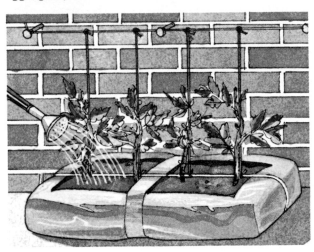

Single-stem plants growing in a peat bag. Support plants with strings tied to a horizontal wire.

Plants grown on stakes in a trench and cloched.

continue cropping until frost checks them. Alternatively, buy young plants for setting out in early summer. After planting in the outdoor bed, cover the plants with flowerpots for several nights, just in case the temperature falls low. When they are growing strongly cover them with a cloche if the temperature falls below 10°C (50°F).

Outdoors, stakes are the simplest method of supporting the plants. Tie the plants to 1.8 m (6′) canes with twine.

Outdoor plants will pollinate themselves without trouble. They will also tolerate temperatures far above 27°C (80°F) if they are given sufficient moisture. If it has been applied, farmyard manure will help to conserve moisture, but during a drought heavy daily watering is necessary, 4-5 litres (a gallon) a day is not too much per plant.

The side-shoots should be pinched out exactly as for greenhouse tomatoes, and the leading shoots should also be stopped after the formation of five trusses or so.

A very rich soil outdoors may provide all the nutrients the tomatoes require, but they are gross feeders, so if the tomato patch is not generously supplied with organic material, liquid feeding exactly as for greenhouse tomatoes will be helpful.

Bush tomatoes

Bush varieties are now available from most seedsmen. They are hardier than ordinary tomatoes and mature more quickly, making them very useful for growing in cooler districts.

The instructions for staking, pinching out side-shoots and stopping leading shoots do not apply to bush tomatoes. Simply allow them to grow freely. They will form small bushes about 45 cm (18″) high and 45 cm (18″) in diameter.

Soil, manuring, watering and general culture are all the same as for ordinary tomatoes. Each plant will produce a mass of fruit, usually much smaller than the ordinary tomato but with a delicious flavour. The stems will sag under the weight of the fruit, so it is advisable to put a layer of straw or plastic over the ground beneath the bushes to keep the fruit clean.

The bush tomatoes include a number of novelties. There are plum-shaped tomatoes, pear-shaped varieties, tomatoes that grow on 'strings' like currants, and yellow bush tomatoes. Some of the smaller varieties may even be grown in pots on window sills or in window boxes.

Growing in a cold frame

Both cold frames and cloches will give a more certain chance of tomatoes developing outdoors. Because the plants can be put out considerably earlier than without protection, the tomatoes thus have a longer period of growth. Choose a slightly shaded, south-facing site, sheltered by a wall if possible, for your frame. Prepare the soil in winter as for outdoor cultivation, and raise the

seedlings in the way described above, or buy young plants. Put the plants in the frame in mid to late spring, or late spring to early summer for bush varieties. Two weeks before planting out, water the soil thoroughly and put the lights on to let the soil warm up. Ten days before transplanting the young plants from their 7.5 cm (3″) pots, give a top dressing of three parts rotted garden compost to one part granulated peat, with 90 g (3 oz) of bonemeal to each bushel of the mixture.

Set the plants towards the back of the frame. Leave 45 cm (18″) each way between single stem (cordon) types and train them along a cane from the back to the front of the frame. Leave the same planting distance between bush varieties. Otherwise, grow as for outdoor tomatoes. Another method of using a frame is to up-end it against a wall and use it to protect three or four tomato plants in pots or boxes.

Growing under cloches

Prepare the soil as for outdoor cultivation. Then, if growing cordon tomatoes, dig a V-shaped trench, 15 cm (6″) deep, 30 cm (12″) wide at the top and 15 cm (6″) wide at the bottom, a week before planting. Add the same top dressing to the bottom of the trench as used for growing under frames.

Set the plants out in mid-spring in warm areas, but a little later in cooler districts. Plant bush types 90 cm (3′) apart and cordon types 45 cm (18″) apart. Extra height can be gained by standing the cloches on bricks, or you could use tall barn cloches for even more height. Remove the cloches from cordon types when the growing tips have nearly reached the tops, and thereafter treat as outdoor tomatoes.

Container growing

Even without a garden, small quantities of tomatoes can be grown in pots, troughs, peat bags or even rings, on patios and balconies. Cultivate the plants in the same way as normal garden tomatoes. All containers except peat bags must hold a minimum depth of 17.5 cm (7″) of a reliable potting compost. Support the plants with canes or by looping a fillis string round the base of each one and tying the other end to a horizontal wire held to a wall with nails. Give regular liquid feeds as well as watering frequently. If using peat bags, water exactly according to manufacturer's instructions.

Exhibition tips

To grow big tomatoes, plants with an unusual number of trusses, or plants with an unusual amount of fruit per truss, try this method: instead of staking the plant, allow it to fall over and grow along the ground. The soil must contain well-rotted manure or garden compost.

Peg the stem down at intervals. At the points where it is pegged it will grow more roots. The plant will then absorb nourishment from perhaps four to eight times as many roots as a normal plant would, and should produce a correspondingly greater weight of fruit. This technique is best employed with indoor tomatoes in a heated greenhouse for an early start, but it can also be successful outdoors.

For a prize-winning truss, select one truss and remove all the others, so that the plant's resources will all be used by the one remaining.

For a single, prize-winning tomato, leave only one on the plant. Spray it frequently with lukewarm water so that it does not burst its skin.

Companion plants

Marigolds, particularly the French variety, help to repel whiteflies, one of the most common of tomato pests, and some commercial growers have marigolds in their tomato greenhouses.

There are also plants which have a detrimental effect on each other. Growing potatoes and tomatoes near each other is to be avoided, because they are members of the same family and therefore attract the same problems.

Pests & Diseases

Tomato moth: the green or pale brown caterpillars of the tomato moth may feed on the leaves and also the fruit, causing great damage. The moths lay their eggs in early to mid-summer, and the caterpillars are seen from mid-summer to early autumn. Caterpillars should be removed by hand and destroyed as soon as they are seen, but if the attack is very bad, spray with fenitrothion.

Eelworm: both the potato root eelworm and the root-knot eelworm can infect tomato roots, causing stunted growth, discoloured leaves and wilting plants. In severe infestations, plants will die. Plants infected by eelworm usually have tiny, cream-coloured cysts on the roots. There is no satisfactory chemical control for eelworm which is available to gardeners. Dig up and burn every scrap of the infected plants, especially the roots, and avoid growing tomatoes on the same ground for at least five years.

Red spider mite: tomatoes grown under glass are especially susceptible to red spider mite. The mites lay their eggs and feed on the undersides of the leaves, producing a reddish mottled look. Fumigation of the greenhouse with azobenzene will help control the pest or spray with derris or malathion.

Whitefly: these can be one of the most troublesome tomato pests, and they can

Serious damage to both fruit and leaves caused by an infestation of white fly.

ICI Ltd.

attack both greenhouse and outdoor plants. The adult flies, which look like tiny moths, lay their eggs on the undersides of leaves. The immature insects feed on the leaves, secreting honeydew which encourages sooty mould to form. The leaves look greyish and curling. As soon as you see whitefly, spray with resmethrin or malathion.

Leafmould (Cladosporium): this very common greenhouse disease is a fungus which causes yellow patches on the leaves. The undersides of the leaves are often covered in a brown or purple mould. The damage to foliage can be quite severe, and the flowers and fruits can also be affected. Leafmould is most likely to appear where the temperature and humidity at night are high, so maintain good ventilation without drought at such times. Keep an eye open for the disease, which tends to appear from mid-summer, and pick off infected leaves as soon as seen. If necessary, spray with benomyl. Some varieties of tomato are cladosporium-resistant.

Grey mould (Botrytis): this fungus thrives in excessively moist atmospheres such as an unventilated greenhouse. Infected parts (leaves, stems or fruit) grow patches of grey fur, beneath which the plant tissue rots, and eventually the whole plant may die. Prevent by careful ventilation; remove and destroy any infected plants, or parts of plants. The cuts on plants which result from this can be treated with benomyl.

Water or ghost spot: this is caused by the spores of grey mould germinating on the fruits but then drying up because of a change to warm dry conditions. It shows as small, transparent rings on the stem of the fruit and does not cause any real damage. Try not to over-water or splash water on the setting fruit.

Potato blight: this disease also attacks tomatoes, which are members of the same family, so take precautions not to grow potatoes and tomatoes in the same ground or too near to each other. Infected plants have dark brown to black patches on the leaves and eventually develop brown black patches on the fruit. Destroy any affected leaves as soon as you see them. Spraying with Bordeaux mixture in mid to late summer is a good preventative measure.

Verticillium wilt: a fungus disease which infects the roots of the plants, and is soil-borne. First symptoms are the wilting of the top leaves in hot weather, then the lower leaves start to turn yellow; gradually the whole plant wilts and becomes permanently limp. If the stem is cut through horizontally just above soil level, there will be a brown stain in the internal tissues. Infected plants cannot be cured, but mulching close round the stem with moist peat will encourage the plant to put out new

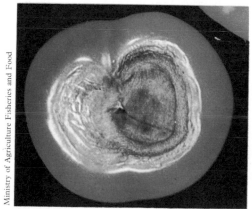

Hard scabs on the fruits produced by severe blossom end rot.

Mottled leaves on a plant suffering from mosaic virus disease.

Ministry of Agriculture Fisheries and Food

ICI Ltd

GUIDE TO TOMATO TROUBLES

Symptom	Probable cause
Irregular holes in leaves, brownish-green caterpillars	Tomato moth
Red mottling on underside of leaves	Red spider mite
Limp, curling leaves, sticky black patches; tiny white flies on undersurface	Whitefly
Small, round leaves; yellow spots, brown fur on underside	Leafmould
Dark brown blotches on leaves, stems and fruit	Potato blight
Mottled yellow and crinkled leaves	Mosaic virus
Bronze brown spots on leaves	Spotted wilt (virus)
Wilting yellow leaves; eventually whole plant wilts	Verticullium wilt
Patches of grey fur	Grey mould
Long, thin, threadlike leaves	Enation mosaic virus
Transparent spots on fruit with 'halo' around them	Water spot
Hard patches on fruit around calyx	Greenback
Yellow patches on red fruit	Blotchy ripening
Hard, sunken dark patch on fruit at blossom end	Blossom end rot
Brown rings around stem at base	Stem rot
Stunted growth; lumps or cysts on roots	Root knot eelworm
	Potato eelworm

healthy roots, which may just save it sufficiently to ripen some of the crop. Spraying the plants daily and lowering the temperature by shading or more ventilation will also help. Destroy infected plants at the end of the season, especially the roots, and sterilize the soil if tomatoes are to be grown there the following season.

Greenback: fruits have hard green patches round the stalk which never colour. The cause may be exposure to too much sun, or lack of potash.

Blotchy ripening: another functional disorder; parts of the fruit remain orange, yellow or pale green and never ripen. Insufficient potash is the cause.

Split fruit: this occurs as a result of irregular water supplies, either because a lot of water has been given after a prolonged dry period in the greenhouse, or because heavy rain follows a drought outdoors.

Stem rot (Didymella): this is a fungus disease which produces a corky infection that girdles the plant stems at soil level. The plants then wilt, and can be completely destroyed. Badly affected plants should be removed and burnt but, if the disease is seen early, spraying with captan may help.

Blossom end rot: this is a condition in which a round, sunken, dark brown or black patch appears on the fruit at the blossom end. It is not caused by a disease but by a severe shortage of water when the fruit is swelling. It can be prevented by regular and adequate watering.

Virus diseases: a good many virus diseases for which there is no cure, can attack tomatoes. Remove any diseased plants immediately. Spotted wilt is the most serious, as it spreads rapidly and can destroy a crop. The young top leaves turn brown, and concentric rings appear on them. The plant stops growing. Thrips spread the disease, especially in the greenhouse, so control these by spraying with malathion, if seen.

Mosaic virus shows as pale green or yellow mottling on the leaves, together with curling and distortion. The fruits will be affected only in severe cases and will show no symptoms.

Yellow mosaic is more serious but rarely seen, with both fruit and leaves mottled with yellow patches. Diseased plants should be dug up and burned.

Enation mosaic is a commonly seen virus trouble, in which the leaves are so badly distorted as to be reduced to long, thin threads, curled and twisted, mainly near the top of the plant. Growth will stop or be slow.

Varieties

Cordon varieties recommended only under glass

Amberly Cross: F₁ hybrid; early and heavy cropper; best for growing under glass; resistant to leafmould and greenback.

Big Boy: F₁ hybrid; enormous tomatoes, each of which can weigh up to 500g (1 lb); excellent flavour. Allow 3 trusses only.

Britain's Breakfast: egg-shaped tomato of excellent flavour; grows best under glass.

Eurocross: F₁ hybrid with several variations; best grown under glass; heavy cropper of large, well-flavoured fruit; resistant to greenback and leafmould.

White: produces yellowish-white tomatoes with a very sweet flavour.

Golden Sunrise: heavy cropper of golden-yellow, medium sized, sweet fruits.

Grower's Pride: vigorous and early F₁ hybrid; reliable indoor variety; excellent cropper; very disease resistant.

Grenadier: new variety; F₁ hybrid; heavy cropper for cold greenhouses; non-greenback; resistant to leafmould.

Britain's Breakfast

Pat Brindley

Eurocross

A-Z Collection

Other cordon varieties, including those for outdoor cultivation

Ailsa Craig: medium-sized fruit of good colour and excellent flavour; early fruiting; can be grown outdoors or under glass.

Alicante: excellent variety which succeeds equally well outdoors or under glass; early fruiting; greenback resistant.

Best of All: large, deep scarlet fruits; heavy cropper; suitable for outdoor growing.

Carters Fruit: grows under glass or outdoors; easy to slice and peel the well-flavoured fruits; very few seeds.

Craigella: form of Ailsa Craig bred for resistance to greenback; reliable cropper of medium-sized, tasty fruits.

Gardener's Delight (Sugar Plum): very popular outdoor variety; long trusses of small but very sweet tomatoes.

Histon Early: one of the earliest of the tall-growing varieties; heavy cropper of bright red, large well-flavoured fruits.

Pixie: very fast ripening; small, compact plants; heavy cropper; hardy, may be grown outdoors.

Sioux: F₁ hybrid; crops early and well; grow outdoors or under glass; medium sized fruits of good quality and taste.

Sub-Arctic Plenty: new type grows very well under most conditions and withstands cold better than most; bite-sized, sweet fruits.

Sunrise: suitable for indoor or outdoor cultivation; medium-sized, well-flavoured fruits.

Sweet 100: new variety; very heavy cropper of tiny, sweet tomatoes; must be staked.

Brian Furner

Yellow Perfection

Brian Furner

Outdoor Girl

Harry Smith

Ailsa Craig

Brian Furner

Tiny Tim

Yellow Perfection: suitable for growing outdoors or under glass; heavy cropper; fruits are bright yellow and well flavoured.

Moneymaker: one of the most popular tomatoes; medium-sized, well-shaped scarlet fruits; extremely heavy cropper but rather bland flavour.

MM: F_1 hybrid similar to *Moneymaker;* very early ripening; resistant to leafmould; good all rounder, but especially suitable for cold greenhouses.

Moneycross: another *Moneymaker* type; matures early; resistant to leafmould; fruits of good shape and colour.

Outdoor Girl: one of the best outdoor varieties; very well-flavoured fruits; grows to about 1.2m (4′).

Ronaclave: one of the best tall outdoor varieties; F_1 hybrid; crops early and heavily; large, fleshy fruits; resistant to leafmould, wilt and greenback.

Bush Varieties

The Amateur: one of the earliest and best bush varieties; can be grown indoors or out; heavy cropper of deep red fruits.

Tiny Tim: dwarf bush type suitable for a windowbox; tiny, bright red, almost seedless tomatoes.

Sigmabush: F_1 hybrid; early maturing; high yield; ripens well under poor conditions.

Sleaford Abundance: F_1 hybrid; dwarf bush type; outdoor variety; produces small, bright red tomatoes.

Fruit

Apples

Malus pumila (fam. *Rosaceae*)
Hardy deciduous tree, with a useful life of about
50 years.
Planting to harvesting time: dwarf trees on M9
rootstock produce fruit when about three years old. More
vigorous trees take a year or so longer.
Size: from about 1.8 m (6′) tall for dwarf bushes to about
7.5 m (25′) for standard trees. Up to 12 m (40′) for crab and
cider apples.
Yield: dwarf bush trees may average about 18 kg (40 lb) a
year; bush trees, 36 kg (80 lb), and mature cider apple trees
may yield 500 kg ($\frac{1}{2}$ ton).

The apple is probably the most widely grown tree fruit because it is reasonably hardy and there are varieties to suit most soil and weather conditions. Even a neglected apple tree will produce some kind of crop, but all too often the wormy or diseased fruit harvested from neglected trees could easily be avoided. With a little care, a mature tree can be restored to vigorous cropping within a couple of seasons and will supply the family with large supplies of delicious fruit.

Apples are a rewarding crop to grow in the small garden. It does not take long for a young tree to start fruiting; dwarfing rootstock can be chosen to restrict the size of the tree so that it will not outgrow its site; a small number of trees will provide all the apples that a family will want, and careful selection of varieties can ensure fruit almost all year round.

The trees will grow happily in most temperate regions. They need a sunny, well-drained site which is sheltered and frost-free at blossom time to ensure that

insects can pollinate. They will not grow in gardens waterlogged for long periods, although there is a way of overcoming this problem (see over). Cooking apples are more tolerant than dessert ones of heavy clay soil, high rainfall and indifferent drainage—and they can survive with less sunshine.

Types of apple

Apples can be divided into four groups: cooking apples, dessert (or eating) apples, cider apples and crab apples. The last two groups can be planted as pollinators for the others.

Cookers are sharply flavoured and are not usually eaten raw. They tend to have a longer season, to keep better and are more tolerant of less-than-perfect conditions than dessert apples, but they do, however, need more nitrogenous fertilizer.

Sweeter in flavour, and mainly eaten raw, are the dessert apples. These are smaller than cooking apples and have a shorter eating season. The trees dislike

A modern dwarf bush apple tree — convenient to look after and ideal for the small gardener.

rainfall of more than 1 m (40″) a year.

Choosing trees

A combination of cooking and dessert apples suits most families best. Nearly all apple trees must have another variety nearby flowering at the same time, if they are to bear fruit, so you should plant a minimum of two. Most varieties have plenty of pollen and will pollinate one another, provided their flowering seasons coincide or overlap. Some have little pollen—they are known as triploid and need a suitable pollinator to set their fruit. Triploids will not pollinate the other tree, however, so in this case there should be a third variety present (not triploid) to ensure a good crop on all three.

A very few varieties are self-fertile but all will give bigger crops if pollinated by another.

Tree shapes: the simplest and most appropriate form of tree for the small garden is the bush. These small, free standing trees are simple to manage and the fruit can be easily harvested. For very small sites they can be obtained in dwarf forms needing as little as 1.5 m (5′) space.

Apple trees can, however, be trained in several different shapes, some of which are particularly useful. Cordons are excellent space savers grown on walls or fences, or can be used in a row as a screen. Fans are also suitable for a large wall, but apple trees should not be placed in too warm a site. The espalier, with branches trained at regular intervals at right angles from the trunk, and dwarf pyramid trees are also popular.

If you want to train a tree into one of these artificial shapes, you must buy a maiden—a one-year-old. The inexperienced gardener may find it easier to buy a ready trained tree, two or three years old, from the nurseryman. Maintaining the shape is then relatively simple. Training cordon trees is described in this chapter.

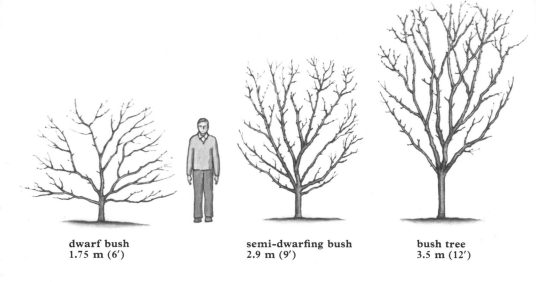

dwarf bush
1.75 m (6′)

semi-dwarfing bush
2.9 m (9′)

bush tree
3.5 m (12′)

Rootstocks: nowadays trees are formed by joining the apple variety to a separate root system or 'stock'. The fruiting habit of the resulting tree is that of the top, called the scion, but the size is determined by the rootstock.

The development of what are called dwarfing rootstocks means that now small trees are available which fruit abundantly. The research was carried out at East Malling Research Station and at Merton in England and their rootstocks, referred to as M (Malling) and MM (Malling Merton), are used throughout the world. By choosing between rootstocks you can select the variety you want at the size you want. For instance, M9 rootstock produces the most dwarf trees, M26 more vigorous ones and MM106 and M7 semi-dwarf specimens. If you are buying a tree, the nursery catalogue will explain the differences in detail.

There are trees available with several varieties (usually three) grafted on to the same roots. These 'family trees' are particularly suitable where space is very limited. The three varieties will pollinate each other and you will have a selection of types of apple.

Age of tree: if you intend to train an apple on a fence or wall yourself, buy a maiden (one-year-old tree). You will, however, get fruit sooner by buying a two or three-year-old cordon or bush. But do not let trees bear more than one or two sample fruit each in their first summer—give the roots time to re-establish.

Preparing the soil
A medium loam, slightly acid and well-drained, is the perfect type of soil.

If possible, prepare the soil in summer by deep digging to improve surface drainage and get rid of perennial weeds. If you cannot prepare the soil so far in advance, firm the ground well by treading or rolling it after digging. Then leave it to settle for two weeks or more before planting.

If the soil is very acid make it less so by applying lime. Improve a neutral or only just alkaline soil by working in manure and use acid fertilizers such as sulphate of ammonia when necessary. The lack of nutrients caused by highly alkaline soil can be corrected by modern artificial fertilizers and foliar sprays.

Work in liberal quantities of manure, garden compost, peat or leafmould to improve the consistency of both light, sandy or gravelly soil, and do the same

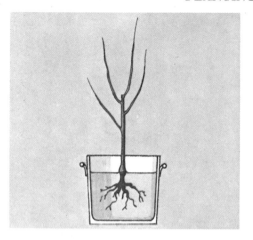

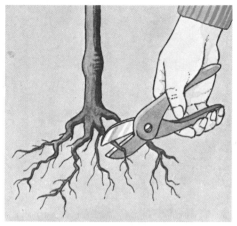

1. If roots have dried out, soak in water for about an hour.

2. Trim back damaged roots. Make a slanting cut in thicker roots.

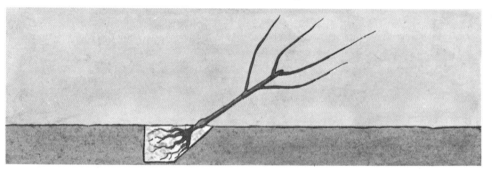

3. If planting is delayed, bury roots in a trench, up to soil mark on stem.

4. Place stick across hole to check planting depth. Soil mark on stem should align with the stick.

5. Drive in upright stakes 23 cm (9″) away from tree. Return soil, making sure it penetrates between the roots.

6. Tread the soil down firmly and level off. Make sure the union of rootstock and scion is above ground.

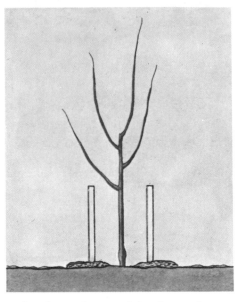

7. Apply surface mulch of rotted compost, manure or peat, but avoid touching the stem.

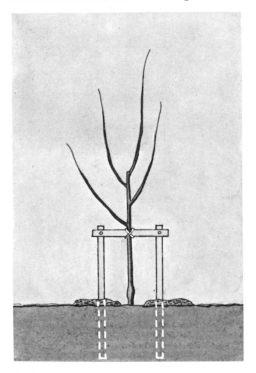

8. Erect a crosspiece between the stakes, to run below the bottom branch of the tree. Tie the tree to the crosspiece.

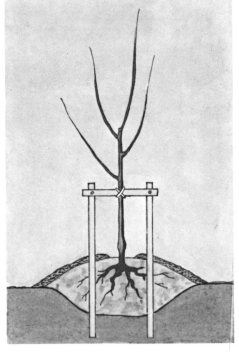

9. Planting method for badly drained ground: create a mound above a shallow hole to raise tree roots above the normal level.

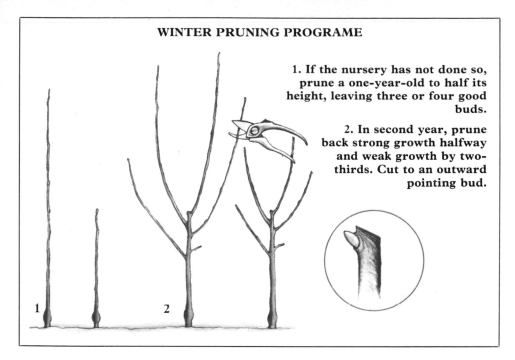

WINTER PRUNING PROGRAME

1. **If the nursery has not done so, prune a one-year-old to half its height, leaving three or four good buds.**

2. **In second year, prune back strong growth halfway and weak growth by two-thirds. Cut to an outward pointing bud.**

thing for heavy clay soils.

If you are planning to grow apples in a kitchen garden where there has been a high level of feeding, beware! Tree growth, especially of dessert apples, will be stimulated to the detriment of fruit blossom. Delay tree-planting for a year, meanwhile do not fertilize the ground but go on growing vegetables.

Planting

Planting is possible at any time during the dormant season—when there are no leaves on the tree—so long as the ground is neither frozen hard nor too wet to work freely. The soil should be crumbly, not pasty. Soon after leaf-fall is best.

Plant the trees as soon as they are delivered, if possible. If the roots have dried out in transit soak them in water in a dustbin for about an hour. Trim back any damaged roots, making slanting cuts on the underside of thicker roots.

If for any reason planting has to be delayed, heel trees in temporarily in the open. Make a trench, with one side sloping at an angle of about 45°, deep enough to bury the roots up to the soil

mark on the stem, which shows the depth to which the tree was growing in the nursery. Lay the tree in this trench and cover the roots with soil just up to the soil mark. Tread in lightly.

The trees should not be planted too close together. For bush trees on MM106 rootstock in average quality soil, allow a radius of 2 m (7′) around each bush. In rich soil, increase this to 2.8 m (9′). Bushes on M26 rootstock need a radius of 1.75 m (6′) space. For the smallest trees on M9 rootstock, allow a radius of 1.5 m (5′) and for vigorous growers on dwarf M9 rootstock, 1.75 m (6′). Family trees need a spacing of at least 4.25 m (14′).

Try to get someone to help you when you plant the trees. An extra pair of hands will make it much easier to position a tree straight and upright. Dig each planting hole wide and deep enough for all the roots to be spread out fully in their natural growing position. When you have finished planting and treading down the soil, the tree should be at exactly the same soil depth as it was when growing in the nursery. The join of the rootstock and the scion (called the union) must not be below ground level, or the scion may put out its own rootstock.

To check that your planting hole is of the right depth, lay a stick across it to show you the ground level and hold the tree in its planting position in the hole. The level of the stick should match the mark on the stem of the soil from its former planting.

All bush trees need staking. Use 5 cm (2″) diameter stakes which have been treated with a copper-based preservative. Drive two upright stakes into the planting hole, each about 23 cm (9″) away from the tree. In light soil they should eventually be buried 60 cm (2′) below soil level, in heavy soil 45 cm (1′ 6″).

Put a spadeful of soil into the bottom of the hole, spread out the roots, sprinkle over a few handfuls of moist peat and start returning the soil. If soil is rather poor, mix a couple of handfuls of sterilized bonemeal with the soil waiting to go back into the planting hole, but not in immediate contact with the roots. Get a helper to wriggle the tree a little so the soil filters well between the roots. Tread the soil down to firm it as you go.

Water with one 12 L (2½ gal) bucketful and, if there is no rain within a week, give it another bucketful.

Level off the soil and surround the tree as far as the branches extend with a surface mulch of well-rotted compost, manure, leafmould or damp peat, but do not let this touch the tree stem or it may rot the bark.

As soon as the tree is planted fix a crosspiece to the two stakes, a little below the lowest branch, and fasten the tree to it. Use a purpose-made plastic tree tie for this job, or wrap a piece of sacking or cloth around the tree to protect the bark and tie over it with soft string. Finish by twisting the string between the tree and stake to prevent chaffing.

During the early months the soil will settle and the tie may need repositioning.

THINNING FRUITLETS

Thin dessert apples to improve size and appearance of fruit. Use a thin pointed pair of scissors and cut out the central fruitlet in each cluster and then any diseased or smaller fruitlets. Leave only one or two fruit on each cluster.

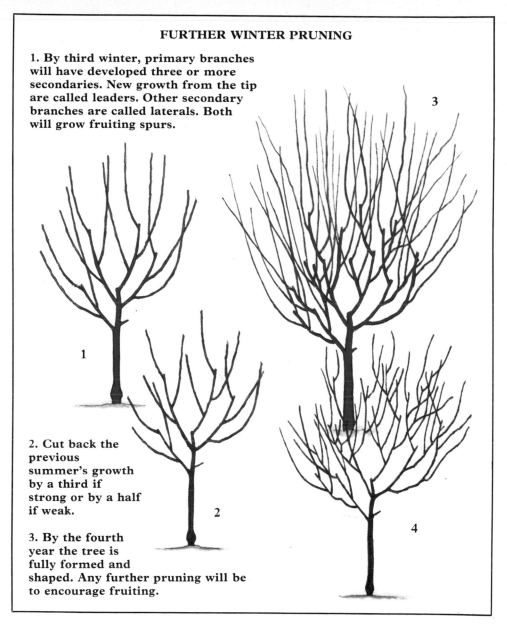

FURTHER WINTER PRUNING

1. By third winter, primary branches will have developed three or more secondaries. New growth from the tip are called leaders. Other secondary branches are called laterals. Both will grow fruiting spurs.

3

1

2. Cut back the previous summer's growth by a third if strong or by a half if weak.

2

3. By the fourth year the tree is fully formed and shaped. Any further pruning will be to encourage fruiting.

4

In two or three years the tree may be able to dispense with support.

Planting on badly drained land
If you want to grow dessert apples and the ground is badly drained, you can plant on a slight mound.

Make only a shallow depression instead of digging a deep planting hole. Stand the tree in this, insert its stakes and then mound up soil from some other part of the garden to the soil mark on the stem. The mound must be wider than the existing extent of the roots to encourage them to grow outwards. Mulching extends further than the branches and therefore each year you will have to topdress further out.

This method can be used also where shallow top soil overlies chalk at a depth

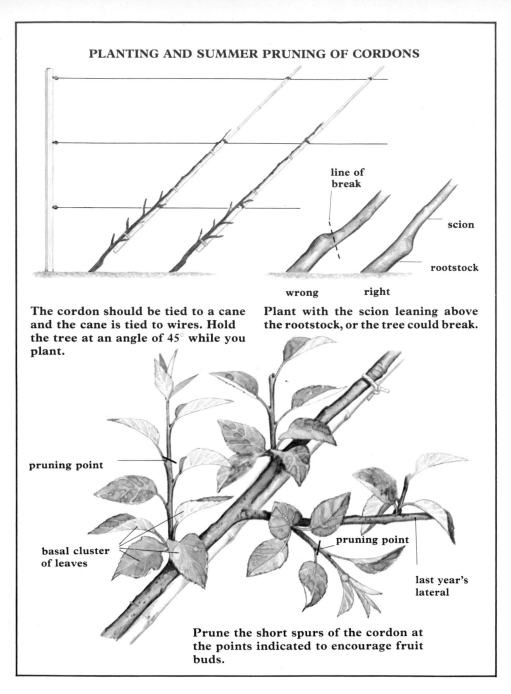

PLANTING AND SUMMER PRUNING OF CORDONS

line of
break

scion

rootstock

wrong   right

**The cordon should be tied to a cane
and the cane is tied to wires. Hold
the tree at an angle of 45° while you
plant.**

**Plant with the scion leaning above
the rootstock, or the tree could break.**

pruning point

pruning point

basal cluster
of leaves

last year's
lateral

**Prune the short spurs of the cordon at
the points indicated to encourage fruit
buds.**

of about 45 cm (1′ 6″).

Trees grown on mounds are more
vulnerable to drought, and plenty of
watering is essential in dry periods,
particularly in early life. A mulch of
garden compost or leafmould to arrest
surface evaporation is very important.

Watering and feeding

The first spring is a critical time for
newly planted trees. In the first few
summers it is essential to water freely

and in adequate quantities, and a surface mulch will do much to conserve moisture in the soil.

Give no more manure in the first season. In succeeding winters, dress the ground around each tree a little further out then the branches extend. Use 38 g per sq m ($1\frac{1}{4}$ oz per sq yd) of sulphate of ammonia and 22 g per sq m (3/4 oz per sq yd) of sulphate of potash. Rake the fertilizers into the surface in late winter.

Thereafter, every other year rake in, at the same time, 52 g per sq m (1 3/4 oz per sq yd) of superphosphate. If the harvest has been heavy, an extra fertilizer dressing is beneficial.

Pruning

Winter pruning is to build a framework of robust main branches. Standards, half-standards and bushes are pruned the same way.

Immediately after planting give the tree its first pruning with sharp secateurs. Hard winter pruning stimulates the wood growth necessary at this stage of the tree's development. If it is an unpruned maiden tree cut it back to half its height, leaving three or four good buds.

If you have bought a two-year-old tree, it will have only three or four branches. If these are strong and long, cut each back half way, making your cut close beyond a growth bud pointing outwards.

If these first branches are thin and wispy and not very long, be more drastic and cut off two-thirds of the length of each. This cutting back will cause growth buds near the cut ends to develop.

By the tree's third winter each of the primary branches will have made three or more secondary branches. Cut back the previous summer's growth by a third if strong, by a half if thin and wispy.

Some sideshoots (the laterals) may have grown from the secondary branches by now. If these laterals are badly placed to make new branches, cut each back to its fourth bud. Any sideshoots springing from the trunk of the tree just below the main branches should be sliced off flush with the stem.

Four-year-old trees are regarded as adult. From now on winter pruning is restricted to the minimum necessary to ensure a continuing supply of fruiting wood, rather than to extend the size of the tree. Remove crossing branches and cankerous or broken ones.

If you do not prune a sideshoot, it will make fruit buds in its second year. These are bigger, fatter and rounder than growth buds and the next year will blossom in spring. Every winter leave at least some sideshoots unpruned to bear fruit. If more sideshoots are needed, cut back some to the second bud from the base. But, in general, cut back just the three-year-old sideshoots which have fruited to a 5 cm (2″) stump.

Do not touch the tips of the branches once fruit-bearing has begun—unless a branch is growing in an undesirable direction and you want to replace the season's new extension growth (the leader) with another one. Some varieties also form fruit buds at the tips of one-year-old shoots. Leave such shoots intact.

This system of pruning will produce a balance of fruiting laterals and vegetating ones to provide fruit later on.

Training cordons

A cordon consists of a single stem bearing fruiting spurs. The tree is planted at an angle to restrict growth and to encourage early fruiting and an even production of buds. Three different varieties can be grown in one 3 m row.

Rows should run from south to north if at all possible. Put in 2.25 m (7′ 6″) sturdy posts, about 3 m (10′) apart. Stretch three 2.5 mm ($\frac{1}{10}$″) gauge galvanized wires between posts at heights of 60 cm (2′), 1.2 m (4′) and 1.8 m (6′). Use an adjustable fence strainer at the end of each wire to keep it taut. Fix a 2.4 m (8′) long bamboo cane to the wires at an angle of 45° where each tree is to be planted.

Plant two to three-year-old cordons 75 cm (2′ 6″) apart at an angle of 45° with the tip pointing away from the midday sun. Space rows 1.8 m (6′) apart.

About 10 cm (4″) from the soil mark there is a swelling where the scion is joined to the rootstock. This is the union. Hold the whole tree at an angle for planting with the scion uppermost on the rootstock. Planted the other way round the tree could break off its roots.

As soon as it is planted, the cordon must be tied to its supporting bamboo cane. Tie in three places—the lowest one 5 cm (2″) above the union.

Pruning cordons

Pruning is necessary in the first winter for tip-bearing types. With these, cut back just the main stem by a quarter of the previous season's growth. Repeat in subsequent winters.

The main pruning is done in mid-summer in warmer districts and up to a month later in cooler ones. Start when you see that sideshoots growing directly from the main cordon stem are maturing–when they are more than 23 cm (9″) long, the leaves have lost their early brightness and become a deep green and the skin of the shoot has stiffened and begun to look bark-like for the lower part of its length.

At the base of such shoots you will usually find a cluster of leaves. Ignore these, count three leaves from the base of the shoot and then cut close after the third leaf. There may also be growths springing from laterals made and pruned in a previous year. Cut each back to the first leaf beyond the basal cluster. If some new shoots are not mature, wait until they are before pruning. If secondary growth occurs in late summer from near the point where you made the first cuts, prune such shoots back to one leaf or bud in mid-autumn.

In about three years, when the cordon reaches the length of its cane, unfasten the cane from the wires and bend the whole tree down about 5 and refasten the cane. Repeat again in a few years

if it appears to be necessary.

Usually there comes a time when the mature tree stops producing further extension growth each summer. But if it reaches the limit of space before this happens, cut it back in spring soon after new growth begins.

Except in the case of tip-bearing varieties, the leader should not normally be pruned until it must be checked for lack of space. If the desired fruit-bearing sideshoots are scarce, however, stimulate the production of more by pruning the season's new extension growth of the leader by one third in winter. To encourage individual buds in a bare length of stem, cut a half-moon notch from the bark just above them.

If after some years there are too many fruiting spurs and they are getting crowded, in winter cut some back and take out others entirely.

Thinning out the fruit

If an apple tree bears a very heavy crop in any one year, it may take a rest the next season. The big crop, too, is likely to be of undersized fruit.

Dessert apples are thinned out to improve the appearance and size of the individual fruit. Cookers tend to be naturally larger and are not usually thinned. Fruit thinning is less likely to be required on dwarf trees growing on M9 rootstock and trees trained as cordons.

Some shedding of fruit occurs naturally about mid-summer or just after, but the earlier you do any thinning the better for the tree. As soon as the fruitlets have 'set' (when a tiny but obvious fruitlet has replaced the blossom and you know a heavy crop is possible) take a thin pointed pair of scissors and cut out the central fruitlet from each cluster. This 'king apple' often proves to be misshapen and of poor keeping quality. Remove any blemished fruitlets and continue thinning until only one or two fruit remain out of each cluster. These fruit should never be closer than 10 cm (4″) to the next cluster.

If the crop is heavy, support the branches with stakes.

Harvesting the crop

When you think an apple is ripe, lift it in the palm of your hand and give it the slightest possible twist. If it comes away easily, it is ready. Take care not to bruise the fruit. Cider and crab apples grown in grass may be allowed to drop off.

Apples intended for storing should be picked just before they are ripe or they will quickly deteriorate but care must be taken not to tear the shoots when picking an unripe crop. Cooking apples may be used before they are ripe but their full flavour will develop with keeping. Cider apples should mature on the tree. Do not leave late crops of dessert apples on the tree after the end of October.

Storing the crop

The ideal storage place for apples is one which is cool—just below 5°C (40°F) – well-ventilated, dark and slightly moist. A loft, garage or shed is usually too dry for this purpose, but by storing the fruit in plastic bags, this problem can be overcome.

Store only sound dry fruit and do not mix varieties in one bag. Use lots of small bags so that any rot cannot spread far. After sealing them snip off a finger-nail sized triangle from each bottom corner to ventilate.

Exhibition tips

Pick ripe perfect fruit and leave on the stalks—all fruit is shown with the stalks in place.

Select only fruit of the same colour, form and size.

Dessert apples should be no more than 7.5 cm (3″) across—about 7 cm (2¾″) is the most favoured size.

Wrap each apple separately in tissue paper and pack in a box of crumpled newspaper to take them to the show.

Stiff paper plates are favoured for displaying fruit. Apples are never polished for shows and usually only one variety is displayed on a plate.

Pests & Diseases

Apples can be attacked by a number of pests and diseases—some of the more common are described below. A regular spraying programme will keep many of them in check: scab, mildew, caterpillars eating leaves (winter moth etc) or fruitlets (sawfly), aphids of various kinds, capsids, apple suckers, red spider mite and scale insects. American blight (woolly aphids), codling moth, canker, brown rot and bitter pit, however, will not be controlled by the spray programme.

Birds may do much damage to buds in winter. A netting fruit cage may be practical for small trees, otherwise, swathe trees in the rayon web sold at garden shops for the purpose.

Every second or third year spray with a tar oil solution during the tree's dormant (leafless) period. This will control the eggs of aphids, winter moth and suckers, as well as adult scale insects. It will also clean the bark of lichen and moss which harbour troubles.

Spraying programme

Each year give the tree three spray treatments. The first is when the leaves are unfolding at 'green cluster' stage: captan to control scab, and malathion against aphids, capsids, apple suckers and winter moth caterpillars.

Brown, ribbon-like scars indicate damage by the maggots of the apple sawfly.

The next spray, about two weeks later when the blossom buds are showing pink, contains captan and dinocap (for mildew).

The third spray is at petal fall when nearly all blossom is off. *Never spray fully opened flowers, because of the danger to bees and other pollinating insects.* This spray is against pests and diseases already mentioned, plus apple sawfly caterpillars.

Pesticides can usually be applied together, *but not all are compatible,* so follow the maker's instructions.

As an alternative to a regular programme of spraying you can spray only if trouble appears and cut out shoots affected by such diseases as mildew or by pests like leaf-curl aphid. Regular feeding of course will do much to aid the tree's resistance to fungal diseases and natural predators may help to keep down pests.

Aphids: these widespread pests cause young leaves and shoot tips to curl. Leaves become sticky and sooty-looking. The insects are small, green or grey in colour, and live on the underside of leaves. Remove and destroy aphids as soon as they appear and spray with an insecticide, for example, malathion.

Apple sawfly: the white maggots of apple sawfly eat into the side of fruitlets leaving a sticky mess at the entrance. The resulting apples bear ribbon-like scars. Spray with malathion when most of the flower petals have fallen.

Apple sucker: attack by this pest shows itself as waxy threads on the flower trusses leading to brown discoloration of petals and a failure to unfold. It feeds on the sap in the same way as aphids and is controlled by the same insecticides: tar oil in winter, or malathion in spring.

Capsid: damage is mainly in the fruitlets, which develop pale scabs and become distorted in shape. Leaves are punctured, puckered and tattered. Control as for aphids.

Codling moth: the grubs of the codling moth have a brown head. From mid-summer they enter the fruit near the eye and eat the centre. Affected fruit becomes highly coloured and drops early. Spray with fenitrothion four weeks after petals fall and again three weeks later. To avoid this pest, tie a band of sacking round the trunk in early mid-summer in which the caterpillars will pupate. Remove and burn band and cocoons in winter.

American blight (woolly aphid): as the name suggests, this pest is covered with white fluff. It commonly feeds on

An infestation of the white fluff-covered woolly aphid, also known as American blight.

Symptoms of canker on a branch, showing shrunken, flaking bark.

the junctions of branches resulting in warty growths; the bark cracks, which allows the entry of canker and other fungal diseases. Malathion sprayed in early summer, repeated two weeks later, or brushing with methylated spirits, will control the aphids.

Red spider mite
These minute pale red insects live on the undersides of leaves and are particularly active in hot dry summers. The leaves become a speckled, dull, pale yellow or grey green, wither and fall early, and new growth is stunted. Spray with derris or malathion.

Scab: this fungus disease produces black or brown spots on leaves and fruit, which later cracks and may become infected with brown rot. It is worst in a wet spring and is treated with captan. Spray at bud-bursting stage and repeat twice at 14-day intervals.

Canker: the most common fungus disease of the wood of branches, trunk and shoots, canker is especially active where soil is badly drained. The bark becomes sunken, and flakes and dies where fungus enters through tree wounds. If it encircles the stem, the branch above will die. Wherever flaking bark is seen, cut back the wood below the infection to healthy growth, making a

clean cut just above a joint. Burn infected wood. Treat any large wound with a fungicidal paint.

Mildew: white powdery patches on leaves and young shoots in spring, and infected flowers which turn cream in colour and do not set, are produced by mildew. Remove infected shoots and spray with dinocap.

Bitter pit: bitter pit causes small brown pits in the flesh, giving it a bitter taste. Spray the leaves with calcium nitrate at two to three-week intervals from early to late summer. Less hard pruning, less nitrogenous fertilizer and regular watering will keep it in check.

Brown rot: this disease infects the fruit, which turns brown then either drops, or remains mummified on the tree to infect next year's fruit. Fruit with brown skin or flesh should be destroyed as soon as seen—not stored.

ICI Agricultural Division, Millbank

The effects of brown rot on fruit—the brown fruit often remains 'mummified' on the tree.

GUIDE TO APPLE TROUBLES

Symptoms	Probable Causes
Holes in fruitlets with sticky mess around them	Apple sawfly
Discoloured petals on partly opened bossom buds	Apple suckers
Misshapen fruitlets	Capsid
Curling leaves and shoot tips	Aphids
Hole at eye end of fruit	Codling moth
Soft warty growth on bark	American blight
Speckled leaves	Red spider mite
Sunken, flaking bark	Canker
White powdery patches on leaves	Mildew
Brown pitting in apple flesh	Bitter pit
Fruit turning brown	Brown rot
Black or brown spots on fruit and leaves	Scab

Varieties

To set a crop, most apples need to be cross-pollinated. Most varieties have plenty of pollen and will pollinate one another, *provided their flowering seasons coincide or overlap.* Some have little pollen—they are known as triploid. They need a suitable pollinator to help them set their fruit, but they themselves will not pollinate the other tree. In this case there should be a third variety present (not triploid) to ensure a good crop on all three. A few varieties are self-fertile though they crop better with a suitable pollinator.

As previously mentioned there are literally hundreds of different varieties of apple. Below are some of the more readily available dessert and cooking apples, and some crab apples.

Varieties of dessert apple

Beauty of Bath: small apple; heavily striped bright red; crops prolifically; ready late mid-summer; not advisable for planting in frosty gardens; does not store, slightly tip-bearing; *flowers early.*

Egremont Russet: medium; yellow, heavily covered in brown russet; crisp and well-flavoured; suitable for the small garden—makes good cordons; ready mid-autumn to early winter; heavy cropper and disease-resistant; *flowers early.*

James Grieve: medium to large; yellow, striped and flushed red; good cropper; ready early autumn; tends to canker on heavy soil; *flowers mid-season.*

Coxes Orange Pippin: medium yellow-orange with red flush and stripes; crisp with superb flavour; ready mid-autumn, stores to late mid-winter; crop moderate to heavy; spurs well but not advisable in wet areas; *flowers mid-season; proven best pollinator James Grieve.*

Winston: medium; green, covered in stripes and flush of dull red; good flavour, slightly sharp; ready mid-winter, stores until mid-spring; crop moderate to light; good as cordon; *flowers mid-season, self-fertile.*

Tydeman's Early Worcester: medium, pale green heavily flushed with red; crops well; ready late summer; slightly tip-bearing; *flowers early to mid-season.*

Fortune: medium; yellow with long red stripes and flushed red; crisp, good flavour; ready early to mid-autumn; crop moderate; *flowers mid-season.*

George Cave: bright yellow and red good regular cropper; juicy and crisp, slightly acid; *flowers early.*

Laxton's Epicure: yellow-green, flushed and streaked with red; sweet and juicy, best eaten as soon as picked; heavy cropper; *flowers mid-season.*

Ashmead's Kernel: greenish-yellow russet; firm with first-class flavour; moderate cropper; *flowers mid-season.*

A-Z Collection

Beauty of Bath

Pat Brindley

Egremont Russet

Orleans Reinetter: yellow-gold, blotched with russet; juicy and well-flavoured; heavy cropper; *flowers late.*

Discovery: medium-sizes greenish yellow fruit flushed with scarlet; crops early autumn; *flowers mid-season.*

Varieties of cooking apple

Bramley's Seedling: large; green but flushed red in the crimson-skinned sort; excellent flavour and cooks very well; ready late autumn and stores until mid-spring; crop mostly heavy, but makes large tree and not suitable for small gardens; *flowers mid-season; N.B. triploid variety.*

Grenadier: medium to large; yellow-green apple; very good flavour; ready late summer to mid-autumn; crop heavy and regular; good for small gardens; not prone to disease; *flowers mid-season; self-fertile.*

Peasgood Nonsuch: large; golden-yellow, flush bright crimson, good as baking apple; crop moderate, needs deep well-drained loam; good for small gardens; *flowers mid-season.*

Lane's Prince Albert: greenish-yellow, streaked red; juicy white flesh; good cropper; suitable for small gardens; *flowers mid-season (flowers for a long time).*

Edward VII: medium; yellow when fully ripe; good cooker (and dessert if kept); keeps very well; *flowers very late* (a 'wise apple' which often escapes late frosts).

Rev. W. Wilks: very large; yellow, striped with scarlet; good exhibition fruit; excellent for baking; rather acid; does not keep long; heavy cropper; *flowers early; self-fertile, (and not a good pollinator as it flowers irregularly).*

Howgate Wonder: large; green, striped red; good tree for the smaller garden; cooks well; heavy cropper; *flowers mid-season.*

Varieties of crab apple

Dartmouth: small; deep red fruit; ready mid-autumn; good for jelly making; forms a spreading head; *flowers mid-season*

John Downie: small; conical shape; yellow, flushed bright red; ready early autumn; good for preserves; upright head; *flowers mid-season.*

Golden Hornet: bright yellow fruits the size of cherries; stiff erect habit; fruits suitable for jelly-making; *flowers mid-season.*

Varieties of cider apple

Tremlett's Bitter: very red fruit; harvested mid-autumn; bittersweet flavour; *flowers early.*

Brown's Apple: harvested mid-autumn; sharp flavoured variety; *flowers early.*

Donald Smith

Bramley (cooking apple)

Harry Smith

James Grieve

Blackcurrants

Ribes nigrum (fam. *Saxifragaceae*)
Hardy deciduous shrub, with a useful life of twelve years
Size: bush about 1.5 m (5′) high and wide
Planting to harvesting time: two years
Yield: 4 kg (9 lb) average per bush

Blackcurrants are an easy soft fruit to cultivate and require a moist climate for best results. These delicious juicy berries are the richest in vitamin C of all the garden fruits and their sharp, tangy flavour has made them popular for pies, puddings and jams.

Four blackcurrant bushes at or near full cropping capacity will probably satisfy the needs of most families. It is a good idea to plant a range of varieties; this is not necessary for cross pollination, but it will spread the picking and flowering seasons, and be an insurance against a single frost causing crop failure. You can plant at any time during winter when the ground is not frozen or waterlogged, but early winter is best, so order new bushes in good time. Make sure you buy healthy two-year-old plants, preferably from ministry-certified clean stock, as supplied by most reputable nurseries. Plants which are not certified are liable to diseases, and they may give diminished yields.

Suitable site and soil

Choose a warm spot, sheltered from cold winds; this is essential because the flowers are prone to frost damage, causing a drop in yield. An open sunny aspect is preferable, but the crop will tolerate partial shade.

Blackcurrants will put up with wetter soils than most other fruits; however, the best results are to be had on deep, rich, moist well-drained sandy loams. A mildly acid soil is the best; on testing you should have a pH reading of 6 or 7, so adjust the content of the soil to give this reading.

Preparing the soil

Acid soils with a pH value of 5.5 and below require sufficient hydrated lime (or ground limestone) to raise the pH to 6.5, to be applied before planting in late autumn or winter. Never mix lime with manure or fertilizer and allow at least six weeks to elapse between working in manure and the application of lime. To

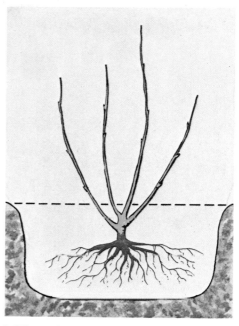

1. Prior to planting, dig the ground thoroughly to a depth of 30 cm (1′), incorporating manure.

2. Plant the bush with enough room for the roots to spread. Place the soil mark about 5 cm below ground.

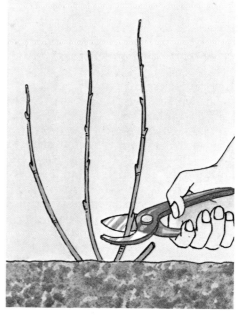

3. After planting, fill in the hole and gently heel in the soil to firm the ground around the bush.

4. Immediately after planting, use secateurs to cut back every shoot to 2.5 cm (1″) above the ground.

Several months after planting, work in a compound fertilizer around the roots of the bush.

Apply a mulch of well-rotted manure or garden compost to nourish the bush and help retain moisture.

raise the pH from 5.5 to 6.5 on a medium loam will require a dressing of hydrated lime at the rate of 400 g per sq m (12 oz per sq yd).

On soils which are alkaline, such as those occurring in chalk and limestone districts, where the soil pH is 7-7.5, be sure to work in plenty of peat before and during planting.

Before digging over the ground, dispose of perennial weeds, such as nettles, thistles, docks and couch grass. Fork them out carefully and remove them from the site. Weedkillers can be used, provided you allow sufficient time so that no harmful residues remain at planting time.

Dig the ground over, to a full spade depth of 30 cm (1'), about six weeks if possible before planting and work in manure, compost or leafmould at the time of digging. The rate of dressing of organic matter should be one wheelbarrow load per 1.7 sq m (2 sq yd) of ground. If this sounds rather heavy, bear in mind

that these plants occupy the site for a number of years.

Blackcurrants respond well to generous dressings of nitrogenous feeds, so, following the digging in of organic matter, provide extra plant food by forking into the surface a dressing of 45 g per sq m (1½ oz per sq yd) each of sterilized bonemeal and hoof-and-horn meal, together with 30 g per sq m (1 oz per sq yd) of sulphate of potash. Alternatively, apply a dressing of general garden fertilizer at 120 g per sq m (4 oz per sq yd). The analysis of the general fertilizer should be approximately 7% nitrogen, 7% phosphate, 12% potassium.

Planting
Space the plants at 1.8 m (6 ft) apart. Dig a planting hole big enough to spread the roots out in their natural directions without being cramped. Blackcurrants, when established, have a number of main stems arising at or just below

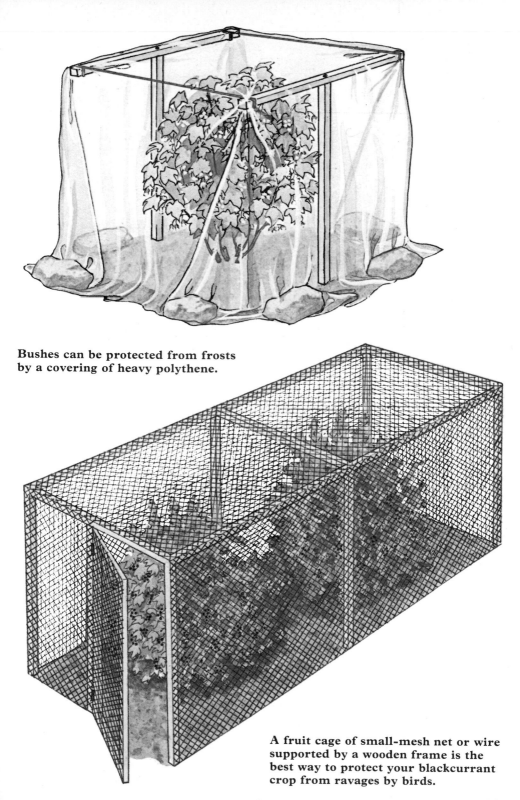

Bushes can be protected from frosts by a covering of heavy polythene.

A fruit cage of small-mesh net or wire supported by a wooden frame is the best way to protect your blackcurrant crop from ravages by birds.

High-yielding blackcurrant bushes are an excellent investment. Be sure to leave adequate space for development when you first plant them.

ground level, unlike gooseberries, red currants and white currants which grow on a leg or single stem. To encourage this habit of producing vigorous stems low down, bushes should be planted 2.5-5 cm (1-2″) deeper than they were in the nursery. The nursery level will be indictated by a soil mark, where the stem changes colour.

When each bush is placed in its planting hole, work in the soil around the roots and firm it with your heel.

Immediately after planting cut every shoot to within 2.5 cm (1″) of the ground to just above the first or second visible growth bud. This cutting back ensures that the bushes develop good root systems and strong vigorous stems, but they will not produce fruit the first year. If there have been some hard frosts after planting and the bushes and soil have loosened as a result, be sure to firm the soil around the roots again.

Aftercare

Water the plants early in the season following planting if the weather is dry. Blackcurrants need moisture more than most fruits. Mulching to conserve moisture and smother weeds should be carried out early. Remove weeds and keep them under control as soon as they appear, to prevent them competing with bushes for moisture and to reduce the risk of other hosts for pests and diseases.

Blackcurrants grow and crop better with generous dressings of manure or compost, or peat and fertilizer. In early spring each year, scatter and work in 30 g per sq m (1 oz per sq yd) of sulphate of ammonia and 15 g sq m ($\frac{1}{2}$ oz per sq yd) of sulphate of potash over the bed. Where the soil is acid, use nitro-chalk instead of sulphate of ammonia.

Working in the fertilizer can be carried out with a rake if the soil surface is crumbly and friable. If the surface has

PRUNING

Pruning from the second year is to encourage new wood, as this bears the most fruit the next year, and to build up a good bush shape. Prune to the ground, or to a low-growing shoot, and ignore new growth at the tip of old wood. Low-growing branches, crossing branches and those which are diseased are cut out first, followed by those branches in the centre of the bush, to let in light and air. Finally, a proportion of old wood is cut to a low shoot, or is removed entirely.

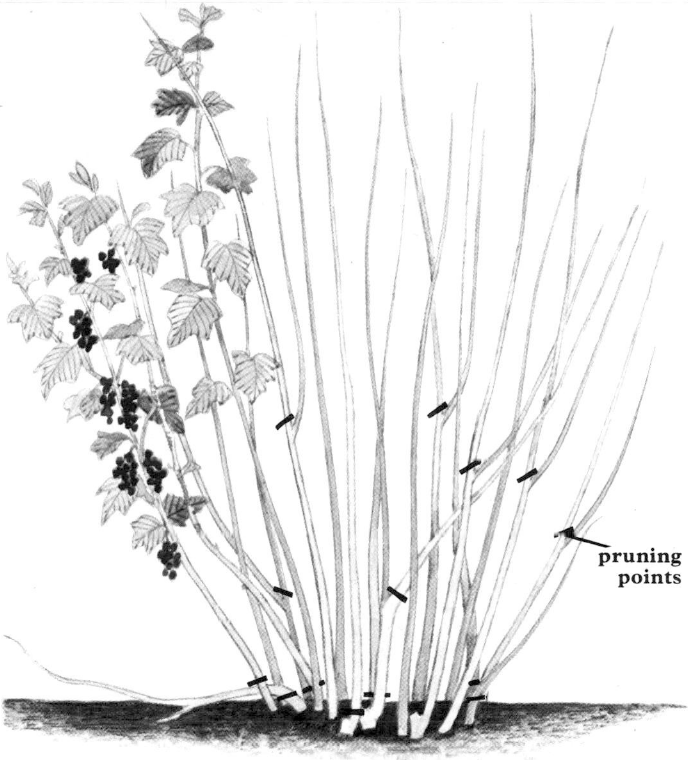

pruning points

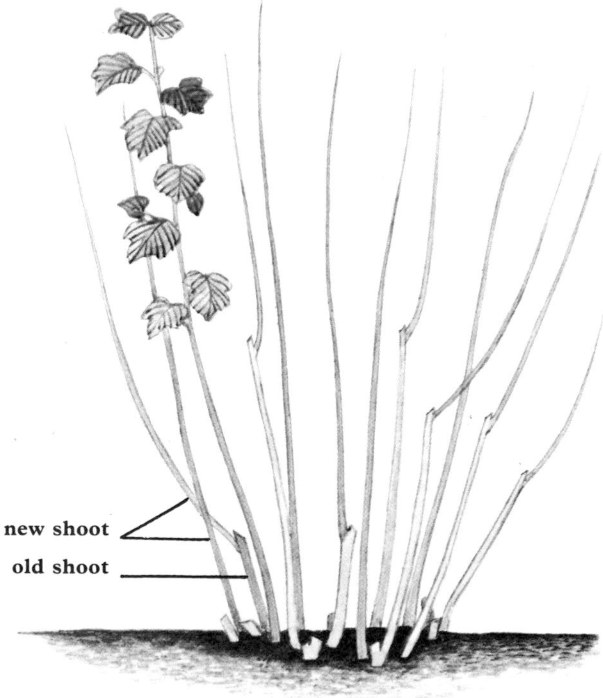

new shoot

old shoot

become rather compacted after the winter rains, then use a hand cultivator or garden fork to do two jobs in one, to loosen the surface and work in the fertilizer before a mulch is applied.

Mulching will feed the bushes, besides its other functions. A mulch of manure or compost laid on top of the soil should be applied at the rate of one wheelbarrow-load to 2.5 sq m (3 sq yd). If no manure is available, double the quantities of fertilizers and mulch with moist peat or pulverized tree bark.

Frost protection
The greenish white flowers are borne in hanging clusters of four to twelve, or even more in early to mid-spring.

To protect the bushes from frost, cover the bushes at night with hessian, cloth or plastic attached to a light framework.

Pruning
In the winter following planting, little pruning will be needed, but any weak growths can be cut back to the first bud above ground level. Immediately after the first harvest, the second winter after planting, pruning should be carried out.

Blackcurrants bear most of their fruit on the new shoots produced the previous summer, so the aim of pruning is to encourage the growth of strong new wood from the base of the plant. Most of the new shoots will be retained, and some of the older wood which also bears a quota of fruit. First cut away low-growing growths which hang down to the ground, also any which are dead or obviously diseased, and any that are crossing or awkwardly placed. If the centre of the bush is crowded, remove some of the shoots there to let in light and air.

Finally, remove about one-fifth of the older wood that remains. Make your cuts above a good new low-growing shoot or close to the ground to encourage new growth lower down, and ignore promising growth at the tips of these shoots.

When the bushes are well established,

after about four seasons, remove roughly one-third of the old wood each winter. Where growth is very vigorous remove less, but if it is weak and needs stimulating, then prune more severely.

Harvesting
The bushes will need some protection, by the use of netting or a wire cage, from the ravages of birds as the fruits ripen. Fruits are ready for picking when they are black or nearly so; the time of ripening depends on the variety you choose. Always pick when the fruit is dry; wet fruit goes mouldy very quickly. For quickness, berries can be stripped off their stalks using a kitchen fork, but fruits picked off a truss or cluster are less likely to go mouldy and will keep for four or five days in cool conditions. Some varieties do not ripen evenly so that on the cluster of fruits some berries are ready for picking while others are still green. In this event stripping off fruits with a fork is not very practical.

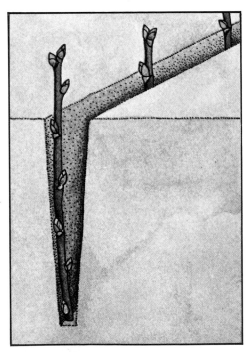

To propagate plants, take cuttings in mid-autumn and insert them in the ground with some buds below the soil.

Pat Brindley

A – Z Collection

Boskoop Giant

The Raven

Varieties

Propagation

Hardwood cuttings, an easy and convenient means of propagation, should be taken in mid-autumn from healthy bushes. Under no circumstances should cuttings be taken from diseased bushes to replace those about to be destroyed.

Cuttings are prepared from shoots of ripening wood, about 20-25 cm (8-10″) long, cut just below a bud. Dig V-shaped trenches about 15 cm (6″) deep. Some sharp sand placed in the bottom of the 'V' trench is a useful aid to rooting. Put in the cuttings, leaving two or more buds above ground, and spaced at 15-20 cm (6-8″) apart. These shoots are then firmed in. Unlike gooseberries and red currants, blackcurrant cuttings do not have any of the buds rubbed off before inserting into the ground.

By the following autumn, the cuttings will be ready for transplanting into their new quarters.

Softwood cuttings (i.e. immature shoot tips) about 7.5 cm (3″) long taken in late spring to early summer and rooted in a shaded frame, is an alternative method of propagation. When the cuttings are rooted, increase ventilation gradually until the frame is removed.

These fall into a number of categories, but are usually classified according to the time of fruiting, namely—early, mid-season, and late varieties. However, the time and habit of fruiting differ within those groups. Some varieties, such as *Seabrook's Black* and *Boskoop Giant* may be set back by frost (possibly because they lack leafy cover for the flowers).

The list is by no means exhaustive, but these varieties are well tried and proven by commercial growers and amateurs. Most have some resistance to diseases.

Early varieties

Mendip Cross: large spreading bush; flowers mid-season; berries medium to large, heaviest cropper of the early sorts; moderately resistant to leaf spot.

Boskoop Giant: a very old, but well tried variety; vigorous habit, between *The Raven* and *Mendip Cross*. Flowers early; large berries, well spaced and easy to pick. The earliest variety to ripen, but tends to have a lighter crop. Moderate resistance to leaf spot.

Tor Cross: similar to *Mendip Cross;* flowers mid-season to late; better quality fruit than *Mendip Cross* and develops

313

Wellington XXX

Blacksmith

Donald Smith

two or three days later; moderate to good resistance to leaf spot.

Mid-season

Seabrooks Black: medium upright growth; late flowering, good for exposed or northern areas; berries medium-sized, fruits about seven days later than *Mendip Cross*; moderately resistant to leaf spot.

The Raven: largest bush of all, open nature, but stiff stems; flowers early, but well protected by the foliage; large sweet fruit of even size and thin skinned. Outstanding for juice and flavouring; not susceptible to leaf spot.

Wellington XXX: open habit, inclined to droop with a heavy crop; flowers early, liable to be damaged by frosts and cold winds in exposed sites. Fruit of good size and quality; crops well in milder areas; susceptible to leaf spot.

Blacksmith: very vigorous, makes a rather uneven bush; flowers late; prolific cropper, large berries at base of clusters, small at the ends; fruit hidden in foliage. Short season, ripens few days before *Baldwin*; moderate resistance to leaf spot.

Brodtorp: a newer variety of considerable promise, but requires further trials before a full assessment is given.

Late Varieties

Baldwin: a very old variety and a good cropper; makes a dense upright bush; flowers mid-season; medium-sized fruits, easy to pick and thick skinned; ripens evenly; berries hang well unless the foliage is poor; succeeds best in mild areas (e.g. southern and western England) where it crops regularly and heavily; stands closer planting; prone to leaf spot.

Westwick Choice: very compact; flowers mid to late season; berries large and firm; ripens a few days after *Baldwin* and hangs well; more resistant to leaf spot than *Baldwin*.

Amos Black: vigorous, upright unbranched stems and dark green foliage; flowers late season; large berries on short branches; variable cropper; moderate resistance to leaf spot.

Daniels September: vigorous open bush, tends to have characteristic leaf mottle; flowers late, after *Baldwin*; two forms of fruit develop, early and late; the latter is the desirable form; large, thick skinned fruits, hang late for about fourteen days after *Baldwin*; moderate resistance to leaf spot.

Malvern Cross: similar habit to *Wellington XXX*; flowers late season; well berried, but tip fruits are small.

Pests & Diseases

Unfortunately, blackcurrants are very prone to attack by a variety of insects, viruses and fungi. However, if you make sure that your plants come from certified stock and follow a sensible preventive spray programme, you have an excellent chance of a healthy crop. It is particularly important to protect your plants from infection by blackcurrant gall mite. Spray with 1% solution of lime-sulphur when the first flowers open, and repeat three weeks later. Malathion or derris sprays are useful against aphids, capsids, blackcurrant sawflies, leaf midge and red spider mites. In all cases, spray exactly at the time stated, and never spray when the blossom is in full bloom.

Blackcurrant gall mite/Big bud: infection with blackcurrant gall mite is responsible for the disease 'big bud'. The gall mite also transmits reversion virus (see below). These mites are minute in size, and thousands of them can be found in a single infected bud. The infected bud then swells prematurely and becomes less pointed (hence the name 'big bud'). There is no completely effective control but spraying twice each spring with lime sulphur,

1% strength, at the rate of $\frac{1}{3}$ litre to 27 litres of water ($\frac{1}{2}$ pt to 6 gallons of water) is a useful measure. Apply the solution as the first flowers open, and again three weeks later. Prune branches which show signs of big bud on slightly infected bushes. Badly infected bushes should be dug up and burned.

Reversion virus: this incurable virus disease is carried by the blackcurrant gall mite. It is difficult to diagnose leaf reversion in its early stages because the infected plant may appear no different from a healthy one, except for a reduction in cropping. In late spring or early summer, closely examine the leaves of those plants which have cropped poorly. If the plants have reversion virus, the leaf structure may have changed. Healthy leaves have five or more veins on either side of the centre rib of the lobe opposite the leaf stalk. Reverted leaves have less than five. Infected plants will never recover. Remove and burn them. Plant healthy replacement stock on a different site well removed from possible sources of infection.

Aphids: the first sign to look for is stunted leaf growth, leaf curling and leaf distortion. Cotton wool-like grubs on

---

GUIDE TO BLACKCURRANT TROUBLES

Symptoms	Probable cause
Unnaturally large, swollen buds	Blackcurrant gall mite
Leaf veins reduced in number, little fruit produced	Leaf reversion virus
Stunted growth, leaf curling and distortion	Aphids
Whitish orange maggots, twisted or folded leaves	Blackcurrant leaf midge
Green and black caterpillars, foliage stripped	Blackcurrant sawfly
Green, winged insects causing disfiguration of leaves, fruits, shoots	Capsids
Minute red or brown mites, yellow, stunted growth	Red spider mite
Buds fail to open in spring, long bare branches	Eelworm
Brown spots on leaves from mid-spring onward	Blackcurrant leaf spot
Yellow pustules on undersides of leaves in early summer	Blackcurrant rust
White felty growths on young leaves, fruits and shoots, growths later turning brown	American gooseberry mildew
Delicate powdery mould on underside of leaves	European gooseberry mould

the roots of the infected plants are due to currant root aphids. To control aphids, spray in mid-winter with a tar-oil spray. As soon as the first flowers open, spray with malathion, thoroughly wetting the undersides of the leaves.

Blackcurrant leaf midge: This pest usually appears in its larval stage as whitish orange maggots which cause the leaves to twist and become folded. *Seabrook's Black*, *Wellington* and *Baldwin* are the most susceptible varieties of blackcurrants. Spray with malathion at the open flower stage.

Blackcurrant sawfly: the green and black caterpillars of this insect will quickly strip a plant of foliage. The damage is usually done on the underside or in the centre of the infected bush. If the caterpillars appear, pick them off by hand, or give an extra spray with derris or mathathion.

Common green capsid: this insect's over wintering eggs hatch out when the flowers are about to open. The emergent winged capsid will attack other garden crops as well as blackcurrants. It sucks the sap from the growing shoot tips; scars are formed and later the leaves become puckered and distorted. Again, a spray of malathion before the flowers

Blackcurrants showing the enlarged buds of 'Big Bud' trouble, caused by gall mites.

open will control these pests. Treat the eggs with tar oil sprays.

Red spider mite: these are minute red or brown mites which suck the sap from leaves, eventually weakening the plant. A sign to watch for is the rapid bronzing of leaves. Spray with malathion at the first open flower stage.

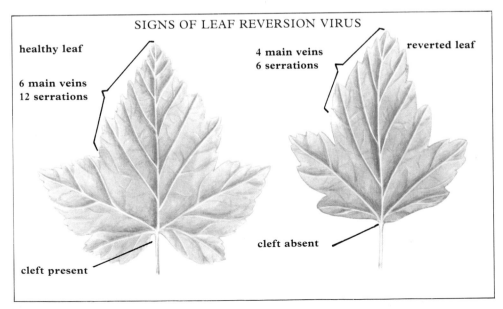

SIGNS OF LEAF REVERSION VIRUS

healthy leaf

6 main veins
12 serrations

cleft present

4 main veins
6 serrations

reverted leaf

cleft absent

Severely distorted leaves caused by an attack of the common green capsid.

Blackcurrant leaves displaying a mild (left) and severe (right) leaf spot disease.

White felty growths on plants suffering from American gooseberry mildew.

Eelworm: damage from this pest is usually worse after a wet season. Buds will fail to open in spring, leaving long, bare branches. *Daniel's Black* and *Westwick* are particularly susceptible blackcurrant varieties. Eelworm is best controlled by avoiding planting on diseased ground, especially following potato crops. This problem is rare.

Blackcurrant leaf spot: this fungus can be fairly damaging unless kept in check. It is likely to occur in higher rain fall areas and in wet seasons. Brown spots appear on the leaves from late spring onwards if the attack is severe, the bush can be badly weakened. Premature leaf fall is an indication of infection by leaf spot. Spray the infected plants with copper fungicide, zineb or thiram immediately after flowering and three more times at four-weekly intervals; you can also apply Bordeaux mixture, if the disease was severe in the last season, but only after picking.

Blackcurrant rust: the symptoms of this disease are yellow, raised pustules on the undersides of the leaves in early summer. Fungicide sprays of copper, thiram of zineb will control blackcurrant rust.

American gooseberry mildew/ European gooseberry mildew: the American mildew is the more dangerous of the two; its symptoms are white felty growths on the young leaves, fruits and shoots. In summer and autumn, the fungal growth becomes brown and felt like. The European mildew shows itself as a delicate, powdery mould on the undersides of the leaves. Both are controlled by lime sulphur or dinocap sprays before the flowers open. Cut out any diseased shoots.

317

Gooseberries

Ribes grossularia (fam. *Grossulariaceae*)
Hardy deciduous shrub with a
useful life of 12 to 20 years
Size: 1 m (3′) high; 1.2-1.5 m (4-5′) wide
Planting to harvesting time: 2-3 years
Yield: 3.5-7 kg (8-15 lb) per bush and more

Gooseberries are easy to grow and are probably the best soft fruit for a small garden. Their cultivation needs are moderate, they give a large amount of fruit for the area they cover, and a well-tended bush will go on cropping for twenty years or more. Three or four gooseberry bushes will be ample to supply the needs of most households. However, gooseberries are self-fertile, so you can grow a single bush in your garden with good results. Gooseberries are very tolerant of exposure and are occasionally grown as windbreaks to protect less hardy crops, though strong winds at flowering time will discourage pollinating insects. They are more shade tolerant than other soft fruits, so gooseberries will thrive in town gardens where other soft fruits fail.

There are many varieties of gooseberry available; if you plant several bushes you can extend the season of cropping from early summer through to early autumn. Gooseberries are usually first picked when the fruits are small and green. These unripe thinnings are cooked and served in pies or puddings or preserved for future use. Ripe gooseberries are highly valued as a dessert fruit, and are delicious when eaten raw. First class dessert gooseberries are seldom seen in shops, so it would be well worthwhile for the amateur gardener to have at least one bush in the garden. Ripe dessert gooseberries can be yellow, white, green or red. The Worcesterberry, a gooseberry hybrid and not, as often thought, a cross between a gooseberry and a blackcurrant, has fairly small, blue-black, gooseberry-like fruit, and it is cultivated in the same way.

Gooseberries are usually grown as spiney shrubs on a single short stem like a tiny tree, although cordons, espaliers and standards are available. A gooseberry grown as a standard is particularly suitable for planting in pots if you have a paved terrace, courtyard or balcony. They make attractive features and will carry good crops if properly cared for.

Suitable site and soil
The best soil for gooseberries is a well-drained loam containing plenty of potash and nitrogen; gooseberries, more than

Gooseberries are best protected from attacks by birds if they are grown in fruit cages.

other soft fruits, are very particular about soil conditions. Generally, light soils or sandy gravel are not suitable because they lack nutrients and tend to dry out in hot weather. Chalk soils are unsuitable because they heat up in the summer, and gooseberries need a cool moist root run. Whatever the soil, it must be moisture retentive because the fruits will not swell if moisture is lacking. If the soil is too rich and fertile, however, sappy weak growth and poor crops will result. Some varieties of gooseberry are more tolerant of difficult soil conditions than others: *Whinham's Industry* is recommended for heavy soils, *Lancer* for light soils. Unfortunately, *Leveller*, which is highly prized for its delicious

dessert berries, needs near perfect soil conditions to crop well.

When selecting a site, much depends on the general geographic location. The best flavoured gooseberries are grown in cooler areas. This is because the berries are less liable to be ripened prematurely by hot sun and they have time to mature slowly. In Britain, the counties of Cheshire and Lancashire and nearby areas have appeared to be particularly good locations.

Some varieties such as *Whinhams Industry* are shade tolerant. Rows of gooseberry bushes are sometimes grown between young apple trees; and are dug up after 15-20 years, when the trees are reaching maturity. Gooseberries, like

1. Dig in well-rotted manure, leaf mould, garden compost or moist peat. Make sure all weeds are removed.

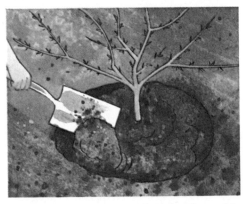

2. Plant in autumn, in a hole about 60 cm (2′) in diameter. Spread the roots out and replace soil firmly.

3. Heel in the soil around the bush, but do not compact it too much or rain will lie on the surface.

red currants, can be grown against north-facing walls and fences in gardens where space is limited. Cordons are the best shape to grow against fences or on their own as a boundary between gardens.

Generally, a sunny site will give a better flavoured crop. In full sun, gooseberries should be grown as bushes so the branches help shade the fruit hanging beneath.

Avoid windy sites, because cold winds prevent insects from pollinating them in early spring. Gooseberries are hardier than plums, apples and pears, and they will probably produce a moderate crop even if the flowers have been frosted. A frost-free site is better, though.

The site must be well drained, because gooseberries will not tolerate any water-logging. Avoid low-lying sites on heavy soil because they tend to be badly drained and form frost pockets in winter.

Soil preparation and planting

Gooseberries fruit on both old and new wood, so it is important that the plant makes good strong annual growth. The best way to ensure this is by preparing the soil adequately prior to planting in early autumn. Ideally, the soil should have been under cultivation for several seasons; if the site is newly cultivated, it is best to double-dig it.

For all soil types, dig into the top spit well-rotted farmyard manure or garden compost, moist peat or leafmould, remembering that the peat will not have any nutrient value. Light soils will then be made more moisture retentive, heavier soils more friable. Also apply sulphate of potash at this time, at the rate of 25 g per sq m ($\frac{3}{4}$ oz per sq yd), forking it lightly into the soil. Make sure the area is completely weed-free. Once couch grass, bindweed or docks grow up into a gooseberry bush they are impossible to eradicate.

If you are buying gooseberry bushes, make sure they come from a reputable source; try to get two or three-year old bushes.

The best time to plant gooseberries is in early autumn, so that the bushes have plenty of time to settle down and become established before making spring growth. If you are planting more than one bush, the distance between planting depends on the variety and the shape grown. Normally, strong growing bushes of varieties such as *Lancer, Lancashire Lad* and *White Lion*, should be planted 1.8 m (6') apart. Less vigorous varieties can be planted 1.5 m (5') apart. Single cordons should be 30 cm (1') apart; double and triple cordons and espalier-trained gooseberries should be 90 cm (3') apart. If you are planting more than one row, leave at least 2.4 m (8') between rows.

Before planting, remove all buds and suckers below the main shoots. If there are any suckers on the roots, take these off also. Gooseberries are usually grown on a single leg, or clear stem, about 15 cm (6") high. You may have to trim off the top-most roots (very carefully) and plant the bush a little higher than the nursery soil mark, to get a good leg. This also helps keep down suckering.

Plant the bushes firmly, and not too deeply. Do not compact the soil too much, or rain will lie in puddles on the surface. Trained specimens should be staked when they are planted. Standard gooseberries will need strong stakes at least 1.2 m (4') tall.

Cultivation

Gooseberries benefit greatly from feeding and mulching annually; greater yields will result if you follow these routines.

In spring or late summer, apply well-rotted garden compost, at the rate of one barrowload per 10 sq m (11 sq yd). This encourages the formation of fibrous feeding roots, and increases crop production. Mulching also helps to keep weeds down and conserve soil moisture.

Because gooseberries need more potash than other soft fruits, they should have annual application of sulphate of potash at the rate of 20-30 g per sq m (¾-1

1. **Each year in late winter or early spring apply sulphate of potash before mulching, and rake it in.**

2. **Mulch annually with well-rotted manure or compost to encourage the formation of fibrous feeding roots.**

3. **If birds are a problem, thread black cotton through the branches in mid-autumn as a deterrent.**

321

oz per sq yd). This should be done in later winter or early spring, but if the edges of the leaves look scorched, brown and fall prematurely the plant is suffering from potash deficiency—apply sulphate of potash at the higher of the above rates immediately and water in. Sandy and gravelly soils are usually deficient in potash, so make sure you apply a potash fertilizer regularly. Ashes from the bonfire contain potash, and a mulch of these can provide additional potash.

Nitrogen is also necessary, to promote strong growth. However, if too much nitrogen is applied, sappy weak growth will result, with an increased risk of mildew. Usually, a mulch of garden compost in spring is sufficient. Every third year apply a dressing of super-phosphate at the rate of 90-120 g per sq m (3-4 oz per sq yd) with the potash.

In winter check the plants frequently; firm down any lifted by frost. To reduce the risk of damage by frost, cover the bushes 'in early and mid-spring with muslin or fine netting.

Birds, usually bullfinches and sparrows, tend to peck the buds out from late autumn to late winter. The variety *Leveller* seems particularly vulnerable to bird attacks. If the fruits are not grown in cages, the best method of protection is winding black cotton thread round the shoots and branches after leaf fall. If your garden is very vulnerable to bird damage, it is best to delay pruning until bud break in spring. In early spring, when bud-breaks occurs, and you find that a shoot or shoots have been largely stripped of buds, cut them right back to the first strong bud near the base of the shoot; a badly-stripped shoot will not recover.

Watering is necessary in dry weather from late spring to mid-summer, otherwise the fruit will not swell and the leaves may scorch. This is particularly important for sandy or other very free-draining soils.

Water the plants at the rate of 20 L per sq m (4½ gal per sq yd).

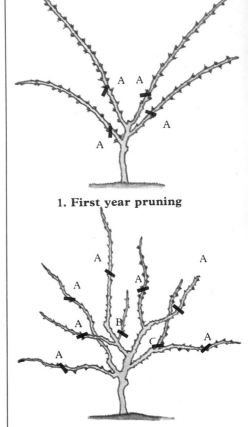

1. First year pruning

2. Second year pruning

1. *The first pruning consists of cutting back three or four strong shoots to an outward pointing bud, three or four buds from the base (A). Remove weak or badly placed buds.*

2. *One year later, cut back 5-8 strong shoots to half their length, to an outward pointing bud (A). Shorten smaller sideshoots to one bud from the base (B); remove completely any weak or badly placed shoots (C). When pruning to form the framework of the bush, aim for an open-centred bush.*

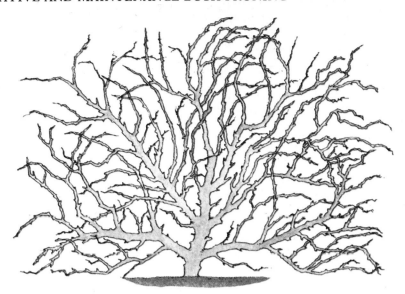

Established gooseberry bush (unpruned)

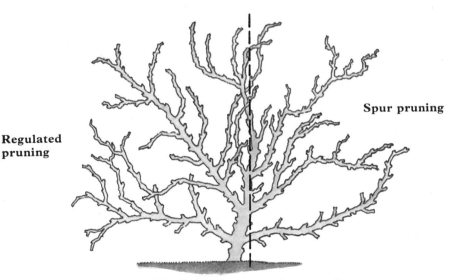

Regulated pruning

Spur pruning

Established gooseberry bush (pruned)

There are two methods of pruning an established bush; regulated and spur pruning. The former consists of removing overcrowded, weak and old wood, pruning branch leaders back by a quarter, and pruning one-year-old shoots by 7.5 cm (3"). To spur prune, cut back all sideshoots to one or two buds, to encourage the formation of fruiting spurs. Spur pruning results in larger, but fewer, gooseberries.

If you removed all the weeds before the bushes were planted, you should have little trouble with weeds later. Should weeding be necessary, however, hand weed or hoe lightly. Never dig between the bushes or hoe deeply because you may damage the fibrous surface feeding roots. Mulching is a good way of keeping weeds down. Watch for brambles in particular seeding in the middle of the bushes.

Check for suckers growing up from the roots and carefully cut off any you find. If the suckers are left, the bush will lose its shape and be difficult to pick from.

Pruning

Gooseberries can be trained into a number of shapes. Although the bush form is the most commonly seen, gooseberries can be grown as single, double or triple cordons, as espaliers and as standards, and even as fans. You may be able to buy a standard gooseberry from your local nurseryman; it will probably have been grafted on to a rootstock of golden currant (*Ribes aureum*). It is quite easy to train a standard yourself. Remove all but one strong straight shoot from a new bush and train it vertically until it has reached about 1.2 m (4'). Remove all the lower side shoots from the stem, leaving the top four or five buds to form the branching head of the gooseberry, which is then pruned as though it was an ordinary bush.

Cordon trained gooseberries are particularly suitable for growing in rows against a wall or where room is scarce. Single cordons are trained by cutting back all side shoots to leave one bud only on each, and cutting the leader back each year to leave about 15 cm (6") of new growth until the desired height is reached, about 1.5-1.8 m (5-6'). Then cut away the whole of any leading shoot each year, so that the spurs lower down continue to be strong. Double cordons are slightly more difficult. Begin by cutting back the main stem to leave two

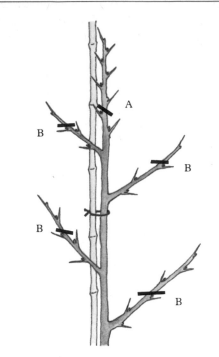

Winter pruning consists of shortening the leading shoot to leave one third of its new growth (A), and pruning laterals back to three buds (B). Pruning laterals encourages the formation of fruiting spurs. In areas where bird damage to gooseberry buds is severe, leave pruning until early spring.

buds pointed in opposite directions, about 22 cm (9") from the ground. Train the shoots which grow out from these buds at an angle of 45° at first, later gradually lowering them to the horizontal. Tie these horizontal shoots on to wires, and then cut them back to leave one bud on the upper side of each. These two buds will produce the vertical framework of the cordon. The formative pruning of specially trained forms is done in early winter unless birds are likely to be a problem when it should be done at bud-break. The early pruning of gooseberry bushes is aimed at establishing a strong open framework able to carry a heavy crop. Once this framework has been formed, there are two methods of maintenance pruning. Regulated

PRUNING ESTABLISHED GOOSEBERRY CORDONS

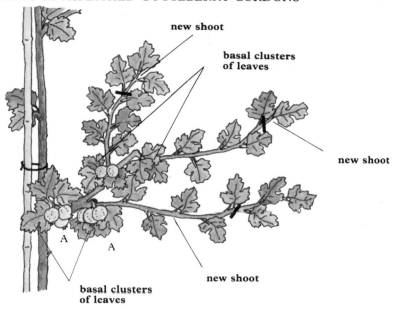

new shoot

basal clusters
of leaves

new shoot

new shoot

A A

basal clusters
of leaves

In mid-summer, prune back laterals to 5 or 6 leaves, not counting the basal clusters (A). This pruning encourages the formation of fruit buds. As American gooseberry mildew appears first on the tips, Regulated pruning at this time helps to control the disease.

If the cordon has reached the desired height, you can cut back the leading shoot during routine summer pruning. Sometimes, sucker-like shoots appear near the base of the cordons; cut these off cleanly as soon as they are seen, as they will drain the cordon of energy needed to produce the fruit.

---

pruning ensures a large quantity of berries, perhaps for freezing or bottling, where perfection and size are not so important. If you want fewer, but larger and higher quality berries, for exhibition or dessert, spur pruning is the best method (see diagram). Spur pruning is also recommended for bushes growing on light soils or where growth is poor.

Growing standard gooseberries in containers

This method is suitable if you have a paved terrace or courtyard. Select a pot 30 cm (12″) in diameter and 30 cm (12″) deep to start with; as the plant grows on you will have to repot into a larger pot, say 35 cm × 35 cm (14″ × 14″). Line the bottom of the pot with a layer of drainage material, such as large stones or broken pieces of clay pots or brick. Then put in a layer of good loam mixed with an equal part of well-rotted garden compost, or use John Innes potting compost No. 3. Carefully spread the roots of the plant out over this layer, and fill the pot with more of the mixture until the top of the soil is 2.5 cm (1″) beneath the rim of the pot. Water in well. Potting is best done in mid-autumn or early spring. Remember that plants in pots dry out very quickly in hot weather, so water the pots frequently— daily in very hot weather.

Do not feed the plant for the first year, as it is still becoming established. Thereafter, feed with liquid fertilizer when the fruits are swelling. If you live in a warm area or if your garden is fairly

325

sheltered, you can leave the pot outside all year round without protection; otherwise plunge the pot in a sheltered border for the winter and mulch heavily, or put some form of lagging round the pot and over the compost surface to protect the roots from hard frost.

Propagation

There are three methods of propagating gooseberries: layering, cuttings and seeds. Layering is the easiest method, and probably the one most suited to the amateur gardener. Peg down suitably placed shoots in early summer and cover with a thin layer of soil about halfway along their length. By late autumn the rooted layer should be severed from the parent plant and moved to its permanent position. Unfortunately, bushes propagated by layering are less symmetrical than those raised by cuttings; they tend to sucker more, and it is difficult to get a clean leg.

The main problem with propagation by cuttings is that gooseberry cuttings do not root easily. If you try this method, prepare more cuttings than you need, as there will probably be some failures. If all the cuttings root successfully, you can share them with friends or neighbours.

One of the main reasons for failure of cuttings is the drying out of the cut end.

Cuttings must not be left around while you prepare the site in which to root them; once the sap has dried the cutting will not root. Dig the trench beforehand in early autumn, selecting a warm and sheltered site. It should be V-shaped in section, and 22 cm (9″) deep. If you are digging more than one trench, make them at least 60 cm (2′) apart. Then spread a 7.5 cm (3″) layer of sand mixed with a little moist peat in the bottom of the trench.

Cuttings should be taken while some of the leaves are still on the bush; the earlier in autumn they are taken, the better provided the wood is ripe. Use only one-year-old shoots (these are lighter in colour than old wood) about 25 cm (10″) long; the shoots should be straight and thick but not sappy. Remove the top 2.5 cm (1″) tip, cutting just above a leaf cluster or bud. The bottom cut should be made just below a leaf cluster or bud. Rub off the lower buds leaving about four or five buds on the upper part of the shoot. Branches will develop from these buds, and the lower portion will form the leg.

Dip the bottom 5 cm (2″) of the cutting in hormone rooting powder, and then insert the cutting firmly against one side of the trench so that about half the cutting is above the soil surface.

PROPAGATING FROM CUTTINGS

1. Take cuttings of one-year-old shoots in autumn; plant immediately in trenches; space cuttings 15 cm (6″) apart.

2. The next autumn, rub out any suckers (A) and cut back side-shoots by half (B). Cut off terminal shoot (C).

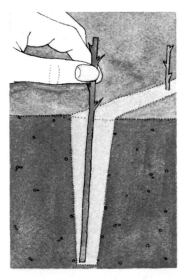
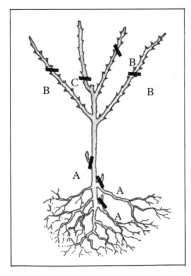

Marshall Cavendish Clay Perry

A standard gooseberry is very easy to train and makes an attractive feature in the garden. They are also very suitable for growing in large pots if you have a paved terrace, courtyard or balcony.

Cuttings should be spaced 15 cm (6″) apart. Press the soil sufficiently firmly around the cuttings so they do not feel loose when given a gentle tug, and make sure the soil does not dry out. Keep the ground well weeded. If you have extra cloches available, it is a good idea to cover the cuttings during the worst of the winter months.

The following autumn, one year later, rub out any unwanted buds or suckers on the stem and roots and replant the rooted cutting in its permanent position.

If you do not mind waiting three or four seasons for the first fruit, gooseberries can be grown quite easily from seed. Sow seeds taken from a fully ripe berry in a 1.2 cm (½″) deep furrow. Keep it weeded and well watered in dry weather. The following spring transplant them so they are 60 cm (2′) apart. If you have planted out more than one row, the rows should be at least 60 cm (2′) apart. The following spring transplant them out again, into their permanent positions. You will find that the seedlings vary greatly in quality; discard all but the best.

327

Harvesting

Harvesting is done in several stages; early thinnings are useful for tarts and jam-making, while the final crops of large, fully ripe fruit are usually eaten fresh. Start picking late in spring when the fruits are about the size of peas. Thinning at this stage leads to larger fruit later on. Because the colours of the different varieties do not appear until the fruits are nearly ripe, all thinnings at this stage will be green. Pick the berries off the bush with a quick jerk; in this way the fruit can be removed from the plant without damaging the spur.

The first picking should be done all over the bush, so that the remaining berries are evenly distributed. The thinned fruit should be at least 3.7 cm ($1\frac{1}{2}''$) apart. The next picking should be done from the centre of the bush and from lower branches. Fruits in these positions are unlikely to ripen completely, because of shading. The best placed fruits on the outer branches are then left on the bush to mature fully, and picked for dessert use when soft and ripe. To obtain the best flavour, pick these dessert gooseberries during the afternoon or early evening, while they are still warm from the sun. If possible, avoid picking while the weather is wet.

Exhibition tips

For exhibition work it is best to spur prune your bush (see *Pruning* above) to get good size fruits of the finest quality. When the fruits begin to set, apply weekly applications of manure water until just before the show date. If there has been a very heavy set of fruit, thin them after they have begun to swell..

Gooseberries, like other soft fruit, should be shown with a stalk still attached. Thirty berries is the usual number called for. They should all be of the same variety and as uniform in appearance and size as possible. Judging is divided into two categories: ripe and unripe gooseberries. Ripe fruits should be fully ripe and of good colour, unripe fruits should be large and fresh.

Pests & Diseases

Gooseberries are relatively pest and disease free, given proper cultivation. It is a good idea, if you have had insect trouble, to spray them with a tar oil wash in winter. Do this when you spray plums and redcurrants. Then inspect your plants in spring and early summer for signs of attacks and spray or dust with pesticides in severe cases.

Caterpillars: the caterpillars of the gooseberry sawfly are very destructive and in bad years can quickly strip a plant of foliage. It is a particularly troublesome pest because there are three generations of sawfly in one season. For this reason it is important to completely kill off the first generation of caterpillars when they hatch out in spring. They eat small holes in the leaves; eventually the whole leaf is eaten except for the main veins and midrib. In mild attacks, pick them off by hand or spread out sacking beneath the bush and shake them out. If the attack is severe, handpick as much as possible as soon as the caterpillars appear, and then spray with derris. Similar damage is done by the black, white and yellow caterpillar of the magpie moth. Treatment is the same.

Gooseberry red spider mite: these do most damage in mid and late spring,

The caterpillars of the gooseberry sawfly can quickly strip a plant of all leaves.

when the weather is fine. They suck the sap from the undersurface of the leaves and are especially troublesome during warm, sunny springs. The leaves become pale or bronze-coloured and may fall prematurely; any fruits which form will be small and unappetizing. In general the mites migrate to the bushes in spring from apple trees and buildings; spray just after flowering with dimethoate or malathion to control them.

Birds: these are particularly troublesome in some gardens; in winter they peck out the dormant buds. If you cannot grow the bushes in fruit cages, twine cotton thread through the branches; alternatively, delay pruning until bud-break in spring (see *Cultivation above*). Harmless bird repellant sprays can also be used, containing quassia, thiram, anthroquinone and other substances unpleasant-tasting to birds.

Capsids: these pests are much more troublesome some years than others. They suck the sap from young leaves and the tips of the new growing shoots. Leaves damaged by capsids are covered with tiny pin pricks and later become distorted, tattered and browned. Fruits and flowers attacked by capsids will be mis-shapen and badly discoloured. If they appeared the previous season, as a precaution spray just after the flowering stage with malathion.

Greenfly: these tiny green 'plant lice' infest the tips of the shoots and new leaves in spring, and can result in serious damage. The new shoots will cease to grow and be stunted and distorted; sideshoots may be produced lower down whose growth is weak. Remove the worst affected tips and spray at once with derris, bioresmethrin or malathion, repeating if necessary. Remember not to spray during the day at flowering time.

Die back: this is caused by the fungus *Botrytis cinerea,* or grey mould. The main symptom is the sudden death of a whole branch or branches, often in full leaf. If the fungus attacks the main stem, the whole plant will die. Infected leaves will turn yellow and then almost white along the margins, they later turn brown and wither. Infection usually enters the bush through a wound or pruning snag. Make sure you prune correctly and paint over large wounds with fungicidal paint. If the bush is only moderately infected, cut back into living wood and burn the infected branches. If a bush is badly infected, dig it up and burn it. Plants grown in poor soils are the most susceptible, so take precautions.

American gooseberry mildew: this infection is probably the most serious gooseberry disease. The symptoms are first: white powdery patches on the young leaves as they unfold, and on the

These pale, powdery growths indicate American gooseberry mildew.

Donald Smith

Royal Horticultural Society, Wisley, Surrey

These leaves are infected with leaf spot, a disease most likely to occur in wet summers.

GUIDE TO GOOSEBERRY TROUBLES

Symptoms	Probable cause
Small holes in leaves; later entire leaf eaten except for main veins and midrib	Gooseberry sawfly or Magpie moth
Leaves pale, bronze coloured, fall prematurely; fruits small, unappetizing	Gooseberry red spider mite
Dormant buds pecked out	Birds
Leaves covered with tiny pin pricks, distorted, tattered, brown; fruits mis-shapen and discoloured	Capsids
New shoots stunted, distorted, weak sideshoots	Greenfly
Sudden death of whole branch or branches, leaves brown and withered, fruit drop off	Die back
White powdery patches on young leaves and stems, later turning brown; fruits small, unpleasant looking	American gooseberry mildew
Bright red or orange patches on leaves and stems, fruit; later cup-like growths on patches	Cluster cup rust
Small, black-dotted spots; leaves yellow, fall prematurely	Leaf spot
Leaf edges curl up, look scorched, rest of leaf green	Potash deficiency

young stems; later the fruits are infected, and at a later stage the patches of fungus turn brown and can be peeled off like thin felt. Infected berries remain small; infected shoots are stunted and twisted.

Bushes grown in the open, and well pruned so that air can circulate freely around them, are less likely to be infected. As with die back, avoid using too much nitrogenous fertilizer which encourages weak sappy growth. If the infection is mild, cut off and burn infected shoots in spring as soon as seen. Any infection still appearing in summer should be cut off in late summer, no later, otherwise new growth may appear, which would not ripen before winter. If your bushes have suffered attacks of American gooseberry mildew in previous summers, a good preventive measure is to spray the bushes with dinocap or a mixture of washing soda and soft soap solution at the rate of 1 kg of washing soda and $\frac{1}{4}$ kg of soft soap mixed with 45 L of soft water (2 lb washing soda and $\frac{1}{2}$ lb soft soap mixed with 10 gal water). If the water is hard, double the quantity of soft soap. Spray before the flowers open, again as the fruit is setting and thereafter at 2-week intervals until it is controlled.

Cluster cup rust: this is another fungal disease likely to occur where bushes are grown in crowded or damp conditions. The main symptom is bright red or orange patches on the leaves, stems and fruits. Late in the summer, tiny cup-like growths develop on these red patches. All infected leaves, fruits and shoots should be burned. If your bushes have been infected with cluster cup rust before, spray them with Bordeaux mixture two weeks before flowering.

Leaf spot: blackcurrants are more susceptible to this disease than goose-berries, although the latter are sometimes infected. It is most likely to occur in wet summers or areas which have high rainfall. The main symptoms are small, black-dotted spots; if the infection is severe, there will be large numbers of spots, the leaves will turn yellow, and fall prematurely. Rake up and burn all fallen leaves and remove infected leaves from the bushes. If the attack is severe, spray with zineb after removing the infected leaves, and again a fortnight later, and follow the manufacturer's directions with regard to precautions.

Potash deficiency: if the leaf edges develop brown bands around them, curl under and look scorched, while the rest of the leaf remains green and the new growth is short, then the plant is suffering from a shortage of potash. A further symptom is small berries which remain unripe. Correct this by applying sulphate of potash at the rate of 30 g per sq m (1 oz per sq yd) immediately. Thereafter apply 22-30 g per sq m ($\frac{3}{4}$-1 oz per sq yd) annually in early spring.

Varieties

Early

Keepsake: dessert or cooking; fruit size depends on picking date; pale green, oval and hairy, excellent flavour if left to ripen; bush vigorous and spreading with early foliage which protects young fruitlets from frost; reliable cropper but prone to mildew and flowers liable to frost damage.

May Duke: dessert or cooking; fruit deep crimson when mature, medium size, smooth skin, roundish oval shape; flavour better when cooked green; upright bush of moderate vigour.

New Giant: dessert or cooking; fruits large, yellowish green, well flavoured; bush upright, vigorous but not rampant.

Whitesmith: dessert or cooking; fruit pale greenish yellow to amber, medium to large, downy; bush upright, moderately vigorous; bush will spread with age.

Mid-season

Careless: cooking; fruits whitish-yellow, downy, large oval shape, veins sharply marked; bush moderately vigorous, spreading with age; resistent to mildew but does not do well under trees, or in poor soil, needs potash.

Lancashire Lad: cooking; fruit deep red, large if not overcropped, oval, hairy, moderate flavour; best picked green for cooking; bush vigorous and spreading, but needs good soil to do well; heavy cropper; *Lancashire Lad* is resistant to mildew.

Leveller: dessert or cooking; fruit large, oval, smooth, yellow-green veins sharply marked; good flavour, very popular variety; prolific cropper, but needs good soil conditions to do well; bush spreading; sulphur shy. Main commercial dessert variety.

Whinham's Industry: dessert or cooking; fruits large, hairy, oval and sweet, ripening dark red; upright vigorous growth later spreading; prolific cropper but subject to mildew; does well in semi-shade and under trees; may get too woody on rich soils; needs careful pruning for best results.

Langley Gage: dessert; fruit small, oval, pale greenish white, smooth, transparent with very sweet flavour; bush upright and vigorous.

Laxton's Amber; dessert or cooking; fruits yellow, medium-sized; bush upright in habit.

Late

Lancer (Howard's Lancer): dessert or cooking; fruit large, smooth, oval, very downy, greenish yellow; strong, vigorous growth and heavy cropper; grows well on most soils.

King of Trumps: dessert or cooking; fruits pale green; bush spreading but moderate growth; one of the latest of the late varieties.

Green Gem: dessert or cooking; fruits dark green with pale veins, medium to large, roundish oval; bush upright and compact; good and reliable cropper, resistant to mildew; worthwhile variety to grow but is often quite difficult to obtain.

White Lion: dessert or cooking; fruits white, large, oval, slightly hairy; growth vigorous and erect; best white variety for picking green and for dessert; very good flavour

Careless

Pears

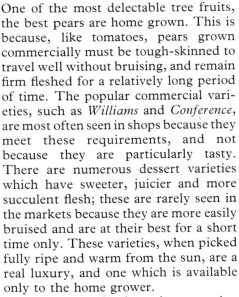

Pyrus communis (fam. *Rosaceae*)
Hardy deciduous tree with a life of
60-200 years
Planting to harvesting time: 5 years
Size: varies according to variety,
rootstock and training, but standard on
quince rootstock 3.6 m (12 ′) high, 2.7 m (9 ′) wide,
Yield: mature bush tree 25 kg (60 lb) fruit, dwarf pyramid
7 kg (15 lb), espalier 12 kg (25 lb)

One of the most delectable tree fruits,
the best pears are home grown. This is
because, like tomatoes, pears grown
commercially must be tough-skinned to
travel well without bruising, and remain
firm fleshed for a relatively long period
of time. The popular commercial varieties, such as *Williams* and *Conference*,
are most often seen in shops because they
meet these requirements, and not
because they are particularly tasty.
There are numerous dessert varieties
which have sweeter, juicier and more
succulent flesh; these are rarely seen in
the markets because they are more easily
bruised and are at their best for a short
time only. These varieties, when picked
fully ripe and warm from the sun, are a
real luxury, and one which is available
only to the home grower.

Pear trees used to have the reputation
of being slow to crop; the old saying,
"Plant pears for your heirs", was often
quoted. Although this was true when
pears were grown on pear rootstock, it no
longer applies. Today pear trees are
commonly grafted onto quince rootstock
which makes them come into crop much

earlier. In one sense, however, the old
saying still applies: pear trees are very
long lived, and a healthy specimen may
live for two hundred years or more. You
can often see ancient pear trees in
country gardens, still producing good-
sized crops.

Another drawback which has largely
been corrected is the problem of size.
Wild pear trees (*Pyrus communis*), found
in hedgerows and copses over much of
Europe, are large trees, growing 15 m
(50 ′) or more in height. Cultivated pears
are descended from *Pyrus communis* and,
like them, make lofty trees, much too
large to prune, spray and harvest easily,
and much too large for today's smaller
gardens. Growing pears on quince
rootstock has a considerable dwarfing
effect, and bush, cordon, pyramid and
espalier trained trees can easily be
accommodated in a small garden.

Pears grown commercially are mostly
open centred bushes, and this is
probably the best method for the
amateur and gives the highest yield in
suitable conditions. However, most
pears can be trained very easily and there

are many other forms available. The dwarf pyramid, or central leader tree, follows the natural shape of the pear, which is upright; it is space saving and convenient for picking. In cool areas, or where shelter is required, it is worthwhile training an espalier against a wall.

Besides producing delicious crops, pear trees make very attractive features in the garden. In early to mid-spring they are covered with masses of white blossom, followed by leaves with a silvery sheen. The foliage of many varieties gives a rich display of autumn colour.

Pears can be divided into three groups according to use. Cooking pears are hard textured, and less juicy and flavourful than dessert varieties; slow cooking with plenty of sugar improves them. They are prolific croppers, however, and tend to keep better than dessert varieties. In the north of England and in cool, exposed sites they are more likely to succeed.

The second category is made up of pears having a very high tannin content. These perry pears are very bitter and are not eaten. They are pressed for their juice, which is then fermented and made into perry, an alcoholic beverage. The varieties planted for perry are not usually available to the amateur grower, although there are commercial perry orchards in southwest England.

Lastly, and probably the best category for the amateur grower, are the dessert pears. These are softer in texture, and often have a sweet aroma. Dessert pears appreciate a warm, sheltered site; in cooler areas these varieties do best when trained as an espalier cordon, or fan, and grown against a wall. Dessert varieties will cook and bottle well if picked before they are slightly ripe; they are the best choice for the small garden.

Suitable site and soil

Because pears are Mediterranean in origin, they thrive in warmer conditions than apples. Pears are therefore more successfully grown in the south of England than the north. It is possible to grow dessert pears in cold areas if they are given wall protection; otherwise select a late cooking variety for growing in the open.

A Conference *pear tree trained as an espalier against a wall. Pears flower about a month earlier than apples, so they are more vulnerable to frost damage. Select a site which is warm, sunny, and fairly sheltered from winds, so insects can pollinate the flowers successfully.*

Pat Brindley

Pears blossom about four weeks earlier in the season than apples, so they are more vulnerable to damage from spring frosts. Avoid low-lying ground or frost pockets. Exposure to strong winds at flowering time can cause considerable damage, as well; insects are discouraged from visiting the blossom, and tender young leaves will be torn or even stripped off the tree. Autumnal winds can dessicate older leaves and cause premature fruit fall. Wind-bruised pear leaves always turn black. Try to site pear trees in as warm and sheltered a position as possible.

Pears will tolerate less well drained soil conditions than apples, but will not survive dry root conditions. The ideal soil for pears is a deep heavy loam which is slightly acid. Extremely alkaline soils may lead to chlorosis (yellowing) of the leaves. Whatever the soil type, there should be at least 60 cm (2′) of rooting depth.

Buying a tree

There are several factors to consider when selecting a pear tree, or trees, if you have room for more than one. Choose wisely because the chances are you will be living with the tree for a long time. It is an expensive and time-consuming proposition to replace unsatisfactory trees with more suitable varieties two or three years later, and much time will be wasted unnecessarily.

There are many named varieties from which to choose; this is further complicated by the fact that these will be grafted on one of several possible rootstocks, each with its own growth pattern. Lastly, pears are available as maidens or in a variety of trained shapes: standards, half-standards, bushes, cordons, espaliers, pyramids and fans.

The main determining factor is the size of your garden; if it is fairly small select a self-pollinating variety, such as *Dr Jules Guyot* or *Marguerite Marillat* trained in bush or pyramid form. Although some pear varieties are self-fertile, most require a second variety to ensure fertilization, and even self-fertile varieties bear heavier crops when there is a suitable pear tree nearby. Some have exceptionally poor pollen, and need two different varieties for satisfactory fertilization, but fortunately there are not many of these. *Jargonelle* is one. For successful pollination, trees must flower at the same time; however, certain varieties will not cross-pollinate each other and' some varieties will not pollinate any others, so check with your local nurseryman.

Pears are either grafted onto quince or pear rootstocks. Malling Quince A is probably the most popular quince rootstock; it produces trees of moderate vigour and high fruit production. Quince C rootstock has a dwarfing effect, producing bushes rather than trees; ideal for the smaller garden. Pears on Quince C come into fruit earlier than on Quince A. Some popular varieties, such as *Williams bon Crétien*, do not unite properly with quince when grafted; they are said to be incompatible. These varieties are double grafted by the nursery, using an intervening compatible variety to prevent a future break at the union; this is why some varieties are more expensive to buy.

Pear rootstocks are used to make large standard trees of vigorous growth. These are not suitable for the small garden because they grow too big to prune and harvest easily; trees on pear rootstock also take much longer to come into crop.

Buy maidens or two or three-year-old trees, if possible. They will settle down more quickly than a four or five-year-old and you can train them exactly as you wish from the beginning.

Planting

Prepare the soil well in advance by breaking up the subsoil and incorporating plenty of well-rotted manure. Correct the pH level if it is below 6.0 by liming, allowing at least two months to elapse between manuring and liming. About two weeks before planting, work

In today's smaller gardens, pears grown as bushes, cordons, or pyramids make the most economical use of space. Besides luscious fruit, the flowers are most attractive, and some varieties have leaves which turn rich shades of crimson in the autumn.

Donald Smith

in a general compound fertilizer at the rate of 60 g per sq m (2 oz per sq yd).

Autumn-planted trees establish themselves quickest; try to plant them as soon as possible after leaf fall. If the soil is frozen or very wet, heel the trees in until conditions improve. Plant, stake, and mulch as for apple (see APPLE). Spread out the roots so they occupy the maximum amount of soil from which to draw water and nutrients.

Take care to keep the union of the scion and the rootstock at least 7.5 cm (3″) above soil level. If the scion roots, the named variety will quickly dominate the rootstock and an over-vigorous, unfruitful tree will result.

Bush trees should be spaced 3-3.7 m (10-12′) apart; pyramids can be as close as 1.8 m (6′). Pears growing against a wall should be allowed a minimum of 2.1m (8′) height and a spread of 3.6 m (12′).

Pruning an open-centred bush

The initial pruning to shape an open centred bush is the same as that for apples (see APPLE) with two important differences. Most varieties of pear, if correctly pruned, carry their fruit on spurs close to the main branches and therefore more main branches can be allowed for each tree, say twelve, where eight would be more suitable for apples. Secondly, pear branches in the young tree are naturally slender and have a tendency to droop. To counteract this, continue to prune the leading shoots on the main branches by one third to one half of the new growth, according to vigour, until the trees approach their allotted height and spread. This will be when they are about eight years old, when leader pruning should cease.

Leaders are pruned back for four reasons: to strengthen the branch, to encourage more side growth, to remove deformed or diseased wood and to remove a branch growing in an undesirable direction. If none of these apply, then leader pruning should cease.

Some pears are tip-bearers, which means that instead of producing fruit on

PYRAMID PRUNING

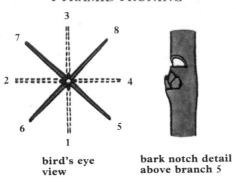

bird's eye
view

bark notch detail
above branch 5

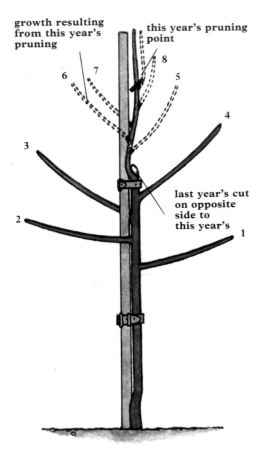

Prune central leader each winter to encourage new tier of branches to form. Cut to a bud pointing in the opposite direction of the previous year's bud; leave about 20 cm (8″) of new growth. Choose four well placed buds to intersect existing branches. Stimulate lowest bud to grow by notching bark over it.

short spurs, these are formed on the end of branches. *Josephine de Malines* and *Jargonelle* are tip-bearers; they should be pruned very lightly, and for this reason are not really good for restricted training. They are also better with a longer trunk than is usual in bush forms, up to as much as 30 cm (12″) longer.

Training and pruning a pyramid

Because most pear trees are upright in growth, they are very suitable for training as pyramids. Pyramids grow with a strong central leader, and are similar in form to a Christmas tree. From this central trunk cropping branches grow away at wide angles with about 30 cm (1′) of trunk between each tier of branches. The resulting tree is a very compact and efficient fruit bearer. Formative pruning is done in winter; pruning to encourage fruiting and restrictive growth is done in summer.

To train a pyramid pear tree, buy a maiden or two-year-old. Cut the tree back to about 50 cm (20″) the first winter it is in your garden, making the cut immediately above a conveniently placed bud. Rub out the first bud below the leader bud. Make sure there are three or four buds left, spaced evenly around and down the stem. These will grow out to form the first tier of framework branches. The lowest bud should ensure that there is a leg of about 23-30 cm (9-12″). Any 'feathers' should be cut off flush with the main stem. The following winter, and each subsequent winter until the desired height is reached, prune the leader, leaving 20 cm (8″) of new growth; cut to a bud pointing in the opposite direction to the previous year's bud. This keeps the leader growing straight. Make sure there are three well-placed buds on the remaining part of the leader to make additional whorls of branches. These buds should be as evenly spaced round and down the stem as possible; ideally they should point towards the gaps between branches on the tier below.

Do not retain a bud immediately above an existing branch, but aim for even spacing both up and around. Rub out all unwanted buds; this can be done by pushing them off with your thumb.

The branches and sideshoots are pruned in summer. Start when the new growth has begun to mature and the shoots are becoming stiff and woody, and brown at the base. Disregarding the cluster of leaves at the base of the new growth, count five or six leaves along the branches and cut beyond a downward pointing one. While the tree is still young flowers may form on the central leader; these should be removed to encourage the production of more side branches.

From late mid-summer, when the sideshoots along the branches begin to mature and are about 30 cm (1 ′) long and woody at the base, cut to the second or third leaf beyond the basal cluster. This helps to build up strong spurs, close to the main branches. Where there has been growth from a sideshoot pruned in previous years, prune back to the first leaf beyond the basal cluster. Spread out the work over a period of three to four weeks. If in winter you find there has been further growth from any of these summer cuts, prune it back to the first bud.

Restrict the final height of the pyramid to about 2.1 m (7 ′), by switching pruning from winter to late spring, just after new growth has begun. Cut the central leader back to within 1.2 cm ($\frac{1}{2}$″) of its new growth. When branch leaders reach the length of those in the tier below, or begin to grow close to branches of adjacent trees, deal with them in the same way, by cutting them back.

Training an espalier

Espaliers can be trained against walls, fences or specially erected posts and wires. An espalier tree has a strong central leader from which branch out horizontal pairs of opposite laterals, each tier parallel to the others. Nurseries usually sell two and three tier espaliers, but these are expensive and if you train your own, you can make it fit exactly into the available space.

Espaliers need wires, whether against walls or in the open, 30 cm (1 ′) from the ground, and additional wires for each tier at intervals of about 30 cm (1 ′). A horizontal space of 4.2 m (14 ′) is best.

To train your own espalier, buy a maiden or two-year-old. Immediately after planting, cut the leader back to a strong bud, about 5 cm (2″) higher than the lowest wire. This bud will produce a vertical shoot. Below this top bud, select two buds, on opposite sides of the stem; these will eventually become the laterals forming the first tier. Notch above the lower bud. Rub out any other buds.

During the first summer, tie the middle shoot to a cane with soft string; attach the cane vertically to the wires. When they become long enough, attach the shoots from the two lower buds to canes as well. Fasten the canes to the wires at an angle of 45°, so that the two lower shoots will be at a 90° angle from each other. Try to keep the two growing equally strongly so they are the same length. If they are growing unequally, lower the cane of the stronger shoot to impede the flow of sap and thus slow it down; raise the cane of the other slightly to encourage growth.

In late autumn or winter, unfasten the two side canes and bring the branches down to the horizontal wires; secure the branches to the bottom wire. However, if they have to be forced down to the horizontal, it is better to leave them and continue to lower them the following summer, finally tying them in when they are two years old, in their second winter. In winter, prune the vertical leader to a strong bud about 5 cm (2″) above the second wire. Proceed as in the first winter, choosing two more buds to fill the second wire. Continue in this way until the required number of tiers has been formed. When forming the final tier, allow only two shoots to form, one on either side of the central leader, and cut the leading growth back to about 2.5 cm (1″) above the highest of the two sideshoots. Prune established espalier branches in summer. Prune the side growths as they mature to the third leaf beyond the basal cluster. Cut shoots from laterals that were pruned previously to one leaf beyond the basal cluster at the twig base (see diagram). When the main branches of each tier have filled the space available, cut them back in late spring as required.

Fertilizers and care
During the first winter, check the trees after hard ground frost and firm any which have lifted. Pears, particularly young trees, are very sensitive to water shortage. In dry weather, water thoroughly. Watering in late spring or early summer tends to encourage shoot growth, while watering in mid- and late summer aids in fruit swelling. Trees planted against walls are particularly vulnerable to drought, as soil near foundations dries out very quickly.

Pears respond more than any other fruit tree to applications of bulky organic matter. For the the first three springs after planting, give an annual mulch of well-rotted manure, 5 cm (2″) thick in late spring; spread it over an area

TRAINING AN ESPALIER

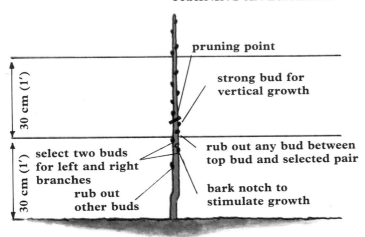

pruning point

strong bud for vertical growth

30 cm (1′)

select two buds for left and right branches

30 cm (1′)

rub out any bud between top bud and selected pair

rub out other buds

bark notch to stimulate growth

1. *Espaliers need wire supports, whether in the open or against walls, 30 cm (1′) from the ground, and at 30 cm (1′) intervals. Immediately after planting, cut the leader back to a strong bud 5 cm (2″) higher than the lowest wire. Select two opposite buds to form laterals, notch the lower one, and rub out the rest.*

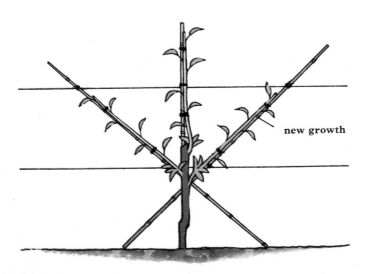

new growth

2. *The first summer, tie middle shoot to a cane with soft string; when they grow long enough, tie the lateral shoots to canes as well. The middle cane should be vertical, and the two lateral canes at an angle of 45° from the ground. If the sideshoots grow unequally, lower the cane of the stronger shoot to slow it down; raise the cane of the other slightly*

equivalent to that covered by the tree's branches. Keep the manure at least 15 cm (6") away from the trunk. Supplement this with an annual dressing of 30 g (1 oz) sulphate of ammonia and 15 g ($\frac{1}{2}$ oz) of sulphate of potash per sq m (sq yd) applied in late winter or early spring.

Pears are very nitrogen greedy; for this reason they should not be grassed down. There is one exception, however. If you wish to retard the growth of over-vigorous cordons or dwarf pyramids, then grassing down is a good method. Trees competing with grass for moisture and nutrients will be slower than those in cultivated ground.

Spur and fruit thinning

Pears make spurs more readily than apples and as the tree gets older the spurs may become crowded. When this happens, spur pruning is beneficial; prune the oldest and least fruitful ones back to their base. Any spurs which are too long can be shortened by about half. All spur pruning is best done in winter.

Pears tend to produce a great deal of

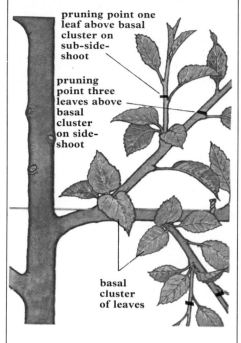

PRUNING ESPALIER LATERALS

pruning point one leaf above basal cluster on sub-side-shoot

pruning point three leaves above basal cluster on side-shoot

basal cluster of leaves

Prune espaliers in mid-summer. Cut mature laterals growing from horizontal branches to three leaves above basal cluster; cut sideshoots back to one leaf above.

3. *In autumn, undo the two side canes and bring the branches down to the horizontal wires, secure the branches to the bottom wire. In the second autumn, the same procedure is followed to produce a second tier, and again until the top tier has filled the top wire.*

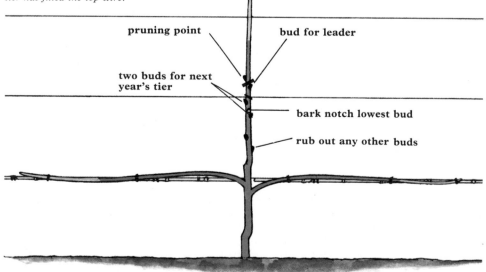

pruning point

bud for leader

two buds for next year's tier

bark notch lowest bud

rub out any other buds

SPUR PRUNING ON OLD TREES

Pear fruiting spurs will become overcrowded in time, and fruit production may diminish. When this happens, cut out the oldest and least fruitful spurs back to their base with secateurs or a sharp pruning knife in winter.

blossom; if all was allowed to produce fruit it would exhaust the tree. Judicious fruit thinning is usually necessary although pears need less thinning than apples. Thin first in late spring, when the young fruitlets are about 2.5 cm (1") long. Remove and burn all mis-shapen ones first, as they probably contain pear midge larvae. A second thinning, after the natural fruit fall in early summer, should be done in mid-summer. There should be a final spacing of 12.5 cm (5") between fruit. This varies slightly according to the age, health and variety of the tree; vigorous mature trees can carry heavier crops than very young or weak-growing ones.

Harvesting

Pears, more so than apples, need to be picked and eaten at exactly the right moment, as most varieties are at their best for a short while only. Very early varieties, which are ready mid- to late summer, can be picked straight off the tree and eaten at once. As soon as the base skin colour begins to yellow or pale, is about the right stage. Early varieties, like *Williams Bon Chrétien*, should be picked before they are fully ripe.

This will mean picking them when the skin at the stalk end of the fruit starts to change colour. If left on the tree for longer, they will become too mature, and although the outside may appear just right, the centre will have started to rot.

Mid-season varieties, ie early to mid-autumn kinds, are picked, and then kept in a cool place for about a week or so before eating. To tell if a pear is ripe, lift the fruit and twist it slightly; ripe pears should part quite easily from the tree. If pears are picked too soon for storing, they will become 'sleepy', when the outer flesh becomes soft but does not develop its flavour, and the inner remains hard. The best criterion for picking for store is the ground colour of the skin; when this begins to change, the fruit can be picked. When harvesting, handle the pears carefully as they bruise easily, particularly at the stalk end. Try to pick the fruit in dry weather, as pears rapidly deteriorate if left wet for any length of time.

Storing

Unfortunately, pears do not keep as well as apples, so if you want a steady supply, it it best to plant several varieties of trees with fruit which ripen in succession. Early and mid-season varieties do not keep for any length of time; it is not worth arranging long-term storage, as you will more than likely be disappointed. Late varieties need to be picked when slightly unripe and stored until they reach their full flavour. If a sharp tug is needed to get the fruit off, they are not ready for storing. Leave them for a couple of days and try again. Be guided also by the change in the ground colour,

340

1. To get healthy, good sized pears, thin fruit in late spring and mid-summer; remove mis-shaped fruit.

2. Ripening pears are vulnerable to attacks by birds; protect the fruit by fixing cardboard squares onto stalks.

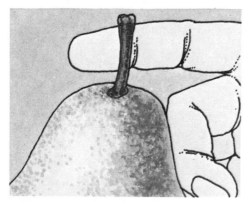

3. If picking pears for storing, pick fruit with the stalk intact, otherwise the pears are liable to rot.

especially near the stalk end; when this begins to change, the fruit is ready for storing. Pick the fruit when dry, with the stalk intact. Store only sound, unblemished fruit; any damaged pears will quickly rot and the rot will spread.

Do not wrap them, but lay them in a single layer on slatted trays in cool 4-7°C (40-45°F) conditions. An empty room or shed will do, as long as there are no severe fluctuations in temperature. They are better in some humidity, and shrivel quickly in a dry store. Inspect them frequently for approaching maturity, which is indicated by a softening of the flesh close to the stalk. Then bring them into a warm room for a couple of days, to finish off the ripening process.

Exhibition tips

Pears for exhibition are divided into two categories: cooking and dessert. The methods of preparation and presentation are the same for both. In both categories the judges will look for large fruits with eyes and stalks intact. The skins should be clear and unblemished, and the colour appropriate to the variety. Six is the usual number shown of the same variety, and they should be as uniform as possible. Do not include one or two enormous pears, which would make the remaining fruit seem small by comparison, and spoil the exhibit. Never display over-ripe pears, small, mis-shapen fruits, or fruits with blemishes.

To get the best pears, thin the crop while the fruits are still small. As the selected pears ripen, expose them gradually to more and more sunshine, by carefully removing the leaves closest to them and tying back the overhanging foliage. Pick more pears than the actual number needed, so that you have a reserve supply when you are setting up the exhibit.

Pears shaped like apples are usually staged with eyes uppermost, and stalk end downwards; place one fruit in the centre and the remaining fruit around it. You can raise the central fruit slightly by placing white tissue paper underneath it.

Varieties

Although *Conference* and *William's Bon Chrétien* are the most popular, there are many other fine flavoured varieties which should be planted more often. Remember that the more varieties you plant, the better crops you will have from each.

Summer pears

Beurré Bedford: large, pale yellow fruit, relatively resistant to scab; fruit ripens late summer or early autumn; erect and compact growth; mid-season flowering.

Doyenné d'Été: small, yellow, conical fruit; one of the first to ripen in mid to late summer; juicy and pleasant flavour; tree has weak but spreading growth; flowers early to mid-season; not very good for restricted training.

Jargonelle: very old variety but still popular; long, greenish-yellow, tapering fruit; relatively scab resistant; heavy cropper; will do well in the north of England or on north-facing wall; flowers mid-season; tree large, spreading growth, tip-bearing; must have two pollinators, *Beurré Superfin* is suitable.

Early to mid-autumn pears

Gorham: long, pale yellow pear with heavy russeting; good flavour; fills the gap between *William's* and *Conference*; scab resistant; tree of hardy and upright growth; late flowering.

Dr Jules Guyot: self-fertile variety; better flavour than *Conference*; yellow fruit, black dotted skin, often flushed scarlet; tree fertile and hardy, upright growth; flowers late in season.

Fertility Improved: sweet, juicy, crisp pear; heavy cropper, often needs thinning; disease resistant; self-fertile; fruit small, yellow, but heavily russeted; tree tall and upright in growth with red autumn foliage; flowers late in season.

Marguerite Marillat: self-fertile pear, although it will not pollinate other varieties; crops well; yellow flesh, skin flushed with bright scarlet; upright, small tree with scarlet autumn leaves; flowers early, so avoid a frost pocket.

William's Bon Chrétien: best known and most widely grown of all pears, also called *Bartlett*; irregular, roundish, pale yellow fruit with red flush; moderate flavour, juicy flesh; very susceptible to scab; upright tree, suitable for training against north wall; needs double working; flowers mid-season.

Merton Pride: green pear of good size; very good flavour; heavy cropper; tree upright in growth; flowers mid-season.

Mid to late autumn pears

Beurré Hardy: large, round, conical, coppery russeted fruit with red flush; very good flavour; fertile; relatively resistant to scab; tree vigorous, full and spreading; prune lightly; leaves scarlet in autumn; flowers late in season; fruits best picked a little before they part readily from the tree; keep two or three weeks before eating.

Beurré Superfin: long, golden yellow fruit patched with russet; less vigorous pear good for small gardens; makes good cordons; fruit does not keep well, pick late in early autumn; mid-season flowering.

Conference: most reliable of all pears; long, pale green fruit with silvery russet; prolific cropper; pick late in early autumn and keep one to three weeks before eating; self-fertile but will do better if cross-pollinated; vulnerable to wind damage and scab; moderate flavour; flowers mid-season.

Doyenné du Comice: large, roundish, golden fruit with light russetting and red flush; superb flavour; not entirely reliable in bad years or bad locations; needs several varieties to pollinate, to ensure regularly good crops; very susceptible to scab and sulphur-shy; vigorous upright growth; good against wall or as cordon; flowers late in season; pick late in early autumn or early in mid-autumn and keep a few weeks.

Louise Bonne of Jersey: greenish-yellow fruit, flushed red; flesh white and delicious; fertile; tree hardy and vigorous; upright in growth; regular cropper; exceptionally beautiful blossom; flowers early in the season.

Durondeau: fruits long, tapering, red russet; good flavour; stores well; tree small, suitable for small gardens; spurs well and is good in restricted forms; red autumn foliage; crops heavily in suitable soil; flowers mid-season.

Packham's Triumph: fruits broad, squat, bright green changing to bright yellow; juicy, very sweet; crops well, and ripens 10 days before *Comice*; moderate sized, tip-bearing tree; flowers mid-season.

Early and mid-winter pears

Glou Morceau: green pears, turning yellow when ripe; sweet flavour, keeps well; does best on sunny wall or in sheltered garden; flowers late in season.

Joséphine de Malines: small, green fruit, yellow when ripe with a russet patch; flesh pink, with delicious scent and sweet flavour; best of all winter pears; stores well; fruit ripens unevenly in store, so inspect regularly; fertile and reliable cropper, especially in warm gardens; tip-bearing and tending to droop; flowers mid-season.

Winter Nelis: juicy, sweet, smallish pear, best eaten while still yellowish green; fertility good and useful for pollinating *Comice*; ripens over a month or more; tree has slender, arching growth; scab resistant; flowers late in season.

Santa Claus: excellent type to choose if growing on a sheltered wall; may not be successful in harsh climates; heavy cropper of well-flavoured brownish-red russet fruits; vigorous, upright growth; very attractive in autumn when foliage turns crimson and purple.

Late cooking pears

Catillac: large, green, cooking pear remaining hard until mid-spring; scab resistant; tree spreading with broad leaves and large flowers; vigorous cropper but needs two other trees to pollinate it; blossoms late in season.

Pests & Diseases

Pears suffer from the same trouble as apples, but generally to a lesser degree. Natural predators and good cultivation, including regular feeding, should reduce the risk of damage considerably. If you have had serious trouble in the past, an annual spraying programme should be carried out, to control the damage done by a particular pest or disease, otherwise follow a system of 'spot' spraying. A tar oil wash applied in mid to late winter will control the eggs of aphids and leaf suckers, but is best applied only once every three or four years, as it also kills many beneficial insect predators. In early spring, at the green cluster stage, spray with captan against scab. In mid-spring, at the early white bud stage, spray with malathion to control aphids, caterpillars and pear midge and apply captan again for scab. Lastly, in mid to late spring, at petal fall when nearly all the blossom is off, apply captan against scab. Never spray fully open flowers, because of the danger to bees and other pollinating insects. Not all pesticides and fungicides are compatible, so follow manufacturer's instructions before applying them together. And remember that these substances can also be dangerous to pets and children, so be sure they are properly stored.

Aphids: these sometimes infest young growth, causing the leaves and shoot tips to curl and the new shoots to be stunted, sometimes severely. The leaves may also become sticky. The insects are small, green, grey or dark brown in colour, and are usually found on the underside of the leaves. The most serious is the pear bedstraw species, which is a mealy-covered, pink aphid; in severe attacks the whole tree may be smothered. Remove and destroy aphid-infested shoots as soon as they appear and spray the tree with derris or malathion; the winter tar-oil wash will kill most of the overwintering eggs.

Pear sucker: in recent years this has been causing a good deal of trouble. It is a small, flat, pale green, sucking insect which feeds on the undersides of the leaves, and the flower trusses, in bud and open. Three generations can occur in a season. Leaves have pale green patches on them, flowers do not develop, and sticky 'honeydew' with black mould on it, covers the leaves and shoots. The winter tar-oil wash will deal with the eggs, or derris or malathion can be used in spring.

Pear midge: if the young fruitlets on your tree do not develop, but become badly mis-shapen, turn black and fall off the tree, then pear midge is the probable cause. The tiny, white maggots, 3-4 mm $\frac{1}{8}-\frac{1}{6}''$) long, live in the young fruit, and later move to the soil where they overwinter.

Thorough cultivation under the trees will expose the maggots to insect-eating birds, the weather and physical damage from hoeing. Remove and burn all infested fruitlets, before the larvae have a chance to get to the soil. If this pest has caused considerable damage in the past, spray with gamma HCH at the white bud stage, but not during flowering.

Pear leaf blister mite: this microscopic insect spends winters beneath the bud scales and during the summer lives inside the leaves. Infested leaves will have numerous yellowish green or reddish pustules on them, from mid-spring onwards. The pustules eventually turn brown to black by mid-summer, and the leaves fall early. If the attack is a mild one, pick off and burn all infested leaves. In general, this is usually all that is needed in the private garden. However, if you have had serious trouble in the past, spray with lime sulphur in early spring as the buds start to open. Do not spray *Doyenne du Comice* with lime sulphur, as it is sulphur shy.

Caterpillars: there are several varieties of caterpillar which may attack pear trees, including the fruit tree tortrix moth, the vapourer, lackey and winter moths. The treatment is the same for all types of caterpillars: hand-pick the caterpillars in the case of mild infestations, or spray with trichlorphon in severe attacks.

Fireblight: this is a very serious bacterial infection which enters the tree through the flowers, and moves from the spurs into the main branches. Dieback occurs and leaves turn brown and black but remain on the tree. It is seen mostly on new shoots which look as though they have been scorched by flame. Cankers develop beneath infected tissues, which ooze a sticky liquid in spring. This liquid contains bacteria, which are then carried by rain or insects to other trees.

If you suspect fireblight, you must notify your local representative of the Ministry of Agriculture, who will then give you instructions about treatment.

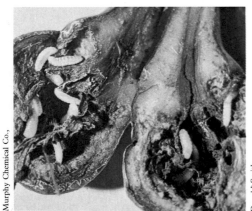

This fruit is infested with pear midge larvae; control with gamma HCH spray in spring.

Pear leaf blister mite infestation: the minute insects live in the leaves and destroy them.

Pear scab: this fungal infection appears as blackish scabs on the fruit, or dark brown blotches on the leaves. Occasionally shoots are infected and they will appear blistery and scabby. Remove and destroy all diseased leaves; do not leave them on the ground, or the infection will spread rapidly. Spray with captan (except for fruit to be preserved) as indicated. For fruit for preserving, use benomyl at bud burst, and at three-weekly intervals as long as necessary. In winter, be very careful to prune off all infested shoots, as the spores overwinter on them and can remain viable for at least three years. The scab lesions also provide a means of entry for the fungus disease canker.

Pear stony pit virus: if the pears are mis-shapen and pitted, and have small, hard areas in the flesh, then the tree is infected with stony pit virus. In severe cases, the fruit will be completely inedible. At first, fruit on single branches will be affected, but eventually the virus spreads through the whole tree, and the whole harvest from that tree becomes useless. Old trees are most susceptible. There is no cure; dig up and burn any infected tree.

Canker: this fungus disease also attacks apple trees, and the symptoms and damage are the same. The bark of branches becomes sunken and cracked; if the canker girdles a stem, it will die above the infection. Cut out all infected parts and paint large wounds with a tree wound-sealing compound.

Pear scab: this is a fungal infection which attacks leaves and shoots as well as fruit.

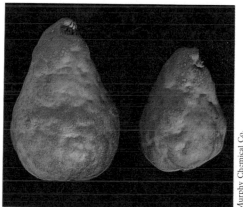

Murphy Chemical Co.

Pears having stony pit virus are mis-shapen and inedible; old trees are most vulnerable.

GUIDE TO PEAR TROUBLES

Symptom	Probable Cause
Leaves sticky and curled, shoots curled	Aphids
Pale green patches and sticky honeydew on leaves, flowers do not develop	Pear sucker
Mis-shapen black fruitlets	Pear midge
Pale green or red pustules on leaves	Pear leaf blister mite
Leaves eaten	Caterpillars
Leaves turn brown or black and remain on tree, oozing cankers on branches and trunk	Fireblight
Dark brown blotches on leaves, blackish scabs on fruit	Pear scab
Fruit mis-shapen and pitted, with small hard areas in the flesh	Pear stony pit virus

Plums

Plum: *Prunus domestica*
(fam. *Rosaceae*)
Damson: *Prunus damascena*
Gage: *Prunus italica*
Bullace: *Prunus insititia*

Hardy deciduous tree with a useful life of 50 years
Planting to harvesting time: 4-5 years
Size: 6-9 m (20-30′) tall; less on trained shapes
Yield: mature standard or bush tree on St. Julien A
rootstock 22-26 kg (50-60 lb), more for a more vigorous
rootstock, less for a pyramid tree. Greengages yield half this
figure.

Plums are among the most delicious and succulent tree fruits, and a freshly picked plum is one of summer's finest treats. The trees are hardier and easier to grow than peaches and cherries, and they will succeed in nearly all types of soil.

Damsons, gages and bullaces are all closely related to plums and their cultivation is basically similar.

Plums are usually divided into cooking and dessert varieties. Cooking plums are mainly dark coloured, with blue-black skins, and have less flesh and a tarter flavour than the dessert varieties. The trees which produce cooking plums are usually larger, hardier and more reliable croppers than the dessert varieties. Dessert plums have a richer flavour, higher sugar content, and may be yellow, green, red, blue-black, or purple-skinned. Most dessert plums are partly descended from the gages and, like the gages, do best in sunny sheltered

conditions, trained against a wall.

Bullace is a species of cooking plum which is sometimes found growing wild in hedgerows and woodlands. Bullace is very similar to the sloe, or blackthorn, and forms a small, hardy, ornamental tree. It is a useful shelter tree, and is sometimes planted in rows along the edge of an orchard. The fruit is very sharp-flavoured, and is usually left on the tree until late autumn, so that frosts can soften the acidity. Bullaces are not eaten raw, but are excellent for preserving and jam-making.

Damson is another cooking variety closely related to the bullace, and is also found growing wild in hedgerows. The trees produce oval fruit in early to mid-autumn, which are smaller and sweeter flavoured than those of the bullace. The fruits are cooked when ripe and are used for tarts, jam-making and bottling. They are very tough trees, and will crop well

A fan-trained plum, newly planted against a wall. All but north-facing sites are suitable.

even on thin soil. Damsons flower later than other plums, and are less damaged by frosts and cold winds. They also keep their leaves late into autumn and like the bullace can be used as windbreaks for less hardy trees.

Closely related to the bullaces and damsons are the gages which are used mainly as dessert plums. These are usually green-fleshed, with green, occasionally red-flushed, skin. Greengages may also be yellow-skinned and yellow-fleshed. Regardless of the colour, they are generally considered to be the sweetest and most deliciously scented of the plums. Unfortunately, gages need more favourable growing conditions

than other plums, and are best grown as a fan-trained tree against a south-facing wall.

Suitable site and soil

Because there are no really effective dwarfing rootstocks, plums eventually make large trees. They are unsuitable for small gardens unless they are fan-trained, or grown as a pyramid or bush. Plums can be grown as standards or half-standards if you have a large garden.

Remembering that you need to plan for the size of a mature tree, you should expect the following heights from the different shapes: fans 2 m (7′); pyramids 2.4 m (8′); half-standards and standards

A lovely crop of golden plums. Three-year-old purchased fans should start fruiting in two years.

6-9 m (20-30′); bushes 3.5-4.5 m (12-15′).

Plums start to flower earlier than most other fruit trees, in mid-spring, so if your garden is in a low-lying area or subject to frosts, it is best to choose a late-flowering variety, and give it wall protection. Although plums do best in full sunshine, they can crop well with less light than pears need. If there is protection from frost, some varieties of plums can be grown against east or west walls, leaving the southerly positions for pears or peaches.

Because plums need a lot of moisture in the soil, do not plant them next to large trees, particularly those which are surface-rooting, like elms. Annual rainfall should ideally be between 50 and 76 cm (20-30″). Although plums need a continual supply of moisture at the roots, the subsoil must never be stagnant or badly drained. A heavy loam or clay soil is preferable, and one that is neither very acid nor very alkaline. Although the trees crop better when some lime is added to the soil, they do not need an enormous amount, and on chalky soils the trees may show symptoms of iron deficiency.

Buying a tree

Because there are so many varieties and shapes available, there are several factors to consider before making your purchase. A major consideration is the ultimate size; this is controlled to a large extent by the rootstock. A few varieties are grown on their own roots, but most plums are budded or grafted onto other rootstocks of known performance. Myrobalan B rootstock will give a large tree, too vigorous for the small garden. St. Julian A rootstock is semi-dwarfing and is more suitable for the small garden. Brompton rootstock is also good for the small garden, as trees grafted onto it will grow steadily and come in to bearing quickly, and Brompton rootstock sends up very few suckers. The common plum rootstock is also semi-dwarfing, and is often used as a rootstock for gages.

The grafting of named varieties onto rootstocks is complicated by the fact that not all varieties are compatible with all rootstocks. If an unsuitable combination is made between the scion, or shoot of the named variety, and rootstock, the tree may break where the two join together. A good nurseryman will choose a suitable rootstock according to the variety, shape and size of the tree to be grown. Make sure you buy your trees from a reputable source.

Size is also controlled, to a lesser extent, by the way the tree is trained. You can either buy a ready trained standard, half-standard, or bush tree; these are either two or three years old. Alternatively, you can buy a one-year-old maiden, and train it yourself.

Pollination

A second point to consider when buying a tree is pollination. A few plums, such as *Victoria,* are self-fertile, but most require a compatible pollinator which flowers at the same time, and even the self-fertile varieties will set heavier crops if cross-pollinated. Timing the cross-pollination is less difficult than with apples and pears, because flowering of all plum varieties takes place within the space of 18 or 19 days; from early spring onwards. Plums are divided into 'early' and 'late' flowering for pollination

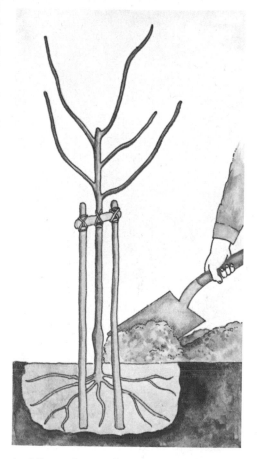

1. Allow plenty of room for the roots. Stake the tree for support. Return soil, making sure it penetrates between roots. Press down very firmly.

purposes. Unless they have been damaged by frost, the trees will remain in flower for exactly 10 days, so the early trees will have just about finished flowering when the late flowering varieties are starting to bloom. Early self-fertile varieties will pollinate early self-sterile varieties, and the same is true for those varieties which bloom later. If you have room in your garden for only one tree, choose a self-fertile one. If you are buying more than one tree, check the Varieties list for suitable pollinators.

If you plan to grow gages, remember that they tend to produce rather small

349

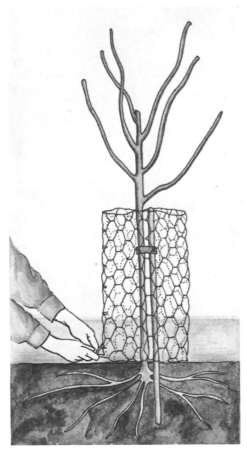

2. If rabbits or other animal pests are likely to be a problem, protect the newly planted tree with wire netting. Leave no gaps at the base.

3. An alternative staking method: make sure the pole is not so long as to interfere with growing branches. Use a soft, strong material to tie.

crops. Hence it is a good idea to plant two trees, either two varieties of gages or a gage and another plum tree.

Planting out

This is best done in late autumn, but an open-grown tree can be planted from late autumn to early spring, provided the weather is suitable. If your soil is heavy, you should work in coarse sand before planting, at the rate of 3 kg per sq m (7 lb per sq yd). Make freely draining soil more water retentive by mixing in rotted organic matter, at the rate of 12 L per sq m (2½ gal per sq yd). This is particularly

important if you are planting the tree against a wall, as the soil near walls tends to be dry. In general, plums will not grow well on light, 'hot' soils.

Plant and stake the trees as for apples (see the relevant chapter on apples), making sure you firm well round the tree. Also, make sure the union between the rootstock and scion is at least 7.5 cm (3") above ground level, or the scion will form its own roots and the beneficial effect of the rootstock will be lost. Be careful not to injure the bark while planting, or bacterial canker may set in. Keep the soil round the tree free of grass

FORMATIVE TRAINING OF PYRAMID PLUM TREE

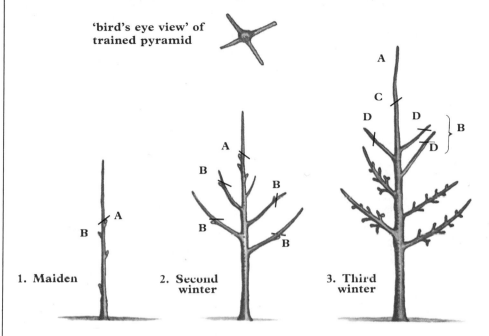

'bird's eye view' of trained pyramid

1. Maiden

2. Second winter

3. Third winter

Pruning young pyramid trees should be done in the winter; because the wounds are tiny, the trees are unlikely to get silver leaf.
1. Cut the maiden back to 50 cm (20")
the first winter the tree is in your garden.
Cut back to a suitably placed bud (A).
Rub out bud immediately below leader bud (B). Make sure there are 3 or 4 buds left spaced evenly around the stem.
2. The next winter, prune the leader to about 45 cm (18") to a bud pointing in the opposite direction from the previous year's pruning; this helps keep the growth straight (A). Make sure there are 3 well-placed buds on the remaining part of the leader to make a second whorl of branches. Prune all branches back to 22 cm (9") (B); this encourages the formation of fruit spurs.
3, 4. Train the leader vertically (A); the second whorl of branches will grow out (B). Cut back the sideshoots formed on the lower set of branches to 4 good leaves during early summer. In the third winter cut back the leader to 45 cm (18") (C) and the new whorl of branches back to 22 cm (9") (D).

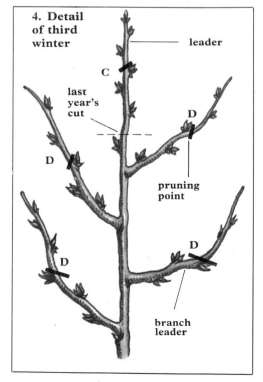

4. Detail of third winter

leader

last year's cut

pruning point

branch leader

PRUNING ESTABLISHED PYRAMID TREE

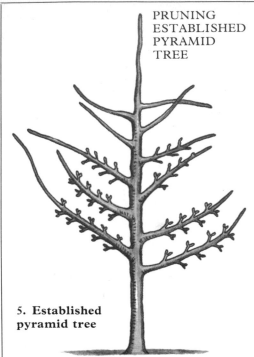

5. Established pyramid tree

5, 6. Plums need much less pruning than older fruit trees because they fruit on old and new wood. Generally, pruning should be done in early summer to avoid the risk of dieback and silver leaf. Pinch out vigorous sideshoots to 4 to 6 leaves from the parent stem (A and B). This encourages fruiting spurs to form. Cut out any dead wood back to living wood (C) and if the wound is larger than 2.5 cm (1″) treat it with bitumen paint. When the branch leaders grow longer than 1.2 m (4′), cut it back by one fourth to one third, depending on the vigour of the tree. Cut back to a suitably spaced spur or sideshoot (D). If the variety has a naturally drooping habit, such as Victoria, *prune the branch leader back to an upward growing spur or sideshoot. Cutting back the branch leaders encourages the formation of new sideshoots. When the leader grows taller than 2.4 m (8′), cut it back into the old wood (E). Do this at blossom time, in mid-spring, every three or four years, as necessary.*

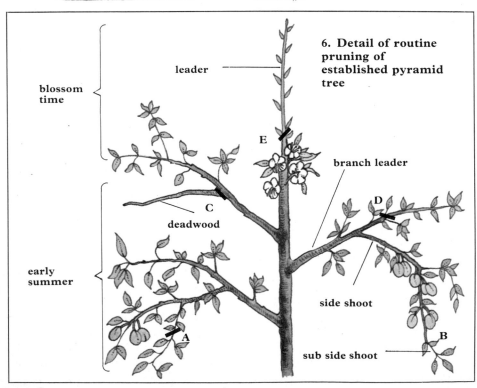

6. Detail of routine pruning of established pyramid tree

blossom time

early summer

leader

E

branch leader

D

C

deadwood

side shoot

A

B

sub side shoot

and weeds, so the plum does not have to compete with them for moisture during the summer.

If you are planting more than one tree, space less vigorous varieties, such as those on St. Julian A rootstock, 3 m (10′) apart. Space pyramid trees and those on Myrobalan B rootstock 5.5 m (18′) apart. Fan-trained trees on St. Julian A rootstock should be allowed at least 4.5 m (15′) wall space.

Manuring and aftercare
Check frequently to make sure that newly planted trees have not been lifted by frost; firm down any which have been lifted. If the summer is dry, water any newly planted trees and also water established trees which are grown against a wall.

Plums need plenty of nitrogen, and should never run short of lime. A good mulch of rotted manure or compost, rich in nitrogen, is especially helpful to young trees, applied in mid-spring every year. Mulch an area of soil slightly larger than the area covered by the tree's branches.

In autumn, fork over the soil very lightly. Do not fork too deeply, because plums have very shallow rooting systems, closer to the surface than pears or apples, and over-vigorous forking may damage the roots.

The amount of fertilizer given varies according to the type of tree and soil conditions. A good general rule for trees growing normally in moderate to good soil is to apply 30 g per sq m (1 oz per sq yd) of nitro-chalk or sulphate of ammonia in late winter, and 15 g per sq m ($\frac{1}{2}$ oz per sq yd) of sulphate of potash in mid-autumn. About three years after planting, apply 30 g per sq m (1 oz per sq yd) superphosphate in late winter, and repeat at three-yearly intervals. Be careful not to overfertilize wall-trained trees, particularly with too much nitrogenous fertilizer, or lush unfruitful growth may result.

If you have no manure or compost available, mulch annually with moist peat to conserve soil moisture, and give twice as much nitro-chalk in the fertilizer mixture.

A major problem with plum trees is the continual production of root suckers, which use much of the nourishment needed by the tree. Check for suckers whenever pruning the tree. Carefully dig away the soil until you can see where the sucker joins the root, then pull the sucker off to remove the adventitious buds around it. Do not cut the sucker, as it is impossible not to leave a bud or two behind. Any injury to the root will heal quickly.

Pruning
One general rule applies to any pruning done to plum trees. Because of the risk of infection by silver leaf disease during the early autumn and late spring months, all pruning should either be carried out in winter on young trees, when the wounds are small and the trees vigorous, or immediately after fruiting in the summer or in the beginning of early autumn for older trees. Whenever you prune, make sure all large cuts (over 2.5 cm, or 1″ in diameter) are flush with the bark and covered with a protective sealer. Remove and burn dead or diseased wood, and shorten any unduly long shoots at this time.

Plums form fruit buds along the whole length of younger branches so, aside from cutting out dead wood and thinning overcrowded branches, pruning should be kept to a minimum. An established plum tree can carry a much larger proportion of wood than other fruit trees, and drastic pruning is never necessary.

Ready-trained bush, half-standard and standard trees are available at nurseries. Pyramid trained trees are smaller than standards and half-standards and can be grown in restricted areas. A pyramid-trained tree has an upright trunk with branches radiating out in all directions, like a Christmas tree. This form is relatively easy to pick and net against birds.

If plums are not thinned, small badly flavoured and colourless fruit will result. Begin thinning in early summer; thin again when fruits have begun to swell and are half size.

The final distance between fruit should be 5–7.5 cm (2–3″), or more for larger varieties, so the fully developed plums do not touch.

Thinning fruit

Plums tend to crop too heavily one year and too lightly the next. An excessively heavy crop usually means small, colourless and tasteless fruit. In varieties with very brittle wood, like *Victoria*, broken branches can result. To get fruit of the best size and flavour, thin the fruit in two stages. Begin thinning in early summer, then thin again after the tree has shed some of the fruit naturally at the stone-hardening stage. The fruits at the second thinning should be swelling and about half their final size. When thinning fruits, always remove diseased, injured or badly shaped plums first. Try to aim for 5–7.5 cm (2–3″) of space between the fruits. Allow 10 cm (4″) or more for varieties with very large fruit, so that plums can develop fully without touching each other. Do not remove the stalk with the top fruit, as the shoot could be harmed and next year's crop may be damaged as a result.

Supporting branches

Any heavy-bearing branches must be supported, because even after thinning the weight of the crop can be considerable. One method of support is to drive in a heavy, upright stake next to the trunk, and support the branches by ropes attached to the top of the stake, like a maypole. You can also support individual branches from below by driving in stakes which are forked at the top. Wrap the branch with sacking where it meets the crotch to avoid

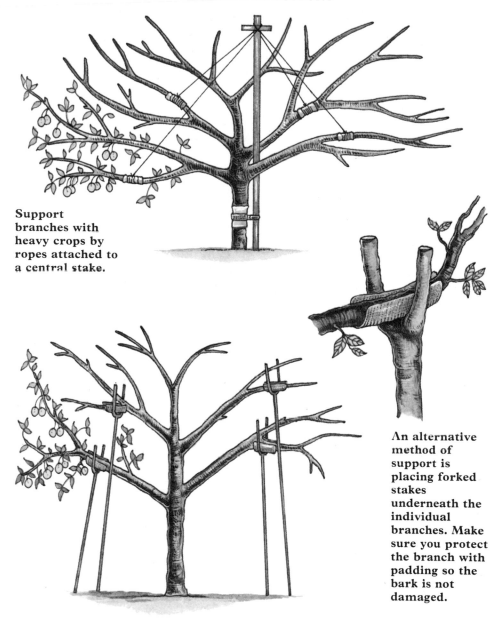

Support branches with heavy crops by ropes attached to a central stake.

An alternative method of support is placing forked stakes underneath the individual branches. Make sure you protect the branch with padding so the bark is not damaged.

chafing and subsequent risk of disease.

Growing plums in pots

Plums, particularly the late-fruiting dessert varieties, are suitable for growing in large pots or tubs. Make sure you select a tree with a semi-dwarfing rootstock. Pyramid, fan-trained or bush are the best sizes for pot culture.

Start the trees in pots in early autumn, preferably in 35 cm (14″) pots. Put crocks or broken bricks at the bottom, so the drainage hole is kept open. For the potting mixture, combine (by volume) five parts fibrous loam, one part decayed manure, one part lime or old mortar rubble, and one-half part peat or leafmould. Add 8 g ($\frac{1}{4}$ oz) sulphate of potash for each pot and mix thoroughly into the compost. When planting the tree, fill the pot to within 5 cm (2") of the rim. Find the sunniest and most sheltered site for the plant, against a wall if possible.

The cultivation for pot-grown plums is similar to that for open grown plums, with a few exceptions.

Make sure the soil in the pots never dries out; water daily in summer if necessary. Syringe the foliage with water from early summer onwards. Mulching the plants with moist peat will help retain moisture. In early autumn of each year, remove some of the old compost from the top few inches and replace it with fresh. In the winter, protect the roots from frost by covering the soil in the pots with leaf litter or dried bracken. Wrap some protective material, such as several sheets of newspaper or fibreglass with polythene, around the pots. From early summer to early autumn, feed weekly with dilute liquid manure. Lastly, you will get a heavier crop if you hand pollinate the blossom with a camelhair brush several times during the flowering season.

Harvesting

Trees begin bearing fruit when they are about five years old, and cropping is from late mid-summer to late autumn, depending on the variety. Leave dessert fruit on the tree until it is thoroughly ripe to obtain the best flavour. For jam-making, bottling, and ordinary cooking, it is best to pick the fruit while it is slightly under-ripe.

Both dessert and cooking varieties should be picked several times as they ripen; do not clear the tree at one picking. Most varieties can be easily detached from the stalk when ripe, but some types, particularly gages and damsons, are easier to pick with the stalks still attached. Take care not to jerk them off, as this can damage the shoots. Always remove and destroy any dam-

aged and rotting fruit you come across while harvesting. Do not allow them to remain on the tree, or brown rot may result.

Gages and some other varieties are liable to split in wet weather. If heavy rain threatens and the fruit is nearly ripe, pick the fruit and bring it indoors to ripen. This may impair the flavour a little, but you will avoid cracked fruits, which are often inedible.

Storing

Ripe plums picked in the ordinary way will not keep for more than a couple of days. If you want to keep plums for a longer period, pick them when they are dry, slightly under-ripe and with the stalks still attached. Use secateurs to cut the stalk from the spur, to avoid the risk of tearing the bark. Wrap the fruit carefully, and place it in one layer in a shallow basket or box, making sure that the plums are not touching each other. Put the box or basket in a cool airy place; the fruit should keep for two to three weeks.

Exhibition tips

For both cooking and dessert plums, the judges will look for large, fully ripe fruits with the stalks intact. They should have a good colour and undamaged bloom. Small, under-ripe or over-ripe fruits or those lacking stalks will be considered defective.

After picking the plums you wish to exhibit, wrap them individually in tissues and store them in a cool place until the show. Make sure your presentation of plums is neat and attractive. Do not, however, polish the plums or the bloom will be lost. Lay the plums in lines across the plate, with the stalks pointing away from the front of the table. Nine is the usual number of plums shown; they all should be of the same variety unless otherwise stated in the schedule. Damsons and bullaces are a separate category of exhibit, but the same criteria apply. Usually, however, thirty damsons or bullaces are shown, instead of nine.

Varieties

As explained above, a number of varieties need to be cross-pollinated by another variety with a coincidental flowering period. Where necessary, we have indicated suitable pollinators.

Gages

Early Transparent: dessert; medium round, apricot yellow fruit; excellent flavour; fruits late summer; *self-fertile.*

Denniston's Superb: dessert; pale green with red flush; delicious flavour; reliable

Victoria

cropper in late summer; *self-fertile.*

Oullin's Golden Gage: dessert; fruits golden yellow; crops late summer; *self-fertile.*

Cambridge: dessert; fruits similar to old-fashioned greengage, but better cropper; crops in late summer; self-fertile but cropping improved by cross-pollination with *Victoria, Czar, Golden Transparent,* or *Laxton's Gage.*

Jefferson's Gage: dessert; yellow-green with bronze markings; juicy and delicious fruit; crops early autumn; *cross-pollinate* with *Denniston's Superb* or *Early Transparent.*

Damsons

Merryweather Damson: cooking; big, well flavoured fruit; good for bottling or freezing; crops early autumn; *self-fertile.*

Quetsche: cooking; medium-sized purple fruit; crops mid-autumn; *self-fertile.*

Plums

Early Laxton: cooking and dessert; very prolific; earliest plum; small, yellowish red fruits, better for cooking than eating; crops mid-summer; *cross-pollinate* with *Czar, Victoria* or *Merryweather Damson.*

River's Early Prolific: cooking; small, roundish purple fruit; reliable cropper in mid-summer, *cross-pollinate* with *Czar, Victoria,* or *Merryweather Damson.*

Czar: cooking; reddish purple fruit; hardy, prolific and frost-resistant; *self-fertile.*

Yellow Pershore: cooking; medium-sized, golden-yellow fruit; crops in late summer; *self-fertile.*

Victoria: cooking and dessert; heavy cropper, excellent flavour; crops early autumn; *self-fertile.*

Warwickshire Drooper: cooking; medium to large yellow egg-shaped fruit; crops mid-summer; *self-fertile.*

Coe's Golden Drop: dessert; golden yellow, spotted red; crops mid-autumn; *cross-pollinate* with *Early Transparent Gage, Early Laxton* or *Denniston's Early.*

Marjorie's Seedling: dessert and cooking; large, oval purple fruit, flesh pale yellow; vigorous grower, good cropper; crops mid-autumn; *self-fertile.*

Ariel: dessert; oval, yellow-green fruit with pink flush; reliable cropper; crops early autumn; *self-fertile.*

Kirke's Blue: dessert; rich flavoured, large, round blue fruit; light cropper; does best in sheltered position; *cross-pollinate* with *Czar* or *Victoria.*

Belle de Louvain: cooking; large, oval rich-flavoured fruit; crops late summer, *self-fertile.*

Giant Prune: dessert; large red fruit crops early autumn; *self-fertile.*

Pests & Diseases

Birds: can do the most damage to both buds and fruit. Net small trees and place glitterbangs or other scaring devices on large trees.

Leaf-curling plum aphids: these are particularly prolific pests, often producing three generations in one season. In spring the aphids completely cover the undersides of leaves, which curl and die. The aphids also excrete honeydew, which leads to infection by sooty mould. Control with tar oil washes in winter. If the aphids appear in spring, spray the trees with derris or malathion before the leaves have curled.

Plum sawfly: caterpillars of the plum sawfly eat their way into the young fruits, and a sticky black substance exudes from the holes they have made. If the infection is severe, cropping will be considerably reduced. Spray with fenitrothion or derris one week after petal-fall.

Red plum maggot: this relative of the codling moth eats its way into the fruit, like the plum sawfly, but it appears much later in the season. Eggs are laid at the base of the fruit stalk, and the emerging red caterpillars attack the young fruits. The best way to control red plum maggot is to kill caterpillars in cocoons in mid-winter by spraying the trees with a tar oil wash. If the moths are seen in early to mid-summer, spray with derris about a week after their first appearance.

Plum gall mites: these microscopic creatures overwinter in the bud scales and emerge in spring to attack the leaves. They produce pouch-shaped blisters in the leaves, which may eventually curl up and die. Spray in late winter with $\frac{1}{2}$ L lime sulphur to $13\frac{1}{2}$ L water (1 pt lime sulphur to $3\frac{3}{4}$ gal water). Check the trees frequently in summer for leaves which have blisters on them. Pick off and burn

Plum leaf sawfly: this pest occasionally attacks plums, feeding on the leaves from early summer to early autumn. The larvae are slug-like, yellowish-white later changing to dark green or black, and they usually attack the upper surfaces of the leaves, which become blotchy and skeletonized. Apply derris or fenitrothion washes or dusts in early summer if you see large numbers of larvae.

Red spider mite: these tiny mites infest the undersides of the leaves and feed on the sap. Infected leaves will turn brown and fall prematurely. Red spider overwinters on the tree as eggs laid in the crevices of bark; a late winter wash of DNOC/petroleum will usually kill the eggs. If red spider mite does appear, from late spring onwards, spray with malathion, dimethoate or derris.

Silver leaf: this disease is caused by a fungus and is a major problem with plum trees. *Victoria* is particularly susceptible. The disease is called 'silver leaf' because leaves of infected trees develop a silvery sheen. A second symptom of the disease is a purple-brown stain in the wood when cut across. A final symptom of the disease is the appearance of brown or purple fungal fruiting bodies on the wood. Once this fungus appears, the tree should be removed and destroyed, as it will never recover. As soon as a tree develops silver leaf, cut back the infected wood until no purple-brown staining can be seen. Then apply lime and fertilizer to keep the tree vigorous, as healthier trees have a better chance of

Iron deficiency: although plums need only a small amount of iron, if it is lacking the trees cannot manufacture chlorophyll and will suffer from chlorosis. This occurs most frequently on very chalky soils. The main symptom is a yellowing of the leaves well before autumn. Correct this by dressing the soil with 120 g per sq m (4 oz per sq yd) of iron sulphate. Try to avoid planting on chalky soils.

Bacterial canker: this is a serious infection, and appears first in early summer as brown spots on the leaves. These spots develop into holes, and this stage of infection is sometimes called 'shothole'. Cankers later develop on the branches or trunk of the tree; these long, cracking areas ooze gum. If the canker encircles the entire stem, the tree will die. The following spring, buds on infected branches may not open; if leaves do appear, they are small and yellow and soon die. There is no chemical way to control bacterial canker. Avoid pruning the tree during autumn and winter, when the infection is most likely to occur. Protect any pruning wounds with a coat of sealer. Always avoid damage to the trunk of the branches by making sure stakes are not rubbing the bark. *Victoria* is one of the varieties most susceptible.

Honey fungus: this very damaging disease attacks the roots of trees and can quickly kill them. Trees on heavy, badly drained soils are most likely to be affected, so make sure you have corrected any drainage problems before planting. Another good preventive measure is to make sure you have removed all nearby dead tree stumps and hedgerows before planting, as the fungus lives in dead and dying wood. Lastly, make sure the stakes anchoring the tree have been dipped in creosote or other wood preservative.

As the fungus attacks the plant via the roots, there are few noticeable signs above ground, however premature autumn colouring and leaf fall may be symptoms. Trees which are seemingly healthy and then die for no apparent reason should be dug up and inspected. Lift the bark just below ground level. If you see among the roots and in the soil long, shiny black strands, then honey fungus is present. It is these black strands which reach out, underground, to infect nearby plants.

Dig up and burn infected trees, including all the root system. Use a different site when replacing tree.

Brown rot: this disease attacks other top fruits besides plums. It appears as small brown patches, inside which are circular rings, whitish or yellow in colour. These rings contain the spores, which spread the disease to other fruit, particularly if the fruit are damaged by birds or insects. Infected plums may drop off the tree, or else remain on the tree shrivelled up. If they remain mummified on the tree all winter, they will reinfect the next season's fruit. Remove and burn any diseased fruit, both on the tree and on the ground. As the infection can spread down the stalk to the fruiting spur, cut off the infected spur when removing mummified fruit.

Pocket plum: this is also known as bladder plum, or plum pocket. It is a fungal disease which causes the young fruit to grow long, swollen and one-sided. The skin of the fruit eventually develops a whitish bloom. Cut off all infected fruit and the attached shoots, as the infection spreads to the wood.

GUIDE TO PLUM TROUBLES

Symptoms	Probable causes
Leaves curl and die	Leaf-curling plum aphids
Holes in fruit oozing sticky black substance	Plum sawfly
Holes eaten in fruit in mid-summer	Red plum maggot
Pouch-shaped blisters on leaves	Plum gall mite
Blotchy, skeletonized leaves	Pear slug sawfly
Bronzed leaves, premature leaf-fall	Red spider mite
Leaves silvery, wood stained brown	Silver leaf
Leaves yellow prematurely	Iron deficiency
Spots on leaves, cracking bark	Bacterial canker
Fruits long, swollen and one-sided	Pocket plum
Trees die, black strands in soil and among roots	Honey fungus
Brown patches on fruit which shrivels up on tree	Brown rot

Raspberries

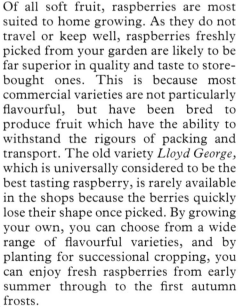

Rubus idaeus (fam. *Rosaceae*)
Hardy perennial prickly cane with a useful life of 12 years
Size: up to 2.5 m (8′) high unpruned; kept to about 1.2-1.5 m (4-5′) when fruiting
Yield: 1.5-3 kg (3-7 lb) per stool or 11-22 kg (25-49 lb) per 3 m (10′) row
Planting to harvesting time: 2 years

Of all soft fruit, raspberries are most suited to home growing. As they do not travel or keep well, raspberries freshly picked from your garden are likely to be far superior in quality and taste to store-bought ones. This is because most commercial varieties are not particularly flavourful, but have been bred to produce fruit which have the ability to withstand the rigours of packing and transport. The old variety *Lloyd George,* which is universally considered to be the best tasting raspberry, is rarely available in the shops because the berries quickly lose their shape once picked. By growing your own, you can choose from a wide range of flavourful varieties, and by planting for successional cropping, you can enjoy fresh raspberries from early summer through to the first autumn frosts.

Raspberries give very quick returns, and are second only to strawberries in the length of time from planting until cropping. Although they will produce some fruit the first season they are planted, it is best not to allow them to do so. By pinching out the flowers as they appear, you are encouraging the young

plants to develop strong stools and root systems instead of fruiting, and the canes should then produce heavy crops from the second season onwards. Unlike strawberries, which are disease-prone and need replanting every three years or so, well cultivated raspberry canes will continue to be fruitful for at least twelve years.

The plant itself, *Rubus idaeus,* is a native of Europe, including Britain, and parts of Asia. It can often be found growing wild in hedgerows and on hilly heathland with acid soils. Many of these plants are garden escapes, the seeds having been scattered by birds. Although most raspberries have red or purplish-red berries, there are richly-flavoured yellow-fruited varieties (sometimes known as white raspberries) and also black raspberries. These black-fruited types, derived from *R. occidentalis,* are much more popular in America than Europe, and are widely cultivated there. Unlike the raspberry, which has a spreading habit of growth, black raspberries are clump-forming, with heavier and more branched canes.

Raspberries flower and fruit on

1. In mid-autumn, plant canes about 7.5 cm (3″) deep; spread roots out and firm soil thoroughly.

2. After planting, cut canes back to a strong healthy bud, about 30 cm (1′) above ground.

laterals growing from canes which were produced the previous year, after which the fruiting canes die, and are replaced by new canes. Although most varieties fruit in mid-summer, there are some types which are specifically cultivated for autumn crops. These autumn fruiting, or everbearing, raspberries produce fruit on the tips of the current season's shoots. Fruit quantity may be smaller than that of summer fruiting canes. Summer and autumn fruiting varieties require slightly different methods of pruning, but neither method is particularly difficult or time consuming. The variety *Lloyd George* can be pruned to crop early, mid-season or in autumn, and traditionally some bushes in the fruit cage were pruned for early cropping and the rest pruned for maincrop and late picking.

Suitable site and soil

Raspberries do best in a sunny site, but being woodland plants, they will tolerate some shade. Because they flower relatively late in the season, frost is not usually damaging and low-lying sites can be satisfactory for growing raspberries in most years, unless there is a very late frost. They will not tolerate waterlogged soil, however, and in very wet winters, excessive water will kill the roots.

Besides soil drainage, shelter from wind is the second major consideration. The canes are fairly brittle and may snap off in high winds, and the point where the fruiting laterals join the canes is also very vulnerable to serious damage from strong winds.

The best soils are deep, rich, well-drained loams, as long as they retain some moisture in dry weather. Shallow sands and gravels can be made suitable, if you are prepared to water them frequently and give a continual supply of nutrients. Likewise, heavy clay soils are not really suitable without careful preparation and maintenance, because they tend to harden and crack in dry summers depriving the shallow roots of water. Raspberries will accept more acid conditions than most other soft fruits, but readily become chlorotic in too alkaline a soil. Shallow soils over chalk should be avoided.

Because some viral infections are soil-borne by eelworms, avoid planting new canes in sites previously occupied by berries of the same genus and plant as far away as possible from old fruiting canes.

Begin soil preparation well in advance. Remember that the plants will remain in the ground for at least 12 years and no amount of aftercare will make up for inadequate preparation. Whatever the soil type, make sure the ground is completely free from perennial weeds, such as couch, bindweed and nettles. If the subsoil is hard and impervious to water, break it up with a fork. Then fork in well-rotted manure at the rate of 12 L (2½ gal) per plant. At the same time, apply superphosphate, at the rate of 30 g per sq m (1 oz per sq yd). If manure is not available, use garden compost, leaf-mould or moist peat. If the soil is very alkaline, and using it for raspberries is unavoidable, work in fritted trace elements at the time of planting at the rates recommended by the suppliers, and thereafter treat the plants as suggested under PESTS AND DISEASES.

Planting out
Buy canes which are certified virus-free and plant in mid-autumn. Because raspberries break into fresh growth very early in spring, later plantings should be avoided. If, however, the ground is very wet or cold when the canes arrive, you can heel them in until conditions are more suitable.

Dig out a shallow trench about 30 cm (1') wide where the row is to be. Space the canes 45 cm (18") apart; if you have more than one row, leave a minimum of 1.5 m (5') between rows. This may seem wasteful of space, but the canes must be exposed to enough air and sunlight for the fruits to ripen properly. Closer planting will also encourage problems with pests and diseases. If you are planting varieties which are slow to sucker, such as *Lloyd George,* you can plant two canes per station.

Plant the canes firmly, with the roots well spread out and about 7.5 cm (3") deep; there should be a soil mark on the stems indicating the right planting depth. After planting, either at once or some time before spring, cut the canes back to a strong healthy bud about 30 cm (1') above ground. This may seem a bit drastic, but if you do not cut the cane back, and allow it to fruit in the first season, the plant's ability to produce vigorous new canes will be seriously

reduced, and it will not crop properly for another two years.

Should there be any heavy frosts after planting, check the newly planted canes; if any have been lifted by frost, firm them down.

Erecting training wires
There are two basic methods of support. The quicker method, as it does not involve tying individual canes, is to have two rows of parallel wires through which the canes grow. To do this, erect stout end posts, at a maximum distance of 5 m (16') apart. At 60 cm (2') and again at 1.5 m (5') bolt on to the end posts cross pieces of wood about 30 cm (1') long, to act as spacers. Then run wires (telephone wire is best) from one cross piece to the other, fixed with a strainer at each end (see diagram). The young canes are then trained to grow up between the wires, and the canes inside the wires tend to support each other. There is one disadvantage to this system: in high winds, serious damage can occur, and if the canes get too overcrowded, they are more vulnerable to disease.

The slightly more time-consuming, but better method of support is to tie the canes individually to parallel horizontal wires as they grow. Drive 2.25 m (7½') poles 45 cm (1½') into the ground at each end of the row. The first autumn after planting, erect horizontal wires at 45 cm (1½'), 105 cm (3½') and 1.2-1.5 m (4-5') depending on the vigour of the variety. Then tie the young canes individually to the bottom wire with soft garden twine, and to the middle and upper wires as soon as they are tall enough.

Training and pruning
The young canes grow from adventitious buds; without training or pruning the plant would quickly form an impenetrable thicket of stems. Because the root system is very wide-spreading, new canes may appear some distance from the parent plant.

The first summer after planting, cut out the old canes entirely when the

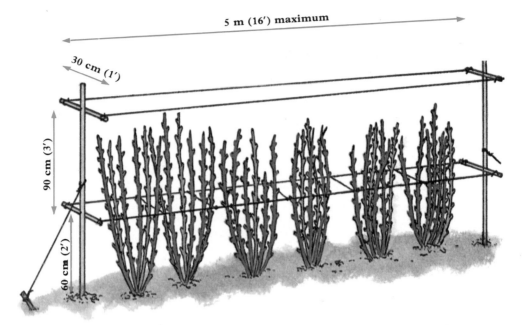

5 m (16') maximum

30 cm (1')

90 cm (3')

60 cm (2')

To support raspberries without tying individual canes, erect two rows of parallel wires through which canes grow; fix wires to cross-pieces at end posts.

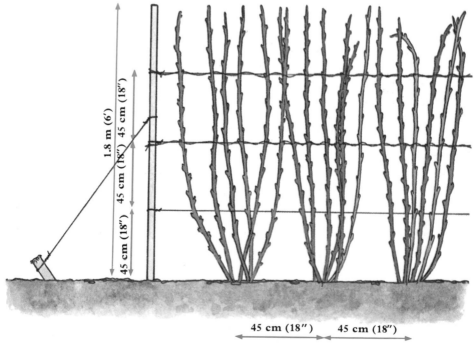

1.8 m (6')

45 cm (18")

45 cm (18")

45 cm (18")

45 cm (18")

45 cm (18")   45 cm (18")

Alternatively, tie canes individually to parallel horizontal wires as they grow. Erect wires at 45 cm (18"), 90 cm (3') and 1.2-1.5 m (4-5') from ground.

1. In the first summer after planting, when the young canes are 25 cm (10″) high, cut out old canes entirely.

2. As the canes grow, tie them to bottom wire with soft twine, and then to middle and upper wires.

young canes reach 25 cm (10″) high. The following late winter, tip prune all the canes slightly. Strong growing ones should be cut back to a good bud about 15 cm (6″) above the top wire; less strong growing canes should have the top 7.5-10 cm (3-4″) removed. This winter tipping, which should be done annually, will get rid of any diseased and damaged cane tips, and it will also encourage the canes to send out more fruiting laterals, thus increasing crop yields.

Healthy raspberry stools will normally produce more canes than are practical for good cultivation, so from the second summer onwards, allow only six fruiting canes per stool, choosing the strongest. If you remove all the weak, damaged or diseased canes early in the season, the selected fruiting canes will have more room to grow and more sunlight. Tie these six to the wires to keep them separated and firm. While these are flowering and fruiting, new shoots will appear and, as before, the obvious weak ones are cut out, and the best of the remainder left as replacements, to bear the following year's fruit.

After cropping, cut to the ground the old fruiting canes; it is a good idea to remove and burn them immediately, to lessen the possibility of disease. Then tie in the selected young canes which have

grown during the spring and summer for next year.

Autumn-fruiting varieties are pruned by cutting the old canes down to ground level in late winter or early spring; the plant will then produce canes in spring and summer on which fruit will be produced in autumn.

Care and cultivation

If dry weather occurs when the plants are flowering, watering is essential. Otherwise the new canes, which are growing at the same time, will be small and sparse, and next year's crop will be poor. An annual mulch of well-rotted compost or manure in mid-spring will help conserve soil moisture. If the soil is dry, water it thoroughly before mulching. Because the roots are shallow and wide-spreading, the mulch should be spread 1 m (1 yd) on either side of the row. A good rule of thumb is to apply 2.5 kg (5 lb) of mulch per sq m (sq yd).

Weeds, which compete with the canes for moisture and nutrients, must be controlled. Over-vigorous hoeing can do more harm than good, though, because the shallow roots are very near the surface. Hand weeding is better. Remove unwanted suckers which may spring up between the rows, unless you want them for propagation, and cut back

3. Mulch in mid-spring with garden compost or well-rotted manure to keep weeds down and conserve soil moisture.

4. If bushes arc not growing in a fruit cage, give temporary protection when fruit begins to form. Use 2.5 cm (1") nylon mesh netting over stout wooden posts. Bricks will keep net from blowing away in strong wind.

5. Harvest on dry sunny days. Support laterals with one hand while picking berries with the other.

6. Put berries in shallow bowls or punnets, so they are not crushed by their own weight.

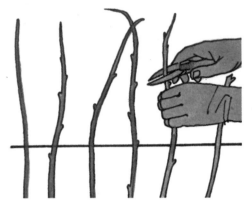

1. Tip prune in winter: cut strong-growing canes back to a good bud 15 cm (6″) above top wire.

2. After fruiting, cut old canes back to ground level in autumn; remove and burn canes immediately.

to the ground all small or spindly canes.

Under good conditions, raspberries will not require extra fertilizer, but if cane production is inadequate, fertilizer should be applied in late winter. Scatter a nitrogenous one, such as sulphate of ammonia, at the rate of 30-45 g per sq m (1-1½ oz per sq yd), and one containing potassium, eg sulphate of potash, at 15-30 g per sq m (½-1 oz per sq yd).

The raspberry is a favourite target for birds, and netting is the only satisfactory long-term solution.

Growing black raspberries

Newly planted canes of black raspberry varieties are best cut off at ground level after planting. Young canes produced during the first growing year are cut back during the summer to 50-75 cm (20-30″) high to stimulate the growth of side-shoots. The following late winter or early spring these are also cut back to leave two to six buds, depending on the strength of the cane; the stronger shoots can support more buds. Fruiting branches are produced from these buds. It is not necessary to provide support for black raspberries, but they can be tied in for convenience. In the second and subsequent years, the primary canes should be limited to four per stool, preferably by early selection or during

the post-harvest clean up. Tipping off the main shoots and cutting back of the sideshoots continues each year.

Propagation

Raspberries can be easily propagated from suckers which spring up at or near the base of the parent plant. This is a somewhat risky business, though, because if the parent plants are not absolutely healthy, the newly propagated canes will be diseased from the start. To avoid all risk, you should not propagate new canes from your own fruiting stock, but buy in fresh certified virus-free stock from a reputable source.

If you do want to propagate new canes from your own stock, autumn is the best time to do so. Gently loosen the rooted suckers which have grown during the season with a fork and sever them from the parent plant. The suckers should have strong, well-developed root systems: discard those without much root and those which have weak or spindly growth. Plant the suckers out in their permanent positions and immediately cut them back to 60 cm (2′) above ground. The following late winter or early spring, cut the canes back again, to a strong bud about 30 cm (1′) above ground. The American black raspberry is propagated by tip layering. Wait until

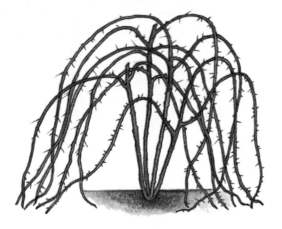

Black raspberry before spring pruning; the main canes have been stopped during the first year of growth.

To prune, cut the laterals back to two to six buds, depending on the strength of each cane.

the side branches are long enough to touch the ground without snapping; this is usually in early to mid-summer. Dig out a 15 cm (6″) deep hole for each branch you are tip layering; the holes should have side slopes of about 45°. If the soil is very heavy, it is best to put a little bit of moist peat mixed with sand into the bottom of the hole; this will encourage root formation. Then gently place the tip of the branch into the hole, against the sloping side, so that about 15 cm (6″) of cane is buried. Backfill with soil and tread down firmly. Peg the cane

The easiest way to propagate new plants is from suckers: sever them with a sharp spade, in late autumn.

where it enters the soil with a metal or wooden peg, to keep it from springing up.

The following autumn, after cropping is finished, sever the rooted cane from the parent plant with a sharp spade, and transplant it to its permanent position.

Harvesting

The early fruiting varieties should be ready for harvesting early in mid-summer, and should continue for three weeks. The maincrop varieties follow, then come the autumn-fruiting types. Pick the berries in dry weather. The fruit does not ripen all at once, so inspect canes every other day. Normally, the fruit is picked without the central core.

Raspberries do not keep for very long, so eat them or preserve them without delay.

Exhibition tips

Thirty is the usual number of fruit required, all of the same variety. Always pick the raspberries with the stalk intact. In taking them to the show, pack in a single layer in a box, and cover with tissue paper. Arrange neatly on a plate to exhibit. The judges will look for large ripe fruit in good condition.

Varieties

Early

Malling Promise: first raspberry to fruit in early summer; good flavour and strong growth (to 2.1 m (7')), but takes a couple of years to settle down; frost-resistant but fruit susceptible to botrytis; large, good for jam.

Malling Exploit: more vigorous than *Malling Promise* and probably more widely planted; fruit very large but tends to be crumbly, very fine flavoured; thrives in a wide range of soils.

Glen Cova: medium-sized berry; excellent for bottling or freezing; crops start early and continue over several weeks with heavy mid-season yield.

Malling Jewel: second early; medium-sized, dark red fruit, somewhat hidden by leaves curling over it; flavour excellent; somewhat frost and botrytis resistant; most popular raspberry for general use; growth compact and less liable to wind damage.

Mid-season

Lloyd George (New Zealand Strain): original *Lloyd George* strain decimated by virus, but replaced by clean stocks from New Zealand; best flavoured raspberry, but difficult to grow well; crops early, mid-season, and again on tips of young canes in autumn; very prone to viral infection and may need replacing after a few years.

Malling Orion: recent introduction; fruit medium large and round; flavour good; consistently heavy cropper over long period of time.

Phyllis King: old variety recently reintroduced; berries large, firm and well flavoured.

Malling 'M': mid- to late variety with fruit excellent for bottling.

Malling Delight: recently introduced heavy cropper with large long berries; not suitable for freezing.

Golden Everest: yellow-fruited variety with mild, delicious flavour; fruits over a long season on both old and young canes.

Malling Promise

Late

Norfolk Giant: crops a week later than maincrop; fruit of good flavour and texture, but a bit acid for dessert; tall-growing variety, susceptible to wind damage, frost damage and virus; particularly good for jam-making and bottling or freezing.

Malling Admiral: recent introduction; heavier cropper than *Norfolk Giant.*

Autumn

September: American variety with very firm, well-flavoured fruit; for autumn cropping, canes must be cut to ground level in winter or early spring; growth thick and vigorous but unsuitable for colder northern districts; will crop well on dry soils and in dry seasons.

Zeva: Swiss variety with unusually large fruit; yields well in first year of cropping; crops from mid-summer until late autumn, with heaviest crop in autumn.

Sceptre: vigorous variety, giving high autumn yields under most conditions.

Heritage: most vigorous of autumn-fruiting varieties; sturdy, self-supporting canes, fruit first class with good flavour.

Black raspberries

Blackie: cross between thorny blackberry and raspberry; limited supplies.

368

Pests & Diseases

Raspberry beetle: raspberry beetle is probably the most serious pest you are likely to encounter, and bad attacks may render your crop inedible. The female beetle, which is light brown and 0.4 cm ($\frac{1}{6}''$) long, lays her eggs in the open flower, in late spring and early summer, and the emerging maggots feed on the developing fruit. One of the worst aspects of this infestation is that it is not likely to be noticed until the raspberries are actually on the table. To control, spray with derris about fourteen days after flowering, at the fruitlet stage.

Aphids: there are several species of aphid which infest raspberries, but the most serious are the raspberry aphid and the rubus aphid, both of which transmit viral diseases. They are present in their largest numbers in late spring and early summer, and their feeding results in the leaves curling a little, but they do not themselves do any great damage. It is their ability to spread virus diseases which is the really troublesome aspect of their infestations. If you have had serious trouble with aphids in previous years, apply a mid-winter spray of tar oil mixture to kill any overwintering eggs. Otherwise, if aphids appear, spray with malathion or dimethoate in spring before the flowers open, and again if necessary, but not while the plants are flowering. Remember to allow the specified time to lapse between spraying and harvesting.

Birds: unfortunately, birds find ripening raspberries particularly tempting, and although bird scarers provide some measure of relief, the only really effective long term protection is growing the crop in fruit cages.

Cane midge: this pest affects primarily young canes, which will have brownish-black blotches if infested. The grubs of the cane midge emerge in about early summer from eggs laid in cracks at the base of the canes and then begin to feed on the internal tissue of the cane. There may be two more broods in the season. Besides causing some physical

Cane spot: a fungal infection which damages canes, and causes spotted, mis-shapen fruit.

Ministry of Agriculture, Fisheries & Food

damage, the scars from the cane midge larva make the plants more vulnerable to secondary fungal infections. Some varieties seem more at risk than others; *Malling Enterprise* is very susceptible. To control cane midge, spray the young canes with gamma-HCH during late spring, and again two weeks later.

Raspberry moth: if the tips of young lateral shoots appear withered and tunnelled in late spring, then it is likely your canes are infested with caterpillars of the raspberry moth. The best preventive measure is keeping the raspberry bed clean and weed free, and removing withered shoots as soon as seen, because the grub, or chrysalis, is likely to be inside it. In severe cases, a winter tar oil wash applied to the soil at the foot of the canes should kill the hibernating larvae.

Capsids: these pests vary from year to year in numbers and the amount of damage done. The tips of young canes are most vulnerable to capsid attack; infested tips may stop growing altogether or form branches. Leaves are injured, and develop puckered brown spots and tiny holes, eventually becoming very tattered. As with aphids, a spray of dimethoate or malathion before the flowers open (treating the ground round the plants as well) is usually the most effective method of control.

Spur blight attacks buds on young canes; the infection spreads back to the stem.

Grey mould *(Botrytis cinerea)*: this is more likely to be troublesome with strawberries than raspberries, but the latter can be infected, particularly if they are growing in wet, overcrowded conditions. Berries with botrytis will be covered with grey, fluffy mould, and the canes can also be infected and even killed outright in severe cases. The best preventive measure is to plant the canes at the correct spacing, so that air can circulate freely. Cut off and burn all infected fruit and canes as soon as you notice them. In severe cases, spray with captan or benomyl when the first flowers open and again a fortnight later, but do not spray if the fruit is to be used for preserving in any way.

Cane blight: this fungal infection appears on the fruiting canes in summer; *Norfolk Giant* and *Lloyd George* are particularly susceptible. The main symptoms are wilted and withered leaves, and very brittle canes with dark basal patches which easily snap off at ground level. Small, dark, round fruiting bodies may appear on the bases of infected canes. Because raspberries attacked by cane midge larvae are very susceptible, the best precaution is to keep the garden clean, and so free of cane midges. All infected canes should be cut out, below ground level if possible, and burnt. This is particularly important in the case of canes which have snapped off, as the stump remaining in the ground can spread the infection. In the following spring spray the remaining canes with Bordeaux mixture or benomyl at bud burst, and repeat just before flowering to protect the young canes. Make sure the new growth is well spaced out and not crowded. Because cane blight is also soil borne, never use canes from infected beds. Buying certified stock will insure that new canes are free from cane blight.

Cane spot: this fungal infection, although not as serious as cane blight, can still reduce raspberry crops. The main symptoms are small, round, purple spots on the canes in late spring or early summer; occasionally the fruits are spotted or mis-shapen. Infected leaves will have pale spots surrounded with a dark border. In time, the spots on the canes grow larger, become elongated and change to pale grey in the centre. Eventually the holes become sunken and cankered, with cracking in the centre. Cut out and burn badly infected canes, and spray the remainder with Bordeaux mixture. If you have had serious trouble with cane spot in the past, spray with a 5% lime-sulphur mixture or benomyl at bud burst, and repeat just before blossoming.

Spur blight: this can be quite serious, as the buds from which the fruiting laterals grow can be killed. Buds on young canes become infected first, and the infection spreads back to the stem. The infected cane nearest the bud turns purple and this patch is the first visual indication that infection has occurred. Later this changes to a greyish white. Fungal fruiting bodies appear in the centre of these grey areas as tiny black dots. By the following spring, the infected buds will either have been killed, or will soon wither and die after opening. As with cane spot and cane blight, cut out and burn infected canes, thin the remainder out and spray with Bordeaux mixture or benomyl.

Chlorosis: this physiological disorder is most often seen on plants which are growing in alkaline soils. Leaf tissue of affected plants will turn yellow, on the youngest leaves first if the trouble is due to a deficiency of iron, and later the older ones; eventually they turn almost white. Lack of manganese shows as a fairly regular, small yellow mottling on the older leaves. Lack of magnesium appears as purple brown patches on the older leaves. The best preventive measure is to correct alkalinity problems before planting. Plants which develop chlorosis can be treated with sequestrenes, applied according to manufacturer's instructions, or fritted trace elements can be applied. Manganese and magnesium sulphate can be applied as foliar sprays.

GUIDE TO RASPBERRY TROUBLES

Symptoms	Probable cause
Fruit tunnelled and eaten; white maggots present.	Raspberry beetle
Young shoots stunted, leaves curled.	Aphids
Ripening fruit torn and holed.	Birds
Brownish-black blotches on base of canes.	Raspberry cane midge
Tips of young shoots withered and tunnelled.	Raspberry moth
Tips of young canes stop growing or form branches.	Capsids
Fruit and canes covered with fluffy grey mould.	Grey mould
Canes brittle, snap off at ground level; leaves wilted and withered.	Cane blight
Small, round purple spots on canes; fruit spotted or mis-shapen.	Cane spot
Canes purple in patches round spurs, later become pale and covered with black fruiting bodies	Spur blight
Leaves yellow between veins; fall prematurely.	Chlorosis
Leaves striped yellow; wither and die; canes with long blue stripe.	Blue stripe wilt
Leaves mottled or spotted yellow; leaves and canes dwarfed or stunted; diminished fruit production.	Virus infections

Blue stripe wilt: this fungal infection lives in the roots and prevents sap from flowing through the plant normally. In early to mid-summer, leaves of infected plants become striped yellow. Eventually the yellow stripes turn brown, and the leaves wither and die; in severe cases the canes become marked with a bluish stripe longitudinally and eventually die back as well. The only option with blue stripe wilt is to dig up and destroy infected plants, so the disease does not spread.

Viruses: there are several types of viral infections to which raspberries are susceptible; this is further complicated by the fact that the same virus may have different symptoms on different cultivars. All virus infections are very serious, and the infected plants must be dug up and burnt as soon as the diagnosis is made. The most common virus is mosaic, which initially appears as yellow and pale green mottling or spots on the leaves. Eventually, the leaves become smaller, crumpled and distorted, the canes become stunted and cropping diminishes considerably. The plant does not necessarily die at once, but it will never recover completely or crop well again. Some varieties are much more vulnerable than others; *Lloyd George* is very susceptible. Less common is raspberry yellow dwarf virus; the main symptoms are stunted canes and linear yellow patterns on the leaves. Lastly, stunt and dwarf virus may cause trouble; infected plants may be only 60 cm (2') tall and cropping nearly non-existant. This virus is spread by leaf hoppers, unlike most other viruses, which are carried by aphids.

With all viruses, the best preventive measure is to control the carriers of the disease: aphids and, very rarely, leaf hoppers. Where soil-living eelworms are the culprits, new stock should not be planted in ground so infested. If you can keep your garden free from these pests, the likelihood of viral infections diminishes. Buying certified, virus-free stock for planting is equally important.

Strawberries

Hybrids of *Fragaria* (fam. *Rosaceae*), derived from *F. chiloensis* and *F. virginiana*.
Hardy perennial herbaceous plant with a cropping life of about 3 years.
Size: 15-30 cm (6-12″) spread by 15-20 cm (6-8″) high.
Planting to harvesting time: 6-10 months.
Yield: from 115-450 g (4-16 oz) per plant.

With its mouth-watering red berries and distinctive aroma, the strawberry is perhaps the best loved of all summer fruits. Although their cultivation requires some care, strawberries are a very rewarding crop for the amateur; they are the quickest cropping of all fruits and summer varieties will give a good-sized harvest in their first year.

Unlike most other fruits, strawberries are produced on low-growing, herbaceous plants. The cropping life of the plants is short; strawberry beds are usually replanted with fresh stock after one to four seasons. However, most varieties readily reproduce themselves from runners; as long as your plants are healthy, you can propagate your own new stocks without any additional cost.

There are two main groups of garden strawberries, summer-fruiting varieties and perpetuals. **Summer fruiters** are by far the most popular, although they generally crop only once in the season. A few varieties may bear a second crop in the autumn if conditions are favourable.

Some of the new varieties produce exceptionally large fruit, weighing up to 90 g (3 oz) each, although many people consider the smaller berries to have a superior flavour.

Perpetual strawberries (or **remontants**) produce fruit all summer, beginning in mid-summer and continuing into autumn. Removing the first trusses of blossoms from the plants prevents overlapping with summer fruiting varieties and ensures a heavier yield from the later flushes. The berries are not as large as those of the summer fruiters, and they tend to produce fewer runners. There is one variety of perpetual strawberry which produces very long runners. It is known as the climbing strawberry. Strictly speaking it does not actually climb, but it can be trained and tied to trellises.

Although they are usually grown in beds, strawberries do very well in containers, such as barrels, window boxes, or special earthenware strawberry

A heavy crop of well grown strawberries is one of the home grower's finest rewards.

pots. This obviously has great potential for a small garden, patio or balcony. The plants have very attractive leaves and flowers, and containers filled with strawberry plants make a delightful feature.

Strawberries are susceptible to a number of serious virus diseases. However, stocks have been improved by the introduction of government certification schemes. Buy disease-free certified stock if this is available. Summer and perpetual strawberries are not propagated from seed.

Suitable site and soil

Because strawberries bloom early in the year and the flowers are carried close to the ground, they are very susceptible to spring frosts. Frosted flowers turn black in the centre, and fail to fruit. The site must therefore be frost free, open and raised rather than low-lying. If your garden is on a slope, try to locate the strawberry bed towards the top, rather than the bottom, where frost and stagnant air would collect.

A sunny site is necessary for any successful strawberry growing, and early

1. Double dig the soil at least a month before planting, digging in plenty of manure or garden compost.

2. If plants are in peat pots, soak pots in water, then plant with rim of pot level with soil surface.

correctly planted   planted too high   planted too deep

3. The crown of the plant must be just level with the soil. If planted too high, the roots may dry out; too deep, the crown may rot.

crops need shelter as well. If the site is too windy, pollinating insects will be less likely to visit the flowers.

Wild strawberries are found in rich woodland soil; cultivated strawberries are most successful if grown in a similar soil. It should be deep, with a high content of organic matter, and well drained. It must be moisture retentive as well, because crops are very dependant on a steady supply of water during the growing season.

A slightly acid soil, with a pH of 6.5 is best; if your soil is too limey, apply moist peat, garden compost or well-rotted manure. Light loams are preferable to very heavy soils, because they warm up more quickly in spring and give earlier crops. Diseases, such as redcore, are also more likely to develop on very heavy soils.

Do not make a strawberry bed on land which is newly dug from turf. There is likely to be a very high wireworm population in such soils, and wireworm can severely damage strawberry plants.

Because strawberry beds should be rotated every three or four years, many people find it most convenient to grow them as part of the vegetable garden. Remember, though, that strawberry plants should not follow potatoes, as they are subject to many of the same diseases.

Preparation and planting

Begin preparing the soil in early spring or mid-summer, at any rate at least a month before planting. If the site has been well prepared for previous vegetable crops, just fork it over lightly and check for weeds. Otherwise, double dig to encourage a good root run, but keep the topmost soil uppermost. Make sure you have removed all traces of perennial weeds. Besides making cultivation difficult, they harbour pests and diseases and a weedy strawberry bed will never crop well.

Dig in well-rotted manure or garden compost at the rate of half a garden barrow load per sq m (sq yd). This opens up a heavy soil and improves the moisture retaining capacity of a light one. If neither is available, work in moist peat or leafmould at the same rate and scatter and rake in an equal parts (by weight) mixture of hoof and horn fertilizer, sterilized bonemeal and sulphate of potash, at 180 g per sq m (6 oz per sq yd). After digging, lightly roll or tread down, and rake the surface smooth.

Plant summer fruiting strawberries in late summer, early autumn, or mid-spring. Plant perpetuals in late autumn, only when soil conditions are first class; otherwise wait until spring. You will not lose a crop by waiting.

Plant in crumbly, friable soil; wait if excessive rain has made the bed sticky, or if the soil is dry. Planting strawberries close together increases the yield from the plot as a whole, but reduces the yield per plant. Also, the size of the individual berries is likely to be reduced. A sensible compromise is to leave 45 cm (18") between plants and 75 cm (2'6") between rows, with 23 cm (9") between plants of compact varieties. Leave slightly more space around plants you intend to use for propagation only, so the runners have room to fully develop.

It is important to plant strawberries at just the right depth. If you plant them too deeply, the crowns rot; if they are too shallow, the roots may dry out. The soil level should be midway up the crown.

Make a shallow hole with a small 5 cm (2") mound in the centre, and set the plant on top of the mound. Spread the roots out over and down the mound to their full extent. If the plants come in peat pots, do not remove them but soak the pots in water for 10 minutes, and then plant at once with the rim of the pot just level with the soil surface. Always plant firmly, then water. Preferably, plant in the evening, but if this is not possible, shade the plants temporarily from strong sunshine.

Cultivation and care outdoors

Water frequently, possibly every day in the early weeks, especially if planted in summer, until the young plants are established. Then judicious watering is called for. Thereafter, unless there is a drought, you will probably not have to water them, once they are established, until the fruits are beginning to swell. Then water once, at the rate of 20 L per sq m (4½ gal per sq yd). This should suffice, unless the weather is very dry.

In late spring the plants will develop stolons, which are long runners with a plantlet at each joint. Cut these off at their point of origin, unless they are needed for propagation.

No feeding is needed as plants come quickly into bearing, but competing weeds should be kept down by light hoeing or hand weeding. If you have cleared the ground of all perennial weeds prior to planting, the only problem will be from annual weeds. The combination of weeding and mulching should be enough; avoid using chemical herbicides.

Removing all the blossom on summer fruiting varieties in their first spring gives more than two seasons' crop the following year, but few gardeners have the patience to wait that long. If planting was done after the beginning of autumn, however, it is essential to take off the first season's blossom. Perpetual varieties should always have their first season's blossom removed to allow them to build up strength for fruiting.

4. If planting after autumn, cut off first season's blossom, so plants build up strength for future crops.

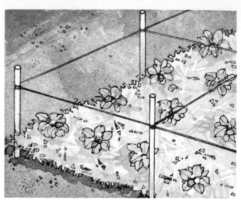

5. To protect crops from birds, make a frame for netting by stretching wires between vertical posts.

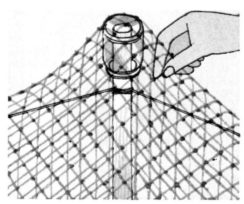

6. Invert jars over posts before putting on netting; this stops the netting from catching on the posts.

7. Water frequently and thoroughly until plants are established, particularly in hot, dry weather.

8. Hoe if necessary to keep weeds down, being careful not to damage roots. Avoid using chemical herbicides.

9. Control greenfly by spraying with derris or bioresmethrin according to manufacturers' instructions.

10. Protect ripening fruit with a layer of barley straw, special strawberry mats, or plastic strips.

11. Pick berries when they are firm and evenly coloured; snap off stem and avoid bruising ripe fruit.

Care of the fruit

To keep the ripening fruit off the ground and free from soil splashes, strawberry beds are traditionally covered with barley straw. Besides keeping the fruit clean, it acts as a mulch, conserving soil moisture. Wheat straw is harder to obtain and oat straw is more likely to carry pests. Try to obtain straw which has been properly thrashed, otherwise grains left in it will sprout. Do not spread the straw until the weight of the developing berries is pulling them down to the ground. Premature strawing cuts them off from ground warmth, increasing the risk of damage from late spring frosts. Spread the straw thickly but evenly round each plant, tucking it under the fruit.

Many gardeners will find it difficult to obtain straw nowadays. Buy special strawberry mats or use black plastic strips instead. Keep the plastic in place with a few stones and make sure that it slopes evenly away from the plants so that pools of water cannot collect around them. If slugs are likely to be a problem, scatter a few slug pellets around the plants before putting down the fruit protector.

Protect the crop from birds with either a permanent fruit cage or with light-weight plastic netting spread over the beds. Drive in short posts and run taut wires between them. These can remain in place for the life of the bed. Invert glass jars over the tops of the posts so that the netting will slide without catching. Protect the plants with netting when the berries begin to swell, because mice and squirrels take while they are still green. Make sure the netting clears the tops of the plants and can be removed easily for picking.

Early cropping

An extra early crop can be grown under cloches or plastic tunnels or in a greenhouse. An unheated greenhouse has no advantage over cloches, although a heated one will give crops from mid-spring. For the best results, hand-pollinate all forced strawberries to avoid mis-shapen unattractive fruits. Use a camel hair brush; dab the flowers daily when they have fully opened.

Outdoors, crops can be forwarded by three or four weeks using glass cloches, or by two or three weeks with plastic cloches or tunnels. Many varieties crop earlier than usual in their first year, so do protect your maiden plants. First year plants will also be smaller, so plant them 23 cm (9″) apart, allowing 90 cm (3′) between rows—the wider spacing makes the placing of cloches and tunnels easier. After the maiden crop has been picked, pull out alternate plants and leave the

1. Begin forcing under cloches in late winter; in warm weather, open cloches or space them slightly apart.

2. For strawberries grown under plastic tunnels, lift the fabric for spraying, pollinating and harvesting.

rest uncovered.

There is no point in using cloches or tunnels too early; the beginning of late winter is quite soon enough. Before covering, weed the bed and scatter slug pellets around the plants. There is no need to 'straw' the beds but the plants must be protected from birds with netting, while the cloches or tunnels are opened during the ripening period.

Using tunnels will lead to poor berry development unless insects are allowed to fly in to pollinate the blossom. Open the tunnel wide in the middle part of the day when the flowers are out. Most glass cloches have spaces through which insects can enter, but in very hot weather, open the cloches or space them 5 cm (2″) apart.

For greenhouse forcing, plant rooted runners singly in 15 cm (6″) pots filled with John Innes No. 3 potting compost, doing this in early summer if possible, and certainly by late summer. Keep the pots indoors until early in mid-winter, making sure that the plants have enough water and are not cracked by frost. Once inside the greenhouse, keep the plants quite cool with no artificial heat until signs of growth can be seen, usually ten days or two weeks later. Now supply heat to raise the temperature very gradually, reaching a maximum of 10 °C

(50°F) by the end of mid-winter. Increase humidity by damping down.

Once the flowers have set and the berries begun to swell, allow the temperature to rise still further, ideally to 18°C (65°F), and maintain moist conditions until the fruit starts to colour, when the air should again be drier. Feed the plants occasionally with dilute liquid manure or fertilizer as the berries swell. Forked sticks or bent galvanized wire can be used to hold the fruit trusses up. Forced plants cannot be used again.

Container growing

There are special pots for growing strawberries but you can make your own container by drilling 5–7 cm (2–3″) holes in the side of a barrel. Put a layer of hardcore in the bottom of the container. Barrels should have a central core of drainage material running up through the middle; make a wire mesh tube, 10–15 cm (4–6″) in diameter; place this in the middle of the container and fill it with clean hardcore. The tube should end 10 cm (4″) below the surface of the compost. Use John Innes No. 3 potting compost, and work upwards, inserting the roots of the plants into the holes from the outside. Water as you proceed with the planting. Water growing plants regularly.

1. Plunge small pots filled with compost into the soil close to the parent plant.

2. Peg down the runners either directly into the soil or into pots; fasten with wire hooks or hairpins.

3. Additional runners may form from the selected plantlet; cut these off as they drain the plant's vigour.

4. Once the plants have rooted, sever the runner from its parent plant with a sharp knife.

Propagation

Strawberries are usually not much good for cropping after three or four years because virus infection has taken its toll by then. However, they are easily increased from runners. Before beginning to replace old stock from runners, make sure the parent plants are free of all pests and diseases, especially viruses. It is not worth propagating from diseased or infested plants.

For the best results, select healthy, one-year-old parent plants, and do not allow them to bear fruits. By removing the flowers, all the plant's energy is channelled into the production of first class runners. The runners should be ready for pegging down from mid-summer to late autumn. Although a healthy growing parent plant will produce numerous runners, select the strongest four or five, and allow only one plant to develop on each.

You can peg down the runners directly into the soil, if it has been lightly cultivated beforehand, or you can peg them into pots. Fill the pots with John Innes No. 1 potting compost and either sink them into the ground so their rims are level with the soil surface, or stand them firmly on the surface. Peg the runners down into the soil and fasten securely with wire hooks or stout hairpins. Once the runner has rooted, a further runner may form at the point of rooting; pinch this out.

About a month after pegging down, the young plants should be ready for moving. Check that the plant has made good leaf growth, which is a sure sign of successful rooting. Then cut the runners from the parent plant. If you are lifting the plants directly from the soil, use a trowel and make sure there is a good ball of soil around the roots. Whether they are open grown or pot grown, the new plants should be planted into their final positions immediately. If you do not want the young plants to crop in their first season, pick off the flowers as they form. An increased second year crop will result. The variety *Royal Sovereign* responds to this treatment well.

Harvesting

Strawberry plants usually crop for three or four weeks. However, in very hot seasons, harvesting may be over after a week or two. Perpetual strawberries carry much smaller crops at any one time, but may continue producing berries for several months.

As soon as the fruits are full sized, they will colour quickly. Pick them when the fruits are firm and evenly coloured all over. Because strawberries go mouldy very quickly, it is best to pick them when the weather is fine and the fruits dry. Pick over the bed daily during harvest time, to avoid over-ripe fruit. As you inspect the beds, remove any rotting or damaged fruit to avoid the spread of disease. Burn any infected fruit, do not leave it on the ground or put it on the compost heap.

Take the strawberries with the stalk intact. Always handle the berry by the stalk, so you do not bruise or discolour the flesh. You can remove the stalk and calyx just before serving. Strawberries for jam-making can be picked with or without the stalk. Use the fruits as quickly as possible, as strawberries do not remain at their best for long.

Aftercare

Late in the season, leaves begin to wither. If you leave the foliage on plants after harvesting, pests and diseases are more likely to be a problem with next year's crops. Cutting the old leaves exposes the crowns to light and air and renews their vigour. Some varieties, like *Talisman*, will crop again in autumn if the leaves are cut after the first harvest.

There are two methods of clearing strawberry beds: burning and mowing. The first is more drastic and more likely to go wrong, although it does kill off many pests. The safer method is cutting off the leaves, and raking them up along with the straw. Use a hand sickle, shears, or, for very long beds, a mower. Remember that the crowns must not be damaged, so if you do mow over the plants, set the cutter for 10 cm (4"). After mowing, clean the beds generally, removing stray runners and weeds. Do not put any of the rakings on the compost heap; burning them in a bonfire is better as it will cut down disease risk.

After the bed is completely cleaned, fork in sulphate of potash at the rate of 15 g per sq m ($\frac{1}{2}$ oz per sq yd). A light mulch put on at this time will also help to build up the crowns and keep the autumn crop of weeds from sprouting. Check your strawberry netting for holes, and do any repairs before you put it away.

Exhibition tips

Because strawberries can be so easily bruised, fruits for exhibition should be handled as little as possible, and picked just before the show. The usual number of strawberries exhibited is 20; use scissors to cut the fruits from the plant. Remember that strawberries can be damaged by their own weight, so when packing them for the show do not put too many in one container. Display the berries on a plate in neat rows, so they can be easily counted. The judge will look for large, ripe fruit with even colour and free from blemishes. The stalks, which should be fresh and green, must still be attached.

Varieties

Early

Cambridge Vigour: first-year plants crop early; older plants crop mid-season. Plant upright, large with vigorous foliage; fruit large, conical, orange-red turning to scarlet later; sweet flesh, fine flavour. Crops best in first year, after which crops diminish. Susceptible to wilt and botrytis, but resistant to redcore. Excellent for freezing; smaller late berries good for jam-making.

Cambridge Rival: tall, open, vigorous plant. Fruits dark crimson, conical shaped, large at first, becoming smaller; firm flesh, scarlet; excellent, sweet flavour. Susceptible to wilt, bruises easily.

Grandee: very large berries, up to 7.5 cm (3″) diameter, 90 g (3 oz) in weight. Heavy cropper, particularly in second year, up to 1.6 kg (3½ lb) per plant.

Gorella: well flavoured, large berries, dark red, wedge shaped.

Maincrop

Cambridge Favourite: reliable, heavy cropper; plant large, spreading; fruits large, pinky red, firm, pale pink flesh; moderate flavour, slightly pine tasting. Most common commercial variety; resistant to mildew, but prone to green petal. Crops well in open, under cloches and in frames, very long season.

Redgauntlet: plant medium large, spreading, vigorous; fruit very large, crimson red; round conical or wedge shaped; firm, dark scarlet flesh. Heavy cropper, but flavour only moderate; can be cropped again in autumn; very suitable for cooler, northern areas. Some resistance to mildew.

Aromel: berries medium red, good size and flavour; crops continually through to mid-autumn.

Royal Sovereign: plant very vigorous and leafy. Fruit medium to large, scarlet berries; sweet-flavoured, light red flesh. First class strawberry, but only moderate crops and is rather subject to fungal and viral infections.

Cambridge Aristocrat: rich flavour, reminiscent of alpine strawberry, long conical fruits; crops over long period.

Late

Cambridge Late Pine: vigorous, open plant; flowers less likely to be frosted; fruit medium to large size; rounded, very sweet, dark flesh; heavy cropper; partially mildew resistant.

Domanil: Belgian variety; berries medium to large; very heavy cropper.

Talisman: mid to late season; vigorous plant, upright dense growth, slow to start growth; fruit scarlet; large fruit getting smaller late in season; crops a second time in autumn; resistant to red core and mildew; needs good soil to do well and adequate moisture.

Perpetual (early summer to mid-autumn)

Hampshire Maid: very good late summer cropper; rounded, conical, large fruit; well flavoured; needs watering in dry weather; produces very few runners.

Gento: continental variety; good crops of very large, conical berries with slight acid flavour; crops heavily late summer to mid-autumn; also crops on runners as well as parent plant.

Sonjana: 'climbing' strawberry; fruits on long runners (as well as parent plant) which can be trained up trellises although runners do not actually climb on their own.

Redgauntlet

Pests & Diseases

Although the number of pests and diseases affecting strawberries is formidable, the amateur gardener is unlikely to meet more than one or two of them. Because many of the infections are not visible in the early stages, and healthy looking plants may in fact be diseased, it is extremely important to buy certified virus-free plants. Remember, though, this does not guarantee that the plants will remain disease-free permanently. It is up to you to keep your strawberry bed in good health.

Aphids: greenfly can infest strawberries from early spring onwards, feeding on the leaves, so that they are curled and twisted and the plants stunted. The main danger, however, is that they carry virus diseases which are incurable.

Watch the plants carefully for any indication of aphids, starting in early spring. If necessary, spray with derris or bioresmethrin.

Strawberry beetle: this is the most damaging beetle which attacks the strawberry. It is mostly black and about 1.3-2 cm ($\frac{1}{2}$-$\frac{3}{4}''$) long. It feeds on the flesh, leaving an open wound in the fruit, and sometimes removes the seeds. Because the beetle lives in rough grass, leaf litter or weeds, the best precaution is to make sure the area surrounding the strawberry bed is well cultivated and any grass is kept mown.

Red spider mite: these are not actually spiders, but tiny, pale red or orange mites which suck the sap from the leaves. The leaves then turn pale yellow or grey-brown, and the plant is generally weakened. Sometimes silken webs are visible on the leaves which are infested. Keep the plants well supplied with water as these pests thrive in hot, dry conditions, and spray with malathion as soon as any signs of spider mite appear.

Strawberry eelworm: these microscopic pests live in the buds, leaf axils and leaves of strawberry plants; the main symptoms of infestation are thickened leaf stalks, puckered leaves and generally stunted growth, but this trouble is difficult to diagnose and may need professional advice. Once the soil has been infested with eelworm, all the plants should be burned and no strawberries grown on that plot for three years. Because runners from infested plants may also carry eelworm, it is best not to propagate from diseased plants. As a further precaution against the spread of eelworm, apparently healthy runners for propagation grown in the same bed should be completely immersed in hot water (43°C, 110°F) for 20 minutes, before potting into sterilized compost.

Snails and slugs: damage from these pests is usually worse on wet, badly-drained soil, or in badly kept gardens full of debris and leaf litter. Rough holes in the leaves and berries, and silvery slime trails are the most usual symptoms. The best precaution is to keep your garden clean and freely drained; controls are either methiocarb pellets or containers of sweetened milk sunk in the soil.

Strawberry weevil: the adults of various types of weevil attack the stalks of the leaves, flowers and fruit, breaking them off, and may feed on the developing fruit itself. In a bad infestation which, however, seldom occurs, the crop can be severely damaged without this being realised until too late. If you see stems hanging limply on many plants, suspect weevils, remove and burn all the

Donald Smith

Pale yellow crinkled leaves with silken webs are symptoms of red spider mite infestations.

damaged parts, and spray or dust the plants and soil with derris.

Tarsonemid mite: these are most destructive in the south of England, during very warm weather. The minute, colourless insects overwinter in the plants and feed on the unfolding leaves which remain small and become brown with down-curled edges. The mites remain inside the folded leaves or low down in the crowns of the plants, and chemical controls available to the gardener are not very effective. Keeping the plants well watered helps; dusting with flowers of sulphur in spring and early summer gives some control.

Botrytis: sometimes called grey mould, this fungus is worse in wet weather, when it can quickly turn berries into rotten, furry fruits useless for eating. Some varieties are more susceptible than others: *Royal Sovereign, Cambridge Favourite* and *Talisman* are particularly vulnerable. It is spread both by spores carried on the wind and by contact with diseased fruit, and so healthy berries can quickly become diseased. Because many weeds are host plants for botrytis, a weed-free garden is less likely to be infected. Plants grown in cramped, badly ventilated conditions, whether in the open or under cloches, are also very vulnerable. Remove and burn any mouldy berries immediately, and, as a precaution, the plants can be sprayed with thiram or captan according to manufacturer's instructions, but not fruit which is to be preserved in any way.

Leaf spot: this fungal disease rarely causes any serious trouble. Tiny, dark red, circular spots appear on the leaves, late in the season. If the infection is severe, the spots join up and the whole leaf withers. Cutting off the foliage after harvesting is a good control, and spraying with Bordeaux mixture in mid-spring the following year, if the attack was bad, is a good preventive measure.

Strawberry mildew: the variety *Royal Sovereign* is most susceptible to strawberry mildew, which appears as dark blotches on the upper surfaces of the leaves, and grey patches beneath. Eventually, the leaf edges will curl upwards, and show the fungal growth beneath. Spray with dinocap just before the plants flower, and two or three times again, at fortnightly intervals.

Red core: this is a serious root disease affecting strawberries, and is most likely to occur on badly drained soils. The soil-borne fungus turns the roots of an infected plant black or brown on the outside, with a red core. Above ground symptoms are stunted plants with wilted leaves, later reddish or brown, and fruiting poorly. Usually only a few plants in a whole bed will be infected to start with; eventually more and more plants look as though they were suffering from drought, wilt suddenly and die. Unfortunately, there is no completely

Strawberry beetles feed on the fruits, and remove the seeds from the undersides.

Botrytis, or grey mould, can quickly turn berries into rotten furry, inedible fruits.

effective cure; affected plants should be lifted and destroyed, and the land left free of strawberries for at least 13 years. Some varieties, however, are more resistant than others, for instance *Talisman, Cambridge Vigour* and *Cambridge Rival. Royal Sovereign* is one of the most vulnerable varieties.

Verticillium wilt: if you are growing potatoes near your strawberry patch and they have verticillium wilt, it is likely your strawberries are also infected. This soil-borne fungal disease causes plants to wilt for no apparent reason; leaves turn brown and die, and any fruits are small and malformed. There is no complete cure, once infected, and plants are best burnt, but soaking with benomyl solution will give some control.

Yellow edge: this virus is spread by aphids; it is also called Little Leaf because the leaves of infected plants gradually become smaller and smaller. The young leaves of infected plants develop yellow edges. The symptoms are most noticeable in mid-spring or early autumn, less so in summer.

Crinkle: there are two forms of this viral infection: mild and severe. Mild crinkle shows as tiny spots on the leaves and may affect cropping slightly. Severe crinkle is much more serious; symptoms are numerous yellow spots on the leaves, which become crinkled and wrinkled.

Arabis mosaic virus: the symptoms of this virus, which is spread by eelworm, vary according to the variety of strawberry grown, but generally the leaves become blotched with yellow, and the plant's fruiting capacity is diminished. Try not to grow strawberries too near hedgerows, as eelworms are much more numerous in the soil near hedges.

Green petal: the symptoms of this disease can first be seen in spring; the leaves are small and curled upwards, and the flowers have green petals instead of white ones. Any fruits which form will be small, mis-shapen and very seedy. In late summer, infected plants will have grey-green leaves which wilt inexplicably; any leaves which form later will be small and yellow. Many garden weeds, particularly clover, are host plants for this virus. Leafhoppers transmit the disease from host plants to strawberries, especially in dry weather.

GUIDE TO STRAWBERRY TROUBLES

Symptoms	*Probable causes*
Stunted plants with curled, twisted leaves	Aphids
Holes in flesh, seeds removed from underside of berry	Beetle
Leaves pale yellow or grey brown, silk webs on leaves	Red spider mite
Stunted growth, thickened leaf stalks, puckered leaves	Strawberry eelworm
Holes in leaves and berries, silvery slime trails	Slugs
Leaves stunted, brown with down-curled edges	Tarsonemid mite
Fruits, leaves covered with grey, furry mould	Botrytis cinerea
Tiny dark red circular spots on leaves	Leaf spot
Dark blotches on upper surfaces; grey mould beneath	Strawberry mildew
Plants stunted with wilted leaves; roots black or brown on outside, with red core	Red core
Plants wilt for no apparent reason; fruits small and malformed	Verticillium wilt
Young leaves develop yellow edges, new leaves small	Yellow edge virus
Leaves have yellow spots, become crinkled and wrinkled	Crinkle
Leaves blotched with yellow	Arabis mosaic virus
Flowers have green petals, fruits misshapen and seedy	Green petal virus
Stalks of leaves, buds and fruit partially or completely severed	Strawberry weevils

INDEX

Page numbers in *italics* refer to
illustrations

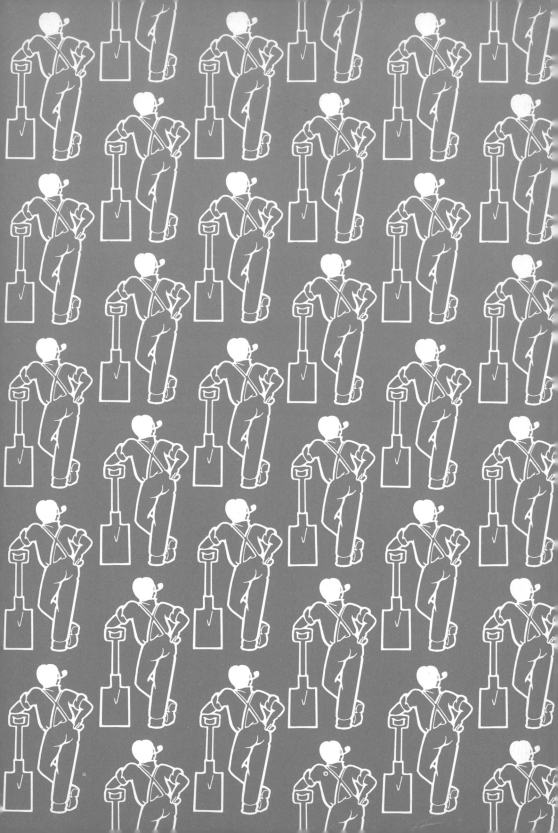